# SOCIOLOGICAL PERSPECTIVES OF DOMESTIC DEVELOPMENT

# SOCIOLOGICAL

Edited by **George M. Beal,**
**Ronald C. Powers,**
and
**E. Walter Coward, Jr.**

Iowa State University
Center for Agricultural
and Economic
Development

# PERSPECTIVES OF DOMESTIC DEVELOPMENT

THE IOWA STATE UNIVERSITY PRESS / AMES, IOWA

*Other publications of the Center for Agricultural and Economic Development are available as follows (work of the Center is supported in part by a grant from the W. K. Kellogg Foundation):*

**Books from the Iowa State University Press (hard-bound)**

Benefits and Burdens of Rural Development: Some Public Policy Viewpoints, 1970
A North American Common Market, 1969
Food Goals, Future Structural Changes and Agricultural Policy: A National Basebook, 1969
Alternatives for Balancing World Food Production Needs, 1967
Roots of the Farm Problem, 1965
Economic Development of Agriculture, 1965
Family Mobility in Our Dynamic Society, 1965
Farmers in the Market Economy, 1964
Our Changing Rural Society: Perspectives and Trends (developedby the Rural Sociological Society under editorship of James H. Copp), 1964
Farm Goals in Conflict: Family Farm Income, Freedom, Security, 1963
Adjustments in Agriculture—A National Basebook, 1961

**Reports from the Center for Agricultural and Economic Development**

CAED 38　Food Costs from Incomes and Crop Yields with Restrictions on Fertilizer Use
CAED 37　Policy Choices for Rural People
CAED 36　Trade-offs in Farm Policy
CAED 34　Analysis of Some Farm Program Alternatives for the Future
CAED 33　Role of the Universities in Social Innovation
CAED 32　Farm Programs for the 1970's
CAED 31　Abundance and Uncertainty . . . Farm Policy Problems
CAED 30T　Capacity and Trends in Use of Land Resources
CAED 29　Implications of Changes (Structural and Market) on Farm Management and Marketing Research
CAED 28　A Recipe for Meeting the World Food Crisis
CAED 26　Weather Variability and the Need for a Food Reserve
CAED 25　International Home Economics
CAED 10　New Areas of Land-Grant Extension Education

© 1971 The Iowa State University Press, Ames, Iowa 50010
All rights reserved
Composed and printed by The Iowa State University Press
First edition, 1971
International Standard Book Number: 0-8138-1405-7
Library of Congress Catalog Card Number: 79-137087

# CONTENTS

Hume

# PREFACE

THE IMPORTANCE of development in all countries appears to be accepted; in fact, development is a major goal. Large portions of national budgets are allocated; complex organizational structures are set up to plan and implement activities for development. The United States is no exception. Billions of public funds are allocated for various development programs and the private sector makes major investments. Such programs and activities are carried out by social systems ranging from local chambers of commerce or development commissions to massive federal bureaucracies.

Most of the discussion and writing about development appears to have been done by philosophers, economists, political scientists, or generalists. Sociologists seem to have played a minor role. Yet, the sociological aspects of development are often mentioned by authors as important ingredients. Further, many sociologists have attempted to play important roles as consultants, advisors, or practitioners in many developing nations. Sociologists may have played less important roles at the policy formation level, as influentials in determining administrative structures, and as advisors to administrative structures in the United States. A relatively large number of sociologists have been actively involved with program implementation at lower administrative levels. Rural sociologists have been actively involved in a large number of programs variously labeled as community development, social and economic development, and resource development. The relatively minor role of sociology has concerned sociologists as well as many individuals in other disciplines including some policy makers and program implementers. Out of this milieu of concern this book was generated.

Two main forces converged to make this book possible. The Committee on the Development of Rural Sociology of the Rural Sociological Society had on a number of occasions discussed various facets of social and economic development. It was agreed that there was a need to attempt to some way focus attention on the sociological aspects of societal development. Holding a conference with invited papers appeared to be a viable starting point. The Iowa State University Center for Agricultural and Economic Development was approached to determine its interest in helping sponsor a conference on the Sociology of Development. Earl Heady, Executive Director of the Center, and

William Stucky, Educational Leader for the Center, agreed that the Center would jointly sponsor the conference with the Rural Sociological Society. This plan was approved by the Council of the Rural Sociological Society and the following committee was appointed to plan and carry out the conference: George Beal, Iowa State University (co-chairman); Howard Beers, University of Kentucky; Emory Brown, Pennsylvania State University; Harold Capener, Cornell University; Archibald Haller, University of Wisconsin; Eugene Havens, University of Wisconsin; Ronald Powers, Iowa State University (co-chairman); and William Stucky, ex officio, representing the Center for Agricultural and Economic Development.

This committee met a number of times and made a number of decisions that have direct bearing on this book. It decided that the general concept of development, with all its ramifications, was not bound to any discipline. However, fully recognizing different philosophical approaches and the many disciplines and specialty areas involved, it decided that within this broad context major emphasis would be placed on the sociology of development.

It also decided that problems of growth are crucial to developing nations. The committee observed that much more has been written about the need for, problems of, and strategies of growth in developing nations than in "developed" nations, e.g., the United States. The decision was made to attempt to focus this first conference on development in the United States. A number of points of view of committee members influenced this decision. The great heterogeneity among developing nations made it difficult to generalize existing conceptualization and research. Further, the low level of conceptualization and descriptive nature of the writings appeared often to lead to "culturally bound" knowledge. There was the belief that attempts were being made to freely export knowledge from the United States to developing countries without first really determining what was available for, or worthy of export. It appeared to some that unique expertise, insight, and personal experience in developing countries were sometimes substituted for conceptual and methodological rigor in discussing improvement in developing nations. There was recognition of the increased emphasis being placed on development in the United States and in many sub-units—region, state, multicounty areas, counties and communities. The committee believed that a relatively common experience area, the United States, would provide a more realistic base for the authors of the invited papers, the discussants, and conference participants to attempt to put their sociological "house in order."

From the beginning, the publication of a book on the sociology of development was a major objective. To this end outstanding scholars were invited to prepare the key papers.

In addition to the authors of the invited papers (whose vitae appear with their chapters) the contribution of the discussants and others playing structured roles in relation to the papers is noted with appreciation: Art Gallaher, University of Kentucky; Lawrence Witt, Michigan State University; John Crittenden, Indiana State University; Helen C. Abell, University of Waterloo; Irving L. Horowitz, Rutgers University; William Kimball, Michigan State University; Howard Phillips, Ohio State University; Gary King, Kellogg Foundation; Albert Krisjanson, University of Manitoba; Frank Santopolo, University of Kentucky; C. Paul Marsh, North Carolina State University; Eber Eldridge, Iowa State University; M. E. John, Pennsylvania State University; Lee Taylor, Center for Urban Studies, University of Louisiana, New Orleans; James Copp, USDA; Archibald Haller, University of Wisconsin; Paul Jehlik, USDA; and Earl O. Heady, Iowa State University.

E. Walter Coward, Jr., formerly of Iowa State University and now at Pennsylvania State University, was the conference coordinator and is mainly responsible for assembling and editing the papers for presentation in their present form. He was assisted in the editing by Ralph Reeder, Editor with the Center for Agricultural and Economic Development. The editors have attempted to provide a general perspective, flow, summary, and some of the challenges inherent in this exploration of the sociology of development. Certainly it is not a definitive work. It is hoped that it will provide a basis for and stimulation to additional conceptualization, research, and writing by sociologists, and perhaps others, on this important subject. It is our hope it will lead to advances in the sociology of development.

G.M.B.
R.C.P.
E.W.C.

# INTRODUCTION

THIS BOOK is concerned with the problems of planned change in the United States herein referred to as domestic development. With Galbraith (2, p. 388) we assume that the present state of American society is not a "terminal phenomenon." It is expected that the future state of the United States will be postindustrial, which will include an increased emphasis on changes which are political, economic, and social in nature.

At a minimum, this book is in tune with the times; times in which numerous resources are being allocated to the support of domestic activities labeled development. As Paul Miller indicates in Chapter 11, "Since World War II, the number of federally sponsored programs within what might be called the development category has reached the 200 mark, and the number of departments and agencies involved is above 20," probably a conservative estimate. Of course, the development activities of other levels of government, universities, foundations, business groups, and other private groups are additional.

Development is nearly a household word. Common adjectives include community, social and economic, area, regional, and the like. Development as operationalized in action program objectives and activities typically suggests one view of development—economic development. The milieu of much domestic and international development has been the economy: negative effects or characteristics of the economy have provided the rationale for change; positive effects on the economy have been the objectives of this change.

Within the "developing" nations development programs have also had a major focus on political development. Political development frequently has taken two directions: a) efforts to increase political participation by the citizens of some state, and b) efforts to increase the ability of government to provide needed social services to these citizens.

There is a second important generalization about the current development scene. Many of the programs being implemented, and many of the discussions about this implementation, deal with the development process in the "developing" nations. Our concepts of "developing" and "developed" have made the discussion of development in a "developed" nation such as the United States an anomaly to some.

The content of this book represents a departure from both of these generalizations. First, the book is concerned with the sociological rather than the economic or political view of development: both development means and development objectives. Second, the book has, as its intended focus, domestic development in the United States.

In planning for this focus it is recognized that we may not achieve the more complete view of development that is a worthy objective. Nevertheless, we pursue the more limited approach and justify it as meaningfully related to the objective of getting the sociological "house in order" with regard to perspectives on development. To some extent the concern with creating a sociological perspective of development arises from the perception that thinking about development has been largely dominated by the economic perspective. We suggest that sociological perspectives of development are related to economic perspectives of development, at a minimum, in that they are offered as alternatives and/or complements to the economic view.

## SOCIOLOGY AND DEVELOPMENT

Within the total scope of development activities are the specialized activities of sociologists examining development phenomena from a sociological point of view. With a play on words, sociological interest in development may be seen as a modernization of the previous habit of examining social change. It is this specialized task within the ubiquitous set of activities of development on which this book focuses. The book is concerned with sociology's contribution to understanding and participating in the phenomenon of planned change that abounds in our nation. The book is also an affirmative response to the important question that Moore (7, p. 765) asks: "Have we, in short, any obligation as social scientists to start taking account not only of the changeful quality of life but also of the fact that some portion of that change is deliberate?"

It seems a viable hypothesis that much of what sociologists have written relevant to a perspective of domestic development has not been labeled as such. There are two broad categories of literature to which we refer: 1) discussions of social change and 2) discussions of social problems. In the first case, what has been written about social change frequently deals at such a macrolevel both with regard to the social group and the social time being considered that its immediate relevance to planned development is ambiguous.[1] In the second case, the prominence of economic development has overshadowed the alternate or complementary views of development as the process of solving societal problems.

A third body of sociological literature has a high relevance to the

[1] See Hobbs's discussion of social change in Chapter 1.

general phenomena of development, but a somewhat more tenuous relevance when the focus is planned change in the United States. This is the literature dealing with change in the "developing" nations.[2] This third body of literature generally treats the social structural modifications needed to achieve systems of production and government of the Western variety. Such literature typically proceeds from the identification of differences between the Western model of social structure and the one being observed. Changes that are analyzed or predicted are an inventory of changes needed to close the gap in favor of the Western model.

### Identifying Change and Development

In these initial paragraphs, as throughout the remainder of this book, two important concepts will recur in the discussion: change and development. As used in the context of this book these concepts generally refer to social change and societal development, respectively.

There is a sense in which the difference between social change and societal development is in the eyes of the beholder. The same phenomenon, for example, the emergence of numerous voluntary associations, may be labeled as change and/or development. In identifying such a phenomenon as change, the focus is on the fact that at some time period numerous voluntary associations exist whereas in an earlier time they did not. In labeling this same phenomenon as development the focus may be altered so that one observes that citizens now have a valued social mechanism for influencing decision-making which they did not formerly have. In general, the development focus differs from the change focus in that the former incorporates concern with both the social alteration and its primary consequences whereas the latter deals only with the form of the alteration. In short, conceptualizing a phenomenon as development implies a social alteration resulting in an improved social condition.

### FORMAT OF THE BOOK

The sociologist's contribution to development is intimately linked with his general role as a social scientist. His best contribution to the sociology of development will derive from his performance as a social scientist.

We presume that the social scientist will deal with the phenomena of development in a manner similar to his approach to other subjects which he analyzes. An initial task is the conceptualization of the

---

[2] Some examples are Eisenstadt (1), Horowitz (3), Hoselitz (4), Lerner (5), Levy (6), Moore and Feldman (8), Smelser and Lipset (9).

phenomenon in abstract terms within a general conceptual framework followed by the task of operationalizing such concepts in a manner that allows empirical observation.

In addition to these tasks, sociologists are increasingly being asked to perform the task of translating such conceptually grounded findings into policies and strategies of action. In fact, what is labeled as the "sociology of development" may not be best characterized as a subfield of sociology that focuses on a particular phenomenon. It may be that the "sociology of development" or "developmental sociology" refers to a fundamental alteration in the hierarchy of objectives for sociology in which sociological knowledge in a form useful for social planning is given increased importance. The sociology of development, in addition to its detailed focus on development processes, implies alterations in conceptualization, methodology, and interpretation that result in sociological knowledge useful as an input for societal decision-making and implementation.

The content of this book attempts to span a large portion of this range of sociological activities. In Part One, Chapters 1–4 deal with the initial task of conceptualizing development from a sociological perspective and identifying sociological factors related to its occurrence. Chapter 5 explores the problem of devising operational measures for development and illustrates one effort to empirically observe the developmental change of community systems.

The three chapters in Part Two are concerned with the transfer of sociological concepts, propositions, and models into the objectives and procedures of action programs. These chapters identify the problems associated with this transfer and illustrate the adaptation of some specific conceptual frameworks into particular program strategy.

The discussions in Part Three deal with the development role of three major institutions of our society: government, the university, and business. The major thesis of this section is that the delivery systems of development are themselves in need of certain modifications if they are to perform these development roles. These chapters provide a feedback to the conceptualization task by warning that sociological models of development must deal not only with the targets of development but also with the agencies and institutions that plan and implement development.

In each of the section introductions the editors provide the reader with a brief overview of the content of each chapter in the section. In the final chapter the editors try first, to bring some parsimony to the wide-ranging discussions of the previous chapters, and second, to further explore some subjects that were either omitted or not discussed in detail.

As a final suggestion before you read the following chapters: we believe the reader can profitably keep in mind three general questions. First: What is the nature of current American society that the author has in mind? Second: What is the definition of development from which the author proceeds? What are the goals that he assumes development is to achieve? Third: What is to be the role of sociology in the pursuit of domestic development?

## REFERENCES

1. Eisenstadt, S. N. *Modernization, Protest and Change.* Englewood Cliffs, N.J.: Prentice-Hall, 1966.
2. Galbraith, John K. *The New Industrial State.* Boston: Houghton Mifflin, 1967.
3. Horowitz, Irving L. *Three Worlds of Development: The Theory and Practice of International Stratification.* New York: Oxford University Press, 1966.
4. Hoselitz, Bert. *Sociological Aspects of Economic Growth.* Glencoe, Ill.: Free Press, 1960.
5. Lerner, Daniel. *The Passing of Traditional Society: Modernizing the Middle East.* Glencoe, Ill.: Free Press, 1958.
6. Levy, Marion J. *Modernization and the Structure of Societies.* 2 vols. Princeton, N.J.: Princeton University Press, 1966.
7. Moore, Wilbert E. "The Utility of Utopias." *American Sociological Review* 31:765–772, 1966.
8. ———, and Arnold S. Feldman, eds. *Labor Commitment and Social Change in Developing Areas.* New York: Social Science Research Council, 1960.
9. Smelser, Neil J., and Seymour M. Lipset, eds. *Social Structure and Mobility in Economic Development.* Chicago: Aldine Publishing Company, 1966.

# PART ONE
# SOCIOLOGICAL APPROACHES
# TO DOMESTIC DEVELOPMENT:
# THEORY-RESEARCH

THE INITIAL BASE from which the sociology of development should proceed is a sociological conceptualization of development phenomena. Thus, we begin with a group of chapters that deal with the general question: How is development defined (or conceptualized) by sociologists? Given the abstract perspectives that sociologists have about the behavior of individuals and groups, what do sociologists perceive are the distinguishing aspects of development?

One approach to this problem is attempting to describe development relative to other sociological phenomena with which sociologists deal—a kind of taxonomic approach in which the family of social phenomena to which development belongs is identified, and perhaps even the specific species. The conceptual identification of development is dependent on the inventory of sociological theory that is available. Sociological theory is used herein to refer to the explanation of social behavior through the use of concepts, propositions, and sets of interrelated propositions or models. By providing development with some conceptual tag we are then able to articulate a number of concepts, propositions, and models that have been previously associated with the concept with which development is identified. Seeking this conceptual home for development may be complicated by at least two factors: 1) development may be so unique that there is no adequate conceptual tag, or 2) there may be several alternative concepts,

1

or forms of the same concept with which development could be identified. The alternative selected may lead to rather different conceptualizations of development (consider the implications of choosing among the varieties of social change discussed in Chapter 1).

Conceptualizing development in terms of existing concepts in sociology is an important, but only a preliminary, step in dealing with the sociology of development. This first step in theory building must be complemented by research in which concepts and propositions are operationalized at the level of observation. Such observations are intended as a feedback process which may lead to the modification of previously held concepts and propositions. This empirical approach to concept building or concept modifying is illustrated in the chapter by Paul Eberts and Frank Young in which techniques of empirical analysis are used to construct conceptual dimensions of development.

Each chapter in this section is concerned with the conceptualization of development from a sociological perspective. Chapter 1 is a review of several theories of social change purported by contemporary sociologists. Chapter 2 deals with the relationship between the concept of progress, used by earlier sociologists, and that of development, as well as the range of definitions of development being used by sociologists. In Chapter 3, a major theme is the conceptualization of development vis-a-vis basic sociological concepts such as social power, social conflict and social control. Chapter 4 gives emphasis to the importance of formal organizations (e.g., agencies and voluntary organizations) as a means for achieving societal development. In Chapter 5 the authors approach identification of sociological components of development empirically through the analysis of data from communities in New York State.

## OVERVIEW OF THE CHAPTERS

### Contemporary Perspectives On Social Change

In Chapter 1 Daryl Hobbs discusses four contemporary approaches to social change: functionalism, modernization, conflict, and social behaviorism. Three of the approaches are directly related to major "schools" of thought in sociology, while modernization, as described by Hobbs, includes the functionalist approach applied to economic growth through industrialization (illustrated by the work of Smelser) and the social behaviorist approach applied to political development (illustrated by the work of Lerner). Hobbs turns to the work of Boskoff (who uses the AGIL model of Parsons) to illustrate the functionalist approach; to Dahrendorf to illustrate the conflict approach; and to Martindale to illustrate the social behaviorist approach.

Each of these approaches is seen by Hobbs as a partial theory of change which both limits their use singularly and suggests their potential complementarity. The differences among social change theories in general, and the four reviewed in particular, are highly related to the different perspectives of social organization from which they begin. The theories reviewed tend to emphasize the structural or relational (as distinct from the cultural) conditions which increase the probability of change-producing factors being articulated—frequently the conditions of structural strains or tensions. The theories of social change discussed suggest that when processes such as conflict, innovation, social mobility, or social differentiation are operative at some level of intensity, modifications in the organization of society will occur over time.

Hobbs identifies development with the concept of social change in the following way: all development is social change but not all social change is development, interpreted to mean that development is one type of social change. Hobbs points out that most current conceptualizations of social change are theories of change rather than theories of changing, consequently perhaps limiting the utility of identifying development with social change.

## The Concept of Societal Development

Following Hobbs's general discussion of social change, H. Kent Geiger, in Chapter 2, focuses on the more specific concept of societal development.

After discussing the inadequacies of the concept progress, he reviews current perspectives of the concept of societal development.

Geiger identifies seven features of progress that restrict its use as a scientific concept. The past use of progress to imply the inevitability of improvement and the finality of some end-state, as well as the current use of progress as an element of community ideology and a prominent value in Western society, are features which Geiger believes discredit its scientific utility.

Societal development is a preferable concept. Among the diverse definitions of development is the common theme that it is inherently relativistic or comparative in perspective—a society is "developed" relative to some former self-condition or relative to some other society. Within this general perspective there exist several more specific approaches to development. Geiger discusses ten such approaches.

These approaches vary from concern with identifying the distinguishing characteristics of developed societies as compared to undeveloped societies, to focus the individual and social psychological variables, to viewing development as an example of intersocietal stratification, to viewing development from the perspective of abstract sociological models of total society.

It is the last view of societal development which Geiger prefers. Geiger views societal development as differentiation and balance in the social system. Using Parsons's AGIL model, Geiger relates societal development to the central processes of differentiation and integration. He identifies a key conceptual component of societal development as managing the magnitude and rate of interchanges between the subsystems of society.

## The Quest for Societal Development

In Chapter 3 Eugene Havens constructs his conceptualization of development from the basic ingredients of social relationships within society. From his assumption that power relations and the concomitant tension or conflict result from the existence of superordinate-subordinate relationships, the chapter suggests a conceptualization of societal development characterized by social mechanisms allowing access to authority roles and the effective management (but not the elimination) of tension and conflict.

Havens suggests that the conditions that will facilitate this societal development are the emergence of voluntary organizations that are successful in attaining instrumental (as opposed to consummatory) goals. The emergence of such interest groups is preceded by two important processes that provide the impetus for change: 1) communication contacts that inform the receiver of alternative opportunities, goals, or means, and 2) relative deprivation by which the receiver values the newly perceived opportunities over the former state of affairs.

The reader is provided with a systematic summary of the chapter in the form of a series of propositional statements. This technique will provide a good overview of the cumulative use of concepts employed and related in the chapter.

## The Structural Matrix of Development

In Chapter 4 Keith Warner suggests that the sociological perspective of development is a focus on the possible increase in an individual's life chances resulting from changes in social organization. In the sociology of development the key scarce resource is social organization—in the form of new or reorganized organizations such as institutional agencies and voluntary organizations.

The achievement of development through the articulation of organizations is constrained by several factors that may inhibit performance: 1) their susceptibility to power groups, 2) the internal problem of "trained incapacity," 3) their heritage of previous commitments, 4) the tendencies to goal displacement, and 5) the trend toward institutionalization.

Social organization for development also leads to a concern with interorganizational analysis since, as Warner indicates, the set of development activities to be achieved frequently is broader than the

**5**

domain of any one public or private organization. The improvement of life chances is dependent not only on the mutual enhancement achieved by individuals acting within organizations but also on the mutual enhancement possible by organizations acting within organizational sets.

An important theme of Warner's chapter is that while increasing complexity of differentiation of social organization may be an indicator of social change, it is only when such differentiation results in improved life chances that change becomes development.

## Sociological Variables of Development

In Chapter 5, Paul Eberts and Frank Young, after briefly commenting on a variety of possible definitions and measures of development, explore its social structural aspects. A major objective of their chapter is to select a "best" measure of development by detailed analysis of empirical data.

Their approach to the problem is consistent with the prior and continuing concern of Cornell sociologists with observing dimensions of the structural complexity of communities.

Applying factor analysis to a set of data representing selected characteristics in communities in New York State they identify the following four components: 1) a socioeconomic status component, 2) a structural complexity component, 3) an industrial base component, and 4) a domestic base component. From the identification of these four components the authors conclude that there is no common factor behind the development measures analyzed and that there is a high probability that these same four factors would be identified even with the use of additional measures. The structural complexity factor is identified as more relevant to the sociology of development.

The selection of development measures is an overriding problem in development research. In the selection of development measures the sociologist needs to consider the following points (several of which are pansociological): 1) the use of aggregated versus structural measures, 2) the use of direct

6

versus indirect measures, 3) the use of social system versus sectoral (subsystem) measures, 4) the use of measures with conceptual meaning and 5) the use of measures with only local versus cross-cultural validity.

Eberts and Young urge that sociological studies of development collect longitudinal data with special emphasis on the structural characteristics of systems. Such analysis would concentrate on the structural changes occurring in the systems over time.

# CHAPTER ONE

# SOME CONTEMPORARY
# SOCIOLOGICAL PERSPECTIVES
# REGARDING
# SOCIAL CHANGE

## DARYL J. HOBBS

USING AS A GUIDE the number of books and articles published by sociologists on social change, this area of sociological concern appears to be experiencing a renaissance. The period of relative dormancy seems to have spanned the first half of the twentieth century. The recent revival of interest has apparently been spurred by extensive national concern with domestic and international development stimulated by the Cold War, the rapid rate of change in society, and by trends within the discipline itself.

Sociologists' relative disregard of change as a feature of theories of social organization during the first half of the century seems to be at least partially attributable to a general discrediting of earlier theories of change. During the initial period of the history of sociology, concern with societal change was predominant. Explanations were sought to account for the emergence and decline of great civilizations and for differences in the rate of development between societies. The early theories (notably those of Comte, Spencer, Marx, Tonnies, Ward, etc.) were characterized by an emphasis on comprehensive conceptions of change and a search for encompassing generalizations and natural laws applicable to all societies. Conceptions of change were

DARYL J. HOBBS is Chairman of the Sociology and Rural Sociology Department at the University of Missouri. He holds the Ph.D. in rural sociology from Iowa State University. He has served as an extension specialist in community resource development and is conducting research on social change in small communities. Publications relevant to his chapter include: "Social Change as a Concept in Rural Sociology" (Theory into Practice 4 [February, 1966]) and Selected Perspectives on Community Resource Development (Agricultural Policy Institute [1969]).

typically deterministic, being viewed as a function of some single cause usually external to society. Emphasis was often placed on variables and analogies borrowed from natural sciences, especially assumptions regarding similarities between biological organisms and social organization. The influence of organicism was especially manifest in expressions of evolutionary tendencies of societies. Darwinian conceptions of natural selection were invoked as a basis for early conflict theories of society, i.e., those societies survived and progressed which were best able to adapt to their environment and compete with other societies.

Other conceptions of society and change, relying primarily on analysis of historical trends, postulated various stages and/or ideal types which at least implicitly assumed linear evolutionary tendencies, e.g., societies "progressed" from states of relative simplicity to states of relative complexity by the action of some forces usually unspecified. Other historically based theories applied the organic analogy in terms of the life cycle of individual organisms to society. Societies were conceived as proceeding through stages of birth, growth and maturation, decline and death.

Because empirical evidence failed to support the conjectures, these approaches were generally discredited and apparently discouraged the next generation of sociologists from seeking general explanations of change. Significant remnants of each of these early theories are to be found, however, as elemental features of contemporary approaches. It is charged by some critics that the remnants constitute the basic apparel of some of the more dominant contemporary theories. (26) Seemingly as a reaction to the difficulties encountered by grandiose conceptions of societal change, there was a tendency within sociology during the first half of the twentieth century to postpone questions of change to concentrate rather on descriptions of social order and to record the fact that social change was taking place with little emphasis on identification of sources or elaboration of processes. The implied strategy seemed to be that it was premature to be concerned with sources of change until the structure and processes of various levels of social organization were more fully understood. This position is enunciated by Martindale who suggests that "the description of these forms (social and cultural) is a logically prior requirement to an explanation of them. In other words, the theory of change is the capstone of sociological theory." (26, p. 495)

Accompanying this trend away from concern with change was a shift also away from analysis of whole societies. The rise of empiricism in sociology brought with it attention to more conceptually manageable units of social organization. Various sociological specialties emerged, representing generally the major institutional sectors of mass complex society. Much of the accumulating literature on social change was ensconced in the terminology and modes of analysis associated with each of the various specialties. Relatively little attention was devoted to broader institutional interrelationships and their relationship to change.

Sociologists' renewed emphasis on social change at the societal level seems to have incorporated several analytical lessons gained from additional experience in analysis and description of social organization. Along with this analytical perspective has emerged greater attention to what is changing—both in terms of level of social organization and the variables undergoing change.

Since change is a concept which does not respect discipline boundaries, it is necessary for purposes of discussion to establish a frame of reference regarding *social* change which distinguishes it from the more general category of change. By social change I shall be referring to relatively enduring modifications of social structure. This definition intentionally excludes ecological, demographic, and technological changes from the category of social change, although as emphasized by Eisenstadt, "they have been frequently emphasized as some of the most important causes of (social) change because each causes changes in the balance between distribution of manpower and resources necessary for performance of social roles and implementation of institutional goals." (13, p. xix) Especially in American society there has been a tendency to confuse social change and cultural change by emphasizing the deterministic character of technology as a primary factor in social change. (38) Williams comments in this regard that "the culture (American) has been characterized by a value system that made it possible for economic and technological activities to change rapidly and hence, to take on special causal significance. In other societies and in other times, the role of technology in social change is definitely minor." (45, p. 571)

Regarding *level* of social change, attention is devoted in this chapter to perspectives regarding *societal* change, recognizing that models of societal change have implications for change of various units of social organization which comprise society. By concentrating on change at the societal level that body of literature specifically related to change in formal organizations, small groups, family, etc., has been deliberately omitted.

## FOUR THEORETICAL APPROACHES

Recognizing that it would be both presumptuous and impossible to review all of the various theoretical perspectives regarding social change, four contemporary sociological approaches were selected for general review. The four approaches chosen are broadly labeled as functionalism, modernization, conflict, and social behaviorism. Of these four, modernization represents an extension of functionalism whereas the conflict and behaviorist approaches exemplified by Dahr-

endorf (10) and Martindale (26) are specifically critical of functionalism and have proposed alternative models for the analysis of the
basis for existence and change of social organization. The objective
will be to cover in broad strokes some of the distinguishing features
of each of these four theoretical perspectives and to identify some of
the typical propositions regarding social change representative of each.
A concluding section is devoted to a discussion of some shared features
of the differing approaches.

Selection of four theoretical approaches for presentation and discussion underscores a characteristic of sociological treatment of change.
There is no single sociological theory of change; rather each identifiable branch of sociological theory has developed its own perspective
and propositions regarding change. Consequently, most propositions
regarding change are inextricably linked to conceptions of social organization, however social organization is defined and described.
Whatever assumptions are made regarding social organization pertain
also to social change and thereby commit the theorist to an analytical
and conceptual approach to change which is logically consistent with
the conception of social organization. Thus, whether change is viewed
as "normal" or "deviant" depends on how social organization is defined
and described.

Emphasizing a variation of this same point, Bealer and Fliegel
contend that it is widely assumed that social change is fundamental
and pervasive and that, therefore, any theory of social organization
which reflects reality is a theory which incorporates propositions regarding change of social organization as well. (4) Therefore, they
contend that social change does not represent a specialized area of
sociological interest and inquiry but rather is part and parcel of
sociological theory. If social change theory is deemed to be inadequate,
then social organization theory is inadequate, since change is a fundamental feature of the reality of all units of social organization.

Theoretical propositions have typically called attention to sources
of change rather than explanation of causes of change. (37) Wilbert
Moore suggests, for example, that "the most noteworthy progress in
the theory of social change has been made in the identification and
analysis of the sources of change. In very general terms, this progress
has resulted from the abandonment of causes primarily external to
social systems and of single-factor explanations, with the correlative
acceptance of imminent changes as the prime mover in social dynamics." (29, p. 811) However, most propositions regarding change have
been correlational and relational rather than specifying cause and
effect and sequences of action leading to specified kinds of outcomes.

In general, sociological theories survive the test of adequacy more
successfully as theories of change (oriented toward prediction) than
as theories of changing (oriented toward identification of variables
instrumental for intervention and control).

Contributing heavily to the failure to identify specific causes and sequences of social change are some methodological limitations involved in the study of society. These limitations include both the sources and nature of data and the element of time. (19) Time is especially critical because, at the level of society, many significant changes manifest themselves rather slowly. Therefore, whether a particular change is described as a short-run fluctuation or aberration, or as a part of a longer-term trend often depends on the span of observation. Thus, the relevant data for analysis of causes and sequences of change extend both into the past and into the future. Search for the cause of change typically begins with the observation that some change has been or is occurring. From this observation, the causes of the change must be inferred from a discontinuous and usually general record of preconditions and sequences. The method of the observer must be longitudinal but ordinarily his data are not.

Further compounding analysis of societal change are imprecisions regarding the boundaries of society itself. Typically the boundaries of societies are taken as those of the political structure which represents only one institutional sector of a society. Although some other institutional sectors are closely aligned with the political boundaries, i.e., the economy, the boundaries of others are less readily established. If boundaries are not clearly defined, difficulty is encountered also in identifying both internal and external forces of change and their repercussions.

Etzioni and DuBow refer to the tendency to view society as a unit complete unto itself as the "island approach" and comment that "it is a mistake to treat countries as autonomous systems, meaning by systems that when a factor outside the system works on one of the members, changes in its behavior are explainable primarily in terms of its relations to other members and changes in them. If one wishes to do a satisfactory systems analysis, it will be necessary to look beyond the boundaries of a particular society to the ties which link it to other societies." (15, p. 153)

Although there are a variety of perspectives on social change, there are some points of a general nature on which there is essential agreement. In some cases these are assumptions and in others they are conclusions based on past research and analysis. However they might be identified, they are set forth as a frame of reference for the more detailed discussion to follow:

*Change is essentially a neutral concept.* Social change is an observable fact of social life which is independent of value judgments regarding good or bad, growth or decline, progress or stagnancy. In the context of this book, it may be suggested that all development involves change but not all change is development regardless of how development may be defined.

The definition of change adopted in this chapter is such a neutral definition. Attribution of direction of change typically involves judgments concerning the appropriateness of change from the standpoint of an observer or participant. An expanding scale of any unit of social organization may be perceived as growth in a society whose value system cherishes size or may be perceived as a cost by one who finds a satisfying relationship disrupted by increased size and complexity.

*Social change is normal and ubiquitous* (10, p. 162; 31, p. 2). It occurs in all societies regardless of how stagnant the society may appear. Probably because of major reliance on ideal type theories, many societies have been typified as traditional, a term often regarded synonymously with nonchange. Gusfield (17), however, contends that most so-called traditional societies have experienced frequent and often radical changes although not necessarily in the *direction* of modernization.

Suggesting that social change is normal and ubiquitous is not intended to imply, however, that all observed fluctuations in social systems are necessarily social changes, e.g., relatively *enduring* modifications of social structure. In this regard, Moore emphasizes that all units of social organization are capable of flexibilities within a limited range without changing their essential nature due primarily to vagaries in socialization and role performance and, therefore, it is important to distinguish between "mere sequences of small actions that in sum essentially comprise the pattern . . . and changes in the system itself, in the magnitude of boundaries, in the prescriptions for action, in the relation of the particular system to its environment." (30, p. 5)

A somewhat different perspective is offered by Tiryakian who differentiates between social change and societal change. He suggests that "social change is essentially a continuous rather than a discontinuous process. It is a quantitative elaboration of structural differentiation. . . . Societal change is fundamentally a qualitative change, a discontinuity or 'leap' in the general normative pattern of the organization, which will be manifested in all major foci of institutional structure. What therefore distinguishes a revolution as a major type of societal change from other social upheavals is not the magnitude of physical violence, as is commonly argued, but its permeation of the social structure." (41, pp. 70–73)

*Structural stress or strain whether described as "tension" (31), "dysfunction" (7), or "conflict" (10), is an inherent quality of social organization and is both a source and a product of social change.* (7, p. 237; 10; 31) In this regard Moore, who is often labeled an "integration" theorist, comments that "there are internal sources of tension and strain in all societies. The model of the perfectly integrated society is a useful analytical fiction for many purposes but ought not to be confused with primitive or agrarian societies. The sources of strain include, at least, uncertainties in socialization from generation to generation, chance innovations, and competing role demands given scarities of time, treasure and energy." (30, p. 162) Similarly Dahrendorf in describing the basic tenets of a coercion theory of society states that "Every society displays at every point dissensus and conflict; social conflict is ubiquitous." (10, p. 162)

The degree of prominence accorded conflict as a factor in social organization and change has been at the heart of one of the recurring controversies in sociological theory. (1, 22, 42, 46) "Integration" and "coercion" theorists do not generally contest the existence of conflict (although integration theorists have a proclivity for terms like "tension," "strain," "deviance," etc., whereas "conflict," "revolution," and "violence" are encountered more frequently in the coercion literature), but do differ on the extent to which conflict is assumed to be endemic to social organization. Coercion theorists in generating propositions regarding social change emphasize internal inequalities in the distribution of power, rewards, and resources as the potential genesis of conflict and hence change. Integration theorists display a greater tendency to seek the causes of change among factors external to the unit of social organization: it is primarily exogenous factors which generate internal stresses and strains which, once set in motion, motivate adaptive responses which lead to social change.

Following from the above, *change of any unit of social organization may occur as a result of forces either within or external to the unit.* This premise is stated only because it has been a rather frequently debated issue in the change literature. Critics of integration theories have argued that a model of social organization based on value consensus and tendencies toward equilibrium and stability commits the model to account for change only by intrusion of external factors. Logically, such a system in isolation would be unchanging. The Parsonsian model of the social system is particularly vulnerable to this charge. (34) However, Parsons conceptualizes the social system as an entity separate from personality and cultural systems which are major sources of innovation and change. Thus, technically, personality and culture systems are external to the social system.

The other theoretical perspectives to be discussed, e.g., coercion and behaviorism, are not logically committed to either endogenous or exogenous sources of change and, therefore, the distinction is of less relevance.

*There is no natural order of social change equally applicable to various societies or to various levels of social organization within society.* By the same token, there are no single causes or determinisms which inevitably lead to change in all situations. Specifically rejected are notions about the effect of race, climate, technology, natural resources, personality, etc., as determinants of either the mode of social organization or its change.

Although rejected as determinisms, social change is generally lacking in literature of analysis of multivariate interaction between changes in such exogenous factors and responses of various types of social organization to changing circumstances. Multivariate interaction is stressed because some writers such as Ogburn (cultural lag) and McClelland (achievement motive) (27) have sought to account for social change by an emphasis on single factors such as technology and personality type.

The routes to social change (or even a more specific directional form such as modernization) are multivarious and the consequences are similarly diverse. This is not to say that there are no predictable patterns of change, but rather to suggest that predictability is based upon specification of the source of change and upon observation and analysis of the unit undergoing change. In this regard, Eisenstadt suggests that "specific processes of change in any concrete society are closely related to the specific characteristics of its institutional structure and can be explained largely in terms of the crystallization of this structure and the problem of maintaining it. Moreover, the directions of change in any given society are greatly influenced and limited by its basic systemic characteristics and by the specific problems resulting from its institutionalization." (14, p. 376)

Following from the above, *social changes are neither temporally nor spatially isolated.* (31) Regardless of the degree of simplicity of the society there are relationships between various sectors within society and, especially in the world today, between societies as well. Changes in one sector change relationships with other sectors, and thereby presumably result in sequences of change. (31)

However, despite the virtually unchallenged assertion regarding interdependence of change, empirical evidence on the path, force, or rate of such repercussions is generally lacking.

*Empirical evidence does, however, support the assertion that social change is more likely to occur in heterogeneous (differentiated) than homogeneous (undifferentiated) societies.* (5, p. 615) The probability of social change appears to be closely related to the range of *perceived* alternatives for action. In general, the greater the range of perceived alternatives, the greater the probability of conflict, innovation, dysfunctions, strains, and other processes identified as sources of change.

*Social change is multidirectional including the possibility of being nondirectional.* Some changes have a tendency to be cumulative such as organization rules (31), or organizational complexity (40); some display cyclical tendencies, e.g., formation and destruction of communities (26); and some are essentially random, e.g., responses to natural catastrophe (26, p. 54). The direction change is likely to take depends, therefore, on *what* is changing. For most qualitative changes, attribution of direction is primarily a value judgment.

## Functionalism

Functionalism has been both a dominant mode of sociological theory and the most criticized version of social change during the past thirty years. Functionalism has been used to describe that "collectivity of theorists who look upon society as a system, the maintenance of which is the function of recurrent social activities, as well as the particular doctrine they profess." (44) The synonyms of "order" or "integration" theory have also been used to describe this theoretical perspective. In the functionalist conception, social systems are viewed as being integrated combinations of interdependent elements with each element contributing positively to the maintenance of the system and which, when taken together, comprise the system. The elements are "functional" to the extent that they contribute the adjustment and adaptation of the system in its environment. The social system is conceived as a natural system and as an entity in and of itself, transcendent to man.

Whether adopted as a generalization or for heuristic purposes, the notion of equilibrium or system maintaining and/or integrating tendencies is fundamental to the functionalist conception of system and system change. As stated by Parsons, "The concept of stable equilibrium implies that through integrative mechanisms, endogenous variations are kept within limits compatible with the maintenance of the main structural patterns and, through adaptive mechanisms, fluctuations in the relations between system and environment are similarly kept within limits." (34, p. 225)

Equilibrium as used by Parsons then means an ordered state of integration in which a society reaches a state of self-sufficiency by virtue of balanced combinations of functions which serve to control both environmental and internal conditions. Functional requisites are those system elements which contribute to the maintenance of stability and include normative consensus and a high degree of social control.

Parsons emphasizes also an important distinction regarding change which is recurrent in the functionalist literature: the distinction between changes *within* the system and changes *of* the system. Changes within the system are identified as small-scale changes which are a normal accompaniment of any ongoing unit of social organization. Of relevance to the theory of social change, however, are changes *of* the system where the basic pattern takes on a new form. Since social systems are described in terms of inertia, the change-producing force must be of sufficient magnitude to upset the "normal" state of the system in order for change of the system to occur. Since systems are organized around the tendency to maintain equilibrium, such forces in an analytical sense must be exogenous[1] and are defined essentially as disturbances. Thus, any change-inducing factor impinging on the system from the outside generates tensions which in turn call forth adaptive responses from mechanisms within the system. In this regard, Boskoff states that "in the functionalist approach changes and tension are intertwined. Innovations initially arise in 'normal' and/or disturbed

[1] It is important to recall that culture and personality systems in the Parsonsian framework are treated analytically as external to the social system.

functioning of social systems. When accepted, these in turn create further tensions traceable to uneven derivative adjustments. And these tensions expressed in terms of social problems incite further, presumably stabilizing, changes." (7, p. 237)

One of the predominant categories of structural change in response to such disturbances is structural differentiation, a process whereby roles and functions become more specialized and distinct, resulting in structural change. The concept of structural differentiation and its prominence in theories of modernization will be discussed in greater detail in the following section.

It has been charged by various critics that the basic features of functional analysis of social organization result in a conservative orientation toward change both because of an emphasis on system-maintaining attributes of social systems and an emphasis on differentiation, adaptation, innovation, and accumulation as processes of change. Parsons however contends that the reciprocal of propositions regarding stability of social organization should be viewed as propositions regarding change. (34) That is, if some element or condition contributes to the stability of a social system, the absence of that same condition or element contributes to its instability and/or change. However, change and stability are not regarded in the functionalist literature as mutually exclusive states. In fact, it is because a system has the capability to adjust or adapt to changing exogenous conditions that it is able to retain relative stability over a period of time. A system which did not adjust or adapt to changing conditions would become increasingly mal-integrated over a period of time, creating conditions leading to probable revolutionary change. (42)

Charges that functionalism does not provide an adequate theoretical basis for dealing with social change have brought forth a variety of responses from its advocates. Included among these responses have been articles by Parsons (33, 34, 35) specifying his considerations on theory of social change and by Boskoff (7) and Cancian (8) who by deductive processes seek to establish the consistency between functionalism and social change.

Boskoff, using the AGIL[2] model of Parsons as a frame of reference, develops a series of hypotheses and propositions regarding social change. (7) In the manner described previously, he differentiates between concepts such as "process" and "development" which are "predictable variations in the operation of social systems based on study of previous phases of their operation" (7, p. 216) and social change "defined as significant variations from procensual and developmental patterns." (7, p. 216)

---

[2] In the Parsonsian framework of social systems, each system is confronted with four basic problems which must be solved for continuation of the system. These functional requisites are adaptive (to the environment), goal-attaining, integration and pattern maintenance.

Taking a cue also from Parsons, Boskoff describes characteristic substructures for the operation of social systems which are incorporated into his propositions. These are: "(1) the primary-technical level . . . (2) managerial level—to mediate and control several specialized but interdependent technical units . . . (3) institutional level—policy-making, legitimation, and coordination of managerial units . . . (4) societal level—provides coordination among specialized units at the institutional level." (7, p. 222) Typically at the societal level, one of three institutional sectors is predominant—religious, governmental, or economic.

Boskoff also distinguishes three analytical states in the process of change which occur in the following sequence: "(a) sources of innovative values or behavior—most likely to be technical or managerial level or external sources . . . institutional levels are uncongenial to innovative roles for itself . . . (b) filtering process or control of contributed innovations— . . . major responsibility of the institutional level . . . (c) derivative structures and functional reverberations." (7, p. 224) Of these three, phase (b) is crucial since phase (a) provides only the possibility of change and phase (c) involves implementation. Therefore, hypotheses and propositions regarding change are most concerned with the source of innovative values and behavior and with the factors affecting legitimation of innovations.

Armed with these conceptual distinctions, Boskoff suggests the following hypotheses regarding structural conditions which are most conducive to innovation. The hypotheses are generally derived from Parsons and from a review of the functionalist literature on change. In general, the opportunity for variation and innovation in social systems is directly associated with:

a) the degree of specialization of roles for discharging the four functional requirements (AGIL)
b) complexity of societal types
c) significant shifts in the proportional effort devoted by the social system to the four functional problems
d) the amount of interpersonal and intergroup conflict within each of the four functional areas, whatever the reasons for the conflict
e) amount of intergroup competition for dominance at the institutional level
f) *perceived* failure of existing practices in meeting the four functional problems
g) *perceived* degree of overemphasis on otherwise legitimate objectives and,
h) other things being equal, adaptive and goal-attaining functions provide more opportunity for variation than the pattern-maintenance and integrative functions. (7, pp. 226–30)

In the tradition of functionalism, hypotheses (d), (e), (f), and (g) suggest "dysfunctional" conditions to which innovative values and behavior are expected to emerge as an adaptive response. Conflict, (d), for example is operative as a source of change to the extent that it results in the emergence of innovations. Left unanswered by such propositions are questions regarding the source of the dysfunctional condition which triggers adaptive responses, viz., change. The other hypotheses implicitly describe conditions which are dependent upon the extent of previous change, e.g., the greater the degree of structural differentiation (heterogeneity of the system) the greater the probability of innovation. Especially hypotheses (c) and (h) and to a degree (f) and (g) do suggest some leverage points for the practitioner or development specialist interested in the introduction of innovations. The above hypotheses relate to the probability of the emergence of innovations, a necessary but not sufficient condition for change.

Regarding sanction of innovations by appropriate institutional levels (the crucial phase), Boskoff suggests the following as some significant conditions:

a) control of innovations is directly associated with success in pattern-maintenance and tension-management.

b) the more diffuse and flexible the system of interaction, the greater the opportunity for diffusion and the greater the likelihood that these (innovations) will be ignored by personnel at the institutional level.

c) one-way communication reduces perception of innovation and also serves to reduce potential diffusion of innovations.

d) institutional groups relying on direct control mechanisms are unlikely to feel congenial toward innovation—unless under their own auspices.

e) achieved criteria in recruitment of institutional elites is conducive to legitimation of innovations.

f) the relative permeability of institutional elites is positively related to facilitation of innovation. (7, pp. 231–33)

Although the above conditions are presented as pertaining to the control and facilitation of innovations, some are essentially redundant of the conditions conducive to innovation. For example, it is not certain how "perceived failure of existing practices in meeting the four functional problems" could be characteristic of a system which experiences "success in pattern maintenance and tension-management." One condition logically negates the other. Consequently often the presence of a condition conducive to innovation implies the presence of a condition conducive to legitimation.

For several of the other conditions which may not be in harmony at various levels, e.g., "perceived failure of existing practices" at the technical or managerial level in association with "direct control" or "ascribed criteria in recruitment," at the institutional level might be conceived as conditions most likely to lead to major conflict or revolution. It would seem predictable that conflict would result where conditions conducive to innovation prevailed in the absence of conditions conducive to legitimation. For most relatively stable and unchanging social structures neither set of conditions prevails. Conversely for most modern and/or rapidly changing societies both tend to prevail.

Although the above do not exhaust the hypotheses and propositions presented by Boskoff, they do include a sufficient sample to indicate some representative generalizations emerging from the functionalist perspective. The hypotheses are generally couched in terms of system attributes and conditions which are described as being conducive to innovation, acceptance of innovation, and, therefore, change. As is generally true of the functional perspective, the source of innovation is identified in only the most general terms. Boskoff notes, for example, that concern with personality variables would be required to understand why some and not all persons innovate in situations conducive to innovation.[3]

Some criticisms of the functional treatment of change have already been alluded to. Perhaps the most frequent criticism has been the lack of fit between systems models and empirical data. Horowitz comments that "the concept of function in sociology has been built up from physiological and biological models in which notions of teleology are central. . . . Functionalism as a sociological credo . . . is not a direct consequence of observations, but rather an indirect consequence of philosophical inference and judgment." (20, pp. 54–55)

In general, functional models attribute change to one or a combination of three sources: adjustment of the system to exogenous change, growth through structural and functional differentiation, and/or innovations by system members. Conceptualizing change in terms of one or more of these three sources results in analysis of change situations primarily in terms of repercussions within the system. Attention is directed to investigation of those adjustments and adaptations that systems make to restore a state of relative integration. This conceptualization has utility in terms of calling attention to those unintended consequences accompanying change. Moore however comments that there are some missing empirical links: "Theoretically innovation may occur at any point in the social structure; functional theory and various 'equilibrium' models do not tell us where or when it is most likely. And although functional theory or 'systems' analysis starts from the assumption that any change has repercussions throughout the system, we do not in fact know either this assumption to be true in detail, or the path, rate or degree of dependent change." (29, p. 817)

[3] Some recent theoretical emphases on identifying psychological (and sociological) factors related to innovation include: E. E. Hagen, On the Theory of Social Change, Homewood, Ill.: Dorsey Press, 1962; David McClelland, The Achieving Society, Princeton, N. J.: D. Van Nostrand & Co., Inc., 1961; H. G. Barnett, Innovation: The Basis of Cultural Change, New York: McGraw-Hill Book Co., 1953.

The emphasis on order and integration and the corresponding indentification of gradual, incremental, and adjustive processes of change which are products of functional conceptions of social organization lead, as suggested by Horton (22), to conservative definitions of social problems and conservative prescriptions for their solution. Left essentially outside the capability of functional models are such sources of change as sudden and profound revolutionary change, structural change generated by conflict and contradiction originating within the system, and nonadjustive responses to extra-systemic change.

Criticisms of functionalism, however, have been fashionable and most often couched in terms which seize on some of the idealistic errors of earlier normative concepts of functionalism. (22) Demerath, in seeking to add clarification to the debate, suggests that much of the criticism of functionalism has failed to distinguish between rather disparate varieties of the breed. He offers a distinction between the "functionalists" of which Parsons is the notable representative and "structuralists," a category which includes Wilbert Moore. The distinction is drawn primarily between concern with the *structural part* (structuralists) or with the systemic whole (functionalists). Many of the more often voiced criticisms of the structural-functional approach to social change have referred to the category of functionalists who, by concentrating their attention on the systemic whole, are more likely to overemphasize system unity or stability, to be concerned with internal process rather than external change, and to be conservative in terms of de-emphasis of change. (11, p. 400) These charges are less likely to apply to the structuralist.

Van den Berghe also rejects the charge that functionalism has not been of value in analysis of change: "far from making analysis of change impossible, functionalism has proven a powerful instrument in dealing with at least two major types of change: growth in complexity through differentiation, and adjustment to extra-systemic changes." (42, p. 697)

**Modernization**

Contemporary emphasis on economic growth and development as a deliberate strategy of change has stimulated a concomitant concern on the part of sociologists with those conditions and processes of change which have accompanied economic growth and expansion of scale. Those theories of change included under the generalized rubric of modernization reflect this emphasis. Most such theories have been empirically derived either from histories of the industrial revolution or from correlational studies involving samples of underdeveloped countries.

Modernization has become a general term for processes of industrialization, urbanization, bureaucratization, and rationalism which are viewed as highly intercorrelated and interdependent processes emanating from the more general process of structural differentiation. Although many of the key concepts employed in modernization models derive directly from functionalism, e.g., structural differentiation, system, integration, etc., several modernization models also incorporate elements of behaviorism. This is especially true of those models which emphasize the role of mass communication in modifying the individual's images, definitions of situations, roles, and therefore also patterns of socialization. (12, 23, 24, 36)

Contrary to models concerned only with change, modernization models are concerned with problems of development and growth and consequently include an explicit specification of the direction of change with the emphasis being on those processes which result in transitions from the simple to the complex, from the traditional to the modern. Concern with the direction of change appears to have been instrumental in stimulating a revival of interest in evolutionary concepts. (3, 6, 33) A recent article by Parsons contributes to this revival. Parsons proposes a series of evolutionary universals which are hypothesized to appear in sequential order and which are defined as "any organization development sufficiently important to further evolution that, rather than emerging only once, it is likely to be 'hit upon' by various systems operating under different conditions." (33, p. 339) Several of the universals proposed by Parsons such as "bureaucratic organizations," "money and market complex," and "generalized universalistic norms" have come to be regarded essentially as defining attributes of the modern society.

For this discussion, a brief review of the basic features of two modernization models will be presented: Smelser's study of social change in the industrial revolution (39) and Lerner's communication theory of modernization. (24)

The basic problem of Smelser's study was to characterize and explain the growth and development of social systems by applying a model of structural differentiation. This model postulates a typical sequence of events which occur when a social system increases in complexity.

Smelser's analysis assumes that the process of passing from a less differentiated to a more differentiated social structure is characterized by definite regularities, and that these sequences of differentiation of the social structure can be analyzed systematically in societies in flux.

The model of structural differentiation is an abstract theory of change. When one social role or organization becomes archaic under changing historical circumstances, it is anticipated that differentiation by a definite and specific sequence of events into two or more roles or organizations will occur with the new structure functioning more effectively in the new historical circumstances. The new social units are

structurally distinct from each other, but taken together are functionally equivalent to the original unit.[4] Any sequence of differentiation
is set in motion by specific disequilibrating conditions. Initially,
this disequilibrium gives rise to symptoms of social disturbances which
must be brought into line by social control. Structural differentiation
is thus regarded conceptually as a mode of system adjustment or adaptation to changing conditions.

The process of change by structural differentiation is defined
sequentially in ideal-type terms as: 1) structural differentiation, or the
establishment of more specialized and more autonomous social units,
2) integration—which changes its character as the old social order is
made obsolete by the process of differentiation (the state, the law,
political groupings, and other associations are particularly salient in
integration), 3) social disturbances—mass hysteria, outbursts of violence, religious and political movements, etc., which reflect the uneven
march of differentiation and integration. (40, p. 259) Such a sequence
may recur, always, however, establishing a new level of integration.
New levels of integration are described by Eisenstadt as the emergence
of new institutional structures which he contends are essential to accommodate higher levels of differentiation. (14)

Although the specific frame of reference of this discussion is societal change, Smelser contends that the model of structural differentiation is a general model applicable to various levels and types of social
structure.[5] Separate models are not required for analyzing changes in
the economy, the family, the class system, etc. The patterns of change
of all these institutions should follow the same general model. It may
be noted that this perspective is in contradiction to one of the points
made in the introduction about the generality of models of social
change to a variety of organizational forms and levels.

Although modernization theories of change are evolutionary in
their emphasis on the continued development of role differentiation,
institutional autonomy, etc., they do not contend that such a path leads
directly to a uniform social structure. Smelser contends for example,
that structural differentiation varies from society to society because of:
a) variations in premodern conditions, b) variations in the impetus to
change, c) variations in the path toward modernization, d) variations
in the advanced stages of modernization, and e) variations in the content and timing of dramatic events during modernization. (40, p. 260)
Thus, the structural differentiation model is not intended to describe
a common end product, but rather to describe a *process* of re-formation

---

[4] It may be noted here that Etzioni (16) in discussing modernization distinguishes
between "preformism" which suggests that differentiation is a process of existing
functions taking on different organizational forms and "epigenesis" where the
process of differentiation involves the emergence of new functions. Smelser's use
of the concept is essentially preformism.

[5] In his analysis of social structure, Smelser makes use of the four functional
requirements of social systems (AGIL) discussed earlier.

of social structure which can be expected to produce a variety of forms.

In Smelser's theoretical framework, differentiation alone is not sufficient for modernization. Rather, modernization proceeds as a contrapuntal interplay between differentiation (which is divisive of established structures) and integration (which unites differentiated structures on a new basis). (40, p. 267) This interplay is conceptualized by Smelser as involving a sequence of seven steps which are involved in a system moving from a point of instability characterized by dissatisfactions to a new more differentiated level of institutional integration.

Illustrating this sequence is his analysis of industrial differentiation which implies that under certain market, value, and other conditions, the existing industrial structure becomes inadequate to meet industrial requirements. 1) The starting point for a sequence of structural differentiation of organization is the historical *appearance of dissatisfactions* with industrial production. The dissatisfaction may be directed at various classes of economic agents, or may be phrased in terms of the misallocation or misuse of the resources of labor, capital and organization. Whatever the specific foci of dissatisfaction, however, it is justified and legitimized in terms of the current values relating to production. 2) Before any specific action is taken to overcome the sources of dissatisfaction *diverse symptoms of disturbance* appear. 3) Next a number of agencies of social control engage in a series of "holding actions" against these disturbances to prevent them from reaching disruptive proportions *(management of tension)*. 4) Simultaneously, there is a reaffirmation of the basic values governing production and an encouragement of ideas designed to implement these values in new, more effective ways (innovations). 5) Inventions and experiments in rearranging the division of labor carry these ideals to a still *greater degree of specification*. 6) Finally, entrepreneurs translate these suggestions into *concrete attempts to reorganize the basis of production* (implementation). 7) If successful, the entrepreneurial attempts lead to an explosive growth of production, capitalization, profits, and reorganization which return gradually to *routine* levels as new methods become consolidated in the organizational structure. (39)

Smelzer suggests that a similar pattern may be observed in the family economy. The family may become, under specific pressures, inadequate for performing its defined functions. Dissatisfaction occurs when it is felt either that performance of roles or utilization of resources falls short of expectations. The symptoms of disturbance resulting from these pressures are first handled by existing mechanisms of social control. Gradually, as the energy is harnessed, it is diverted to the more positive tasks of legitimizing and specifying ideas for social action, and transforming these ideas into social experiments. If successful, these produce one or more structurally distinct social units.

The steps described by Smelser will be recognized as incorporating many of the same points emphasized by Boskoff, namely that innovation is most likely to occur when there is a perceived failure or inadequacy of existing means and, further, that innovation to effectuate social change must be legitimized and implemented to achieve a new level of system integration.

Smelser emphasizes dissatisfactions attributable to failures of existing patterns of organization to meet expectations as one of the principal factors stimulating a sequence of differentiation. Given the presence of such dissatisfactions, most attention is directed toward internal processes of adjustment and adaptation. Several recent modernization theories, however, have focused more directly on social psychological variables and the impact of such external factors as mass communications as a means of modifying individual expectations, images, and definitions and consequently triggering a modernizing process similar to that described by Smelser. (12, 23, 36) Theorists emphasizing mass communication as a crucial variable in modernization essentially accept the conceptual framework of structural differentiation but emphasize in addition the significance of social mobilization which "is the name given to an overall process of change which happens to substantial parts of the population in countries which are moving from traditional to modern ways of life," (12, p. 493) and which finds expression in social, psychic, and physical mobility. Such mobility stimulated by mass communication reduces isolation and autonomy of societies, units of social organization within societies, and individuals, and serves to expand the range of perceived alternatives, thereby enhancing the probability of innovation and structural change. The reduction of isolation is viewed also as stimulating physical movement with an accompanying spatial redistribution of population.

Lerner's communication approach to modernization emphasizes that "modernity is an interactional behavioral system . . . whose components are behavioral in the sense that they operate only through the activity of individuals." (24, p. 239) He emphasizes, also, that "there are two sets of problems that confront the development process: mobility and stability. By mobility is meant the problems of societal dynamism; by stability is meant the problems of societal equilibrium. Mobility is the agent of social change . . . social change in this sense is the sum of mobilities acquired by individuals." (24, p. 332)

Given this frame of reference regarding social organization and change, Lerner's position may be stated as follows: Economic growth is most likely to occur under those conditions where individual effort is associated with reward. If this does not occur, then the "rising level of expectations" becomes instead a "rising level of frustration" which perpetuates the cycle of poverty.

Establishing the association between effort and reward is a communication process. "People must learn to make this association in their daily lives—linking what they see with what they hear, what they want with what they do, what they do with what they get." (23, p. 346)

Communication is the principal means of socialization and socialization the primary means of social change. Therefore, the modernization process must begin with new means of communication intervening in existing processes of communication. Such communication is instrumental in diffusing new ideas and information and modifying images in such a way as to stimulate desires to act in new ways. Such new desires and patterns of behavior are incorporated into socialization processes, thereby conditioning future generations. As suggested by Horowitz, "Consciousness of underdevelopment produces emphasis on social change, whereas consciousness of being highly developed produces emphasis on stability." (21, p. 437)

However, the new interests and innovations, in order to result in modernizing social change, must be translated from private interests into public institutions. Such public institutions ideally represent aggregations of private interests. However, public institutions depend on modifications of patterns of recruitment. New generations socialized in terms of new interests must be recruited so that "the new aggregation of interests into institutions may be accomplished and sustained. So it is that starting from a breakthrough in communication, reinforced by new ways of socialization, a new political class is recruited that aggregates the new interests articulated within the society in such fashion as to create its new institutions—its version of modernity." (24, p. 348)

Lerner takes into account that there are a number of necessary conditions which must be met in order for mass communication to have the predicted effect. He acknowledges that "mass media function effectively only in modern and rapidly modernizing societies." (24, p. 330) The reason for this is that a society must have a capacity to both produce and consume (which is determined by cash, literacy, and motivation) media products. Thus in describing conditions necessary for mass communication to stimulate modernization he virtually concludes that modernization is necessary for modernization.

As mentioned, there has been some tendency for modernization to be viewed as the antithesis of traditionalism, replacing it in total as the process proceeds. Some notes of caution, however, have been sounded by Gusfield who writes, "the all too common practice of pitting tradition and modernity against each other as paired opposites tends to overlook the mixtures and blends which reality displays. Above all, it becomes an ideology of antitraditionalism, denying the necessary and usable ways in which the past serves as support, especially in the sphere of values and political legitimation to the present and future." (17, p. 362) Gusfield's observation is offered support by a recent report of differences in the rate of modernization of two Israeli villages. The authors' research leads them to conclude that the

type of modernization attempted is a crucial factor. Where modernization is individually oriented such as industrialization or urbanization,
then dispersion and disintegration of traditional structures become
essential strategy. However, where the change involves community
some adherence to traditional structures is necessitated. (43)

## Conflict

As noted in the introduction one of the persistent polemics in
sociological theory concerns the distinction between "coercion and
consensus" (1), or alternatively "conflict and order" (22), or "interests
and values" (32) as the basis of integration and change or social organization. The distinction in its more recent forms does not involve
denial of the presence of each of these paired alternatives in all actual
social organization but rather the degree of emphasis placed on each as
the cohering force of society. As has been discussed, various functionalists do not deny the existence of conflict nor do various champions of
conflict theory, e.g., Dahrendorf, Coser, Horowitz, Van den Berghe,
etc., deny the presence of consensus or order as a feature of social organization. In fact each of the conflict theorists has sought to synthe-
size the conflict perspective with various features of integration theory.
Coser especially emphasizes that it is unwise to sharply differentiate a
sociology of order from a sociology of conflict, contending that exclusive emphasis on one or the other tends to obscure social reality. (9)

Although conflict theorists do acknowledge the presence of order,
they cite coercion rather than consensus as a more realistic basis of such
order. Illustrative of how coercion is viewed as a basis of social integration, Adams suggests that "social control . . . whether through
socialization or through differing access to society's rewards is basic
to any level of societal integration. Conflict thus becomes a rebellion
against coercion, and viewed this way consensus becomes more a
group *imposed* phenomenon than the basic aspect of social existence.
In other words . . . it is coercion which maintains society and its sub-
divisions and it is conflict which changes them." (1, p. 717)

Regarding coercion as the integrating force of social organization
has led conflict theorists to emphasize the dialectic as a basic process
of change: the absence of effective means of internal regulation and
the existence of a volatile rather than stable system of values. Distinctions between changes *within* the structure and changes *of* the structure are of little relevance to the conflict theorist since predicating
social organization on coercion and conflict as the basis of both order
and change firmly fixes the source of change within the unit of social
organization. In general, conflict theories share with integration
theories a holistic approach. (42)

Although there are a variety of viewpoints included under the general heading of conflict theory, perhaps one of the more heralded recent contributions to conflict theory and its treatment of social change is Ralf Dahrendorf's *Class and Class Conflict in Industrial Society.* (10) Although Dahrendorf is chosen as representative of conflict theory, he does not consider his theory to be a general theory but rather is intended to apply to industrial society only.

The development of Dahrendorf's theory of class conflict and social change begins with an explication of the difference between the "integrative" image and the "coercion" image of social structure and change. Dahrendorf's contention is that the integrative approach is concerned with consensus which results in a tendency to focus on normative aspects of social structure whereas the coercion approach is concerned with conflict which tends to focus on behavior. While insisting that each is a side of the same coin (that societies are always ordered and are always changing), Dahrendorf chooses to develop his theory of structural change on the latter. As he suggests, "None of the theoretical approaches of modern sociology . . . succeeds in superseding Marx's theory by a new and similarly comprehensive formulation. . . . Our problem is the explanation of systematic social conflicts in industrial societies. . . . It appears advisable to base this formulation on an image of society that permits the explanation of conflicts in terms of structural, not individual, conditions. . . . Finally the theory will have to be capable of accounting for the society with which Marx was concerned as well as for contemporary society and for the changes that have transformed the former into the latter." (10, pp. 114–16)

The basic tenets of the coercion theory of society are:

1. Every society is at every point subject to processes of change; social change is ubiquitous.
2. Every society displays at every point dissensus and conflict; social conflict is ubiquitous.
3. Every element in a society renders a contribution to its disintegration and change.
4. Every society is based on the coercion of some of its members by others. (10, p. 162)

The obverse of these will be recognized as the tenets of the integration theory of society. The above tenets of a coercion theory indicate acceptance of two basic Marxian assumptions about society which have a bearing on social change: 1) social structures contain the seeds of their own change, and 2) conflict groups are the means through which change occurs.

The coercion theory of society is predicated on the notion that all forms of social organization (imperatively coordinated associations) in industrial society are based on the exercise and allocation of power rather than normative consensus. Since power is a scarce resource, competition emerges regarding the distribution of power which eventuates in conflict and change. If there are conflicts of ends among actors then their behavior is determined less by shared norms than by relative power.

Dahrendorf conceptualizes power primarily in terms of authority with relationships being dichotomized as domination and subjection. Contrary to Marx, however, Dahrendorf does not limit his conception of conflict to economic interests alone but rather to interests centered around the distribution of authority and power which embraces all institutional sectors. His explication of conflict includes competition and is considered to vary along dimensions of intensity and violence.

The type of conflict of specific concern in Dahrendorf's analysis is that which occurs between *conflict groups*. It is such conflict groups, once they have organized themselves, which engage in conflicts resulting in structural change. Conflict groups are formed and organized on the basis of interests arising out of domination-subjection relationships. Thus conflict groups are more specifically delimited than the general category of interest groups.

Since conflict leading to structural change occurs as the result of the formation of conflict groups, then those structural conditions which lead to the formation of such groups are of central concern. Among the necessary conditions specified are the following:

1) Personnel—"the availability of possible organizers, founders, and leaders is essentially a technical prerequisite which must be satisfied for unorganized quasi-groups to be transformed into organized interest groups." (10, p. 185)
2) Charter—"there must be a person or circle of persons who take on themselves the task of articulation and codification, or alternatively, an ideology, a system of ideas, must be available which in a given case is capable of serving as a program or charter of groups." (10, p. 186)
3) Freedom of coalition—"Where a plurality of conflicting parties is not permitted and their emergence suppressed by the absence of freedom of coalition and by police force, conflict groups cannot organize themselves even if all other conditions of their organization are present." (10, p. 186) Thus suppression can be a means of thwarting conflict.
4) Patterned recruitment—"the formation of organized interest groups is possible only if recruitment to quasi-groups follows a structural pattern rather than chance, e.g., the lowest stratum of industrial societies is frequently recruited in manifold but structurally *irrelevant* ways; by delinquency, extreme lack of talent, personal mishaps, physical or psychological instability, etc. In this case, the condition of structural recruitment is not satisfied, and conflict group formation cannot be expected." (10, pp. 187–88)

Given these conditions, conflict groups within industrial society, organized around interests, may be expected to emerge.

Structural change is defined in terms of "changes involving the personnel of positions of domination in social organization." (10, p. 231) Change in personnel results in structural change since authority is structural and, as will be recalled, authority is manifest in the behavior of role incumbents. Therefore changing either the *incumbents* or their *behavior* changes the domination-subjection relationship. Dahrendorf emphasizes also that if personnel in positions of domination incorporate the proposals and interests of those in positions of subjection into their policies then structural change has occurred without change of personnel.

Dahrendorf differentiates between suddenness and radicalness of structural change, contending that suddenness, which can range from slow evolutionary change to revolution, can vary independently of radicalness of change. He cites the case of the industrial revolution as an example of radical but relatively slow structural change. In general "radicalness of change co-varies with the intensity of conflict" (10, p. 240) and "suddenness of change co-varies with the violence of conflict." (10, p. 240) Both the relative degree of intensity of conflict, which is defined in terms of "energy expenditure and degree of involvement of conflicting parties" (10, p. 211), and violence of conflict, expressed in terms of manifestations, are attributable to various kinds of structural conditions. Those structural conditions which account for variation in the intensity and violence of conflict therefore are expected to account also for variations in structural change.

Dahrendorf proposes the following structural conditions as being related to the intensity of conflict:

1) Degree of pluralism—in general the greater the degree of pluralism the lower the intensity of conflict. This is in contrast to superimposition where the individual is totally involved in an encompassing social structure. Since such a structure represents all aspects of his life, he is totally involved and, consequently, intensity of conflict, when it emerges, would be expected to increase. Pluralism is only slightly related to violence of conflict. A corollary of this condition is emphasized by Coser (9) who suggests that the closer (and therefore the more encompassing) the relationship the more intense the conflict. However in close relationships there is a greater tendency to suppress conflict: although intensity is greater, frequency is lower. The degree of pluralism can be interpreted also as degree of structural differentiation. Thus although intensity of conflict as a source of change may be reduced by greater pluralism, the functionalist hypotheses offered by Boskoff suggest an increase in innovation with greater differentiation.

2) Relative deprivation—the greater the dissociation of socioeconomic status and authority in associations the lower the intensity of conflict. This condition is derivative from the first condition. It suggests that the greater the extent of bifurcation of power as well as other rewards of "an imperatively coordinated association" the

more intense the conflict. If the "haves" have everything and the "have-nots" nothing, conflict, when it becomes manifest, is likely to be intense and resulting structural change radical.

Dahrendorf concludes also that violence of conflict is closely related to degree of deprivation. The greater the extent to which deprivation is absolute the more violent conflict is expected to be.

3) Mobility—the greater the extent to which classes are open the lower the intensity of conflict. Conflict itself is a means of mobility, especially as defined by Dahrendorf. Thus the degree of conflict as a means of mobility for those in positions of subjection is a reciprocal of the extent to which mobility may be achieved by means other than conflict. In general terms the degree of mobility was emphasized by Boskoff as a condition conducive to institutional legitimation of contributed innovations. Thus it can be interpreted that the conditions under which conflict is expected to be less intense are conditions under which innovation is most likely to be a primary source of change.

4) Organization—the intensity of conflict decreases to the extent that the conditions necessary for conflict group formation are present. Dahrendorf qualifies this condition however by suggesting that organization serves to reduce violence of conflict to a greater extent than intensity: "for individuals concerned, involvement in conflicts decreases as the legitimacy of conflicts and, by implication, their issues become recognized. However in the ensemble of factors affecting intensity of conflict, the specific weight of the conditions of organization is not very great." (10, p. 213)

The above structural conditions relate primarily to variations in intensity of conflict rather than violence and therefore are most relevant to predictions regarding radicalness of structural change. Violence of conflict is discussed more in terms of institutionalized means of conflict regulation. Dahrendorf defines conflict regulation as "those forms of conflict control which address themselves to *expressions* of conflict rather than their causes and as imply the continued existence of antagonisms of interests and interest groups." (10, p. 225) Since conflict regulation is concerned primarily with expressions of conflict it is concerned with violence rather than intensity. Order then is essentially conceived in terms of the presence of institutional means of conflict regulation (mechanisms of maintenance) which outweigh mechanisms of conflict.

The conditions necessary for effective conflict regulation and, therefore, decreases in violence of conflict and of the probability of sudden structural change include:

1) Recognition—"both parties accept their conflict for what it is, namely an inevitable outgrowth of the authority structure of associations." (10, p. 225)

2) Organization—"so long as conflicting forces are diffuse, incoherent

aggregates regulation is virtually impossible." (10, p. 226) In this regard Dahrendorf suggests that guerilla warfare is the most violent expression of conflict precisely because it is not organized.

3) Rules—"the conflicting parties have to agree on certain formal rules of the game that provide the framework of their relations." (10, p. 226) Coser emphasizes that conflict itself is a relationship and as the relationship develops norms emerge to regulate the conflict. As a result of such norms over a period of time conflict either is resolved or becomes institutionalized.

Insofar as these conditions of conflict regulation are present the degree of violence of conflict is reduced. As suggested by Dahrendorf, "Those who have agreed to carry on their disagreements by means of discussion do not usually engage in physical violence." (10, p. 228)

Thus social change in the Dahrendorf perspective occurs as a result of conflict, which is always present as a cohering force, but which with increases in intensity or violence leads to changes in domination-subjection relationships. Included in his analysis of associations are units ranging from the major institutional sectors of society (including for example the political institution) down to specific associations. Such units typically include within them both the means of conflict regulation which contribute to stability and the potentiality for the emergence of conflict groups leading to structural change.

Comment on Dahrendorf's contribution to social change theory must be made in terms of previous comments regarding functionalism and also in terms of the qualifications Dahrendorf attaches to his theory. Intentionally he proposes an alternative to the "integration" approach to analysis of change but in so doing acknowledges the validity of both perspectives. His alternative is slanted toward accounting for change-inducing forces *within* social structures and in terms of interests and behavioral considerations rather than value and normative considerations. His contention is that the former is more empirically justifiable.

In proposing an alternative Dahrendorf specifically refrains from identifying his as a general theory of either conflict or change. Rather, as he suggests, the model is intended as an extension and refinement of the Marxian model: application being to imperatively coordinated associations within already industrialized societies. Thus his theoretical perspective is based on the existence of bureaucracy, industrialization, and relatively rapid social change and his propositions are intended to apply to such a setting. His model does not for example provide insight regarding the impetus to change-producing conflict in relatively undifferentiated societies and social structures. A more general application of a conflict perspective to social change in relatively underdeveloped as well as in developed societies may be found in Irving Horowitz's *Three Worlds of Development*. (21)

Dahrendorf by limiting his theory to authority relations in industrial society establishes boundaries which are more amenable to an analytical treatment of change than where society as a whole is the unit of analysis and where relationships of domination and subjection are less discernible. However some analytical difficulties are encountered in application of his model. His use of the concept class is somewhat unorthodox and the distinction between classes and conflict groups is unclear. It is questionable also whether the limited perspective of authority relations is adequate as a basis for understanding and predicting the emergence and outcome of conflict. There are many other bases for dissensus and conflict. (42) In proposing an alternative to the integration model he also tends to exclude the value system from consideration which, as Lockwood suggests, is of signal importance in understanding the genesis and direction of conflict. (25) Level of aspiration and therefore perception of relative deprivation for example may be regarded as significantly influenced by the value system.

It has been the contention of several recent writers that conceptualization of social organization and its change exclusively in terms of either the dialectic process or principles of integration and consensus is untenable and omits a significant part of social reality. Rather each represents a partial theory adequate to account for some kinds of changes but inadequate for others. As commented by Robin Williams, "much controversy has raged over the question which of these doctrines is correct? My answer is quite direct: all are correct in part, all are partly wrong, none is wholly adequate. Actual societies are held together by consensus, by interdependence, by sociability, and by coercion." (46, p. 721) This viewpoint is shared by Moore who comments that "Predominant institutionalization of one alternative does not dispel or dismiss its counterpart" (29, p. 815), and by Van den Berghe who calls attention to a number of shared attributes of the two approaches in his development of a synthesis. Van den Berghe emphasizes that both approaches are holistic in that they look at social organization as systems of interrelated parts; that both share an evolutionary notion of social change, i.e., the synthesis stage of the dialectic represents a new stage of adjustment and adaptation of the social structure, and that both are essentially based on equilibrium notions—again the synthesis representing restoration of a relative state of order following conflict. (42)

Recognition of the dual existence of forces of negation (dialectic) and forces of integration or maintenance has lead to expression of empirical questions regarding the relative balance of the forces which describe both the content and movement of social structure. Indeed as proposed by Horowitz, "The ratio between coercion and consensus at any given time determines the character of the political structure just as the mix between public and private investment of capital determines the economic structure." (21, p. 435) It is an empirical question then whether at any point in time forces of negation are equal to, greater than, or less than the forces of maintenance. Van den Berghe observes that if the forces of maintenance are greatly superior in an environment which is rapidly changing then the very forces of maintenance lead to increasing maladjustment of the social structure with its environment, thus making revolutionary change virtually inevitable. (42, p. 698) Under such circumstances continued failure in adjustment and adaptation actually causes forces of maintenance to become forces of conflict or negation. Conversely Coser has emphasized the integrating effect of dissensus, demonstrating that cohesion within a social structure may be attributable to conflict between structures. In general it may be suggested that under conditions of rapid exogenous change, if *either* forces of maintenance or negation clearly predominate, discontinuities of change may be expected.

The factors emphasized by both Boskoff and Smelser could also be interpreted in terms of a balance of forces of integration and negation. The conditions described as conducive to innovation and/or structural differentiation could be interpreted as forces of negation which under the conditions specified are barely superior to forces of integration and maintenance. Under such conditions a rather orderly and continuous process of change could be expected. Returning to Boskoff's propositions, such would likely be true where both the conditions conducive to innovation and legitimation were simultaneously present. However, if the conditions for innovation were present without the conditions of legitimation, conflict and discontinuity of change would be a more probable outcome.

## Social Behaviorism

Both the order and the conflict perspectives as noted share a holistic orientation to conceptualization of social organization and change. Although the conflict perspective is more behavioral, i.e., emphasis on interests and/or on authority relations, the attention of both perspectives is most directly addressed to questions of structural relations. Both perspectives attribute importance to the role of elites and/or the effect of innovation as factors stimulating social change but do not concentrate on the actions or motivations of either individual innovators or elites. However, some recent theories of modernization have sought to bridge this gap by devoting attention to the effect of modifying the socialization process on long-term social change and development. This emphasis was briefly discussed in relation to Lerner's communication theory of modernization. Lerner (23, 24), Deutsch (12), and Pool (36) generally equate the "participant" society with modernization,[6] a process mediated through mass media which is effective in modifying images and reaches fruition as changed images are incorporated into socialization of future generations with resulting structural change at all levels of interaction.

Recently some attention has also been devoted to identifying various personal and behavioral attributes of innovative persons. Hagen (18) and McClelland (27) have both developed models of change which are based primarily on the kinds of socialization experiences and settings most likely to produce creative and achievement-oriented individuals. Their theories both emphasize that economic growth and development are aggregate products of individual creativity and achievement motivation.

As implied by the above comments, the behaviorist perspective with regard to social organization and change is more atomistic than either conflict or functional models with emphasis being placed on structural change as a result of individuals incorporating changed perceptions, images, and definitions into their behavior.

Of essential importance to the behaviorist perspective is the concentration on social behavior as the unit of analysis rather than social structure in the manner of both functionalists and conflict theorists. This distinction suggests that behaviorists view social structure merely as characteristic ways in which individuals interact rather than as entities separate from interaction. Units of social organization such as communities are the ways people act—communities do not themselves act. Change is embodied in the fact that people act or cease to act in certain ways. As Martindale describes it, "social behaviorism places primary emphasis on what are defined as the basic units of social life. Social behaviorism is thus comparable in sociology to atomism in physics and chemistry and the cell theory in biology. Like these theories, it conceives of other structures in terms of units presumed to be more basic." (26, p. 32)

Martindale has recently expressed the behaviorist perspective as a basis for understanding and prediction of social change on a macro scale. His is essentially a behaviorist's interpretation of history with social change being viewed primarily in terms of the emergence and demise of various social structures and life styles. Martindale suggests that the central concepts of the behaviorist approach are social behavior defined as "meaningful interactions of individuals" (26, p. 32); groups, defined as "systems or structures of social behavior which arise when pluralities pursue their separate and collective aims in common" (26, p. 32); and society, which is treated as synonymous with community, and is defined as "a complete system of social interaction, i.e., a set of social groups sufficiently comprehensive to solve for a plurality of individuals all the problems of collective life falling in the compass

[6] See the chapter by Havens in this volume for a more detailed discussion of the relationship between development and participation.

of a normal year and in the compass of a normal life." (26, p. 33) Following from these definitions social change, which Martindale distinctly separates from cultural change, is defined simply as "the formation and destruction of groups and societies." (26, p. 33) In the course of history the formation and destruction is viewed as essentially a cyclical process for reasons incorporated into the theory.

In developing his theory of social change Martindale sets forth a number of propositions:

1) The individual and only the individual is the source of all innovation. The fact that all patterned behavior is learned carries with it the possibility that at any time any individual can potentially transform the social patterns in which he participates. (26, p. 39)
2) While the biological conditions of dependency and sex virtually guarantee the "natural" condition of man is one of society, no single form of social behavior can be conceived to be ultimate or basic. Social behaviorism rests uncompromisingly on the position that any given form of social life is relative to the natural and socio-cultural conditions of a given time and place. (26, p. 39)
3) The three main areas of social life that are inescapably organized into groups, in which the solutions to collective problems are embedded, are socialization, the mastery of nature, and social control. (26, p. 44)
4) There are no grounds for assuming that the solutions to the problems in any one of these areas are any more fundamental than the solutions to those in any other. (26, p. 44)
5) The established solutions to any given institutional area define both the circumstances of socially significant innovation in a particular society and the areas of resistance to innovation. (26, p. 44)
6) The processes of social life inescapably lead to the inter-adjustment of the main institutional spheres to one another. Contrary to some theories of social and cultural change, the main wave of such inter-institutional development may proceed from any of the basic areas. (26, p. 48)
7) The social and cultural changes accompanying community formation have lower limits in the impairment of the basic efficiency of the institution and upper limits in the completion of a community's style of life. (26, p. 48)

Based on these propositions, community formation is considered to involve the operation of three principles—stabilization, consistency, and closure—which occur in that sequence. The formation of communities begins with innovation or a solution to one of the problems of collective life. Such solutions are *stabilized* and become the basis for the formation and organization of groups. Such groups, organized around solutions to problems intersect in their operations and the possibilities of conflict, lead to mutual modification or the establishment of *consistent* relations among groups and institutions. As the final principle and stage of community formation such consistent relations among a variety of groups are *closed* into a style of life which represents the community. It is at this point that the last of the propositions indicated above is especially relevant. Each of the stages of community formation results in the loss of efficiency as accommodations are made in the process of mutual modification. Thus energy is taken from solution of problems of collective life and is diverted instead to the maintenance of community.

Martindale's analysis of social change centers on the intellectual or system innovator and, in a manner similar to others discussed in this chapter, is concerned with identifying those social conditions which are most conducive to innovation and to community formation.

In Martindale's perspective, the innovators of society tend to be differentiated along the lines of the collective problems identified in proposition three. The technical innovator is an innovator of solutions to the mastery of nature: politicians, statesmen, military leaders, etc., are innovators in social control; and moralists, religious leaders, teachers, etc., are innovators in socialization. Although innovators and intellectuals may be identified with a particular institutional problem area, each of these is in interaction with the other and consequently innovations in one area influence the others as well.

Regarding the role of the intellectual in the process of change, Martindale suggests that "while the intellectual is never the sole source of change his peculiarity is that of system innovator. Though his primary institutional location is most often in some branch of socialization, his special tasks include acting as a representative and justifier of the whole." (26, p. 58)

Martindale's analysis is essentially historical with an emphasis on those kinds of conditions which lead to the emergence of great civilizations and to the major advances of man. In general he suggests the following hypotheses as defining attributes of such creative periods:

1) The creative epochs of human kind are the periods of the formation of new communities. At such times the sphere permitted for individuality of the intellectuals tends to be widened, and its products tend to be rewarded. (26, p. 91)

2) The quality and quantity of creativity are related to the type of community in which they occur. In general the brilliant creative periods have been coincidental with the creation of the more complex human communities. ( 26, p. 91)

3) During the periods of the maturity of a community and the completion of its cultural synthesis the encouragement of free creativity tends to come to an end. The sphere of social life left open for the free construction of individuals is narrowed, and a restricted array of intellectual forms tends to be fixed. (26, p. 91)

4) The standards of acceptability of thought or truth in this restrictive sense tend to vary as between the creative and conformist epochs of human civilization: a) during creative epochs there is a strong tendency to determine the truth in terms of standards and criteria established in the proper conduct of the thought processes, and b) during conformist epochs of human civilization there is a tendency to establish socially acceptable truth by institutional procedures. (26, p. 91)

Martindale's interpretation of social change visualizes periods of creativity during which time new social forms come into being. As the new social forms become stabilized, codification of procedures and innovations results in stifling further creativity. The stabilization of social forms is suggestive of the conditions discussed by Boskoff as being antithetical to the generation and legitimation of innovations. In this regard also Martindale's interpretation appears to at least implicitly rely on dialectic processes. As the community establishes its style it is necessary to siphon off energy for the purpose of maintenance of the social form which leads to increasing inadequacy of the community as a solution, thus establishing a basis for emergence of alternative solutions.

Although the symbolic interactionist perspective is particularly suited to analysis and conceptualization of change at the interpersonal level, reservations must be expressed regarding suitability of the approach for analysis of change at a macro level. The problem of societal change for the symbolic interactionist involves primarily a problem of aggregation and accumulation of a myriad of changed bases for interpersonal interaction.

## SUMMARY

It has been intended to review briefly some of the contemporary sociological conceptions of change as a means of indicating both the variety of concepts employed and some sample propositions regarding both sources and consequences of modification of social structure. Although the perspectives chosen are all concerned with social change, there are several reasons why no one of them can be selected as being more basic, relevant, or applicable than another. Each is concerned with somewhat restricted aspects of change, restricted primarily by the conception of social organization of the theory or by the change-inducing factor emphasized, i.e., structural differentiation, innovation, conflict, etc. At least to this observer, it does not appear possible to select any of these perspectives over another on the basis of any valid criteria of correctness. Researchable hypotheses have been generated from each perspective. Rather, as emphasized previously, it would seem that there are several partial theories of change suggesting both the limited applicability of any of these perspectives and also the possibilities of synthesis of some of these partial theories into more general theories of social organization and change.

Although the various perspectives have been represented as alternative conceptions of social organization and change, there are a number of areas of commonality and apparent consensus. Although emphasis on description of structure has been criticized as having directed attention away from analysis of change, it is generally regarded by the theorists discussed as being a necessary step in the analysis of change. To quote Dahrendorf, "No theory of social change or conflict can forego the description of the structural entity which undergoes change." (10) Boskoff similarly states that "analysis of change is inseparable from identification of analytically separable social systems." (7) Martindale was previously quoted regarding theory of change as being the capstone of sociological theory. (26) Thus each emphasizes that intimate connection between theory of social organization and theory of social change, implying that further developments will not proceed independently. Indeed analysis of social change has come to be regarded as a complement of analysis of social structure. One effect has been to emphasize the more dynamic aspects of social structure rather than dwelling on static concepts which limit the kinds of changes studied. Another effect seems to have been a recent trend toward an emphasis on objective and factual study of change. This is manifest in a number of recent works, including those of Smelser and Lerner discussed in this chapter, where a change model has been developed as a means of organizing and interpreting a study of social change.

Following from the above, the perspectives discussed in this chapter share a common approach to the analysis of change. They are all essentially concerned with specifying conditions which are most conducive to the emergence of change-producing factors whether it be conflict or innovation. Especially with regard to innovation, it is emphasized by both functionalists and behaviorists that innovation is essentially an individual phenomenon which is more likely to occur in some settings than others. Here again some agreement may be found between the functionally derived hypotheses suggested by Boskoff and Martindale's propositions. They both emphasize that innovation is a necessary but not sufficient condition for change—that innovations must be accepted and/or rewarded in order to eventuate in change. This condition is also emphasized by Lerner who cites the necessity for aspiration to be coupled with reward and new interests and ideas with public institutions in order for modernizing change to occur. In regard to innovation, the perspectives discussed, all of which are contemporary, exemplify a trend in the social change literature to more clearly distinguish between social and cultural change. Although each acknowledges the interrelation and correlation between cultural change and social change, explicit efforts are made to regard them as analytically separate.

Although variously labeled, it would appear that all the perspectives discussed emphasize that dissatisfaction with existing conditions and/or solutions is a necessary condition for social change although not all dissatisfaction leads to change. Such dissatisfaction for Dahrendorf involves the domination-subjection relationships, for Boskoff perceived failure of existing practices, for Lerner rising expectations and the gap between aspiration and realization, and for Smelser as the crucial factor or the impetus to structural differentiation, with structural differentiation leading to further dissatisfactions and change-producing tendencies. The central position assigned to dissatisfactions in the functionalist perspective of change is emphasized by Merton who comments that "the key concept bridging the gap between statics and dynamics in functional theory is that of strain, tension, contradiction between the component elements of social structure." (28, p. 122)

However, again there is rather general agreement that just as innovation is a necessary but not sufficient condition, so dissatisfaction is emphasized as being necessary but not sufficient. In order for dissatisfaction to result in structural change it must be translated into perceived and acceptable alternatives. It is emphasized by all the theorists discussed that totalitarianism can be an effective means of suppressing alternatives. (This does not suggest that social change does not or cannot occur under totalitarian conditions—it can, very effectively, by means of force or coercion. However, it is notable that the theories discussed devote relatively little attention to such forced change.) Boskoff views the effect of suppression in terms of failure to legitimize innovations and Dahrendorf in terms of preventing formation of conflict groups.

Another point of essential agreement among the theories presented concerns a point emphasized by omission. Although Lerner stresses communication which is heavily dependent on literacy and Martindale stresses the likelihood of the more significant changes occurring in the socialization sector, no one of the theories discussed views any particular institutional sector as the prime mover of change or more specifically of modernization. Rather, significant patterns of societal change can begin in any of the sectors and be attributable to either endogenous or exogenous factors.

Although used in somewhat differing ways, the notions of differentiation of social units and mobility are incorporated into the discussion of each perspective. To the theorists who place principal emphasis on innovation (functionalists and behaviorists) as a necessary condition of change, both mobility and relative differentiation of functions and units of social organization are described as conducive to innovation. However, in the coercion perspective, intensity of conflict (and thus radicalness of structural change) is described as inversely related to mobility and differentiation of function. The difference in interpretation of the effect of mobility again underscores the previous discussion regarding innovation and conflict both being sources of change but with differing bases and outcomes. Despite differences in hypothesized effect, these two variable conditions of social existence are accorded a prominent place in the analysis of change.

Again common to the perspectives discussed is the apparent tendency to view change in terms of discrete incidents (perhaps attributable to the prominence of discrete incidents in recorded histories) rather than as continuing processes. Such an "incident bias" seems to pertain to both the functionalists and the conflict approaches to analysis of change. While such a bias is to be readily understood in terms of the methodological problems involved in maintaining a continuous record of change, it is probable also that regarding change in terms of critical incidents has focused attention away from ongoing processes which may be both predictive of "critical incidents" and more fully account for the range of social change.

Although contemporary sociological theory reflects an increased sophistication in synthesis and identification of sources of change, this sophistication has not necessarily been reflected in theories of *changing*. Essentially missing from the sociological arsenal are models which identify sequential cause and effect relationships among controllable variables as a requirement of theories of changing. Thus as a final point of consideration, it has been emphasized on several occasions in this discussion that concentration on modifications of social structure only in terms of sociological variables results in the omission of a wide range of variables which are the legitimate concern of other social science disciplines. All societal change involves interaction of individuals, social organization, culture and environmental settings, and change in any of these can probably be best understood in terms of others. Thus, it is observed that some additional breakthroughs in the understanding of societal change may well come about as a result of concentrated efforts to merge the perspective of several disciplines around the more general problem of change.

## REFERENCES

1. Adams, Bert N. "Coercion and Consensus Theories: Some Unresolved Issues." *American Journal of Sociology* 71 (May 1966): 714–17.
2. Barnett, H. G. *Innovation: The Basis of Culture Change.* New York: McGraw-Hill Book Co., 1953.
3. Barringer, Herbert, Blanksten, George I., and Mack, Raymond W. *Social Change in Developing Areas.* Cambridge, Mass.: Schenckman Publishing Co., 1965.
4. Bealer, Robert C., and Fliegel, Frederick. "A Reconsideration of Social Change in Rural Sociology." In *Our Changing Rural Society,* edited by J. Copp. Ames, Iowa: Iowa State University Press, 1964.
5. Berelson, Bernard, and Steiner, Gary. *Human Behavior.* New York: Harcourt, Brace and World, 1964.
6. Bock, Kenneth E. "Evolution, Function and Change." *American Sociological Review* 28 (1963): 229–37.
7. Boskoff, Alvin. "Functional Analysis as a Source of Theoretical Repertory and Research Tasks in the Study of Social Change." In *Explorations in Social Change,* edited by George Zollschan and Walter Hirsch, pp. 213–43. Boston: Houghton Mifflin Co., 1964.

8. Cancian, Francesca. "Functional Analysis of Change." *American Sociological Review* 25 (1960): 818–27.
9. Coser, Lewis. "Social Conflict and the Theory of Social Change." *British Journal of Sociology* 8 (September 1957): 197–207.
10. Dahrendorf, Ralf. *Class and Class Conflict in Industrial Society.* Stanford: Stanford University Press, 1959.
11. Demerath, N. J., III. "Synedoche and Structural-Functionalism." *Social Forces* 44 (March 1966): 390–401.
12. Deutsch, Karl. "Social Mobilization and Political Development." *American Political Science Review* 55 (September 1961): 493–514.
13. Eisenstadt, S. N. *Comparative Perspectives on Social Change.* Boston: Little, Brown and Co., 1968.
14. ———. "Social Change, Differentiation and Evolution." *American Sociological Review* 29 (1964): 375–86.
15. Etzioni, Amitai, and DuBow, F. L. "Some Workpoints for a Macrosociology." In *The Study of Total Societies,* edited by S. K. Klausner, pp. 147–61. New York: Praeger, 1967.
16. ———, and Etzioni, Eva. *Studies in Social Change.* New York: Holt, Rinehart and Winston, 1966.
17. Gusfield, J. "Tradition and Modernity: Misplaced Polarities in the Study of Social Change." *American Journal of Sociology* 72 (January 1967): 351–62.
18. Hagen, E. E. *On The Theory of Social Change.* Homewood, Ill.: Dorsey Press, 1962.
19. Heirich, Max. "The Use of Time in the Study of Social Change." *American Sociological Review* 29 (1964): 386–97.
20. Horowitz, Irving. *Philosophy, Science and the Sociology of Knowledge.* Springfield, Ill.: Charles C Thomas, 1961.
21. ———. *Three Worlds of Development.* New York: Oxford University Press, 1966.
22. Horton, John. "Order and Conflict Theories of Social Problems as Competing Ideologies." *American Journal of Sociology* 71 (May 1966): 701–14.
23. Lerner, Daniel. *The Passing of Traditional Society.* Glencoe, Ill.: The Free Press, 1958.
24. ———. "Toward a Communication Theory of Modernization: A Set of Considerations." In *Communication and Political Development,* edited by Lucian Pye, pp. 327–50. Princeton, N. J.: Princeton University Press, 1963.
25. Lockwood, David. "Social Integration and System Integration." In *Explorations in Social Change,* edited by G. Zollschan and W. Hirsch, pp. 244–57. Boston: Houghton Mifflin Co., 1964.
26. Martindale, Don. *Social Life and Cultural Change.* Princeton, N. J.: D. Van Nostrand Co., 1962.
27. McClelland, David. *The Achieving Society.* Princeton, N. J.: D. Van Nostrand Co., 1961.
28. Merton, Robert. *Social Theory and Social Structure.* Glencoe, Ill.: The Free Press, 1957.
29. Moore, Wilbert E. "A Reconsideration of Theories of Social Change." *American Sociological Review* 25 (1960): 810–18.
30. ———. "Labor Attitudes Toward Industrialization in Underdeveloped Countries." *American Economic Review* 45 (1955):156–65.
31. ———. *Social Change.* Englewood Cliffs, N. J.: Prentice-Hall, 1963.
32. Neal, Sister Marie Augusta. *Values and Interests in Social Change.* Englewood Cliffs, N. J.: Prentice-Hall, 1965.

33. Parsons, Talcott. "Evolutionary Universals in Society." *American Sociological Review* 29 (1964): 339–57.
34. ———. "Some Considerations on the Theory of Social Change." *Rural Sociology* 26 (September 1961): 219–39.
35. ———. *Structure and Process in Modern Society.* Glencoe, Ill.: The Free Press, 1960.
36. Pool, Ithiel de sola. "The Role of Communication in the Process of Modernization and Technological Change." In *Industrialization and Society,* edited by B. F. Hoselitz, and W. E. Moore. UNESCO, 1966.
37. Rose, Arnold. *Sociology: The Study of Human Relations.* New York: Alfred A. Knopf, 1965.
38. Ryan, Bryce. "The Resuscitation of Social Change." *Social Forces* 44 (September 1965): 1–7.
39. Smelser, Neil J. *Social Change in the Industrial Revolution.* Chicago: University of Chicago Press, 1959.
40. ———. "Toward a Theory of Modernization." In *Social Change,* edited by A. Etzioni and E. Etzioni, pp. 258–74. New York: Basic Books, 1964.
41. Tiryakian, Edward A. "A Model of Societal Change and Its Lead Indicators." In *The Study of Total Societies,* edited by S. K. Klausner, pp. 69–97. New York: Praeger, 1967.
42. Van den Berghe, Pierre. "Dialectic and Functionalism: Toward a Theoretical Synthesis." *American Sociological Review* 28 (October 1963): 695–705.
43. Weintraub, D., and Bernstein, F. "Social Structure and Modernization: A Comparative Study of Two Villages." *American Journal of Sociology* 71 (March 1966): 521.
44. Whitaker, Ian. "The Nature and Value of Functionalism in Sociology." In *Functionalism in the Social Sciences,* edited by D. Martindale, pp. 127–43. Monograph No. 5. Philadelphia: American Academy of Political and Social Sciences, 1965.
45. Williams, Robin. *American Society, A Sociological Interpretation.* New York: Alfred A. Knopf, 1960.
46. ———. "Some Further Comments on Chronic Controversies." *American Journal of Sociology* 71 (May 1966): 717–21.

# CHAPTER TWO

# SOCIETAL DEVELOPMENT: NOTES ON THE VESTMENTS OF A CONCEPT

## H. KENT GEIGER

WHAT IS SOCIETAL DEVELOPMENT? Can we attach precise meaning to it? If so, how do we discover the meaning of such a concept as this, which has in a brief span of years captured the attention of millions of men?

### WHAT IS WRONG WITH PROGRESS?

It has been said that each age has its favorite concept. But a concept also has its age, in the other sense of that word. The concept of progress, born of the Christian doctrine of salvation and the rise of experimental science in the eighteenth century, may have been favored during recent centuries. However, today it suffers from absence of leanness, an excess of overly fanciful associations, and a precipitous decline of activity. Few of the items now being published on the economic, political, and social affairs of the newer nations make use of the word progress.

It would appear that progress has been retired, its place taken by the younger, freer, promising but still immature notion of development. What is the relationship of development to progress? Are they father and son, as suggested by their respective ages? Or are they even closer as relatives, perhaps identical twins, born by some freakish twist

**H. KENT GEIGER** is Professor of Sociology at the University of Wisconsin. He holds the Ph.D. in sociology from Harvard. His research experience includes work at the Russian Research Center, Harvard University. Publications related to his chapter include: **National Development, 1776–1966; A Selective, and Annotated Guide to the Most Important Publications in English.** Metuchen, N.J.: Scarecrow Press (1969).

with 200 years between them? Were the latter true, of course, to know one would be to know the other. But since the former is more surely the case, we are well advised to become acquainted with both concepts, and to know them by their differences as well as by their sameness.

The proper starting point in our problem is to sketch out a set of reasons why progress is no longer serviceable, an operation which should at least put us on the road to a clearer view of what we ought not to mean by development. If the older concept's undesirable accretions of many years can be identified, then perhaps they can be prudently put aside by the younger one. Our contribution to the achievement of this goal will be in the form of seven features of the concept progress which appear today more as liabilities than assets in the quest for a central conception for observers of the new nations. These features are necessarily provisional and of varying weight, listed, according to my guess, in approximate order of importance.

According to the dictionary, progress carries as a central component of its meaning the notion of improvement or betterment. Mankind, society, or some other entity is conceived in two different states and chronological periods, and the second of these, coming later chronologically, is judged better, more advanced, more perfect, or otherwise seen more positively than the earlier one. Why not? What is the objection? In general, it is not a good idea for the scientific observer to pass judgment about the general "standing" or "quality" of two different historical epochs. Such judgments ordinarily strike us as inappropriately arbitrary, for there is seemingly no way to subject the judgment to any kind of test.

A second, very substantial, connotative accretion to progress is found in the emphasis placed upon the property of inevitability. Particularly after the middle of the nineteenth century, and under the influence of Darwin's theory of organic evolution, the idea of progress was generally accepted as axiomatically true; "the world was obviously better than it had been, obviously would be better than it was." (4, p. 498) Though many who believe in progress would insist that improvement in some inner condition of man's life is central to their belief in it, such as prosperity, happiness, or human nature, it was the rapidly changing external circumstances—the growth of cities, wealth, medicine, etc.—that captured the imagination. Moreover, these external conditions were typically seen as completely convincing indicators of concomitant changes in the inner condition. A wiser view balks at such an unwarranted extension of evolutionary thought, urging that far from constituting evidence that progress is "true," Darwinian theory had best be confined strictly to the province of organic affairs. Improvement in man's state is far from guaranteed. A soberly accurate assessment would see his changing external circumstances as a process "simultaneously creative and destructive, providing new opportunities and prospects at a high price in human dislocation and suffering." (6, p. 27) Rather than inevitability, which entails foretelling of the future, the best that can be proposed by science of directionality in the experience of human societies is conveyed by the notion of irreversibility, which is quite a different matter.

As a third liability, progress must be reckoned as unduly committed to the idea of finality. Some ultimate objective, end-state, or goal has usually been a part of the concept of progress. Hegel, Compte, and Marx, to name three prominent exponents, had such final "stages" in mind; so do many proponents of more modern theories, by implication if not explicitly. Clearly, to the extent that finality is present, progress is not acceptable to the modern thinker, for constant change and an uncertain future for society are both generally accepted as axioms of modern social science. From this perspective, the wise decision for students of development is to shift the focus of attention in time-perspective, placing less emphasis on "moving toward" and more on "moving away from."

To continue our listing of the liabilities of progress, we turn to the East. Encumbered with the residues of strong wishes and great thoughts from the past, progress has also become a minion of the world's most lively political movement. Communism in all its varieties has appropriated the idea of progress, using it in a particular and uncongenial way. According to the *Great Soviet Encyclopedia*, "the only scientific theory of progress is that conceived by Marxism-Leninism, which expresses the interests of the proletariat, a class standing at the fore of all toilers and vitally committed to the progressive development of society." Further, "the victory of socialism in the USSR and the successful building of socialism in the countries of peoples' democracy is a remarkable instance of social progress." (7, p. 593) We need not dwell on the details to agree that even if one does not wish to prefer charges for misappropriation, the canonization of a particularized view hinders good communication.

Further defects can be treated more briefly. It is widely agreed that progress bears the stigma of its origin in the early childhood of Western civilization. As the heir to the Hebraic-Christian doctrine of messianic intervention and salvation, progress can be made to appear in part at least as an accident of historical sequences. The Hebraic-Christian view of history, which entails a radical transfer of attention and hope away from the current world and time to a distant if not other-worldly future, must be understood in its relation to the ancient world, most notably to the decay of the Roman Empire. Thoughts of an ultimate happier fate, we know, stand in striking contrast to the views of history and human destiny held by most peoples. During the bulk of human historical experience, the world, society, and man have been much more likely to be seen in essentially static terms, or as a result of deterioration from a previous imputed golden age. (24, p. 296).

If it is indeed true that the peculiar combination of circumstances surrounding the ancient Jews and early Christians produced Western monotheism, then it can also be argued that the central doctrine of salvation by messiah or faith, by its historical uniqueness, must be counted as a largely accidental factor in the generation of the idea of progress. Thus, as one writer notes, even after the Christian view was gradually discredited as historical truth, Christian philosophy had "so thoroughly habituated men to the thought of an ultimate happy destiny that they could never be content with a pale imitation of Greek pessimism." (4, p. 497) In consequence, the concept of progress seems to stand in what is for us an uncomfortably close link with its metaphysical forbear, and invites the verdict of "guilty by association."

My sixth reason for questioning the scientific utility of progress is that in Western civilization progress is a prominent value. Like any other general value, it is notably abstract in content and elicits much fervor. Its abstract quality makes its meaning diffuse and controversial; its quality of eliciting heavy emotional commitment makes people want to promote it rather than study it. Both qualities detract from its scientific utility.

Finally, the notion of progress, as it has evolved over the past centuries, seems usually to carry a reference to "mankind as a whole" or to "all of humanity" or perhaps to the people of Western Europe. As such it has constituted in the main a term suitable for use in a larger frame of discourse than that with which most development scholars like to work. For the present, at least, the largest manageable grouping of human beings for discussion and analysis is the national society or nation state. In this respect, as well as in those preceding, the term societal development, which refers explicitly to a single society, seems preferable to the term progress.

There can be little doubt that the concept progress has many faults. We can probably agree that for most purposes "societal development" or "modernization" is preferable. But a nagging thought persists. Can we, in spite of all, assign a clear and useful meaning to the concept of progress? Rather than summary execution or incarceration, perhaps a final hearing is in order. Perhaps progress can be rehabilitated.

In my opinion, the most important meaning to progress is that found in the first of those seven described above. Shorn of items 2–6, progress is still recognizable so long as the judgment of "better" or "improved" is offered about the later of the two states presumed in any comparison. This being the case, why not make the best of it, accepting the evaluative component as vital to the meaning of progress. Then there is this question: Can a concept built upon evaluative judgments be scientifically useful? My answer to that is yes, so I would propose that progress be henceforth defined as that property which makes it better than some one or more other societies or better than it was itself in an earlier era. A scientific view of "better" presumes broad agreement: judgments should not be arbitrary. What might be the basis for such agreement? I would seek them among the fundamental presuppositions of human existence everywhere. I propose four criteria as universally acceptable for evaluative judgments about human societies. The first is based on one distinction between the affairs of humans and those of animals. It is the extent in each case of preoccupation with, or obtrusion of, physiological or anatomical considerations into social situations. The basic premise is simple: human is better than animal, and "human" behavior is better than "animal" behavior. Restricting the comparison to purely human societies, one of the most striking differences between one kind and the other is found in the amount of time, attention and interest given to such things as the seclusion of women, puberty rites, head-hunting, torture, blood sacrifice, preoccupation with the dead body, and multitudinous varieties of bodily deformation found throughout history. Some (progressive?) societies react to these patterns with disgust and aversion. In these societies such activities as concern blood, death, and decay are kept largely private rather than existing as public affairs. In this, humans outrank animals, adults outrank children, and societies I would label progressive outrank those I would label retarded or regressive.[1]

A second criterion is based on the organic version of the principle of entropy, namely, the tendency for systems to collapse or dissolve, with loss of control and boundary, into the environment. The basic axiom here is that life is better than death. In more problematic terms this postulate takes as a corollary the principle that a healthy organic system is better than a sick one. This leads, in turn, to the intimate association in humans between the organic and psychic levels of being and to the idea of mental health and illness. Taking things one step further, we can propose the degree of disengagement from magic and superstitition—belief in shamans, superstitions, and the like—as a specific indication of mental health, where this latter is defined as careful separation of objective and subjective phenomena, of reality and illusion.

As the originator of the idea expresses it, this seemingly dogmatic judgment is "based on the observation that beliefs in magic, such as are normal in backward societies, do recur in cultures that have discarded magic, but chiefly among individuals whose social fortune is backward or who are psychotic, mentally deteriorated, or otherwise subnormal. When the sane and well in one culture believe what only the most ignorant, warped, and insane believe in another, there would seem to be some warrant for rating the first culture lower and the second higher. Or are our discards, insane, and hyper-suggestibles perhaps right and the rest of us wrong?" (24, p. 298)

[1] A good part of this idea and those following comes from Kroeber (24), especially "The Idea of Progress," pp. 296–300 and "More about Progress," pp. 300–304.

My third and fourth criteria for evaluating societies are extensions of the first two. If humans are different from animals in one way, and this difference can be ordered along a quality dimension, then other modes of differentiation are also eligible. One such is the human capacity for culture. Culture is communicable and cumulative among us humans. Animals lack it. Can there be too much culture? I think not. Therefore, societies with "more culture" are better than those with less. The most variable and putatively quantifiable realm of culture is the realm of science. Thus, societies with more science are higher, better, and more progressive than those with less.

We may, in our self-congratulation, have overstressed the property of science in question, namely, its cumulativity. See Kuhn, where the principle of substitutability of scientific paradigms is stressed. However, the dimension of quantitative differentiation in respect to the "amount of science" in a society can be seen as lying within the number of distinct disciplines at hand and established, rather than in the concepts and propositions of any one discipline taken individually. On this, see especially p. 169. (25)

A final criterion for judging society has a long history in social philosophy. Human happiness or welfare ought to be included among the criteria for judging society. Whether happiness is an aggregable attribute and, if so, whether it is well conceived as a true societal variable (or, in contrast, a constant factor over a sufficiently extended period of time) are moot issues. If it is both aggregable and variable, then surely human welfare must be reckoned in among the criteria of progress.

The answer to our initial query "What is wrong with progress?" is that nothing is wrong with it that cannot be cured. Let the cure be the decision to employ the term only for the task of judging the worth or quality of a society. Who will deny the need for such a concept? But what of societal development? If we can accept the meaning proposed for progress, then we can also argue that the term development could well be divested of the responsibility for meeting this need. As a first approximation, then, let us conclude that progress involves an index of societal worth based on four explicit, widely shared value judgments about man's condition, and that development does not, or should not.

## FRAMES OF REFERENCE FOR THE CONCEPTUALIZATION OF SOCIETAL DEVELOPMENT

### An Initial Pattern and Theme

A brief acquaintance with the published literature is sufficient to convince the reader that there is no standard definition of the concept development. Indeed, within publications as well as between them there is a tendency to use such terms as growth, industrialization, modernization as equivalents to development. And in referring to that group of nations of primary concern, the newer ones, we find in common and interchangeable usage such terms as developing, underdeveloped, less developed, poor, emerging, modernizing, industrializing, and transitional. From time to time, the words "backward" or "less civilized" appear, but, like their opposites "progressive" and "civilized," they are in less frequent use than they were ten or twenty years ago.

We can read discussions of the different nuances of meaning attached to these various terms. For example, fifteen years ago Myint, arguing from the Marshallian tradition of distinguishing between man and his environment, recommended that "backward" be used solely to refer to the "economically unsuccessful" people of an area and that "underdevelopment" refer to the existence of unused natural resources.[2]

In 1966 Nettl and Robertson proposed the following distinction between the terms industrialization, "the process which involves a changeover from either agriculture or domestic activity to factory production on a growing scale," and development, "the general term for the process of economic and directly consequent social change involved." (33, pp. 279–80) The authors further argue that a third concept, modernization, be used primarily to refer to a nation's efforts at "goal-setting" and "goal-attainment in an international context."

In the previous year political scientist Apter had proposed definitions of the same three terms. (2) Industrialization is defined as the appearance of new functional roles linked with machine technology, modernization as the direction and control of the consequences of industrialization, and development as the emergent consequent of the two preceding terms. If industrialization is economic differentiation and modernization is political integration, then development is the process by which societies achieve both differentiation and integration.

As reasonable or useful as such distinctions might be, the fact remains that the next writer to be consulted will be found recommending a different set of them. The only conclusion for the moment is that terministic usage is in a chaotic state. Whether this fact is inevitable and trivial or evitable and deplorable is a matter of opinion; I tend to favor the former view.

However unhappy the condition of formal definitions, amidst the clutter there is a unifying thematic premise: whatever develop-

[2] Myint (32). The claim is further made that the two dimensions can be independent of each other. If so, a four-class typology of nations is generated. However, the bulk of the author's interest was concentrated upon one of the four possible cases, the nations which are both backward and underdeveloped, a condition tending to produce interaction between the two factors and result in a "vicious circle."

ment may be, it must emerge out of a sense of the possible through some process of comparison. Viner, for example, noting that the economics of development literature is "extraordinarily lacking" in explicit definitions and that the implicit definitions show a wide range of different and often conflicting concepts, argues for a definition stressing a country's "good potential prospects for using more capital or more labor or more available natural resources . . . to support its present population on a higher level of living." (36, p. 12) Thus, one variety of this idea looks to the country's economic potential, say as judged by the professional economist. Another stresses the notion of a relative or comparative frame of reference by pointing to the contrast between the wealthier and the poorer nations. The latter are judged "underdeveloped" primarily in terms of a comparison between them and the former, and the view that this need not be the case is frequently left as an entirely implicit presupposition.[3] The most sophisticated form of the view that societal development should be seen always in a relative or comparative sense is expressed by Lagos-Matus, who conceives of the world as a community of nations stratified along a continuum of "real" status positions which contrast with the widely accepted belief that all sovereign nations enjoy equal "formal" status. Development is therefore defined explicitly as a result obtained by comparing two previously executed comparisons of one country with others. It is a relationship between real status and formal status in which the former is a composite of wealth, power, and prestige.

Let us start our survey by accepting two preparatory conclusions. First, it seems that an extremely complex phenomenon with many independently varying dimensions, such as the topic of this chapter, cannot be captured with a concise nominal definition. Let us, therefore, give up the effort, concluding that at this stage at least, and perhaps permanently, nominal definitions are of little help. Second, there is something inherently "relative" or "comparative" to societal development. It will be the task of the next three sections to elaborate this point in terms of what are variously called perspectives or models, all of which define the concept by placing it in a large context of meaning.

## The First Round of Consistent Perspectives

Once the view is accepted that development is hard to define but is well conceived in terms of a relativistic or comparative perspective, the logical next step is to adopt an inductive approach. In what terms do writers on development compare and evaluate countries?

[3] See for a good example the writing of Celso Furtado who, along with many other Latin American writers, seeks an explanation of the cited fact in terms of structural defects in the domestic economy and in the international market situation. (12)

*Trait Lists.* The first approach to be considered focuses on the points of contrast between the less developed countries and those more developed. This procedure eventuates in a set of traits. These can be couched in terms of the factors or conditions shared by the more developed countries, seen as favorable to development, in terms of those shared by the less developed countries, in which case they are presented as obstacles or barriers to development, or in terms of general variables which can serve as either facilitators or barriers depending on the specific values they assume. A typical example of the depiction of barriers is the set presented in two subgroups by Hauser. (16) The first, under a heading of "The Colonial Heritage," includes the following handicaps: truncated social orders, pluralistic societies, over-urbanization, resurgent nationalism, and mass disillusionment because of the slow pace of economic development. The second subgroup is discussed under the heading of "Elements of Indigenous Culture" and here the difficulties include value systems which conflict with material aspirations, highly stratified societies with a relatively small but powerful elite and minimal social mobility, age prestige and deference, prescientific mentality, atomism in interpersonal and intergroup relations, and actual or potential demographic imbalance.

Trait lists vary in length, level of generality, and in the extent to which the particular traits or the procedures for selection of traits are rationalized. To the extent that the basis for selection is clarified, trait lists approach the status of theoretical models. Most of them, however, at least in the earlier years of inquiry, were in good part reflections of rising scholarly dissatisfaction with the economic growth models based on analysis of the experience of capitalist economic systems. As such, trait lists represent a natural and vigorous quest for some way of encompassing the large bag of "noneconomic" variables which economists had traditionally taken as givens. A good example of this order of response is found in the trait list contributed by Hoselitz. (19) It is more systematic than most, and it eventuated in an eight-fold ideal typology. Three variables are identified as particularly important—the relation between population and natural resources, the degree of dependence of one country upon another, and the degree of active intervention by the government.

As useful as trait lists are for giving a first approximation, they share a major defect. The selection of traits seems random or arbitrary, for without some explicit model of society the selection of one rather than another trait is hard to justify.

*Microsociological.* A second approach to the meaning of development is found in a large body of publications focusing intensively on a single factor, condition, variable, or component of a society. The purpose of such investigations is to come closer to the facts, employing the micro focus for the most of the fact-gathering but seeking to clarify the significance of what is learned for the development of the entire society, which endows the whole effort with more of a "macro" flavor. An extraordinary variety of "key" phenomena has been inspected—sustained growth in GNP per capita, psychic participation in societal affairs by individuals, organizaton for the accomplishment of local economic and political tasks, social mobilization of a country's population, the accumulation of knowledge, etc.

Many of the local community field studies belong here, as do those by sociologists and political scientists which fasten upon one component of the total picture for intensive scrutiny. In *Peddlars and Princes,* Geertz analyzes two Indonesian towns and their nascent economic organizations in terms of their distinctive problems of organization. (14) Entrepreneurship in each town manifests characteristic liabilities; the specific weaknesses are explained in terms of the local culture and social structure and are evaluated for their relevance to Indonesian national economic policy. The outer limit to the microsociological approach is reached when the focus of attention is upon a single factor, but the analyst includes more than one society in his discussion, or treats an extended historical period. Johnson does both in elaborating the thesis that "the middle sector" plays an important role in developing the Latin American societies.[4]

What is here termed a "micro" focus could as well be given another name. Coleman refers to it as the single factor or "reductionist" approach, and in a brief discussion of political development mentions the following "single" factors which competent writers recommend: capacity or capability, differentiation, institutionalization, national integration, participation, populism, political culture, social mobilization and various psychological traits, and socioeconomic correlates. (9, p. 396) The string of factors or conditions which have been or could be defended as important for development would seem to be literally endless, and in this respect the micro approaches taken as a whole add up to another pathway to a more or less arbitrary set of development traits. In defense of the trait approach it should be noted that traits do provide a wealth of factual detail about the context, patterning, and interrelated nature of the phenomena they treat.

*Toward the Western Model.* Standing out among the group I have labeled the "first round of consistent perspectives" is the contemporary heritage of a famous Marxian premise: "The industrially more developed country presents to the less developed country a picture of the latter's future."[5] Extending the idea, perhaps without Marx's permission, we are led to the position that societal development is

---

[4] The term "middle sector" is not a happy one, for it calls to mind the "middle class," which is not what the author intends. Modern or functional elite would be more appropriate. (21)

[5] From the preface to the first edition of *Das Kapital,* cited in Gerschenkron, p. 6. (15)

well conceived as the process whereby the less developed countries increasingly take on the shape of the already developed societies. Some of the most influential writers in this field have defended such a view, or at least can easily be so interpreted (1; 28), and one of the most provocative current controversies about the futures of the U.S.A. and the U.S.S.R.—the so-called convergence hypothesis—is a close relative. While this is not the place to take up a detailed description and critique, we can at least note the following points. At a very high level of generality, it is probably accurate to think of all nations as tending toward a standard, or what we can loosely term a Western, model. That is, in the modern age, certain general trends seem to be everywhere present. I include such trend patterns as institutional, role, and status differentiation, the proliferation of formal organizations or bureaucratization, the multiplication of communication channels, the sharing of a common culture, especially that made available through scientific discoveries and increasing scale of social organization and individual involvement in it.

Such generalizations are true but not very informative, for they omit from consideration the problems and questions of most concern, which must be posed and answered in more specific terms. Thus it is not the trend toward institutional differentiation which most interests us, but the fact that it occurs at different rates and under varying conditions at different times and places. Similarly, the sharing of scientific knowledge has come to be pretty much a routine business, but the zeal exerted in devising, institutionalizing, and promoting certain types of political culture is a very problematic matter of great interest throughout the world.

The main criticism of this perspective is that it does not adequately provide for the fact of historical emergence. The less developed countries today are faced with conditions in their quest for modernity which the already developed countries never had to confront, not the least important of which is the increased pace of technological and cultural change as a worldwide experience, observed if not shared by almost all of the world's peoples.

*Searching for More Complex Models: Stages of Development.* The impressive number of empirically observable regularities in the development experience of the advanced nations and the poignant desire for emulation felt by the leaders of the less developed countries have combined to produce a more complex model of the development process. Stages of development schemes furnish powerful assistance to the individual's increasing desire to place his nation and his personal fate in historical perspective, and they buttress the search of national leaders for an explicit orienting point for policy formation.

The list of different schemes and terminologies is long. The two best known in the contemporary world, the Marxist and that proposed by Rostow (35), have five distinct stages. A laudable system of stages of development proposed by Galtung has four—primary or primitive, traditional, modern, and neo-modern. (13) The model used most commonly today, however, has three stages, and probably the terms most acceptable to all would be traditional, transitional, and modern. On the other hand, some of the models which have shown greatest longevity have only two stages, such as the "classical" schemes proposed some decades ago by such writers as Durkheim, Tönnies, and Redfield. Perhaps there are two contradictory principles at work—the greater the number of stages the more "interesting" and dramatically compelling the model, and the fewer the number of stages the more valid and durable.

It could, by the way, be argued that the functionally relevant number of stages in both the Marxist and Rostow schemes is two— capitalist and socialist, and pre- and post-take-off.

Stage perspectives have great utility. They arrest the inherently continuous nature of historical change so that comparative analysis is possible. They elicit and make possible the testing of specific hypotheses. Perhaps most important of all, they challenge the historian and area specialist to produce evidence and explanation of why a particular society or group of societies fails to meet the specifications of the model.

The main defect of stage schemes is similar to that of the model described in the preceding section: stages do not allow sufficient room for the unique historical experience of the societies still to develop. As one notably unenthusiastic observer puts it, the only proper conclusion is that societies which came late to the process of modernization "will not follow the sequence of their predecessors, but will insist on changing it around or on skipping entirely some stages as well as some 'preconditions.'" (17, p. 41)

Increasing dissatisfaction with schemes which ignore or too rigidly treat one or another side of the historical experiences of societies has produced two additional perspectives. Both of them involve descriptive categories which are more highly differentiated than those found in the stage models. The first is largely the response of those most conscious of historical diversity, in the main anthropologists and historians. The second is a sociological answer to the main weakness of the stages perspective—the provision of abstract formal models of society.

*Typologies of Adaptation.* Human society, it is often held, is made possible by culture. Moreover, culture is the means whereby the past is perpetuated. If both of these assertions are true, then one cannot fail to be impressed with the position that "no human society can exist without substantial reliance on patterns which must be regarded as traditional and not rational. (29, p. 15) Full acceptance of such a view leads toward concomitant acceptance of the responsibility for treating each nation as a unique case, and prepares the analyst for the

discovery that previous general formulations of the typical development experience are faulty.

For instance, in the case of Japanese development Bellah was led
to the conclusion that neither the Marxist nor the Weberian formula—
neither the mode and relations of production nor the implication for
work attitudes of the religious value system—was adequate for explanatory purposes. Rather, the strength of the Japanese government has
been fundamental. "Of all the major non-Western societies Japan
stands out as unique in its possession of a strong polity and central
political values, and it is this above all, in my opinion, which accounts
for the differential acceptance of industrialization." (5, p. 193) Correspondingly, Japanese development constituted a "reversal" of the supposed predominance of economic, or religious, over political factors.
Such a reversal could only be properly understood in the light of the
specific experiences and patterns of Japanese history and culture.

To the extent that one accepts the weight of history and the deep
embeddedness of culture, his image of the development experience is
one stressing the adaptation to new conditions of existing social institutions, and the preferred model of the process, if he can be led to
generalize, would tend toward an adaptation model. Historian Cyril
Black provides an appropriate definition, though he prefers the term
modernization to development. Modernization is "the process by
which historically evolved institutions are adapted to the rapidly
changing functions that reflect the unprecedented increase in man's
knowledge, permitting control over his environment, that accompanied
the scientific revolution." (6, p. 7) We could, I propose, alter and short-
en this to "development is the process by which nations adapt to new
conditions in the modern world."

The next step, of course, is to search for a way to identify and
describe these new conditions or, as Black puts it, the "rapidly changing functions." Black himself emphasizes the political problems at
stake, choosing five criteria for comparing the modernization of nations, and he proposes a typology of seven patterns of adaptation. The
first is shown by the earliest countries to modernize, Britain and
France; the second is composed of their offshoots in the new world,
U.S.A. and Canada; the third includes those European countries
which modernized under the impact of the French example; and so on.

Simon Kuznets restricts his analysis to sixteen countries which
are already developed, ten in Europe, five European descendants, and
Japan. (26) Like Black, Kuznets recognizes the crucial importance of
expanding knowledge, but focuses on the economic implications of
this fact. He conceives of an addition to knowledge so major in its
implications that it dominates an entire age, labeling it an "epochal
innovation." An epochal innovation produces an "economic epoch."
We are currently in the midst of one variety of economic epoch, the
"scientific epoch," in which the basic, epoch-making innovation is the

application of science to the various problems of economic production.

As to the role of different countries in this process, rather than a stages-of-development model, Kuznets stresses the interdependence of all countries, and a sequence pattern by which the epochal innovation breaks through in one or two typically small "pioneer" countries. It then spreads gradually to the "follower" countries at a rate dependent upon their geographical and historical distance from the pioneer country.

Still another variety of adaptive typology is that proposed by Moore. His analysis covers the political solutions for a crucial economic task—the transformation of agriculture from a subsistence level into a commercialized activity providing a large surplus. His argument is that development hinges upon the changeover from a feudal to a modern pattern of land use, that there is always a high social cost involved, and that among the most interesting features of the process is how this cost is allocated. According to Moore's model there have been three historical routes to modernization: bourgeois revolutions leading to capitalist democracy, in England, France, and the U.S.A.; abortive bourgeois, ultimately conservative revolutions leading to fascism, as in Japan; and peasant revolutions leading to communism, as in China. (31)

It is quite evident that the rich complexity of the nations' concrete historical experience leads different writers to emphasize different variables and to propose differing typologies of their development experience. From the policy-making point of view such models are of scant help because they, like stage theories, are too general to use in defining particular problems and, like the trait list approach, too unstable or arbitrary to use in selecting problems of greater importance from among those of less importance. From a theoretical point of view adaptive typologies based on detailed historical analysis have much to recommend them. They constitute the macrosociological version of middle range theory. That is, they involve a limited number of interrelated variables which lend themselves to reasonably operational definition.

*Abstract Portraits of the Total Society.* The third variety of "more complex model" to be described is the most ambitious. It is the description in abstract terms of the component parts of a national society. In this task sociologist Parsons has taken the lead, and has promoted the view that a society can be characterized in terms of the adequacy with which it creates solutions for four omnipresent functional problems or tasks faced by all social systems. More will be said in the next section about the details of Parsons's approach, and how it might be adapted to produce a rigorous definition of development. (34) A similar approach is taken by Levy in a two-volume publication devoted to a thorough analysis of the structure of society with specific reference to the problems faced in development. (30)

The main argument in favor of the characterization of society in abstract terms is that the first step in the scientific analysis of any phenomena is accurate description. We must, it is urged, understand the details of social structure before we can learn about its patterns of change. The most important argument against such an approach is that a cumbersomely large or unmanageably abstract set of categories is generated, which does not lend itself to orderly thinking or to productive research activity.

*Returning to Simpler Models: Focusing on the Individual.* The subtitles — "An initial pattern and theme," "The first round of consistent perspectives," "Searching for more complex models," and the present — suggest a chronological order to the predominance of one or the next approach to the meaning of development. In point of fact, such a sequence pattern may indeed exist, but it is probably better to treat the possibility gingerly and to think of the various approaches or perspectives as relatively concurrent and look upon the subtitles as mainly an expositional device.

The present section may indeed be a complete misnomer, for many writers have preferred "simpler" models from the beginning of their concern, and it is by no means clear that the field as a whole has "returned" to them out of distaste for the more complex creations of the preceding section. In any case, the first of the simpler models is the social psychological one. In two of the most significant early contributions, those by the Banfields and by Lerner, personality traits are extremely important variables. (3, 28) In Doob's *Becoming More Civilized,* the psychological experience of development is the complete center of attention, and comparisons are made among individuals grouped as "unchanged," "changing," and "changed." (10) These three groupings are easily seen as correlative with traditional, transitional, and modern stages of societal development. Similarly, Inkeles has proposed a set of psychological traits distinctive of "modern man" because they are intimately related to his successful adjustment as a citizen in modern industrial society, which Inkeles in turn describes in terms of societal traits—urbanization, education, mass communication, industrialization and politicization. (20) The corresponding attitudes, values, and feelings include readiness for new experience, an openness to innovation and change, a disposition to form opinions about many problems and issues both in and outside his immediate environment, a democratic bias, an orientation to the present or the future rather than the past, a favorable attitude toward planning, a belief that man can learn to dominate his environment in order to advance his own purposes and goals, a confidence that the world is calculable, an awareness of the dignity of self and others, faith in science and technology, and a great belief in distributive justice.

Focus on the individual personality provides a lively dimension to the study of societal development. It "humanizes" what in other respects often appears as a formidably abstract realm of ideas. Enthusiasm for this perspective should be tempered, however, by the fact that social psychologists, like other social scientists, differ among themselves as to which variables of personality are most relevant. In a recent publication describing the values of modern men in Brazil and Mexico, Kahl identifies seven variables constituting the "core" of modernism. (22) While not in contradiction to those of Inkeles, there is little conceptual or terministic correspondence. Thus, the subhead to this section may be misleading in another sense—there is some doubt that the individual psychological frame of reference constitutes a "simpler" model.

*International Stratification.* Even if only in implicit fashion, the next approach to be described has also been at hand for many years. If a field of knowledge has an origin, perhaps it is here that societal development received its start. The attention of almost every writer has been captured by the marked inequality in wealth, power, etc., among the nations of the world. The Marxist writers have made the distinction between capitalist and colonial countries a central part of their theory of imperialism. One of the best known recent theories, associated with the names of Hans Singer and Raul Prebisch, takes as a point of departure the premise that certain nations, those at the "center," are prospering at the expense of others, those at the "periphery," because of the terms-of-trade on the international market.

Myrdal, Kuznets, Horowitz, and Lagos are other prominent exponents of what I will term the international stratification approach. (18, 27) These writers all accept the view that the nations constitute units in a larger world system or world community, and propose various conditions and propositions governing the rank order and particular position of one or a group of countries. I consider this approach a promising one, and deal with one version of it in more detail in the final section of the chapter.

*Specific-goal Oriented.* One of the simplest models of the development process is found in the goal-oriented approach. The definition of development is couched in terms of the goal to be achieved; underdeveloped societies have not reached the goal, whereas developed societies are those which have achieved it. Marxism in its realistic or functional sense falls largely into this group. Capitalist societies are judged underdeveloped on the basis of their property institutions; socialist societies with public ownership of the means of production are seen as more advanced. A close relative is the position taken by anticolonialists, of which Fanon is a prominent spokesman, who agree that the single most relevant experience for the former colonial countries is to throw off the hegemony of colonialist rule. (11) Development in this case is equivalent to the experience of emerging from colonial domination.

Specific goals can be couched in quite sophisticated ways. Consider the following definition: "socio-economic development is that kind of social change that leads in the direction of the liberation of man from direct contact with nature in the production process and permits him to pursue other interests." (13, p. 6) It is also true that many of the goals or end-states in forming the content of such definitions are consonant with widely shared values about social organization. Many writers, for example, give the impression that equality with other nations and equality among the peoples within a nation are the paramount criteria for evaluating a country's level of development.

*As a Shared Value.* The final model to be described treats development as a value in itself. In this view the concept development originated in a judgment increasingly shared throughout the postwar world. It has been widely accepted that the impoverished condition of the bulk of the world's countries is both regrettable and remediable, a sentiment which in turn has justified the value-laden term "underdevelopment." Once all are agreed that some countries are "under" developed, the way is open to common acceptance of the desirability of development itself.

From such a perspective, development joins concepts like "freedom" and "democracy" in the Western world, "communism" in the countries of Marxist faith, and "progress" in both places. And, like all general values of that species, the word development will continue in the future to manifest properties with which it is well endowed today—great abstractness, vagueness of meaning, and enjoyment of the greatest esteem in the minds of men. If this be so, the task of "defining" development must be recognized as a pseudo-task, for values are notoriously undefinable. The scientist is better occupied trying to explain how they come into being, and describing their functions. One functon of development is certainly that of providing an incentive—a grand organizing, rationalizing god-term—for the massive task of integrating the nations of the world into a community which will prevent or control the outbreak of international conflict. Indeed, it could well be argued that a number of difficult problems of worldwide scope—population growth and movement, atmospheric pollution, etc.—can be creatively dealt with only at an international level, and that the concept development provides as good a covering term for international cooperation as can be found.

From the national point of view also, the mobilization and organization of peoples of diverse backgrounds and conditions into cooperative communities of larger scale represent a major challenge to political leaders everywhere. In both cases, it is of secondary importance that development "means all things to all men"; it is of primary importance that men everywhere are talking together and working together toward its achievement.

Perhaps the reader is by now weary of our inspection tour. The listing of perspectives can be like a sight-seeing tour extended too long —the sights lose their appeal, the unique features of different structures blend together into a formless mass, and the traveler longs for a resting place devoid of new stimuli. If such is the case, I offer the following conclusion in the hope that the reader will find at least a modicum of refreshment for the moment, and be prepared to resume his travels in the next section.

The proper conclusion to be drawn from the depiction of various approaches to the meaning of the term development is that the word development in itself has no consensual meaning, unless it be that of a world value. When so many men, from so many intellectual backgrounds, with so many different purposes in mind, fasten upon a single word so eagerly, the chief meaning, if one is to be selected, is in their simultaneous commitment to it. Beyond this, meaning is to be found in their perspectives or approaches rather than in the word itself. We could of course state the conclusion less epigrammatically; development has many different "scientific" meanings, depending upon the social background, intellectual experiences, political purpose, cognitive mapping, etc., of the user. The conclusive point to be made is the same—as the scientific tool the clothing of the concept is more important than the concept. In either version, the practical implication is that the framework, conceptual scheme, perspective, is what merits careful study and explicit rejection or acceptance, for on this basis alone can we aspire to know what is meant by development.

## SOCIETAL DEVELOPMENT AS DIFFERENTIATION AND BALANCE IN THE SOCIAL SYSTEM

In the literature of societal development it is common to find the idea expressed that the different parts of society typically develop at different rates or in different stages of the society's historical past. In explaining this notion writers frequently use, or could use, the concepts of "lead" and "lag" or "gap." To give a convenient example, one writer states that during the "Oncenio" in Peru from 1919 to 1930, President Leguía ran a dictatorial regime, detested by labor and liberal groups, but that he also engaged in forced-draft development of the economy, stressing infrastructural construction projects such as highways, port facilities, and public buildings. Thus, in terms of the development of Peru this politically backward eleven-year period must "be accorded a progressive role as far as economic development is concerned." (8, p. 9) Similar statements and evaluations pertaining to the past experiences and present situation of other countries, the reader will agree, can be found quite easily. In decades past, it seems, there was a widespread tendency for the political and social development of a society to lag behind its economic development. Today the typical pattern of developmental disharmony is more apt to be described as a tendency for political development to lead economic and social development. Constitutions, mass movement parties, and other innovations of political life are more easily imported from developed countries or created domestically than are the capital, skill, and entrepreneurial talent required for economic growth, and the wealth required to raise the level of welfare.

This image of society is one which presupposes a substantial degree of structural differentiation. If a society's institutions were undifferentiated or fused, in the manner of most preliterate societies, then such lags and leads would be hard to detect. Thus, it is generally presumed that development goes hand in hand with differentiation.

A large proportion of such writers also propose the idea that such lags or leads must not become too great, or they will produce tensions, problems, perhaps revolutionary tendencies. This conclusion does not have to be stated explicitly, for from a scientific point of view it is implicitly contained in the concepts of lag and lead. That is, either this mode of analysis is simply a value judgment about "how society ought to develop," and thus should be ruled out of bounds, or it can and should be reconciled with, or interpreted in terms of, some larger conceptual framework in which the central propositions at stake must be stated either as axioms or as testable propositions.

In fact, such observers share the view that society is well-conceived as a system of interrelated and interdependent parts. There is less agreement about how best to classify and label the parts, whether they ought to be stated at a high or low level of generality, whether the model of the social system and its presumptive parts are ready to be "closed" as a theoretical system or should remain "open," and so on.

One of the most explicit and elaborate models of society as a social system is that proposed by Talcott Parsons. This is not the place to describe the model in detail, but there are two features of it which have special relevance in our discussion. The first is the grouping of attention into four categories of functional specialization—adaptation, goal-attainment, integration, and latent-pattern maintenance, or, abbreviated, A, G, I, and L—to correspond with the generalized problem or task areas which any social system confronts. A second feature is the tendency for more emphasis to be placed upon one or the other of these foci over time, in a pattern of typical phase movements or phase sequences. In various places in Parsons's work the idea is conveyed that a social system tends to specialize as a matter of relative primacy on particular system problems or tasks at particular times in a typical AGIL order. Further, this phenomenon, sequential specialization, tends to produce time-leads and time-lags. While one problem is receiving more attention, the rest of them are necessarily neglected. Finally, as a paraphrase of Parsons's ideas puts it, "a society is heading for trouble if its leaders are preoccupied *only* with its power position or its Gross National Product, neglecting such problems as friction between institutions, competition between covetous groups and individuals, and personal unhappiness and anxiety among its members. Yet, merely to keep a society harmonious or in high spirits is likewise self-defeating, since essential work would not get accomplished." (23, p. 93)

It appears that Parsons's model could help us in our quest for a systematic definition of development. It includes a manageably simple set of component parts and it explicitly recognizes the lead and lag problem.

With these preliminaries recorded, the stage is prepared for the adaptation of the model to a general conceptualization of societal development. What is a "developed" society? A developed society is one with a social system maximally differentiated with respect to the roles, institutions, general values, and elite groupings which attend to the four functional problems or tasks of the system, but which is also maximally integrated. The main vehicle or general "mechanism" for the production of integration vis-à-vis the functionally differentiated task areas or subsystems is found in the interchanges between subsystems. Such interchanges, across the boundaries separating the subsystems, have as variable properties both magnitude and rate. These are large and rapid, respectively, in a developed society; the larger and more rapid, the more developed the society.

It is further proposed that these interchanges between subsystems perform an emergent function or task, namely, that of maintaining the social system in balance. While stated at a very high level of abstraction, the idea is a simple one. Such interchanges are both a condition of the successful differentiation of subsystems and a measure of the correspondingly necessary integration. In what form do such interchanges occur, at the level of the total society as a social system? In the form of institutional structures, traits, and patterns which are widely recognized as crucial features of the development process. I refer to markets, money, taxation, bureaucratic structures, voluntary specific-purpose organizations, the political franchise, and the like, which serve to identify, aggregate, symbolize, process, and transfer demands, claims, interests, services, etc., from one subsector to another.

The number and performance capacity of such institutions may well be regarded as in themselves measures of the magnitudes and rate of interchanges among subsystems. For example, numerous, well-located and efficiently organized markets for labor and for the purchase of items of consumption effectuate a large and fast interchange between the adaptive subsystem (the economy) and one part of the latent-pattern maintenance subsystem (the family and the individuals in it) in which income, prestige, and style of life appear as products "exchanged on the market" for labor services. When attention is directed to the *number* of different specialized types of institutions, organizations, agencies, etc., in a society, or to the extent to which they perform specific tasks—manifest functional specificity—the term which has come into common use is structural or functional differentiation. It is widely believed that such differentiation is positively correlated with development.

Well and good, but differentiation is only half the picture; performance capacity is not yet gauged. Now the adequacy or efficiency of performance of social institutions and organizations is to be judged in diverse ways, according to varying criteria, and these are extremely difficult to standardize and aggregate, therefore also difficult if not impossible to measure. Without the likelihood of measurement, comparison of different social systems with a view to rating level of development is not possible.

I propose, therefore, an indirect measure of societal development, the products of a large magnitude and rapid rate of subsystem interchange, namely, the absence of lags or gaps. Positively phrased, the measure is the degree of balance of concern and attention simultaneously accorded the four major subsystems.

In a small-scale interaction system such as a face-to-face group, the process of interaction tends to assume the typical AGIL phase movement sequence. Under one condition it does not—when the new element introduced into the system fails to upset the equilibrium of the system because it has been "discounted" in advance. (34, p. 71) In large-scale social systems, such as advanced modern societies, the anticipation of changes, both endogenous and exogenous, is a major preoccupation. Indeed, one of the fundamental latent functions of any interchange process or institution is, in effect, to discount the emergence of disturbing problems. More generally, science, knowledge, and intellectuals assume an ever more central role in the cultural systems of complex societies, where one of their main functions is to promote the anticipation, appropriation, and control of environmental and endogenous sources of change.

Therefore, the more developed the society, the more will its subsystems be "in balance," and the less prominent any sign of the phase movement sequence, those "oscillations around equilibrium" found in simpler social systems and in the differentiated but less developed societies. Another way of putting the idea is—the more developed the society, the more stable is its equilibrium. Institutional or structural differentiation is great, and so is the level of integration of the differentiated components, because of the presence of highly effective interchange processes. National problems, or system tasks are identified and attended to concurrently rather than in phase-sequences. This is, in part, what is meant by a complex system with efficient control and feedback mechanisms.

## SOCIETAL DEVELOPMENT AS A PROPERTY OF THE NATIONAL SOCIETY IN THE WORLD COMMUNITY

The best approach to the solution of a problem is often to conceive it in terms of the largest analytic framework at hand. Consider the world of nations as a global community or giant social system. There is interaction, with problems of order and control, recruitment of new members and their socialization, evaluative assessment by each nation of the actions and qualities of every other, an emergent common culture of cognitions and values and, inevitably, a world stratification system in which the nations take rank according to their several virtues and vices.

Societal development can then be formally defined in terms of three properties familiar to those acquainted with the tradition of sociological theory and research in social stratification. The development of a society is a function of its:

1) static status position—current rank in a hierarchy of nations;
2) dynamic status position—a society's rank at a given time in relation to its rank at some previous time, a comparison which produces a property with two dimensions or subproperties, direction of rank change and magnitude of rank change. Nations can then be ranked in terms of the comparison, such that nations which have moved upward the greatest distance rank high, and those moving downward the greatest distance rank low;
3) dimensional consistency—the degree to which a nation's ranks on different dimensions or criteria of evaluation are highly associated or consistent. Other things equal, the more consistent the dimensional ranks, the more developed the society.

These properties of a nation have for some time been identified, measured, and analyzed as properties of individuals, families, and organizations within society, usually being referred to as social status, social mobility, and status consistency or congruence. The main advantage to applying such an approach to our task, to the search for a good definition of societal development, is that it leaves to an empirical decision the question of deciding precisely what are the criteria of judgment for ranking nations. That is, criteria which are indeed shared as world or international values will lend themselves to a determinate rank ordering of the nations by the nations; criteria or values which are not shared will produce evaluations which will work at cross purposes and lead to seemingly random assignment of nations to particular ranks. Thus, the question of whether there are enough shared values present in the world today can be subjected to test. If the nations can be ranked with reasonable consensus, then the answer is yes, and it is then justifiable to speak of "societal development" as a concept scientifically acceptable to all. If the nations cannot be ranked, then it is inappropriate to conceive of a world system of inter-action and common values, and no universally acceptable definition of "societal development" is possible from this perspective.

A further advantage of the world stratification approach is that it provides an axiomatic point of departure for the generation of additional propositions about the situation of the nations. Thus, na-tions ranking high on the second dimension above having manifested such qualities as national determination, effort, and the like, may be expected to rank relatively low on the third dimension, because the exhibition of such qualities can be interpreted as linked with unusual stress placed upon political coordination or "mobilization," and rela-tive neglect of other dimensions of concern, a pattern leading to what was termed a societal gap or lack of balance in the preceding section. Similarly, nations ranking high on all three dimensions can be ex- pected to place greater emphasis on international stability and delib-erate, orderly change than will those ranking lower. Lower status na-tions would find it to their advantage to press for changes in the pat-tern of distribution of wealth and power in the world, to seek coali-tions and other cooperative devices, to try to mobilize their peoples be-hind national goals, and so on.

Finally, such a scheme makes a clear case for the study of develop-ment policy, for this can be seen as the consideration and evaluation of a nation's efforts to raise its rank in the world community. From this point of view failures and successes of national policy, and therefore of national leadership, can be objectively assessed. This assumes, of course, that judgments of a country and assignment of rank to it are in very large part rendered in terms of performance *relative to poten-tial*. Current rank, or what I term "static status," is also, from the perspective of a given time, ascribed status, and thus the basis for further achievement or failure. Consequently, evaluations of dynamic status position involve considerations of national effort and develop-ment potential, and it is far from true that nations enjoying high cur-rent or "static" status will receive correspondingly high rank on the dynamic side. Similarly, as already noted, dimensional consistency deals with what was referred to in the preceding section as "societal balance," and produces evaluations oriented in large part to the most difficult weaknesses or "social problems" of the societies often judged "highly developed" on the first two properties. For example, there is the widespread opinion that the U.S.A., and the Union of South Africa have not solved (are lagging on) the question of racial integra-tion, and that cultural and political freedom are important minuses on the Soviet scene. Such conditions depress a country's overall rank in the world community—i.e., its level of development—and also consti-tute the setting for a portion of its own explicit or imputed develop-ment tasks.

## REFERENCES

1. Almond, Gabriel A., and Coleman, James S., eds. *The Politics of the Developing Areas.* Princeton: Princeton University Press, 1960.
2. Apter, David. *The Politics of Modernization.* Chicago: University of Chicago Press, 1965.
3. Banfield, Edward C., and Banfield, Laura F. *The Moral Basis of a Backward Society.* Glencoe, Ill.: Free Press, 1958.
4. Becker, Carl. "Progress." In *Encyclopedia of the Social Sciences,* edited by E. R. A. Seligman and A. Johnson, Vol. 11, pp. 495–99. New York: Macmillan, 1933.
5. Bellah, Robert N. *Tokugawa Religion: The Values of Preindustrial Japan.* Glencoe, Ill.: Free Press, 1957.
6. Black, Cyril E. *The Dynamics of Modernization: A Study in Comparative History.* New York: Harper and Row, 1966.
7. *Bolshaia Sovetskaia Entsiklopediia.* Vol. 34. Moscow: Gos. Nauch. Izdat., 1955.
8. Chaplin, David. "Peruvian Stratification and Mobility—Revolutionary and Developmental Potential." In *Structured Social Inequality: A Reader in Comparative Social Stratification,* edited by C. S. Heller. New York: Macmillan, forthcoming.
9. Coleman, James S. "Modernization: Political Aspects." In *International Encyclopedia of the Social Sciences,* Vol. 10, pp. 395–402. New York: Crowell, Collier and Macmillan, 1968.
10. Doob, Leonard W. *Becoming More Civilized: A Psychological Exploration.* New Haven: Yale University Press, 1960.
11. Fanon, Franz. *The Wretched of the Earth.* Paris, 1961. Translated by C. Farrington. New York: Grove Press, 1966.
12. Furtado, Celso. *Development and Underdevelopment.* Translated by Richard W. de Aginar and Eric Charles Drysdale. Berkeley and Los Angeles: University of California Press, 1964.
13. Galtung, Johan. "Socio-economic Development: A Bird's-eye View." In *Members of Two Worlds.* Mimeographed. Oslo: International Peace Research Institute, 1962.
14. Geertz, Clifford. *Peddlars and Princes: Social Change and Economic Modernization in Two Indonesian Towns.* Chicago: University of Chicago Press, 1963.
15. Gerschenkron, Alexander. "Economic Backwardness in Historical Perspective." In *Economic Backwardness in Historical Perspective: A Book of Essays,* pp. 5–30. New York: Praeger, 1965.
16. Hauser, Philip M. "Cultural and Personal Obstacles to Economic Development in the Less Developed Areas." *Human Organization* 18 (1959): 78–84.
17. Hirschman, Albert O. "Comments on 'A Framework for Analyzing Economic and Political Change.'" In *Development of the Emerging Countries: An Agenda for Research,* edited by The Brookings Institute, pp. 39–44. Washington, D.C.: Brookings Institute, 1962.
18. Horowitz, Irving L. *Three Worlds of Development: The Theory and Practice of International Stratification.* New York: Oxford University Press, 1966.
19. Hoselitz, Bert F. "Patterns of Economic Growth." *Canadian Journal of Economics and Political Science* 21 (1955): 416–31.
20. Inkeles, Alex. "The Modernization of Man." In *Modernization: The Dynamics of Growth,* edited by M. Weiner, pp. 138–50. New York: Basic Books, 1966.

21. Johnson, John J. *Political Change in Latin America: The Emergence of the Middle Sectors.* Stanford: Stanford University Press, 1958.
22. Kahl, Joseph A. *The Measurement of Modernism: A Study of Values in Brazil and Mexico.* Latin American Monographs, No. 12, Institute of Latin American Studies. Austin: University of Texas Press, 1968.
23. Keller, Suzanne. *Beyond the Ruling Class: Strategic Elites in Modern Society.* New York: Random House, 1963.
24. Kroeber, Alfred L. *Anthropology: Race, Language, Culture, Psychology, Prehistory.* New York: Harcourt, Brace, 1948.
25. Kuhn, Thomas S. *The Structure of Scientific Revolutions.* Chicago: University of Chicago Press, 1962.
26. Kuznets, Simon S. *Modern Economic Growth: Rate, Structure and Speed.* New Haven: Yale University Press, 1966.
27. Lagos-Matus, Gustavo. *International Stratification and Underdeveloped Countries.* Chapel Hill: University of North Carolina Press, 1963.
28. Lerner, Daniel. *The Passing of Traditional Society: Modernizing the Middle East.* Glencoe, Ill.: Free Press, 1958.
29. Levine, Donald N. *Wax and Gold: Tradition and Innovation in Ethiopian Culture.* Chicago: University of Chicago Press, 1965.
30. Levy, Marion J., Jr. *Modernization and the Structure of Societies: A Setting for International Affairs.* Vols. 1 and 2. Princeton: Princeton University Press, 1966.
31. Moore, Barrington, Jr. *Social Origins of Dictatorship and Democracy: Lord and Peasant in the Making of the Modern World.* Boston: Beacon Press, 1966.
32. Myint, Hla. "An Interpretation of Economic Backwardness." In *The Economics of Underdevelopment,* edited by A. N. Agarwala and S. P. Singh, pp. 93–132. New York: Oxford University Press, 1958.
33. Nettl, J. P., and Robertson, Roland. "Industrialization, Development and Modernization." *British Journal of Sociology* 17 (1966): 274–91.
34. Parsons, Talcott; Bales, Robert F.; and Shils, Edward A. *Working Papers on the Theory of Action.* Glencoe, Ill.: Free Press, 1953.
35. Rostow, Walter W. *The Stages of Economic Growth: A Non-communist Manifesto.* New York: Cambridge University Press, 1960.
36. Viner, Jacob. "The Economics of Development." In *The Economics of Underdevelopment,* edited by A. N. Agarwala and S. P. Singh, pp. 9–31. New York: Oxford University Press, 1958.

# CHAPTER THREE

# QUEST
# FOR SOCIETAL DEVELOPMENT

## A. EUGENE HAVENS

AT THE END of the twentieth century when historians analyze our times, they may record that one of the most impressive trends of the post-World War II period was concern with economic development. A large number of countries have embarked on the planning and execution of economic development programs. The Western world and Communist-bloc countries have demonstrated a willingness to assist less advanced countries by providing technical and investment assistance to a degree uncommon to other historical eras. At the same time, the more advanced countries are still struggling with the development of the lagging sectors of their own economies. Social scientists have responded to this concern in their research activities. Yet this response has been far from satisfactory. There is little articulation between the idealized future state of affairs that is supposedly desired and the theories advanced to take us there. A large portion of this failure lies in the fact that there is little interaction between the proponents of the theories of *economic* development and the more general theories of societal development.

The purpose of the present study is to make a miniscule beginning to bridge the gap between these groups. In doing so, I have attempted to keep in mind Popper's description of scientific theories by the

**A. EUGENE HAVENS** is Associate Professor of Rural Sociology and Director, Center for Developing Nations Programs at the University of Wisconsin. He is chairman of the sociology of development program in the Department of Rural Sociology. He holds the Ph.D. in sociology from Ohio State University. He has been on the staff of the National University of Bogota, Colombia. Publications relevant to his chapter include: "The Use of Socio-Economic Research in Developing a Strategy for Change in Rural Communities: A Colombian Example" (**Economic Development and Cultural Change** [January, 1966] pp. 204–16) and "Goal Displacement and the Intangibility of Organization Goals" (**Administrative Science Quarterly** [March, 1968] pp. 539–55).

metaphor of the searchlight. "What the searchlight makes visible will depend upon its position, upon our way of directing it, and upon its intensity, color, etc.; although it will, of course, also depend very largely upon the things illuminated by it." (26, p. 260) I hope that I have directed it in some of the right directions and that some of the things illuminated will represent a plank or two in the bridge.

Theories of economic development which use economic growth as the sole measure of development are unsatisfactory with regard to a theory of societal development. This point is amply demonstrated by the committee reports accompanying the passage of the Title IX Amendment to the 1966 Foreign Assistance Act of the United States. While economic growth may be a necessary condition for societal development, it is not societal development. Therefore, it is necessary to determine what societal development is.

Contemporary concern for societal development followed a period of dramatic social upheaval—a social upheaval precipitated by the attempt of one society to impose its will upon others. Of course, prior to the German society's attempt there had transpired the internal struggle for the consolidation of power so that one group within the society could impose its will on all other groups within the society. Indeed Hitler's entire justification for his acts seemed to center upon the conviction that the chosen society's existence depended upon the imposition of wills, or as Nietzsche argued, upon the taming of a beast and the breeding of a specific species. (29, ch. 4)

Even after witnessing the results of such a grotesque philosophy, it seems difficult to avoid periods in history where groups within a society and a given society's treatment of other societies essentially turns upon the imposition of wills. For example, the Russian treatment of the Hungarian Revolt and the United States's attempted squelching of the Cuban Revolution are post-World War II cases in point where one society has either imposed or attempted to impose its will upon another society. It is interesting to note that a society's organization seems to be a crucial variable in determining the extent to which it is possible for one group or individual to impose its will upon others. Of course, the existence of a given society where it is totally impossible to impose one's will upon others is viewed herein as an unattainable goal but the role of social organization as a *limitation* on the imposition of wills occupies a central place in the definition of societal development to be presented subsequently.

In addition to these moral complexities, the world is no longer a simple place within which to live. A society's tenacity is partially based upon its ability to cope with the environment, particularly in a society like that of the United States. We are constantly bombarded by technological advances of vast social consequences. Transplanting vital organs from one person to another may prolong life. At the same time, it may require a redrafting of laws concerning the pronouncement of death in order to salvage the organ prior to the donor's currently legal expiration. The shortened work week, coupled with relatively full employment and high wages, has brought about a degree of leisure and affluence and we seem woefully unable to cope with it. Almost every index of social disorganization in the United States (e.g., crime rates, drug addiction, suicides) is rising. The feeling of powerlessness to influence our immediate surroundings and a divisive conflict over international affairs, both coupled with the apparent lack of consensus vis-à-vis ideological commitments, seem to characterize our times.

One of the pivotal assumptions of the present study is that current theories of economic development have overlooked the ideological relevance of organizations as an effective mechanism for coping with the environment. Moreover, it will be argued that a certain type of social organization is implicitly assumed by most economic theories of development. And finally, it is suggested that the structural conditions under which organizations become effective mechanisms for coping with the environment are sufficient conditions for having a society that is economically just and at the same time politically fluent and free. But before these structural conditions can be specified, it is necessary to seek some clarification concerning the concept of development.

Some clarification of concepts may be attained if economic considerations are coupled with sociological ones. This is not a new idea. Economists have been asking for some time that the sociologists assist them in their study of development. Dusenberry (7) and Kuznets (14) especially have presented cogent arguments for the need of including factors from other disciplines in economic development. Hagen has gone a step beyond this and actually attempted to include such factors in a search for a theory of social change. (10)

Sociologists probably rankle at the work of Hagen and at statements such as the following: "In particular, economists have come to consider factors and influences which previously have been relegated to institutional literature or left to other disciplines . . . we think that economic propositions of some generality and depth can be established about them and their interaction with the variables and influences usually studied by economists." (2, p. 11) One of the factors which Bauer and Yamey include is family obligations. Some sociologists might argue that the economists are invading their field and that the economist is poorly equipped to study these areas.

But the plain truth is that sociologists have been slow to respond to the questions economists have been asking us. (21, p. 57) Sociologists have studied development but we have tended to argue polemically in attempts to show that other than economic motives are involved in human behavior. Many economists are willing to grant the point, but they want to know not only *what* these noneconomic considerations are but *how* they operate either to retard or to enhance development. And by development they are willing to employ societal development rather than economic growth. However, most developmental economists wish to deal with quantifiable parameters of development so as to construct a formal theory. Noneconomic social scientists dealing with development generally weave abstractions of pre-science character; their notions concerning societal development are usually unanalyzable abstractions. (12, pp. 14–21) However, let us investigate these pre-scientific considerations.

## SOCIETAL DEVELOPMENT: PRE-SCIENCE AND UNANALYZABLE ABSTRACTIONS

If concern with development is paramount in the twentieth century, it is not the only century of mankind so preoccupied. In fact, concern with societal development is one of the most pervasive themes of mankind. Just what is the future of society and how can man assure its attainment? This question has not only occupied the energies of social scientists but philosophers, activists, and theologians as well. However, the very phrasing of the question has led us into metaphysical and pre-scientific formulations. The question of what is our ultimate destiny does not lend itself to scientific interpretation. The more important question for social scientists is, Toward what tangible goals should society be oriented that will allow the maximum contribution of all mankind to these goals? Of course, this phrasing is not perfect and it too may include unanalyzable abstractions. But it focuses our attention on tangible goals and the selection of means to attain these goals.

In taking this position, I have, using Popper's metaphor, focused attention away from a particular branch of early philosophical thought. I do not agree that there is a natural order of societal development that is discoverable through the cannons of science. While Mill significantly advanced us toward a science of development, his position on historical method is almost identical to that of Marx: "the method now characterized is that by which . . . the laws . . . of social progress must be sought. By its aid we may hereafter succeed not only in looking far forward into the future history of the human race, but in determining what *artificial means may be used . . . to accelerate the natural* progress in so far as it is beneficial." (18)

This conception of history appears much like the Marxian conception which asserts that 1) the economic structure of society is not and cannot be deliberately planned and controlled, but develops independently of human will, 2) this developing economic structure determines what takes place in other spheres of social life, and 3) the course of history is inevitably punctuated by violent revolutions, each marking the transition to a more advanced stage. Such a conception led Marx to state, "When a society has discovered the natural law that determines its own movement, even then it can neither overleap the natural phases of its evolution, nor shuffle them out of the world by the stroke of a pen." (15) However, Marx was certainly no fatalist. Man could shorten and lessen the birthpangs and assist history in ushering in a Utopia that is absent of political or economic conflict and thus the state withers away. As Popper indicated, "The historicist can only *interpret* social development and aid it in various ways; his point, however, is that *nobody can change it."* (27, p. 52)

While I do not agree with Marx's assumption, he must be credited with being one of the few theorists who attempted to advance a theory of social development. Consequently, his theory should be examined in some detail. Starting from three empirical observations, Marx spins his theory and tells us what is a fully developed society. The empirical observations are 1) the presence of conflict between social classes, 2) the presence of ownership of private property, and 3) the presence of relations of domination and subjection. (5, p. 30) Since Marx is forced into a holistic view of society due to his conception of distinct historical periods, he must build a system in which everything fits. Thus, as Dahrendorf points out, if private property disappears, then there are no longer classes. This, of course, is a play on words. Since Marx views society as divided into two classes, those who own property and those who do not, if private property disappears, then, by definition there can be no classes. Marx continues by arguing that if there are no classes, there is no conflict and the realm of liberty is realized. (5, p. 31) But here he has slipped out of the realm of science and into the realm of the metaphysics of an unanalyzable abstraction. What constitutes liberty? This is essentially undefined in the Marxian analysis. (12, p. 17)

However, Marx did give us some clue to the goal toward which society should be oriented. It should be oriented toward the abolition of authority where man existed in a conflict-free society and contributed according to his capacities and earned according to his needs. It is necessary to investigate the possibility of a conflict-free society.

First of all, it must be recalled that Marx thought that the abolition of private property was a necessary and sufficient condition for abolishing authority relations. In a fascinating critique of Marx's sociology, Dahrendorf has shown the logical inconsistency of this belief. As Dahrendorf concludes, "Power and authority are irreducible factors from which the social relations associated with legal private property as well as those associated with communal property can be derived. . . . Whoever tries, therefore, to define authority by property defines the general by the particular—an obvious logical fallacy." (5 p. 137)

If property does not define authority and power, then authority cannot be eliminated through the abolition of private property. But can authority be attacked directly? Is it possible to have society without authority relations? Once again Dahrendorf has provided a convincing answer to this question. It is not conceivable to think of organization without relations of power and authority. (5, pp. 165–79) In order to buttress this conclusion, an examination of what constitutes power and authority is in order.

In most sociological formulations, relations commonly entail ties of mutual dependence between parties. A depends upon B to the extent that his goals or gratifications are contingent upon appropriate actions of B. "By virtue of mutual dependency, it is more or less imperative to each party that he be able to control or influence the other's conduct. At the same time, these ties of mutual dependence imply that each party is in a position, to some degree, to grant or deny, facilitate or hinder, the other's gratification. Thus, it would appear that the power to control or influence the other resides in control over the things he values, which may range all the way from oil resources to ego-support." (9, p. 32)

If such a definition of relation is utilized, then the definition of power becomes explicit. Power resides implicitly in B's dependency upon A. It does not reside *in* A; that is, it is not an attribute of A but rather a property of the social relation. Thus, the power of A over B is equal to, and based upon, the dependence that B feels upon A. (3, ch. 5) Therefore, in all social relations, there is a tendency for power to exist.

Concurrent with the tendency for power to exist in all social relations, there is an equal tendency toward some sort of balance in relations. Thus, if the power of B over A is equal to the power of A over B, we would have a simple balance model. This does not imply that since the power of both is equal, that power is cancelled out. Rather than cancelling out power, we may speak of reciprocal power and the tendency toward balancing power relations. As we move to the societal level of analysis, there is still a tendency toward balancing vast networks of power relationships. This balance often takes the form of coalitions in order to guard against subjugation or dependence. In viewing coalitions, a key point emerges. Groups that may be in conflict in one area may coalesce in another to attain their goals in the other area. This does not eliminate power nor does it eliminate conflict. Both are ubiquitous in all society. (5, p. 165)

On the other hand, authority relations are always determined by positions not by persons. While authority also involves relations of super-ordination and sub-ordination, its use is based on the legitimate right of the person due to his position, not to his caprice. All known social organizations entail positions that carry authority and positions that are excluded from the exercise of authority. Noncompliance with decisions taken by those in positions of authority can be punished; indeed this is the function of the legal system.

Holders of the positions of authority may change without altering the authority of the positions. In order to change the authority of the position, it is necessary to change the sanctions coupled with non-compliance. As long as those excluded from positions of authority desire to attain authority, conflict will exist. And as long as social organization requires the institutionalization of authority, some, perhaps the majority, will be excluded from authority positions.

However, these statements should not be construed as supportive of Michels's "iron law of oligarchy." (17) Even though authority is vested in the hands of a minority, as long as those excluded from authority may form groups to place demands on the holders of authority, society is dynamic, changing and personal liberties are attainable. This does not eliminate authority nor does it eliminate conflict. Conflict is not resolved but it is regulated. Nor should it be resolved for it is conflict which engenders change and provides society with a mechanism for establishing those preconditions necessary for development. As Dahrendorf concludes, "all that is creativity, innovation, and development in the life of the individual, his group, and his society is due, to no small extent, to the operation of conflicts between group and group, individual and individual, emotion and emotion within one individual." (5, p. 208) Given this inherent conflict present within any society, attention to the regulatory mechanisms is required. The key to these regulatory mechanisms lies in the centrality of social relations to all human behavior. Since social relations are governed by normative prescriptions for behavior in general and by role expectations for occupants of positions in particular, the regulatory mechanisms are largely based upon the Parsonsian notions of the double contingency and the complimentarity of expectations in social action.[1] Since both parties (or better yet, *all* parties) hold expectations for their own and each other's behavior, and since these expectations become more sharply defined through the interaction process, there exists the possibility for the *mutual enhancement of effort* in goal-directed behavior.[2] That is, individuals and groups, through the interaction process, become aware of their dependence on others in order to obtain the maximum output at the least cost in social exchanges. (3) While this reciprocity in social relations is a strain toward balance, it is never achieved. The ever-present conflict perceived by the actors in social relations, coupled with the desire to improve one's status even at the expense of others, brings about a gradual and continual change in expectations, which precludes maintaining balanced relations.

In societies where the actor in social relations must behave in rather isolated conditions, he almost always gives up more than he receives. Social relations are typified by superordination of a relative few, who may or may not obtain access to certain reserves of power

[1] Parsons's use of the double contingency and the complimentarity of expectations was an attempt to cope with the Hobbesian problem of order. It was initially formulated in his *The Structure of Social Action,* New York: McGraw-Hill, 1937.
[2] I am indebted to Daryl Hobbs for inclusion of this concept.

from other societies, whose major goal is to exploit the isolated individuals that form the mass of the society. Such is the case in a feudal society and in most instances that we currently refer to as the underdeveloped countries of the world. In other societies where individuals can group collectively to bargain for their social and economic rights, the aforementioned strain toward the balance of power relations occurs and the structural conditions of such a society provide for the mutual enhancement of effort on the part of the individual members of the society. This mutual enhancement is one of the indices of a sociological definition of development which will be presented shortly.

Based upon these contentions, it is possible to free the notion of societal development from its pre-scientific roots and convert it to an empirical question rather than an unanalyzable abstraction. Once we surrender the dogmas of an unalterable human nature or inevitable laws of organizational progress or corruption (17, 22, 24), we can do something about shaping societal development. This, of course, was the position of the early institutional economists. They accepted the *Deweyan* notion that freedom and authority can live together happily only in a society where scientific method is applied not merely to problems of physical control but to questions of human value as well. (11)

Thus, assuming that the laws of societal development are alterable and that man is somewhat rational, it is possible to specify some empirical indicators of societal development. In doing so, it must be granted that using rationality to imply the selection of the best available means to attain the desired ends is highly dependent upon the knowledge present at any given time. However, we are at least using the available knowledge by putting it to practical use. As Dewey pointed out, there is nothing wrong with burning down the barn to roast the pig if that is the only way we know to attain the goal of roasted pig. Hopefully, if we can specify tangible goals, the application of scientific methods rather than pre-scientific dogmas will lead us to the development of more efficient means.

Efficiency, alone, may be a dangerous concept. Total efficiency is not the goal of a developed society. As Hook said, "When efficiency is a desideratum, it is easy to palm off injustice as a necessary evil." (12, p. 125) Purging all those who disagree with the current holders of authority may be efficient in order to attain some goals, but it is hardly the mark of a developed society. (6, pp. 11ff.)

Up to now the discussion has largely centered around the elimination of certain indicators for the measurement of societal development. Thus, it was argued that the absence of authority relations and the corresponding conflicts between those in positions of authority and those excluded from positions of authority was not a measure because it is a logical impossibility. Rationality and its corresponding concern with efficiency were eliminated as sole indicators of development since efficiency alone could lead to blatant social injustices.

Societal development occurs when through instrumental, voluntary associations, political participation on the part of all members of a society is enhanced. This enhancement is in terms of access to various positions of authority, on the one hand, and the ability to influence policymaking and decisions on the other. (1,8) Secondly, the ever-present conflict between groups is low in intensity and its regulation is low in violence. (5) Since individual members of a society have the opportunity to belong to these instrumental organizations, the potential exists for the mutual enhancement of effort on the part of all members. While these indices may define societal development, they do not tell us how to achieve the goal. In order to take some tentative steps toward specifying the necessary conditions for societal development, we must turn our attention to the interrelationships between economic models of growth and societal development.

## SOCIOLOGICAL ASSUMPTIONS UNDERLYING SOME MODERN THEORIES OF ECONOMIC DEVELOPMENT

While it is true that other social sciences have been spinning theories of development that are replete with unanalyzable abstractions, economics has not enjoyed any great consensus concerning models of economic growth. Current and recent literature is full of loose ends, unrealistic assumptions, yet revealing insights and penetrating bits and pieces of analysis. Consequently, there are some who argue that a theory of growth may be developed that is elegant and precise and others who feel all that can be hoped for is a loose framework of general propositions and ad hoc theorizing. Whichever position the economist takes, inevitably somewhere during his theorizing he is forced to fall back to the convenience of *ceteris paribus*. It is this area of "all other factors being equal" approach that will first occupy our attention.

The *ceteris paribus* condition is a variant of heuristic assumption which transforms potentially operative variables into random variables. Economists explicitly assume, for instance, that in many economic analyses various noneconomic factors have a random effect; that is, they may be treated as parameters. The most frequent noneconomic variables assumed to be parameters are institutions. Economists also have traditionally assumed some version of the postulate of economic rationality. By extensive use of this method of simplifying sources of variation, economic researchers have been able to assume away certain potential variables and then, by assuming all remaining variables but one to be constant, isolate the effect of changes in one variable.

The method of heuristic assumption has been helpful in fields such as economics, but it is in many respects inferior to the method of experimentation since the method of heuristic assumption rests on no form of situational or conceptual manipulation other than simplifying assumptions. Rarely are serious attempts made to establish the empirical validity of the assumptions or to "correct" for the degree to which the assumption is not valid. Thus, much precision may be lost by the convenience of *ceteris paribus*. Nevertheless, in spite of the fact that heuristic assumptions are rarely empirically informed, they provide the investigator the same kind of service as the experimental method. This service is to transform operative conditions into parameters to permit the isolated investigation of a limited number of selected operative conditions.

It is necessary, however, to examine some of the assumptions made under *ceteris paribus*. First is the assumption that the all-powerful concepts of supply and demand adjust output, distribution, and prices. While such an assumption is undoubtedly viable in highly industrialized economies, it is not viable in other parts of the world. Polanyi and others have demonstrated that economic activities actually fall into three main patterns of exchange. (25) They suggest *reciprocative* exchange as illustrated by ritualized gift-giving among families; *redistributive* exchange where economic goods and services are brought to a central source, such as government, and then redistributed throughout the populace; and *exchange* which is the familiar pattern of the free market. While the latter pattern is viable in most economic situations of the Western world, it is not always present even in the 1960s in any society.

While the assumption of a market exchange economy may account for a portion of the lack of isomorphism between economic theories and the real world, some other crucial assumptions should be investigated.

Economic growth theory deals in part with the increase of inputs as a result of a change in the quality of inputs, not the quantity, or the addition of new kinds of inputs. Spengler argues that in most modern societies, growth is of this sort and since the creation of new inputs or the improving of the quality of old inputs is more of an evolutionary process, growth of this sort parallels social development. (30, p. 244) The argument runs that capacity for technical progress depends upon the state of the art (i.e., the application of scientific knowledge to practical problems), the availability of entrepreneurs to innovate coupled with their freedom and desire to do so, and upon an economy's being flexible and characterized by a high degree of factor mobility. He concludes, "Capacity for technical progress cannot, therefore, become significant until a society and its labor force have been appreciably modernized; it is absent from a traditional society, and it is not very notable in a handicraft society." (20; 30, pp. 250–51)

Sociologically speaking, one of the major differences between traditional and modern societies is the absence of instrumental voluntary associations that allow for maximum political participation in traditional societies. So we return again to the same key variable in societal development: instrumental voluntary associations. It should be noted that this variable is the crux of the definition of societal development presented in the previous section of this study. One way to increase the political participation on the part of all members of a society is through instrumental voluntary associations that operate in the political sphere. Of course, the operation of instrumental voluntary associations in the political sphere is almost always based upon an economic motivation. Consequently, if the previous arguments are tenable we have isolated a convergence between the theories of economic development and societal development. It is now necessary to present a rationale for how voluntary associations arise and their impact upon societal development.

## SOME POTENTIAL SOCIOLOGICAL CONTRIBUTIONS TO THE THEORY OF SOCIETAL DEVELOPMENT

Bruton's article on some theories of economic growth concluded, "It must be recognized that in a long-run period analysis the distinction between 'economic' and 'noneconomic' factors loses significance, and it becomes necessary to acknowledge that economic growth must be seen as a special aspect of general social evolution rather than as a process which can be factored out of the social system and studied in isolation." (4, p. 298) Such a convergence was readily possible during the height of political economy and institutional economics; however, the fields have grown apart in recent years. Two significant developments are presenting the opportunity for another convergence: the sociologists' use of market models to study social exchange and the economists' use of modern economic theory to study institutions.

One of the major points demonstrated by the recent literature dealing with the convergence of the economic and sociological traditions is that planning for economic development is faulty unless the blueprint includes changes in the social structure and cultural values of the society. In other words, economic development is part of social and cultural change. Economic development specifically involves three interrelated kinds of social action: 1) the establishment of increased wealth and income as a perceived, attainable goal for the society, 2) the creation and/or selection of means to attain this goal, and 3) the restructuring of society so that economic growth is a persistent feature of the social system. (23)

While these three kinds of social action are interrelated, one must be chronologically first. Goals must be decided upon and stated in somewhat tangible terms before means can be selected for their attainment. (31) Who then establishes economic development as one of the goals of a given society? An answer to this question is largely dependent upon the structure of the society prior to the establishment of the goal. As Nash indicated: "If the wealth, power and prestige of a given society is strongly polarized between two groups with relatively little mobility between them, it appears that social change on the structural level is unlikely and that new economic opportunities will not be a chief concern of the dominant group and hardly even a perception of the subordinate group." (23, p. 139)

Obviously, in this type of social structure little emphasis for any type of change such as economic development is likely to spring from either group. Marx has aptly explained why the lower group will not be change oriented. "The small peasants form a huge mass, whose members live in similar conditions without, however, entering into many and varied relations with one another. . . . This isolation is promoted by the poor means of communication in France. . . . Every individual peasant family is almost self-sufficient; it produces directly the greater part of what it consumes; and so earns its livelihood more by means of an interchange with nature than by intercourse with society. . . . In so far as there exists only a local connection among these peasants, a connection which the individuality and exclusiveness of their interests prevent from generating among them any unity of interest, national connections, and political organization, they do not constitute a class." (16, p. 63)

The other group, let us call them the traditional elite, may not desire change since they enjoy complete control of the situation. Change can bring about a realignment of the stratification system of the society. Why risk losing status for a potential increase in wealth when you are currently the wealthiest group of the society? How then does concern for economic growth develop which becomes one of the goals of the society?

The answer to the source of leadership for reorienting society's goals was succinctly presented by Nash. "It is generally conceded that the 'take-off' is led by a particular segment of society, either an elite . . . or a class blocked in social or economic mobility. . . . The success of the dissident social segment and elitist reorientation of goals is closely tied to the group's administrative abilities and to their skills in enlisting the energies and sentiments of a good part of the population in a program of development. . . . If we accept the widely held and frequently repeated generalization that economic development involves some industrialization and some use of new technology, then part of the process is dependent upon the relations of the developing region to the developed countries." (23, p. 138)

The dependency of the developing region to the developed countries, and we might add the dependency of developed countries upon developing regions and other developed countries, is the key to the impetus for change. In today's world, it is impossible for any country to exist in isolation. Developing countries, and developing regions within developed countries, are continually bombarded with new knowledge, new sources of communication, assistance programs for education, industrialization and agricultural production whether they want such attention or not. Consequently, there is a built-in potential for generating feelings of relative deprivation on the part of both the elite groups and the dissident social segment.

If the impetus for redefining societal goals comes from a dissident social group, the leadership for such a group almost always comes from the universities. The quest for change springs largely from rebellion against the existing order, particularly in traditional societies. Also, students who become introduced to idealistic and utopian models for development and wish to work toward such a goal for their society find that post-university prospects for finding a position in the existing structure that will allow them to do so is close to absolute zero. Their usual response to such a bleak outlook is to attempt to work for change within the existing structure or to migrate to other countries. If they attempt to work within the existing structure and continue to have access to the intellectual milieux surrounding their university life, and if their attempts to instigate change are repeatedly blocked, revolution becomes a real alternative. Such is the case to stronger and lesser degrees of the Fidel Castros, Che Guevaras, and Camilo Torres in Latin America and the Menons, Nkrumahs, and Bandas of Africa.

Whether the United States likes it or not, revolution is a viable alternative for structural change. And in many cases, the forms of social organization that make for a successful revolution are highly consistent with the conditions required for societal development as defined herein. However, it is also a more difficult road to development. The difficulty lies partly in the fact that during armed conflict many physical resources such as roads, industrial plants, planes, and land may be rendered unserviceable. Also, human resources are sacrificed through casualties and people fleeing the country. Those who flee do not leave empty-handed. They take with them vital capital reserves and technical skills that will be needed desperately during the post-revolution reconstruction. Moreover, it is apparent from recent historical developments that certain assistance from some developed countries given during the process of waging revolution, will not be forthcoming after the revolution.

Before leaving this alternative for bringing about structural change necessary for economic growth, it must be clearly stated that revolution that merely produces a change in the *occupants* of authority positions and does not also produce a change in *positions* and access to these positions is abortive. It is not revolution in the sense of intense and violent conflict used as a means of bringing about structural change. Moreover, revolution is not societal development. This is, of course, indicated by the definition of societal development presented herein, since it was argued that in a developed society conflict was low in intensity and violence. However, revolution may be one of the means in the means-ends pyramid that ultimately leads to the attainment of the goal of societal development. And it cannot be denied that historically it has been a viable means. The critical point in the revolutionary-based means-ends chain that leads toward economic growth and subsequently societal development is the period immediately following the armed conflict. If the revolutionaries do not 1) increase per capita income, 2) create new employment opportunities, 3) insure that mobility channels are kept open, 4) develop new skills through an educational system open to all, and 5) institutionalize the opportunity to voluntarily affiliate with organizations[3] that can present their demands to the new government so that new economic organization and technology is invented or adapted, then conflict will increase in intensity and violence at another time, the mutual enhancement of effort will be retarded, and the maximum political participation will not be obtained. Such a condition is the antithesis of societal development as defined in the present study. All of this cannot be accomplished without external assistance, at least in the short run. And if it is not accomplished in the short run, the organized groups within the society attempt to take the next step in the means-ends chain leading toward societal development which is best described as a tutelary democracy. (28, pp. 47–84)

Tutelary democracy as a path toward societal development may start without a revolution but it always follows the armed conflict phase of a revolutionary-based means-ends chain if the country is to become developed. Classical examples are the means-ends chains employed by France, Mexico, and Cuba. First, the case of the nonrevolutionary means-ends chain will be presented.

If a tutelary, quasi-national government desires to stimulate economic growth and simultaneously not seriously disrupt the balance of power within the social system, then certain conditions are most likely to be present at the time of emergence. These conditions are 1) local communities are relatively isolated, with few communication or transportation ties to the larger urban center, thereby limiting the possibilities for local residents to perceive their situation as being relatively deprived, which precludes the possibility for developing meaningful local concern for economic growth and societal development, 2) national elite are concerned with increasing economic growth, generally in the agricultural sector, since they feel that any further advancement in their own or others' positions might be inhibited, 3) educational levels are low with a high rate of illiteracy, 4) most of the economically active are either directly or indirectly engaged in agriculture, 5) agricultural production is largely at the subsistence level with locally based mar-

---

[3] For the reader who is not convinced that revolutionary-based means-ends chains toward development begin with local and regional level voluntary associations, see Mao Tse Tung, *On Guerrilla Warfare*, New York: Praeger, 1961 and Che Guevara, *On Guerrilla Warfare*, New York: Praeger, 1961.

kets,[4] 6) mobility tends to be lacking with positions largely assigned by ascription, and 7) authority is vested in a relatively few paternal institutions.

Under such conditions, early attempts to stimulate economic growth and societal development are likely to meet with little success, since the clientele are not initially concerned with change. The elite are concerned because even though they personally tend not to employ land as an income property they recognize that their own economic activities may be limited if the agricultural sector is not more productive. Most underdeveloped countries' balance of payment situation depends upon agricultural exports (such as coffee, rice, cotton, sugar, etc.) in a precarious balance with imports for industry and consumption. The elite may own land but it is for prestige and a hedge against inflation more than an income property. Therefore, the elite's own tastes must be satisfied by either inherited wealth or income from urban industrial and professional occupations. The elite know that any further industrial growth depends upon agriculture's ability to supply this sector or upon the exportation of minerals or petroleum. Since not all countries are blessed with these resources, agricultural production is viewed as the limiting factor.

As the tutelary government begins to press for economic growth, it may either consciously or inadvertently establish the conditions sufficient for moving toward a structural change which will allow for sustained growth. On the other hand, if the tutelary regime desires to maintain the existing power balance and not disrupt seriously the social structure, start and stop growth is most likely to occur. One reason that growth may not be continuous is that no tutelary regime is sufficiently able to consolidate power without recurring intense conflicts.[5] As these conflicts occur, certain human and capital resources are diverted from the productive process and invested in the conflict regulation. As a result, growth tends to increase, while power is consolidated and slow-down or actual decline occurs during conflict regulation. Therefore, the tutelary beginning of development is not sufficient for sustained economic and social development. Of course, if a tutelary regime successfully maintains power consolidation, it is no longer tutelary; it is totalitarian.

If a structural change occurs which leads to the development of a

[4] This does not imply that all markets are locally based or that the products that the peasants produce do not find their way to national markets or international markets. Rather, it indicates that the peasant does not orient his production toward national market price fluctuations but toward family consumption. Any surplus would be sold, but to local buyers.

[5] If it were, then it would be a complete totalitarian state. But not even totalitarian states have been able to reach full development with a sustained economic growth pattern. The Soviet Union is usually classed as an intermediately developed country, and where growth has been most dramatic, the state has relaxed its control; Soviet science is a good case in point.

pluralistic society demanding economic growth, then a certain social process must have occurred which establishes the conditions for sustained economic growth and societal development. This social process and its subsequent consequences may be described in the following manner. Two factors are viewed as necessary preconditions if the sufficient conditions to be detailed subsequently are to emerge. These are communication contacts and relative deprivation. Communication contacts must be present if individuals are to gain knowledge of new alternatives to their present situation. Lack of knowledge about new alternatives undoubtedly is functional from the point of view of the traditional elite since ignorance of other alternatives reduces conflict and lessens the demands for change. (19) Without these sources of knowledge about alternative patterns of behavior, there is no basis for relative deprivation. To be relatively deprived, one must be able to compare himself with others and feel that his position is inferior. If an individual does not feel relatively deprived (or concerned for improving his present position), there is no logical basis for expecting him to be interested in change.[6] Change, then, would most likely come as a result of the activities of a tutelary regime and not a revolutionary-based means-ends chain. If relative deprivation on the part of the rural population is high and a tutelary democracy does not emerge to decrease this relative deprivation, then revolution, given leadership availability, is a viable alternative.

But if these two necessary conditions exist, then the following sufficient conditions may emerge. The communication contacts and feelings of relative deprivation allow for the growth of concern about how to express the demands of the individual. Since many of the individuals who feel relatively deprived also feel that the interests of existing authority structure conflict with their own interests, they may group around this perceived conflict and attempt to attain collectively what individually they would be barred from accomplishing. That is, voluntary associations may emerge that become new power contenders and place demands on the existing authority structure which necessitates some type of response. The response may be 1) a reconsolidation of power which would indicate that the voluntary associations did not attain their goals through currently defined legal means and they may turn to the revolutionary beginning for the means-ends chain, or 2) concessions granted on the part of the authority structure. The set of sufficient conditions then are the formation of voluntary associations,

---

[6] Relative deprivation is used herein to also connote concern for differences between one's conception of self and one's definition of what he should be, that is, a difference between real and ideal self definitions. This might lead to a self-actuated concern for change without comparisons to other reference groups. But one's ideal self definition must be based upon some knowledge of other ideologies or styles of life. Such knowledge must come through some type of communication contact.

that seek to attain instrumental goals,[7] which either by accident or design are consistent with the broad goal of development, and these voluntary associations are somewhat successful in attaining their goals.[8]

If the voluntary associations are not somewhat successful in attaining their goals, they will not emerge as new power contenders. The traditional power structure will reconsolidate its power and maintain the subjugation of the less privileged individuals. If they are successful in attaining their goals, then these voluntary associations will become new power contenders and there will be the creation of new positions and different expectations for behavior. That is, the structural change will be tenacious and institutionalized into the prior structure. If this occurs, then governments will tend to be more stable with less intense conflicts which divert productive resources to conflict resolution, and economic growth will be self-sustaining and simultaneously the probability of attaining the goal of societal development is enhanced.

The set of sufficient conditions may be considered as one side of an equation that, by definition, yields growth. If voluntary associations emerge, that seek instrumental goals that are consistent with the goal of economic growth and these voluntary associations are successful in attaining these goals, then economic growth must accrue. Such a formulation is a logically closed system. The lack of any part will not yield growth. Most frequently, the part of the equation that refers to attainment is lacking. It is not sufficient to form voluntary associations that seek instrumental goals consistent with growth. These associations must also be able to attain their goals.

There is no implicit argument that this set of conditions is the only set that will yield economic growth. Others may be stated that will also yield growth. However, it is argued that the set hypothesized herein perform other latent functions that, in turn, are important for societal development. One such latent function is that societies that are pluralistic are less subject to manipulation by central governments. (12, pp. 125–27; 13) Government's ability to stay in power depends upon its ability to serve the demands of its constituents. Of course, demands can be met by force and individuals can be coerced into acquiescence. However, if the societal values are consistent with a democratic ideology, then effective voluntary associations may serve as a

[7] Not all voluntary associations are necessarily concerned with social change and economic growth. Some may be totally consummatory. Cf., Arthur P. Jacoby and Nicholas Babchuk, "Instrumental and Expressive Voluntary Associations," *Sociology and Social Research* 47 (July 1963): 461–71; and Arnold Rose, *Theory and Method in the Social Sciences*, Minneapolis: University of Minnesota Press, 1954, p. 52.

[8] For a partial indication of why voluntary associations may not attain their goals, or why goals may become displaced, see David L. Sills, "Voluntary Associations: Instruments and Objects of Change," *Human Organization* 18 (Spring, 1959): 17–21.

check on government's power and may lend stability to a developing country.

Finally, it should be recalled that whether the means-ends chain established to lead toward societal development begins with revolution and then tutelary democracy or it skips the revolutionary phase and begins with tutelary democracy, they must converge through the establishment of instrumental voluntary associations if societal development is accomplished.

## SUMMARY

Before attention is turned to the specific case of the societal development of the United States, some sort of summary is needed. There is an inherent danger in writing a chapter that is supposed to deal with the "general setting of development." The danger is that the presentation also tends to be general. This chapter is no exception. Many of the points that have been mentioned in the present study were treated quite superficially. However, the chapters that follow will be treating most of the points in detail. Nevertheless, the following summary is presented as a modest attempt to introduce some formalization of ideas dealing with societal development. The systematic character of the summary does not make it theory. I have no illusions concerning the deficiencies of the attempt, but they should be easier for the reader to detect due to the systematic presentation.

1. The basic postulate of the present study is that a natural order of societal development that is discovered through the canons of science does not exist.

1.1. Development is a social product, thus its attainment depends upon the organization of a society.

1.2. The pivotal assumption of the present study is that viewing organization as an effective mechanism for coping with the environment is a key ideological commitment of a developed society.

1.3. The structural conditions under which organizations become an effective mechanism for coping with the environment are sufficient conditions for having a society that is economically just and at the same time politically fluent and free.

2. Within this frame of reference, society is viewed as an organization attempting to attain certain goals.

2.1. One of the goals of society is societal development.

2.2. How organizations are structured is a key variable in assessing the probabilities of goal attainment.

2.3. The structure of a social organization is discovered by a study of social relations.

2.3.1. In all social relations, there is a tendency for power to exist.

2.3.2. All social relations entail a sense of dependency of one actor upon another.

2.3.2.1. Power resides implicitly in B's dependency upon A.

2.3.2.2. Power does not reside in A; it is an attribute of the social relation and not a property of A.

2.3.2.3. The power of A over B is equal to, and based upon, the dependence that B feels upon A.

2.4. Concurrent with the tendency for power to exist in all social relations, there is an equal tendency toward some sort of balance in relations.

2.4.1. If the power of B over A is equal to the power of A over B, power is balanced.

2.4.2. Power is not cancelled out in social relations, rather we have reciprocal power and the tendency toward balancing power relations.

2.5. Where individuals can group collectively to bargain for their social and economic rights, strain toward the balance of power relations occurs and the structural conditions of such a society provide for the mutual enhancement of effort on the part of the individual members of the society.

2.6. All known social organizations entail positions that carry authority and positions that are excluded from the exercise of authority.

2.6.1. Holders of the positions of authority may change without altering the authority of positions.

2.6.2. In order to change the authority of the positions, it is necessary to change the sanctions coupled with noncompliance.

2.7. As long as people desire to improve their status and as long as status is conferred upon those that occupy positions of authority, conflict is ubiquitous.

2.7.1. The regulation of conflict is largely accomplished by the regulatory mechanisms governing social relations which are largely based upon the Parsonsian notions of the double contingency and the complimentarity of expectations.

2.7.2. Individuals and groups, through the interaction process, become aware of their dependence on others in order to obtain the maximum output at the least cost in social exchanges.

2.7.2.1. This reciprocity in social relations, coupled with the desire to improve one's status even at the expense of others, brings about a gradual and continual change in expectations for behavior.

2.7.2.2. Since expectations vary through time, there is a continual formation and abolition of instrumental voluntary associations composed of individuals, with shared interests and expectations, who attempt to enhance the ability of the society to attain the goal of societal development.

2.7.3.  Since there are varying expectations and multiple associations, each with different perceptions concerning how to attain societal development, conflict between groups is assured.

3.  Societal development is not a unidimensional variable.

3.1.  The degree of societal development varies on a scale depending on the presence or absence of certain unidimensional factors.

3.1.1.  Development is enhanced if the opportunity exists for members of a society to voluntarily affiliate with instrumental organizations.

3.1.1.1.  Through instrumental voluntary associations, political participation on the part of all members of a society is enhanced.

3.1.1.2.  This enhancement is in terms of access to various positions of authority, on the one hand, and the ability to influence policymaking and decisions on the other.

3.1.1.3.  Through instrumental voluntary associations, the potential exists for the mutual enhancement of effort on the part of all members of society.

3.1.2.  Development is enhanced if the ever-present conflict between groups is low in intensity.

3.1.3.  Development is enhanced if the ever-present conflict between groups is low in violence.

3.2.  Economic growth is a necessary but not sufficient condition for societal development.

3.2.1.  Models for economic growth assume that certain societal conditions are present.

3.2.1.1.  These societal conditions enhance factor mobility.

3.2.1.2.  Factor mobility necessary for economic growth is dependent upon a strong central government during the take-off phase.

3.2.2.  Strong central government is dependent upon the will of the people.

3.2.2.1.  People support central government when they can influence its decisions.

3.2.2.2.  Decisions are influenced by the opportunity to exert power; that is, make government realize its dependency.

3.2.2.3.  Influence upon government may start through tutelary democracy.

4.  Tutelary democracy may start with or without revolution.

4.1.  Tutelary democracy starts without revolution when the following conditions are present.

4.1.1.  Local communities are relatively isolated with few communication or transportation ties to the larger urban centers, thereby limiting the possibilities for local residents to perceive their situation as being relatively deprived which precludes the possibility for developing meaningful local concern for economic growth and societal development.

4.1.2.  Mobility tends to be lacking with positions largely assigned by ascription.

4.1.3.  Authority is vested in a relatively few paternal institutions.

4.1.4.  National elite are concerned with increasing economic growth since they feel that any further advancement in their positions is limited without further growth.

4.2.  Tutelary democracy is ushered in by revolution under the following conditions.

4.2.1.  Through communication, relative deprivation is perceived by those divorced from access to positions of authority.

4.2.2.  The existing central government is not responsive to the new demands that arise from those feeling relatively deprived.

4.2.3.  The universities of the society provide a leadership for revolution.

4.3.  Revolution is successful when the opportunity to influence those in positions of authority is created.

4.4.  Revolution is abortive when the occupants of positions of authority are changed but access to these positions is not changed.

4.5.  Regardless of how the means-ends chain leading toward societal development begins, the chains must converge through the establishment of instrumental voluntary associations if societal development is to occur.

4.6.  Without instrumental voluntary associations there is no way to insure access to positions of authority.

4.7.  Without access to positions of authority, there is no effective mechanism for limiting the imposition of wills by a minority.

## THE UNITED STATES AND SOCIETAL DEVELOPMENT

In the few paragraphs that remain, I will attempt to relate the ideas treated in this study to the specific case of development in the United States. The United States was colonized under a tutelary regime. Each colony was under the direction of a Governor appointed by either 1) the Crown in royal colonies, 2) the proprietor in proprietary colonies, or 3) freemen in charter colonies. However, each colony (except Pennsylvania which was unicameral) had a lower house that consisted of elected representatives and an upper house which was appointed except in Charter colonies where they were elected. In all cases, the assembly could exert influence upon decisions taken by the Governor. As the societies developed, the local populace, through their elected representatives, began to place demands upon Governors. These demands were, in general terms, an attempt to limit the extent to which England could impose its will upon the colonists.

Granted that different groups had different bases for their grievances and international political factors led to encouraging the colonists to revolt, the central fact remains that the grievances, whether
economic or ideological, centered around who had the right to limit
the imposition of wills. When the assembly was unsuccessful in its
attempts to reserve this right, revolution became a viable alternative
and this alternative was taken.

Immediately following the armed conflict phase, a constitutional
democracy was established. However, as the frontier expanded, locally
and regionally based tutelary regimes stood in lieu of the federal
government.[9] At the local level, community members voluntarily
associated to obtain certain goals. Admittedly, these were primordial
goals during the early history of the United States. But this was an
advantage since, being primordial, they were very tangible. Thus, the
evaluation of organizational effectiveness in terms of goal attainment
was relatively simple. If the goal of the organization is to provide
protection for life and limb, the question of measuring effectiveness
is as simple as a head count.

Little by little, the federal government absorbed locally based
tutelary regimes, largely through co-option. Through federal concentration of power, or by allowing firms and/or industries relatively
total control over their domains, economic growth started. Prior to
1880, it was virtually impossible for the local tutelary regimes to over-
impose their will; there was free land just over the mountain where
a strong man could escape and carve out a free life for himself. However, with the closing of the frontier and increased industrialization,
it became relatively easy to impose one's will upon others. As this
imposition of wills reached its zenith, organizations arose to limit the
extent to which wills could be imposed. Labor unions arose in industry,
farmers' organizations were strengthened, and demands were effectively
placed upon federal government to take the necessary steps to insure
basic rights.

Today, we are faced with an environment that has changed
dramatically. While the goals of societal development are still the
same, and organizations still state these goals, the milieux within which
such organizations operate present conditions that make old means-
ends chains inoperative or ineffective. Probably today, more than
ever before, the potential for imposing one's will upon others is best
measured in mega-units. And the means available for imposing one's
will are much more insidious than in earlier times. All of this makes
the public definitions of goals less tangible and, consequently, the
ability to develop new means-ends chains diminishes.

Much of this confusion stems, in part, from the lack of consensus
on what societal development is and, in part, from the failure to recognize that effective organization is a viable means for limiting the im-

---

[9] A good example of a locally based tutelary regime standing in lieu of federal
government is the Mormon Church during the settlement of Utah.

position of wills. Of course, wills must be imposed to a certain extent or else anarchy prevails. What constitutes a necessary limitation of wills for society to maintain itself does not exist in nature; it is a social definition and, consequently, subject to change as the environment changes. It is hoped there will be maximum participation on the part of all members of a given society in establishing this definition. Such a task will be replete with conflict, but this should not be viewed with alarm. Rather, it should be welcomed because freedom is part and parcel of conflict. However, it should be remembered that agitation is easy but organization is difficult. The time has come to cope with the difficult.

## REFERENCES

1. Anderson, Charles. *The Political Development of Latin America*. Boston: Little, Brown and Co., 1967.
2. Bauer, Peter T., and Yamey, Basil S. *The Economics of Underdeveloped Countries*. Chicago: University of Chicago Press, 1957.
3. Blau, Peter M. *Exchange and Power in Social Life*. New York: John Wiley and Sons, 1964.
4. Bruton, Henry J. "Contemporary Theorizing on Economic Growth." In *Theories of Economic Growth*, edited by Bert F. Hoselitz and others. New York: The Free Press at Glencoe, 1960.
5. Dahrendorf, Ralf. *Class and Class Conflict in Industrial Society*. Stanford: Stanford University Press, 1959.
6. Djilas, Milovan. *The New Class: An Analysis of the Communist System*. New York: Praeger, 1958.
7. Dusenberry, James S. "Some Aspects of the Theory of Economic Development." *Explorations in Entrepreneurial History* 3 (1950):63–102.
8. Eisenstadt, S. N. *Modernization: Protest and Change*. Englewood Cliffs: Prentice-Hall, 1966.
9. Emerson, Richard M. "Power-dependence Relations." *American Sociological Review* 27 (February 1962): 32.
10. Hagen, Everett. *On the Theory of Social Change*. Homewood, Ill.: Dorsey Press, 1962.
11. Hook, Sidney. *John Dewey: An Intellectual Portrait*. New York: John Day, 1939.
12. ———. *Reason, Social Myths and Democracy*. New York: Harper, Torchbooks, 1966.
13. Korhauser, William. *The Politics of Mass Society*. New York: The Free Press of Glencoe, 1959.
14. Kuznets, Simon. "Toward a Theory of Economic Growth." In *National Policy for Economic Welfare at Home and Abroad*, edited by Robert Lekachman. Garden City: Doubleday, 1955.
15. Marx, Karl. *Capital*. Vol. 1. Preface. New York: New World Press, 1954.
16. ———. "The Eighteenth Brumaire of Louis Bonaparte." In *The Communist Manifesto*, edited by Samuel H. Beer. New York: Appleton-Century-Crofts, 1955.
17. Michels, Robert. *Political Parties*. New York: Hearst's International Library, 1915.
18. Mill, J. S. *A System of Logic*. Chap. 10, Sec. 8. London: Longmans Green & Co., 1949.

19. Moore, Wilbert E., and Tumin, Melvin. "Some Social Functions of Ignorance." *American Sociological Review* 14 (December 1949): 787–95.
20. ———, and Feldman, A. S. *Labor Commitment and Social Change in Developing Areas.* New York: John Wiley and Sons, 1960.
21. ———. "The Social Framework of Economic Development." In *Tradition, Values, and Socio-economic Development,* edited by Ralph Braibanti and Joseph Spengler. Durham: Duke University Press, 1961.
22. Mosca, G. *The Ruling Class.* New York: McGraw-Hill, 1939.
23. Nash, Manning. "Some Social and Cultural Aspects of Economic Development." *Economic Development and Cultural Change* 7: 137–50.
24. Pareto, Vilfredo. *Mind and Society.* New York: Harcourt, Brace and Co., 1935.
25. Polanyi, Karl; Arensberg, Conrad; and Pearson, Harry. *Trade and Market in the Early Empires.* Glencoe, Ill.: The Free Press, 1957.
26. Popper, Karl. *The Open Society and Its Enemies.* 2nd ed. London: Oxford University Press, 1952.
27. ———. *The Poverty of Historicism.* New York: Harper, Torchbooks, 1964.
28. Shils, Edward. *Political Development in New States.* 's-Gravenhage: Mouton and Co., 1962.
29. Shirer, William L. *The Rise and Fall of the Third Reich.* New York: Simon and Schuster, 1960.
30. Spengler, Joseph. "Social Evolution and the Theory of Economic Development." In *Social Change in Developing Areas,* edited by Herbert R. Barringer and others. Cambridge, Mass.: Schenkman Publishing Co., 1965.
31. Warner, W. K., and Havens, A. Eugene. "Goal Displacement and the Intangibility of Organizational Goals." *Administrative Science Quarterly* 12: 539–55.

# CHAPTER FOUR

# STRUCTURAL MATRIX

# OF

# DEVELOPMENT

## W. KEITH WARNER

THE GENERAL THESIS of this chapter is that understanding the development of society is fundamentally a problem of understanding social organization. By adapting and using ideas from a variety of sources, I have attempted to sketch the foundations of a conceptual model for studying the structural matrix of development, and to indicate, at least in abstract terms, how this general line of thinking can orient a program of sociological research on problems of societal development.

Societal development is not a unitary variable. The concept designates a category of quite diverse variables, or "kinds" of development. I believe the structural matrix may vary considerably from one kind of development to another. Rather than exploring one or two of these specific relationships, the discussion takes a more general approach.

I wish to acknowledge the helpful comments of Daryl J. Hobbs, A. Eugene Havens, and Michael S. Taylor at various stages in the preparation of this chapter.

W. KEITH WARNER is Professor of Rural Sociology at the University of Wisconsin. He holds the Ph.D. in rural sociology from Cornell University. His research has focused on organizational analysis, particularly organizational effectiveness and membership participation in voluntary associations, and more recently on organizational problems in environmental resources management. Publications related to his chapter include: "Problems in Measuring the Goal Attainment of Voluntary Organizations" (Adult Education 19 [Fall, 1967] pp. 3–14), "Feedback in Administration" (Journal of Cooperative Extension 5 [Spring, 1967] pp. 35–46), "Problems of Participation" (Journal of Cooperative Extension 3 [Winter, 1965] pp. 219–28), and (with A. Eugene Havens) "Goal Displacement and the Intangibility of Organizational Goals" (Administrative Science Quarterly 12 [March, 1968] pp. 539–55).

## CONCEPTS OF DEVELOPMENT AND SOCIAL ORGANIZATION

### A Concept of Development

By societal development, I mean certain kinds of changes in society. The concept of "life chances" found in the social stratification literature (34, p. 151) is a way of referring to these kinds of changes: the ability of people to reach goals they value, and to avoid what they view as misfortunes. Societal development, then, refers to an increase in the life chances of people in society.

Defined in this way, development is clearly grounded in the culture; it contains elements of purpose, value, and norm, without which there is no way to judge whether a given change constitutes development or the opposite. What one society might consider development, another might not. And within a particular society, individuals and groups may differ in what they consider valued goals and misfortunes. Hence, even though there will be broad areas of agreement that must not be underestimated, societal development will not be an object of complete societal consensus.

The meaning of life chances alters as there are alterations in such things as experience, deprivation, satiation, and available social and material technology relating to such goals or misfortunes. For particular persons or groups at a given time, and in relation to their life chances, there are tendencies to 1) value more goal attainment than is possible with available resources or technology, 2) value contradictory goals, 3) be unsure of the full nature, range, and priority of the goals, or the means of attaining them, and 4) pursue familiar patterns of activity without much clear basis for understanding how these actions relate to their general life chances.

Some of the scope and complexity of the changes in society that are believed to have important relations to life chances can be illustrated by a few more specific examples: urban renewal, industrialization, automation, education, welfare programs, medical research, health care, agricultural production, control of air and water pollution, civil rights legislation, disaster relief, employment level, and income level. Whether we recognize the diverse kinds of development in such terms as the foregoing, or in terms of the more general concept of life chances, societal development is not accomplished, or measured, by only a handful of dominant changes.

Furthermore, changes occur at differential rates among these various kinds, with material changes appearing to proceed farther and faster than nonmaterial ones, at least in American society.[1] Progress along some lines often slows or prevents progress along others. An imbalance results, the consequences of which include considerable

[1] This observation is similar to the culture lag hypothesis, but does not refer specifically to it (see 21).

stress and strain in society; thus, some negative effects on people's life chances are the unintended and unanticipated outcomes of intended changes along other lines.

## A Concept of Social Organization

Social organization represents the outcome of attempts to accomplish collectively what cannot be done as well or at all individually. This familiar general function has two somewhat less familiar parts: organization is a way of protecting people from costs that would be incurred without such organization, and it is a way of gaining additional benefits through a mutual enhancement of effort. (5, pp. 43–46)[2]

The protection function is illustrated by internal and external security (police and military forces), fire protection, and insurance enterprises. Illustrations of the mutual enhancement function are manufacturing, education, and transportation and communication systems. Certain kinds of pressure, bargaining, or mediation organizations may represent both functions, by protecting from domination by other organized interests, and by obtaining preferential benefits from employers, public agencies, etc., for their own members. Both functions permit a division of labor and specialization resulting in expertise, as well as a pooling of effort.

These two functions correspond quite closely to the concept of life chances; protection from costs is a way of helping people avoid life's misfortunes, and mutual enhancement of effort is a way of attaining those valued goals that can profit by collective activity.

Organization is the opposite, in a sense, of Mills's "sociological concept of fate." Using a kind of marketplace concept of society, he viewed fate as the unintended outcome of innumerable intentions. (31, pp. 181–83) Organization, then, consists of a coordination of intentions and actions in order to make the actual outcome correspond more closely to the intended outcome. The degree of organization varies, depending upon the completeness with which fate is displaced and the programs of activity and products are made predictable and controllable.

An understanding of organization requires attention both to those consequences that are anticipated and intended, and to those that are not. Since we cannot be certain about such consequences and their causes, uncertainty becomes a fundamental element of realistic organizational models, and dealing with uncertainty becomes a fundamental problem in the design and operation of organizations. (43, pp. 1–13) The more intangible and nonmaterial are the intended

[2] Daryl J. Hobbs uses the term "mutual enhancement of effort" to speak of gains produced by organization, such as those deriving from division of labor and specialization.

products, the greater uncertainty there is in the organization, and the less basis there is for organization leaders to administer rationally. (44, 45)

Just as we can imagine life chances that cannot be specified or attained, so we can imagine organizational forms and procedures that are not, or cannot be, implemented. This idea sensitizes us to a variation in the degree to which imaginary organization is transformed into reality. Students of organization discovered long ago that publicly avowed goals are not always the objectives actually guiding daily decisions and activities, that formal descriptions of statuses, roles, and unit functions are not completely reliable descriptions of actual activities or outcomes, and that organizational programs become mixtures of illusion and reality. In fact, much of the accumulated literature regarding complex organizations consists of an indirect and one-sided dialogue between those who wrote about the formally stipulated doctrine of organizational structure and programs, and those whose studies showed how the "real," informal organization differed from the prescribed doctrine.

Some administrators and students of organizations, alike, still have great difficulty in distinguishing between the image and the reality. As a consequence, organization is frequently regarded as more real than it is, resources are invested, and hopes for attainment kindled, when the degree of organization is inadequate to the tasks.

Organization varies not only in degree, but also in effectiveness. Organization involves a variety of economic, social, psychological, or other kinds of costs that presumably are justified only by the production of more valuable benefits so that there is, over some period of time and for some people, a net gain. But effectiveness is the most problematic of all organizational variables, and we cannot take it for granted.

Not every form of organization is equally instrumental or efficient in producing every kind of outcome. Thus, the question is not simply one of the degree to which organization displaces fate with predictable and controllable intentions, activities, and outcomes; it is also one of the extent to which alternative forms of structure and process yield outcomes that are desired, rather than some other, and that are in some way worth the cost.

Forms of social organization do not spontaneously arise and change in every time and place to insure an increase or maximization of people's life chances. The formation, growth, and change of social structure is significantly an outcome of human purpose and will, and especially of the purpose and will of leaders and entrepreneurs who can mobilize others. (23, pp. 261–76) There is some basis for a "great man theory" of organizational development in that the genesis and at least early character of many organizations reflect the unique contributions of one man.

In fact, leadership is, in a certain sense, a kind of alternative to organization. It is animation and coordination of activity by individuals rather than by structure. The routinization of charisma, for example, is a transformation from leadership to organization.

## The Relation between Development and Social Organization

In the context of the preceding discussion, societal development can be further defined by reference to social organization. In such terms, development has two main aspects: 1) it is a *product* of social organization, and 2) it is a particular *kind of change in social organization*.

Most fundamentally, development is a product of social organization, and as such its most valid measurement will be a direct one. Thus, the general question is not whether organizations exist that specialize in development, or how much of the national or state budget is allocated to programs that can be labeled "development," or even how many people have worked how many hours in "development programs." Rather, that general question is at least sevenfold: 1) how much increase, 2) in which life chances, 3) of which people, 4) has been produced by which organizations or sets of organizations, 5) at what costs, 6) to which people, and 7) in relation to what alternatives?

As a particular kind of change in social organization, development refers to those alterations assumed to produce more life chances. Progress is being made if changes in structure or programs are being made that will increase the desired product. Measurement of development in these terms is no better than the assumption of predictability or causality between such changes and particular kinds of life chances. That is, an increase in the number and vigor of organizational programs for development, for example, can be counted as progress toward development only to the extent that the number and vigor of such programs are predictively or causally related to changes in the developmental life chances of some people.

One kind of change in structure is a more complete implementation of it, or a more complete transformation of the image into reality. For example, increasing development of certain aspects of American society may require only that we implement more fully and effectively what have long been salient parts of the American dream (11, p. 253), that we take steps to insure a closer correspondence between imagined or claimed outcome and real outcome from our institutional agencies.

Another kind of change is some alteration to decrease problems or enhance productivity. Katz has pointed out, in another context, three characteristic ways of responding to problems. The first and most frequent is to try harder to make the system work. A second approach is to add structural parts or units. Last and least frequent is an examination of the structural sources of the problem, with a resultant change in organizational patterns. (26, pp. 105–14)

I indicated earlier that the life chances are not wholly consistent with each other for any given person or group of people. Attaining one objective often comes at the expense of rendering another desired objective unattainable, and success for one person or group often means failure for someone else. These inconsistencies are reflected in strains and inconsistencies in social organization—both within and between organizations and groups of various kinds.

I have also suggested that the general function of social organization is to increase people's life chances by providing a collective protection from costs that would be incurred without organization, and by providing benefits through mutual enhancement of effort. But social organization is also a chief source of decreased life chances for particular individuals and groups.

Political tyranny and oppression, war and other violence, deprivation of property, inequities in the distribution of costs and benefits in society, and other familiar social problems are products of social organization. This includes the idea that persons can, and do, use social organization intentionally as a means of depriving others of some margin of life chances. It is such aspects of development as these that are "sensitive" and tend to be relatively neglected by policy makers, administrators, and researchers in favor of emphasis on material technology and change.

## INSTITUTIONAL AGENCIES AND DEVELOPMENT

### Institutional Agencies as Keys to Development

Social organization does not simply exist in undifferentiated form. Among the kinds of social entities in it, institutional agencies represent the central forms of organization in society. Their centrality is defined primarily through their relation to what are considered the most important life chances.

These are the organizations through which much of the work of government, the economy, education, and religion is done, for example. In our society, the institutional agencies of government have assumed an increasingly prominent place. They, particularly, are keys to development.

Linked to these organizations in a variety of ways are the secondary, voluntary associations that mediate between those agencies and individuals or other agencies, perform supplementary work, coordinate federations or coalitions of organizations, and influence the programs and procedures of the agencies. Thus, the institutional agencies not only create their own output, but they also promote, support, regulate, and otherwise interact with other organizations. And to an important degree, they are guided by these secondary associations.

Primary claim on the resources, power, and other assets of society rests with the institutional agencies. Societal development cannot proceed far without directly dealing with both the products of these organizations, and the changes in their structure and programs that would enhance progress. Thus, although voluntary associations have a vital part to play in development, their utility will be primarily indirect, and dependent on their ability to influence the institutional agencies.

## Institutional Deficiencies and Constraints

One constraint against development is that the very organizations whose business it is to promote the central aspects of development are those most likely to hinder or block particular kinds of it. We do not need to theorize a "conspiracy of the elite" or other leadership conspiracy to understand this, however.

Any organizational pattern that promotes life chances for someone thereby establishes an interest by the major beneficiaries to resist changes that would lead to decreasing their differential advantage. (17, pp. 51–53) These beneficiaries may not be only, or even primarily, the personnel who staff the organizations. And the organizations may be those seeking change, as well as those resisting it. Differential interests arise and are defended even in protest groups.

Institutional agencies necessarily respond to power groups, and power groups already have some differentially good life chances. Thus, these central organizations respond most favorably to those groups and individuals who have differential advantage at any given time. We do not have an adequate organizational basis for facilitating or insuring any other kind of response. Both organizational and personal costs are too great to risk the demise of the organization, as a regular procedure in society, by consistent rejection of the interests of organized power groups in favor of unorganized interests.

Another constraint against developmental change is "trained incapacity" of the organizational personnel. The knowledge and skills for operating a bureaucracy according to present procedure seem unlikely to constitute the best basis for making those organizational changes that would increase the productivity of life chances for particular people. But the organization has already invested its resources in its present personnel whose knowledge, skills, and interests tend to promote status quo, rather than any major improvements.

Commitments hinder development in other ways. They reach beyond tenure considerations for employees, and include the interests of organizational sponsors, clients, the public, and others. They reach across generations—backward to founders or early leaders of an organization, for example, or forward to those who in the future will pay the costs or obtain the benefits of present activities. (28, ch. 3, 4)

Any form of social structure represents a set of commitments that produces predictability and therefore permits calculations of exchange in interaction. Programs of change often require repudiation of commitments which, in turn, weakens the basis of the social order. Reasonable calculations of future benefit to derive from present contributions, for example, are the basis for much developmental activity in society. To repudiate these commitments is detrimental to the life chances of some people, just as failure to change is detrimental to the life chances of other people.[3]

Finally, the ubiquitous tendencies for goal displacement and emphasis on survival and maintenance are characteristics of institutional agencies of society, particularly as they deal with relatively abstract and intangible life chances. (45) These are major factors in decreasing the developmental output. Organizational maintenance and survival are, by definition, necessary conditions for organizational productivity over a period of time, but they are far from being sufficient conditions.

The leaders of these organizations tend to lack understanding of the nature of the objectives they are supposedly promoting, and to lack understanding of the causal relations that would produce the goals they can specify fairly well. Compounding matters, they react negatively to the kind of research that would be most useful, in the long run, in helping to provide them with this vital knowledge.

## Power Groups

To the extent society is relatively unorganized, there exist large masses of people whose actions are not coordinated to provide mutual protection from costs or enhancement of effort. To the extent society is more highly organized, there are quite different alternatives. One is centralization of power in one of the institutional areas, typically government. The other is the mediation of power between the individual and the central power.

Some of the most serious costs from which individuals need protection are those relating to oppression or deprivation by other people. The mediation of power groups helps provide that protection, as well as influencing the agencies to provide other desired benefits.

Therefore, a key point of leverage in the structural matrix of de-

---

[3] The "commitments" may be either explicit or implicit, of course. For an example of how technological change may have more negative consequences for the life chances of persons who accept or make greater social commitment to the community, compared to those with lesser community commitment, see (9).

velopment is the organization and operation of power groups to represent the interests of individuals in the context of organized action. But at a given time, these power groups will likely represent a position something like status quo. They will not be promoting basic changes that will greatly increase the life chances of large numbers of people not presently among their membership, unless such an increase would be nonthreatening to them or unless they have some means of compelling support from such people. They will not, in other words, be primary sources of developmental change in social areas (though they might be in material areas), but will be sources of structural continuity.

A pluralist view of mediating groups in society must include not only the number of groups and their power but also the extent of their effective representation of all the people. A plurality of organizations can exist, within each of which a small oligarchy exploits the organization and mobilizes the mass of members as needed to further programs detrimental to the life chances of many of those members.

Of particular concern are the organizational forms and methods of "coercing consent." (17, ch. 6; 25, pp. 31–32; 35, ch. 8) The development of society, the promotion of people's life chances, is no longer adequately protected by guarding against overt and blatant force and tyranny. Subtle new forms of coercion, with outward appearances of democracy, have been developed that can manipulate the social structure against the interests of the people who participate and give their consent.

## Sources of Change

Among the numerous sources of change in social structure are changing communication content and experiences that produce a sense of relative deprivation, and the expanding size and diversity of the cultural base.[4] Only a few important factors can be given brief attention.

[4] Important changes may derive from the emergence of challenge groups into positions of power, and from the actions of power groups as they establish an accommodation to the social structure. Changes may also derive from conflicts of interests among power groups, though these seem more likely to be shifts within the general framework of the larger system than changes of that general framework. On the other hand, one cannot assume that all organizations of a particular kind seek either to promote or hinder social change. For example, some voluntary associations do deal with change, but others are consummatory or expressive and, for them, issues of social change are largely irrelevant.

My purpose is not to offer a comprehensive discussion of social change, nor is it to present a detailed discussion of key issues, such as the operation of power groups or particular sources of change. For a general overview of the topic of social change, see (32).

Relative deprivation, as an example of an important source of change I have not specifically addressed, is discussed by Denton E. Morrison in "Relative Deprivation and Rural Discontent in Developing Countries: A Theoretical Proposal," paper presented at the annual meeting of the American Association for the Advancement of Science, Washington, D.C., December 1966. (33)

The unanticipated and/or unintended consequences of technological change constitute a major source of change in social structure. This suggests an interesting point of leverage for societal changes. Suppose some groups could devise ways of foreseeing more accurately than others the changes in social structure that would likely result from alternative changes in material technology. They might then be able to obtain support for the desired material change from those groups that would resist the social change to follow, if they knew about it.

Another important source of change is crisis. People and organizations tend to do what they have to do. (7, p. 374; 10, pp. 195–98; 17, pp. 10, 28–29, 44; 22; 43, p. 1) Crisis forces action, usually on an ad hoc basis that necessarily lacks the prerequisite preparation for effectiveness and efficiency. Particularly in the more intangible areas of life chances and with respect to public goods,[5] it appears that institutional agencies are administered, or at least changed importantly in structure or program content, somewhat from crisis to crisis. In this case, the reason is not necessarily or wholly that the administrators fail to anticipate and prepare; the supporting units and general public typically remain too apathetic to permit, or require of, the administration a more rational approach.

A third source of change is the entrepreneurship of individuals. I have already indicated that this is an important element in social organization. The agitation, mobilization, recruitment, and coordination of individual action into collective action can result from the initiative of one or a few people. The result can be either the formation of a new organization or changes in the old forms.

Social movements constitute a related source of change. They are usually stimulated by dissatisfaction with some institutional agencies, and seek to resolve that dissatisfaction by changing the organizational forms and programs. It is noteworthy that social movements tend to be directed toward *social* change and adjustment. Institutional agencies seem to be able to promote technological change easily enough, but often promote important social changes only under strong pressure from social movements (protest) and interest groups that have finally gained enough power to require attention.

We might speak of *challenge groups* as those organizations that seek changes in the social structure but that do not yet have enough power to command significant response. Challenge groups initially have relatively little power, and must rely primarily on ideological or normative bases for inducing people's support. (14, ch. 1–3) As their power grows, they can move toward more utilitarian and even coercive bases of organization, and vice versa. If and when they obtain suffi-

---

[5] Public goods present particularly difficult problems not only in administering but also in organizing groups to work for such goods and support administrative efforts to get them. Yet public goods are certain to be involved in societal development. Regarding collective action toward such goods, see (36).

cient power to compete with the other relevant power groups of society, they come to lose their reason to challenge the basic configuration of the present structure. They are then well along in the process of institutionalization, and of becoming targets for new challenge groups.

## The Institutional Cycle and Development

There is considerable basis for expecting development organizations and their programs to undergo a cycle of institutionalization. By whatever means they begin, social movements can protest a given allocation of life chances in society, and urge changes. But if these social movements generate challenge groups, and if the challenge groups come into power, we can predict that 1) they will accommodate their operating objectives toward the existing structural arrangement, 2) they will fall short of attaining their major avowed purposes, 3) they will recognize interests in survival and maintenance that will hinder their accomplishment of development aims, and 4) they will become the objects of subsequent protests in society. Similar predictions can be made for new development organizations sponsored by the institutional agencies of society.

An important question, therefore, is how the institutional cycle might be broken for organizations engaged in societal development.[6] And one important implication of these considerations is that programs for increasing societal development must be concerned not only with how to increase the product but also how to change existing organizations with their commitments, interests, and power. Questions of *reorganization*, then, are at least as important as questions of organization. We cannot implicitly assume, in suggesting solutions to the institutional cycle or other organizational problems relating to development, that we can deal only with the formation of new organizations. The reorganization of existing groups and agencies is in many ways both more difficult and more important for solving practical problems in society.

## INTERORGANIZATIONAL ANALYSIS AND THE STUDY OF DEVELOPMENT

The sketchy discussion thus far has put together in an abstract way a series of ideas, assumptions, and generalizations. In the discus-

---

[6] That is, we need systematic, continuous means for organizations to "renew themselves." (17) It should be added that concern for societal development does not require organizational renewal for all institutional agencies in society. Not all such organizations will be crucial to development, but most of those central to development will be institutional agencies.

sion to follow, I will try to move a step closer to the kind of conceptualization that might actually guide research on the structural matrix of development.

## Development as an Interorganizational Problem

Societal development in the general sense, and many specific kinds of development, are beyond the domain of any public or private organization. At the same time, society does not act as a single corporate entity in the pursuit of development. Consequently, the structural matrix of development can be approached usefully as an interorganizational problem. It involves a consideration of several public and private organizations interacting as units in a social environment.

One of the most important interorganizational issues in development is that of the relations between public and private organizations. If public organization is the only medium for societal development, there is no way to prevent political domination and attendant depression of life chances for large numbers of people. If private organization is the only choice available, there is no way to obtain voluntary support for many kinds of development that are collective or public goods, and especially support with the necessary scale of resources. Thus, some kind of public-private coalition seems essential. (12, pp. 81, 86–88; 37, pp. 3–15; 47, p. 245)

Studies in the sociology of law become an essential part of research in this area. Law reflects critical aspects of public organization not only in regulating and prohibiting but also in permitting, facilitating, and supporting private organizational activities. In addition, law constitutes a major dimension in the design and control of public organizational structure and programs. The sociology of law seems to converge with the study of public administration, public policy, and voluntary interest groups in the analysis of how the interorganizational matrix relates to development.

It is increasingly apparent that societal development can be better attained, and for some purposes must be attained, in ecological areas larger than a neighborhood, community, or county. Multicounty, area, and regional organizations for development will increase in number and importance.

This newer ecological approach, by involving interorganizational matters, will face two critical problems. One is the problematic character of interorganizational[7] structure. If organization is coor-

[7] It remains to be determined how much relationship exists, and what kinds, among the various organizations and groups in any given ecological area. Merely indicating that there are "linkages" of some kind explains little. To what extent are the apparent relationships real or imagined? To what extent are they important or trivial either for outcomes internal to the relevant organizations, or for outcomes from their interaction?

dinating and controlling collective actions to reduce the divergence between actual and intended outcomes, organization is more problematic in its interorganizational aspects than in its intraorganizational aspects. And if a fundamental problem of social organization is how to induce individuals to participate and fulfill their role obligations, the problem of organizing organizations into larger collectivities is more difficult. Thus, to the extent the structural matrix of development consists of diverse organizations, and other kinds of social entities, the outcome is less predictable, or less amenable to rational control toward developmental change, and more a matter of fate.

In the balance between autonomy and interdependence, the saliency of the latter indicates a greater degree of coordinated organization. But we expect more autonomy among organizations in society than among subgroups in an organization. Thus, interorganizational outcome is more problematic, other things equal.

The second problem is the relative lack of research, analysis, and theory on these aspects of social structure. (19, p. 838; 42, p. 143)[8] More attention has been given to intraorganizational matters, or to individuals in society. Knowledge sufficient to guide large-scale interorganizational programs of development is expensive and slow to accumulate. It cannot be obtained quickly and simply in response to crises, whether of riots in the cities, strikes in the schools, or holding actions on the farms. We need the chance to obtain necessary data, try alternative modes of conceptualization, make alternative interpretations of findings—particularly in a substantive area that is both more complicated and less well understood than many other areas.

### Conceptualizing the Structural Matrix

In moving from abstract discussion toward a more concrete basis for empirical research, we need ways of organizing our approach to the mass of phenomena involved. One important step is to recognize differences in the *relevance* of various sectors of the social structure. Some part of the social structure is relevant when it significantly influences the activities of a given organization, or when those activities are in some way contingent upon it. (43, pp. 58–61) The question, then, is how to conceptualize differences of this kind.

The concept of "social system" has received widespread use in sociology, and it has been applied to the consideration of multiorganizational complexes. In fact, one of the appeals of the concept is its flexibility; it appears to be a more or less uniform way of approach-

---

[8] There are, nevertheless, many materials available on interorganizational analysis. Some of the variety of approaches and substance in these materials can be seen in the following: 1; 2, pp. 20–28; 3; 4, ch. 8; 8; 13, pp. 435–47; 16; 20; 24, ch. 4; 27; 29; 40, pp. 520–25; 46).

ing greatly different kinds of social entities, varying from small groups to total societies. At least it has been applied in those diverse ways.

One of the utilities of this concept is its reminder of interdependence among the parts of a system. Changes in one part are assumed to evoke adjusting changes in the others. When a multiorganizational or multicommunity sector of society is conceptualized as a social system, the internal relations of that system obviously include interorganizational relations. Thus, system interdependence is one basis for defining other relevant entities in the environment of a given organization.

The interdependence is problematic, however, in a complex organization. (18, ch. 8) It is more so in an interorganizational matrix, such as an area or region, that may be labeled a social system. Nelson, Ramsey, and Verner have distinguished between elements and dimensions as a way of considering differential interdependence in communities: changes in some aspects of the community have a more pervasive impact than others on the remaining parts of the community. (34, pp. 89–91, 215–17) Their distinction merits further attention in interorganizational research.

Some of the master processes of the social system model, as advanced by Loomis (30, pp. 30–37), are particularly important objects for interorganizational analysis, e.g., communication, boundary maintenance, systemic linkage, and social control. Conceptualizing what these processes mean and which groups might be involved with a given organization in these processes is another way of defining, for that organization, the relevant sectors of the social structure.

There is a question about the concept of social system that merits attention: Does the system model, as developed by Loomis for example, apply to interorganizational analysis in the same way it applies to intraorganizational analysis? (30, p. 5) If so, it may provide a conceptual link for helping build on the large body of accumulated literature on intraorganizational studies. But if the model applies differently, considerable clarification of that difference is needed.

*Sets in the social structure.* Another general approach to delineating relevant segments of the social structure for the study of organizational development programs is in the following use of the term "sets."

*Organizational sets* have been discussed by Caplow as consisting of organizations that are of a similar kind and are visible to each other. Within such a set, there is a prestige order, some communication, some personnel interchangeability, and some important activities by each organization that are common to all the others. In a certain sense, these other organizations serve as comparative reference groups. (6, ch. 6)

We can use *affiliative sets* to refer to groupings of organizations having some explicitly joint enterprise. The relations among the organizations may be those of local units of national organizations, temporary coalitions cooperating for limited purposes, or some contractual relationships in which one organization arranges for certain portions of its work to be done by another organization. Some of the differences in these relationships are treated by Warren in his discussion of the interactional contexts of organizational decision making. (20, 37, 46)

I will use *task set* to describe a structural matrix similar to what Thompson calls the task environment of an organization. (15; 43, pp. 27–29) This consists of those collectivities that 1) supply resources, 2) compete with the organization for its supply of resources, 3) use the products and services of the organization, 4) compete for its market for products and services, and 5) have some regulatory relation to the organization. For given tasks, these collectivities constitute the relevant portions of the social structure or environment. When multiple products are produced, and multiple populations served, the overall task set accordingly becomes more complex in composition. Put another way, we can envision different task sets for different development objectives.

*Ecological* sets can be used to designate areas within which a variety of organizations have at least certain locality-based interests in common. The "development districts" being discussed in terms of multicounty areas would exemplify this kind of set. (12, p. 88; 38; 39, ch. 10) One difficulty to be worked out is that the ecological areas for one development problem (e.g., flood control or water pollution control) may differ from the area most instrumental for dealing with another problem (e.g., certain specialized medical services requiring a large population base, or employment problems tied to manufacturing or business trends). Therefore, how does one delineate appropriate boundaries for ecological sets having multiple development problems, each of which may have different relations to geographic space? This is a problem requiring more than arbitrary administrative decisions or casual research attention.

For some purposes, it may be more useful to begin with a particular kind of desired developmental change and ask what organizations are actually or potentially related to successful accomplishment of that change. We can call this a *development set*. It can be restricted to a local or regional area, but the nature of the problem will help determine the ecological bounds.

Organizational, affiliative, and task sets each conceptualize interorganizational structure in terms of an organization in an environment of others. The units of these sets are more widely distributed in different sectors of society, and may (or may not) be composed of organizations specializing in particular development problems. In contrast, ecological sets of organizations are, by definition, tied to particular localities, and necessarily have relevance to numerous development problems. Development sets, by definition, are problem-oriented, and focus on the interorganizational structure relevant to a given problem. They may include parts or wholes of any (or all) of the other kinds of sets. These kinds of sets are not always mutually exclusive; for a given organization, the same environmental groups may appear in several of the kinds of sets.

Each of these kinds of sets has usefulness for particular kinds of problems, though not for others. One potentially useful conceptualization of the structural matrix of development is to consider the *overlay of two or more of these sets*. Thus, to view a particular interorganizational segment of the social structure we might begin with one of the sets and add the others as overlays. The beginning point is a matter of our own purpose. For example, if we are interested in the structural matrix for a particular kind of developmental change, we could begin with the development set, and add the other sets as overlays. Or, if we were interested in delineating a development district and wanted to understand its place in the interorganizational realm of the social structure, we could designate that district as our ecological set and add the other sets as overlays.

The formation of these overlays of sets would reveal a universe of relevant organizations constituting the social environment of a given organization and simultaneously would define large portions of the total social structure as (relatively) irrelevant for a given analysis. The more frequently a particular organization appeared in the series of overlays, the more relevant or salient it would seem to be as a component of the structural environment. This method determines relevance, however, and not importance. By that I mean it determines the part of the structural context that needs to be taken into account in the analysis. But since the relevant organizations will not have equal influence on the given organization, a second question must be asked: What is the relative importance of the relevant organizations, or which have more influence? The method of overlays may be useful, therefore, in determining relevance in the structural matrix, which is the first step, but not necessarily in determining the further issue of relative importance or influence.

The foregoing discussion has assumed the analysis of an organization in an environment of other groups, but the utility of the sets and overlays is not limited to that approach. For example, it could just as well take the network of organizational relations as a point of focus.

Thus, I am suggesting that the diffuse phenomena of social structure might be studied usefully by means of looking at organizations in a variety of sets, even though many important interorganizational problems may not be addressed adequately by this approach.

## SUMMARY AND SUGGESTIONS FOR RESEARCH

### Summary

To recapitulate, I have suggested that understanding the development of society is fundamentally a problem of understanding social organization. Societal development was defined broadly as an increase in people's life chances, i.e., in their ability to reach desired goals and avoid misfortunes. Social organization was defined broadly as the opposite of fate, and consisting of the coordination and control of interests and activities to make actual outcomes correspond more closely to intended outcomes. The general intended functions of such organization are protection from costs that otherwise would be incurred, and mutual enhancement of effort. Development, then, is a product of social organization. Progress toward development can also be measured by considering those alterations in social organization that are assumed to produce more life chances. The change may be a more complete implementation of the "blueprint" for organization, or some alteration in the existing structure.

Institutional agencies were identified as keys to development, with voluntary associations having a more indirect role that depends on their ability to influence the agencies. Several institutional deficiencies and constraints against development were suggested: the interests of present beneficiaries against changes that would relatively diminish their benefits, response to power groups, trained incapacity of organizational personnel, commitments, and the ubiquitous tendencies for goal displacement and emphasis on organizational survival and maintenance.

A key point of leverage in the structural matrix of development was hypothesized to be the organization and operation of power groups to represent the interests of individuals in the context of organized action. But making that leverage work for development is hindered by the tendency for power groups to avoid changes in social structure.

Several sources of change in social structure were reviewed: the unanticipated and/or unintended consequences of technological change, crisis, the entrepreneurship of individuals, social movements, and challenge groups. New organizations deriving from these sources will, if they survive very long, tend to undergo a cycle of institutionalization that enhances the priority of system maintenance over attainment of avowed goals. Hence, the new organizations will fall short of serving the purposes for which they were formed, and will subsequently become the objects of protest and challenge in society. An important question, therefore, is how to break the institutional cycle.

The structural matrix of development can be approached usefully as an interorganizational problem. Relations between public and private organizations, studies in the sociology of law and related topics, and delineation of ecological regions emerge as salient issues in interorganizational analysis. Two critical problems become apparent at once: the more problematic nature of interorganizational structure (compared with intraorganizational structure), and the lack of interorganizational research.

One way to deal with interorganizational structure is to focus on differences in the relevance of various parts of the social environment for understanding the actions of a given organization. This relevance can be identified by means of the interdependence concept in social systems analysis, and master processes in Loomis's social system model.

Another approach to delineating relevant segments of the social environment is to use one or more of the "sets" suggested: organizational, affiliative, task, ecological, and developmental sets. In this context, the structural matrix of development can be conceptualized by means of the overlay of two or more of these sets.

### Needed Research

In the context of the foregoing discussion, I can now suggest some areas of needed research on the structural matrix of development. First, it would seem worthwhile to know how consistent and useful are the concepts briefly sketched in the preceding pages, and how they could be operationalized. Research is needed, as well, to test the validity of the assertions in those pages about relations among variables.

Many problem areas have been suggested and implied, including the following sample:

1. Why the social organization we imagine is not more fully transformed into reality, and how it could be.
2. How challenge and power groups can represent adequately the interests of new categories of people in society with minimum conflict, and without violence.
3. How the cycle of institutionalization can be broken and organizations can become self-renewing, self-adjusting mechanisms for more attainment of valued objectives.
4. How public organization can be designed in the legislative process and administered through the agencies with more instrumental rationality in specifying and attaining objectives, and with less political and administrative expediency—with more advance planning for the future, and less response from crisis to crisis.
5. How the organizational and interorganizational structure could be rationalized further by developing measures of input, output, and exchange for organizations dealing with the relatively intangible aspects of development.

6. How the methods of using system interdependence, social system master processes, and sets and overlays of sets to delineate relevant aspects of the structural matrix could be operationalized and tested for utility.

7. Why institutional agencies and other organizations do not make more adequate use of available social science knowledge regarding the relations between variation in social organization and variation in the development of society—and how such knowledge could be used more adequately.

Perhaps as much as anything, we need studies with adequate scope, depth, and completeness to provide even tentative solutions to important problems of societal development. Social science knowledge tends to accumulate in a piecemeal, often disconnected fashion, and at least in sociology we have been slow to put the pieces together into very complete pictures about important social problems.

There are substantial differences in the progress of different sectors of society toward increasing people's life chances. Generally material science and technology and its related organization have developed further and more rapidly than have similar aspects related to nonmaterial concerns. In the nonmaterial sector, the importance of discovering or devising more effective forms of social organization is matched by the relative neglect of the broad, intensive, and expensive studies needed. Accepting and implementing the results already available lag even further.

One of the chief problems is that people in the sectors of society able to exert routine control over pushing forward with such development efforts are constrained both by the sanctions of our present institutional procedures and by the risks of losing some relative advantage in major changes in the social structure. Hence, development requires of them a certain subordination of personal interests in order to promote societal development, which presumably further enhances their and other people's personal interests. In this sense, the issue of societal development is precisely the historical issue of how society is possible in the first place—how personal interests can be furthered by collective, organized action.

Obviously, society is possible, and so is societal development. The question of "how" still is far from being answered adequately. A crucial part of the search for further answers lies in methods of reconciliation of the relations of individuals to not only organizations but also interorganizational complexes. Particularly, we need more knowledge about the nature, measurement, and distribution of the costs and benefits of collective action for individuals in various circumstances (i.e., for leaders, members, and nonmembers of organizations, public agencies, minority groups, poverty groups, etc.).

An important next step is to deal with this problem for those persons who lead the major organizations and institutional agencies of society. For example, under what conditions will it be in a leader's interest to give more concern to "critical decisions" rather than to "routine" ones (7, pp. 374–82; 41) or to emphasize organizational productivity rather than maintenance or survival, or to cooperate rather than compete with other organizations in a development program even when resources are scarce? Understanding the inducements and constraints operating on those persons who control and allocate resources to and within the major organizations and agencies of society is a leverage point with far-reaching implications for our knowledge of the structural matrix of development.

## REFERENCES

1. Aiken, Michael, and Hage, Jerald. "Organizational Interdependence and Intraorganizational Structure." *American Sociological Review* 3 (December 1968): pp. 912–30.
2. Barton, Allen H. *Organizational Measurement and Its Bearing on the Study of College Environments.* New York: College Entrance Examination Board, 1961.
3. Beal, George M.; Klonglan, Gerald E.; Yarbrough, Paul; Bohlen, Joe M.; and Dillman, Don A. *System Linkages among Women's Organizations: An Exploratory Study of Membership and Leadership Linkages among Women's Formal Organizations in a Local Community.* Rural Sociology Report No. 42, 1967. Ames, Iowa: Iowa State University, Department of Sociology and Anthropology, 1967.
4. Blau, Peter M., and Scott, W. Richard. *Formal Organizations: A Comparative Approach.* San Francisco: Chandler Publishing Co., 1962.
5. Buchanan, James M., and Tullock, Gordon. *The Calculus of Consent: Logical Foundations of Constitutional Democracy.* Ann Arbor: University of Michigan Press, Ann Arbor Paperback, 1965.
6. Caplow, Theodore. *Principles of Organization.* New York: Harcourt, Brace & World, 1964.
7. Chandler, Alfred D., Jr. *Strategy and Structure: Chapters in the History of the Industrial Enterprise.* Garden City, N. Y.: Doubleday & Co., Anchor Book, 1966.
8. Clark, Burton R. "Interorganizational Patterns in Education." *Administrative Science Quarterly* 10 (September 1965): 224–37.
9. Cottrell, W. F. "Death by Dieselization, A Case Study in the Reaction to Technological Change." *American Sociological Review* 16 (June 1951): 358–65.
10. Crozier, Michel. *The Bureaucratic Phenomenon.* Chicago: University of Chicago Press, Phoenix Book, 1967.
11. Deutscher, Irwin. "Words and Deeds: Social Science and Social Policy." *Social Problems* 13: (Winter 1966): 253.
12. Economic Development Division. *Rural People in the American Economy.* Agricultural Economic Report No. 101. Washington, D.C.: Economic Research Service, U.S. Department of Agriculture, 1966.
13. Emery, F. E., and Trist, E. L. "The Causal Texture of Organizational Environments." In *Readings in Organization Theory: A Behavioral Approach,* edited by Walter A. Hill and Douglas M. Egan. Boston: Allyn and Bacon, 1966.

14. Etzioni, Amitai. *A Comparative Analysis of Complex Organizations: On Power, Involvement, and Their Correlates.* New York: The Free Press of Glencoe, 1961.
15. Evan, William M. "The Organization-set: Toward a Theory of Interorganizational Relations." In *Approaches to Organizational Design,* edited by James D. Thompson. Pittsburgh: University of Pittsburgh Press, 1966.
16. Finley, James R., and Capener, Harold R. "Interorganizational Relations: Concepts and Methodological Considerations." Paper presented at the annual meeting of the Rural Sociological Society, August 1967, at San Francisco.
17. Gardner, John W. *Self-renewal: The Individual and the Innovative Society.* New York: Harper & Row, Colophon Book, 1964.
18. Gouldner, Alvin W. "Reciprocity and Autonomy in Functional Theory." In *Symposium on Sociological Theory,* edited by Llewellyn Gross. Evanston, Ill.: Row, Peterson and Co., 1959.
19. Greer, Scott, and Orleans, Peter. "Political Sociology." In *Handbook of Modern Sociology,* edited by Robert E. L. Faris. Chicago: Rand McNally & Co., 1964.
20. Guetzkow, Harold. "Relations among Organizations." In *Studies on Behavior in Organizations: A Research Symposium,* edited by Raymond V. Bowers. Athens: University of Georgia Press, 1966.
21. Hart, Hornell. "The Hypothesis of Cultural Lag: A Present-day View." In *Technology and Social Change,* edited by Francis R. Allen, Hornell Hart, Delbert C. Miller, William F. Ogburn, and Meyer F. Nimkoff. New York: Appleton-Century-Crofts, 1957.
22. Hermann, Charles F. "Some Consequences of Crisis Which Limit the Viability of Organizations." *Administrative Science Quarterly* 8 (June 1963): 61–82.
23. Hughes, J. R. T. "Eight Tycoons: The Entrepreneur and American History." In *New Views on American Economic Development: A Selective Anthology of Recent Work,* edited by Ralph L. Andreano. Cambridge, Mass.: Schenkman Publishing Co., 1965.
24. Joiner, Charles A. *Organizational Analysis: Political, Sociological and Administrative Processes of Local Government.* East Lansing: Institute for Community Development and Services, Continuing Education Service, Michigan State University, 1964.
25. Kaplan, Abraham. "Power in Perspective." In *Power and Conflict in Organizations,* edited by Robert L. Kahn and Elise Boulding. New York: Basic Books, 1964.
26. Katz, Daniel. "Approaches to Managing Conflicts." In *Power and Conflict in Organizations,* edited by Robert L. Kahn and Elise Boulding. New York: Basic Books, 1964.
27. Leadley, Samuel M. "Relations among Formal Organizations: A Study of Collaborative Relations among Formal Voluntary Organizations in a Central New York Rural Community." Ph.D. dissertation, Cornell University, 1967.
28. Lippmann, Walter. *Essays in the Public Philosophy.* Boston: Atlantic Monthly Press and Little, Brown and Co., 1955.
29. Litwak, Eugene, and Meyer, Henry J. "A Balance Theory of Coordination between Bureaucratic Organizations and Community Primary Groups." *Administrative Science Quarterly* 11 (June 1966): 31–58.
30. Loomis, Charles P. *Social Systems: Essays on Their Persistence and Change,* Princeton, N.J.: D. Van Nostrand Co., 1960.
31. Mills, C. Wright. *The Sociological Imagination.* New York: Oxford University Press, 1959.

32. Moore, Wilbert E. *Social Change*. Englewood Cliffs, N.J.: Prentice-Hall, 1963.

33. Morrison, Denton E., and Steeves, Allan D. "Deprivation, Discontent, and Social Movement Participation: Evidence on a Contemporary Farmers' Movement, the NFO." *Rural Sociology* 32 (December 1967): 414–34.

34. Nelson, Lowry; Ramsey, Charles E.; and Verner, Coolie. *Community Structure and Change*. New York: The Macmillan Co., 1960.

35. Nisbet, Robert A. *Community and Power*. New York: Oxford University Press, Galaxy Book, 1962.

36. Olson, Mancur, Jr. *The Logic of Collective Action: Public Goods and the Theory of Groups*. Cambridge, Mass.: Harvard University Press, 1965.

37. Pifer, Alan. "The Nongovernmental Organization at Bay." In *Annual Report for 1966*. New York: Carnegie Corporation of New York, 1966.

38. Powers, Ronald C. "Multi-county Units as a Basis for Domestic Change Programs: A Conspectus of Theoretical and Operational Considerations." Paper presented at the annual meeting of the American Sociological Association, August 1966, at Miami.

39. President's National Advisory Commission on Rural Poverty. *The People Left Behind*. Washington, D.C.: U.S. Government Printing Office, 1967.

40. Scott, W. Richard. "Theory of Organizations." In *Handbook of Modern Sociology*, edited by Robert E. L. Faris. Chicago: Rand McNally & Co., 1954.

41. Selznick, Philip. *Leadership in Administration: A Sociological Interpretation*. Evanston, Ill.: Row, Peterson and Co., 1957.

42. Stinchcombe, Arthur L. "Social Structure and Organizations." In *Handbook of Organizations*, edited by James G. March. Chicago: Rand McNally & Co., 1964.

43. Thompson, James D. *Organizations in Action: Social Science Bases of Administrative Theory*. New York: McGraw-Hill Book Co., 1967.

44. Warner, W. Keith. "Feedback in Administration." *Journal of Cooperative Extension* 5 (Spring 1967): 45–46.

45. ———, and Havens, Eugene A. "Goal Displacement and the Intangibility of Organizational Goals." *Administrative Science Quarterly* 12 (March 1968): 539–55.

46. Warren, Roland L. "The Interorganizational Field as a Focus for Investigation." *Administrative Science Quarterly* 12 (December 1967): 396–419.

47. Wurster, Catherine Bauer. "Framework for an Urban Society." In *Goals for Americans*, edited by President's Commission on National Goals. New York: Prentice-Hall, Spectrum Book, 1960.

48. Zetterberg, Hans L. *Social Theory and Social Practice*. New York: The Bedminster Press, 1962.

# CHAPTER FIVE

# SOCIOLOGICAL VARIABLES OF DEVELOPMENT: THEIR RANGE AND CHARACTERISTICS

## PAUL R. EBERTS and FRANK W. YOUNG

A MAJOR PROBLEM confronting development studies is to define the problem. There is in fact little agreement on what is to be explained. The commonest conceptualization views development in terms of some aspect of growth. But which aspect? Is population growth the best criterion of development? At least it can be given a biological rationale and is relatively easy to measure. Or is long-term improvement in family welfare a better criterion? This standard has the major

We wish to record our appreciation for the able and loyal work, often beyond the call of duty, of our clerical and secretarial assistants: Pat Gaines, Nancy Iglesias, Pluma Kluess, Jane Malizia, Jean Massey, Edith McCrimmon, Carolyn Nolan, and Marilyn Schnell. In addition, we express appreciation for the financial support as provided through the Experiment Station of the New York State College of Agriculture at Cornell University, State Grant No. 828 and Hatch Grant No. 257.

PAUL R. EBERTS is Associate Professor of Sociology at Cornell University. He holds the Ph.D. in sociology from the University of Michigan. His current research is concerned with problems of regional development. Publications relevant to his chapter include: "Metropolitan Crime Rates and Relative Deprivation" (Criminologica [Fall, 1968]) and "Community Control Structures and Regional Development" (paper presented at Rural Sociological Society Meetings, Boston, 1968).

FRANK W. YOUNG is Professor of Rural Sociology at Cornell University. He holds a Ph.D. in social anthropology from Cornell University. His research activities have included field work in Mexico and Puerto Rico. Publications related to his chapter include: "Structural Differentiation of Communities: An Aerial Photographic Study" (Rural Sociology 32 [September, 1967] pp. 334–45) and "Reactive Subsystems" (American Sociological Review 35 [April, 1970] pp. 297–307).

virtue of interesting many laymen. Moreover, changes in welfare levels can usually be measured by income or industrial output shifts which, in turn, tie into a considerable body of economic theory. A third type of growth or development may be set in terms of changes in the structure of industry. Such a conception builds on the historic facts of industrialized and then "service" centers, drawing on time perspectives given us by economic historians. Yet a fourth position regards development as increasing complexity in the division of labor. Since this conception is not confined to economic or productive institutions, it has appeal to many sociologists.

Although these four positions indicate a range of ideas about development, the actual indicators used in measurement show an even greater diversity. When these indicators are combined into complex indices, variations are at once not only so great as to be unmanageable, but at the same time blur important differences. Thus, it may be that all indices of development measure the same thing—that the indicators are highly correlated if not actually interchangeable. It is certainly possible that all concepts of development and their measures merely tap the same phenomenon from different angles. On the other hand, it may also be that measures and hypotheses are still so crude that variations in conceptualization and interpretation do show up as empirical differences.

Although the range of concepts and measures of development just outlined somewhat set the limits of this chapter, there are in fact other positions. Perhaps the idea of growth should be put aside in favor of a concept such as optimum health, as suggested in the work of some ecologists and political sociologists. The ecologist Duncan (6) would view development as optimum distributions of income and services for a given set of populations. And, political sociologists such as Almond and Coleman (1) and Cutright (3), writing primarily about developing nations, but whose concepts may be useful in understanding domestic development, would view development as maximizing political stability, political complexity, political participation, or competitive political institutions. An extension of the latter theoretical posture suggests that the dominance of a developmental consciousness in society's various institutional sectors may be the key. Thus, Eisenstadt (8, pp. 246–66), Lerner (15), Deutsch (4), Janowitz (14), and Friedmann (10) examine changing relations of "centers" to "peripheries" in the development of a "national identity within a nation" as a critical variable in development if not as development itself. A further variant of this position is to think in terms of a general development picture. Leslie White (21) first sketched rough outlines for this scheme, and Sahlins and Service (18) filled in details in their discussions of the interplay between general and specific evolution.

The analysis presented in this chapter contrasts with these last positions. Our primary aim here is not with strategies of development, nor with related or correlated problems in causal factors in development. But we are concerned with understanding some dimensions in the nature of development when it is used as a dependent variable. Furthermore, the nature of development is not simply changes in attitudes of people, although such changes undoubtedly occur. Our view is that changes in the objective or structural conditions and properties of social units are either a reflection of development or development itself, and that in any case development does not occur without changes in such properties. It is to these structural properties, then, that we turn our attention.

Given such limitations we propose to attack the problem of choosing a best measure of development in the following way: first, we review some operational characteristics of selected measures of development, in our case for a set of New York State communities.[1] Then the matrix of intercorrelations for these variables is presented and analyzed. In passing we will note some potentially significant findings, although this is not our major purpose. With such an empirical illustration, it will then be possible to define and discuss basic issues in selecting development measures. Finally, it will be possible to suggest an appropriate course for development sociologists to pursue in their future research.

## AN EMPIRICAL ANALYSIS OF SELECTED MEASURES OF DEVELOPMENT

The data for this analysis consist of all cities or towns[2] in New York State which had a population of 2,500 or more as of 1950 and on which information for our measures of development was avail-

[1] Some question can be raised whether New York, generally considered a highly developed state, is an appropriate source of data. First, we can note that it does contain underdeveloped communities, with fourteen of its sixty-two counties being officially included as part of Appalachia. Moreover, as Myrdal pointed out in *The Rich and the Poor*, as early as 1957, most regions do not develop uniformly —certain centers develop much more rapidly than others. Finally, our purposes require only a set of communities which exhibit a range of characteristics with regard to development, which the communities in New York State certainly provide, as will be indicated below in the data analysis.

[2] Because what most states refer to as "towns" New York State refers to as "villages," the actual units of observation in this study are cities, villages, and urbanized areas with over 2,500 population in 1950. In New York State "towns" technically refer to what other states call "townships."

One other technicality should be noted. Unfortunately some of the changes in the data from 1950 to 1960 reflect changes in the boundaries of these communities due to annexations. Seventy communities or 21 percent of the number in our sample fall into this category. Only eight such annexations involved more than 10 percent of the population for 1960, so that their effects were probably negligible. Moreover, the similarities of the correlations between the data for 1950 and 1960 presented below make us think they are not significantly affecting our correlations.

able. Although 326 New York State communities had attained a population of 2,500 by 1960, only 225 had reached this point by 1950. Inasmuch as data are not readily available for places below that figure and since, in order to study the changes from 1950 to 1960, it was important to have the 1950 baseline, the number of cases was reduced accordingly. Still another small reduction came through the absence of information on some measures. The final sample was 221. Although this is probably the appropriate universe for the present analysis, it is clearly biased toward larger places and, more important, it omits fast-growing smaller places. Since the latter are likely to be middle class suburban areas, the universe probably leans toward somewhat poorer and more stable areas.

The measures of development about to be reviewed may be ordered according to the degree to which they tap overall structure in the community. Thus, the list begins with what, at least on the face of it, are aggregate measures of individual or family attributes. The relationship to social structure is indirect. It then moves to characteristics of industry and of the overall division of labor in the community, and concludes with more direct group-level or structural measures.

Our goals in reviewing these measures are, first, to delineate the various types of measures which have been or might be used in development analyses and, second, to discover at least the broad outlines of their empirical interrelations, both synchronically and diachronically, on a set of diverse communities probably typical of those in many industrializing regions.

*Population:* The first obvious aggregate measure of growth is a count of the number of people. Although of great practical importance, it holds an uneasy position in the range of development measures. From a biological point of view, it is an indicator of something in that a large number of human beings are surviving in one place. Sociologists tend to be uncomfortable with this rationale, and are more inclined to argue that a community which has a large population compared with other places in the same region must necessarily reflect a more complex social organization. Durkheim (7) argued for this view by observing that biological density led to a social or moral density, and thus a link is established between the biological and the social. It goes without saying that simple population size is not social density, and it would be preferable to compute the latter if an appropriate operational definition could be found. But population size is the object of customary attention if for no other reason than that is what is readily available in the census. An additional reason for including population size as a measure is that economists use it as one crude index of the volume of economic activity in a community. (17, p. 4)

*Median Family Income:* A second obvious, and perhaps the most commonly used measure of growth, is an income index. In a money economy such as the United States, it is probably true that income in dollars reflects the general social status and level of consumption of families. Using the median avoids some of the distorting effects of skewed income distributions. It is possible to have population growth without income growth or total income growth in a community without growth in family income. But change in median family income takes into account "the interplay between population growth and the growth in total income" in a given unit of observation, thus more adequately measuring growth in the monetary resources available to a family, assuming inflation is a constant in all our communities. (Cf. 17, pp. 4, 25) Also pertinent is the easy availability of this figure.

*Affluency-Poverty Ratio:* In addition to a central tendency measure like median income, some measure to reflect the distribution of incomes similar to a standard deviation is also informative. Operationally, the present measure is a more easily calculated and simplified version of a standard deviation, namely the proportion in a community who have incomes in a high census category ($6,000 or more in 1950 and $10,000 or more in 1960, which captures 16.0 percent of the New York State population in 1950 and 19.9 percent in 1960) divided by those in the poverty categories ($2,000 or less in 1950 and $3,000 or less in 1960 which captures 30.5 percent in 1950 and 26.1 percent in 1960). Although it has some obvious errors in it, dependent upon the comparative size of the two extreme categories, this measure should catch a sense of an apparent development ideal in our society, namely that all people in a community should be self-sufficient, so that the best communities are more affluent communities.

*Per Capita Availability of Flush Toilets in Dwelling Units:* One criticism of income as an index is that it says nothing about how money is spent. It is therefore useful to have a more direct measure of consumption, and a thing like flush toilets is as good an indicator of domestic well-being as one is likely to find in public statistics.

*Per Capita Housed in Dwelling Units:* Another measure of consumption and domestic well-being is the amount of space available in housing units for each occupant. Developed societies, incidentally, whether capitalist or communist, in contrast to underdeveloped societies, have increased the percentage of people living in single family dwelling units, and reduced the number of people in each unit.

*Median Education Level:* Inclusion of education as a measure meets the criticism made of indices of material consumption that important intangibles are not being taken into account. Moreover, level of education is also a sensitive index of general quality of the social environment.

*Proportion of Labor Force in Professional, Technical, or Skilled Occupations:* This measure is somewhat more refined than average educational level because it reflects the proportion of people who are actually in jobs which require sometime extensive, specialized training in order to attain a proficient skill level. Although its basis is still individual attributes, it clearly reflects a general characteristic of the community. It consists of the combination of the census categories "Professional, Technical and Kindred" and "Foremen, Skilled and Kindred," and is therefore quite easy to obtain for places in the United States.

*Proportion of Labor Force in Secondary Industry (Manufacturing):* Although this measure is still partly aggregative, the emphasis shifts from aggregated individual characteristics to characteristics of the community social structure. The index assumes the importance of careful classification of industries into primary, secondary, and tertiary which stand for roughly, extractive, manufacturing, and service. Colin Clark (2) argues the importance of this typology for nations and it is generally accepted for the United States. The only problem is to decide whether to put the emphasis on secondary or tertiary activity. Given the importance of what has been called the second industrial revolution, it is probable that service and other white collar occupations are better indicators of development; on the other hand, secondary industry is not to be discounted, and certainly is considered important in the eyes of many small communities attempting initial steps to bring about local development.

*Proportion in Tertiary Industry (Service):* Given the foregoing rationale, it remains only to note that the operational definition of tertiary industry is the proportion of the labor force employed in transportation, communication, public utilities, wholesale or retail trade, finance, insurance, real estate, business or repair services, personal services, entertainment or recreation, professional services and/ or public administration.

*Proportion of Managers, Proprietors, and Officials:* Although the inverse of the MPO ratio has attained some currency following its introduction by Hawley as a measure of concentration of community influentials, we believe that when it is used as a direct measurement it is a useful measure of growth, albeit one that is partly aggregative and partly group-level. In effect, Hawley's argument is that the offices (or roles) of managers, officials, and proprietors in a population function "to mobilize the personnel and resources of the community. . . . For it is those functions that coordinate the several other functions in their respective subsystems and articulate the latter with the larger system." (13, p. 424) In a larger sense, then, it is these roles in a community which capture the enterprising spirit which some theorists feel is necessary to represent development. In the capitalist sense, development is a function of business activity, and the characteristics underlying this measure are either businessmen or those concerned to coordinate community affairs, the latter also presumably critical in development. Thus, the indicator at least in part catches "high need achievement," "spirit of capitalism," or "individual initiative" which Adam Smith (19), Max Weber (20), and David McClelland (16) regard so highly in development.

*Number of Economic Establishments:* As is well known, the firm of Dun and Bradstreet maintains, in connection with its credit services, a complete listing of firms and businesses in the United States according to community. If growth is viewed from an institutional point of view and, in the present case, with an emphasis on economic institutions, then a simple count of Dun and Bradstreet listings gives a measure of development. With this measure, the shift from individual to community-level attributes is fully made. The measure necessarily assumes that a community is the organization of organizations rather than of individuals alone.

*Scale of Institutional Differentiation:* The obvious next step after counting Dun and Bradstreet listings is to widen the basis for the count and, at the same time, to refine the technique of scoring. While a simple count may be defended as organizational growth, it is of interest to know how many different kinds of organizations (or institutions) exist in the community. It is probably impossible to determine precisely how many different kinds of organizations actually exist in a community, inasmuch as it turns on the question of defining "differences" between organizations. But the technique of Guttman scaling from a diversified list of types of organizations tends to yield stable measure along these lines. The particular scale built for these communities, which holds for both 1950 and 1960, consists of the following items: at least one grocery store, a plumbing contractor, newspaper, household appliance store, furniture store, local general hospital, chamber of commerce, wholesale druggist, and the presence of a television station. The coefficient of scalability (in contrast to reproducibility) is a satisfactory .82 for 1950, and .79 for 1960.

*Scale of Medical Specialties:* A possible refinement of the scale of institutional differentiation is the scale of diverse medical specialties. From time to time the American Medical Association publishes a list of all its members along with their locations and specialties. The uniformity of such information makes it especially attractive for index-building purposes, and in this case, it provides a known universe of specialties. It is true of course that the range of specialties for 1950 and 1960 varies considerably. In the latter year there are many new specialties such as therapeutic radiology, thoracic surgery, pediatrics, cardiology, pediatric allergy, occupational medicine, and seven more of a similar nature. Moreover, the 1950 list contained some eight labels that are not used in 1960. Since they are probably subsumed in the present specialties, the new specialties undoubtedly represent new levels of complexity in this area. Also, there is some changing of names. In 1950 there were general surgeons and practitioners of internal medicine, but no general practitioners, whereas the latter is a very common label in 1960. Thus the usable pool of items consisted of those 20 specialties with identical labels in the two time periods. Using these, it was possible to devise a Guttman scale of 14 items with a coefficient of scalability of .72 that applied to both the 1950 and 1960 periods.

The initial items in the scale is the presence of any of the 20 medical specialties in the communities. Even using such a broad category, nearly one-third of the communities scored zero on the scale. After the first item, in ascending order, the items are internal medicine, pediatrics, obstetrics and gynecology, pathology, dermatology, urology, pulmonary diseases, allergies, proctology, neurosurgery, plastic surgery, physical medicine, and neurology. Although this scale may be useful primarily to investigators of medical services, it is included here because we hypothesize that the diversity of specialties in one institutional sector is equivalent to the range of variation in any other. This proposition will be denied by those who believe that community organization consists of the interplay of institutional sectors, with some leading and others following, but in terms of the simplified point of departure taken here, namely, that "growth is growth" and, in terms of considerable previous experience, it is expected that this measure will index the role of differentiation in the whole community.

The contrasting methodological characteristics of these indicators will be reviewed below. A characteristic that deserves mention here is that all the measures can be obtained for an earlier time period so that indices of change can be computed. The particular derivation of the change measures ranges from a shift in absolute number to shifts in proportions or of scale steps when the communities for both time periods fit a single scalogram pattern, as they do in the present case. It is acknowledged that these measures of change are crude, and that much future methodological work is necessary. Even so, they provide a purchase on the problem of discriminating among measures of development. That is, in addition to the synchronic comparison for 1950 and for 1960, it will also be possible to compare the diachronic measures.

*Findings:* The matrices of intercorrelations for 1950 and 1960 are given in Tables 5.1 and 5.2.

The main facts are immediately apparent. First, there are no overall intercorrelations; and second, the 1960 matrix is highly similar to the 1950 matrix.

The various measures of development are by no means interchangeable. There are, however, some clear-cut clusters. As might be expected, median income, affluency, mean educational level, the percent of the labor force who are managers and officials and the percent of the labor force in service industries appear intercorrelated.

TABLE 5.1.  Intercorrelation Matrix of Development Measures for 221 New York State Communities, 1950

| Development Measures | 1 | 2 | 3 | 4 | 5 | 6 | 7 | 8 | 9 | 10 | 11 | 12 | 13 |
|---|---|---|---|---|---|---|---|---|---|---|---|---|---|
| 1. Population Size | 1.0 | | | | | | | | | | | | |
| 2. Median Family Income | −.01 | 1.0 | | | | | | | | | | | |
| 3. Affluency-Poverty Ratio | −.05 | .83 | 1.0 | | | | | | | | | | |
| 4. Per Capita Flush Toilets | .05 | −.02 | −.04 | 1.0 | | | | | | | | | |
| 5. Per Capita in Dwelling Units | .03 | −.15 | .17 | .40 | 1.0 | | | | | | | | |
| 6. Median Education | −.09 | .41 | .50 | .06 | −.02 | 1.0 | | | | | | | |
| 7. Highly Trained Labor Force | −.05 | .21 | .34 | .04 | −.04 | .60 | 1.0 | | | | | | |
| 8. Percent in Manufacturing | .05 | .00 | −.21 | −.06 | −.21 | −.45 | −.28 | 1.0 | | | | | |
| 9. Percent in Service Industry | −.03 | .03 | .25 | .07 | .23 | .48 | .31 | −.98 | 1.0 | | | | |
| 10. Percent Managers, Proprietors, Officials in Labor Force | −.07 | .62 | .62 | −.05 | −.09 | .65 | .21 | −.43 | .45 | 1.0 | | | |
| 11. Number Dun and Bradstreet Listings | .98 | −.04 | −.08 | .04 | .01 | −.09 | −.06 | .05 | −.03 | −.08 | 1.0 | | |
| 12. Institutional Differentiation Scale | .30 | −.20 | −.11 | .01 | −.11 | −.10 | −.09 | .01 | −.01 | −.06 | .32 | 1.0 | |
| 13. Medical Specialties Scale | .61 | .07 | .06 | .08 | .06 | .09 | −.07 | −.13 | .17 | .12 | .61 | .45 | 1.0 |

TABLE 5.2. Intercorrelation Matrix of Development Measures for 221 New York State Communities, 1960

| Development Measures | 1 | 2 | 3 | 4 | 5 | 6 | 7 | 8 | 9 | 10 | 11 | 12 | 13 |
|---|---|---|---|---|---|---|---|---|---|---|---|---|---|
| 1. Population Size | 1.0 | | | | | | | | | | | | |
| 2. Median Family Income | −.04 | 1.0 | | | | | | | | | | | |
| 3. Affluency-Poverty Ratio | −.04 | .74 | 1.0 | | | | | | | | | | |
| 4. Per Capita Flush Toilets | .03 | .04 | .19* | 1.0 | | | | | | | | | |
| 5. Per Capita in Dwelling Units | −.01 | .15 | .26 | .85* | 1.0 | | | | | | | | |
| 6. Median Education | −.11 | .46 | .54 | .24* | .25* | 1.0 | | | | | | | |
| 7. Highly Trained Labor Force | −.09 | .29 | .16 | .24* | .33* | .57 | 1.0 | | | | | | |
| 8. Percent in Manufacturing | .04 | −.03 | −.23 | −.03 | .01* | −.45 | −.19 | 1.0 | | | | | |
| 9. Percent in Service Industry | −.02 | .06 | .25 | .01 | −.02* | .46 | .19 | −.99 | 1.0 | | | | |
| 10. Percent Managers, Proprietors, Officials in Labor Force | −.08 | .63 | .73 | .10 | .12* | .66 | .18 | −.43 | .44 | 1.0 | | | |
| 11. Number Dun and Bradstreet Listings | .98 | −.07 | −.07 | .01 | −.04 | −.13 | −.10 | .04 | −.02 | −.11 | 1.0 | | |
| 12. Institutional Differentiation Scale | .30 | −.28 | −.25 | .09 | −.02 | −.12 | −.14 | −.06 | .04 | −.12 | .33 | 1.0 | |
| 13. Medical Specialties Scale | .53 | .13 | .08 | .10 | .06 | .11 | .00 | −.16 | .18 | .14 | .54 | .47 | 1.0 |

* This correlation differs from the 1950 correlation, given in Table 5.1, by ±.15.

125

Similarly, another cluster may be temporarily labeled the structural dimension, consisting of the count of economic establishments, the scale of institutional differentiation, the scale of medical specialties, and population. Of particular interest is the very strong relationship between population and the number of economic establishments (.98 in both years), suggesting that the multiplicity of such establishments is a direct response to population size.

The two measures of domestic welfare—per capita use of flush toilets and single dwellings—are also highly intercorrelated, .85 in 1960, although only .40 in 1950, and are not highly related to the other measures. It was anticipated that these measures would be highly and negatively associated with other socioeconomic indicators, and the fact that they are not is somewhat puzzling. It is in these measures also that the major differences in size of correlations between Tables 5.1 and 5.2 appear.

Several things may be noted regarding these findings. First, the means and standard deviations in the per capita ratios for both measures were reduced between 1950 and 1960. The means of per capita in dwelling units were 3.31 for 1950, and 3.09 for 1960; and the standard deviations were .66 for 1950 and .38 for 1960. The means for per capita flush toilets were 3.49 for 1950 and 3.17 for 1960; and the standard deviations were .58 for 1950 and .44 for 1960. Second, a case by case examination, however, showed that 34 cases actually increased in per capita dwelling units and 18 cases of these 34 also showed an increase in per capita flush toilets. Third, an examination of these measures in the matrices for 1950 and 1960, comparing Tables 5.1 and 5.2, shows that the major differences in the size of correlations between the two matrices all fall in correlations of these two variables. And, fourth, the major differences in correlations occur mainly in relation to socioeconomic variables, with the correlations becoming positive in 1960, rather than the expected negative, and higher.

These findings probably indicate the following things: first, that since the standard deviations are reduced from 1950 to 1960, communities are becoming more alike with regard to domestic well-being. Second, since the means are being reduced in most cases, family sizes are probably not increasing between 1950 and 1960. The 34 communities which are exceptions to this trend, however, may be experiencing an influx of lower income and larger size families, since 23 of these cases are in metropolitan counties of New York State. Third, the changes in correlations between 1950 and 1960 in these domestic well-being measures and socioeconomic status variables are probably not spurious, but recognize an increasing trend toward a positive correlation between family size and socioeconomic status. (Cf. 11, pp. 214–22) This would be especially so in communities which do not have large in-migrations of people in the lower socioeconomic categories, such as suburban or rural communities, which constitute the majority of communities in our data.

A final isolated pair are the two measures of type of economic activity. The proportion of the labor force in manufacturing is negatively related (in 1950 —.98 and —.99 in 1960) to the proportion in service occupations. In both years, they are also moderately related to median education, and percent managers, proprietors, and officials, but not to income or affluency, of the first cluster mentioned above. This reflects the oft-noted finding that communities specializing in manufacturing have populations with lower education and occupational structures, compared to the proliferation of specialized, often professionalized services offered in centers of tertiary industries. (Cf. 5, p. 219 ff.)

In order to document more fully the lack of overall correlation and, at the same time, to underscore the four dimensions underlying the development measures, several factor analyses were performed on the data. The factor analyses for 1950 and 1960 by an orthogonal varimax rotation method are presented in Tables 5.3 and 5.4. As readily observed, the factor analyses by this method for the two years show highly similar results. Four factors appear above the eigenvalue of one, with the high loadings appearing in the same variables for both years. The major difference between the two tables is that the four factors appear in different order in the two years with regard to total variance explained by the factor. This probably indicates predominance of industrial base in affecting communities under conditions of a growing gross national product, as seen in Table 5.4, the 1960 matrix.

Moreover, the four factors correspond closely to the clusters of variables just reviewed. In each table, one factor may be labeled socioeconomic status, a second one may be labeled structural complexity (which includes population size), a third is industrial base, and a fourth is domestic ease. Furthermore, the correlations with the factors noted in discussing the clusters above continue to be found in the matrices, albeit more clearly than in the correlation matrices of Tables 5.1 and 5.2.

Interest naturally turns to the positive associations, but it may be that lack of association between certain variables is the most important fact of this analysis. For instance, the low negative correlations in the two factors of socioeconomic status and domestic ease on institutional differentiation tend to indicate that some cities have a high level of development in terms of multiplicity in services and institutions, but that development in terms of domestic amenities or median income of people living in the communities is lower than in cities with lower differentiation. An explanation of this may be that larger, more structurally complex cities have become ghettoized as a result of the middle class exodus and the influx of the poor, but that small or middle-sized cities, perhaps suburbs, might show a positive relationship. The empirical follow-up to this interpretation, namely, to re-run the matrices for different "types" of communities,

TABLE 5.3. Factor Analysis (Orthogonal Varimax Rotation) on Development Variables for 221 New York State Communities, 1950

| Development Measures | One Socioeconomic Status | Two Structural Complexity | Three Industrial Base | Four Domestic Ease | Communality |
|---|---|---|---|---|---|
| 1. Population Size | .01 | .93 | −.12 | .10 | .88325 |
| 2. Median Family Income | .93 | .01 | −.09 | −.09 | .87424 |
| 3. Affluency-Poverty Ratio | .91 | −.06 | .12 | .13 | .87072 |
| 4. Per Capita Flush Toilets | −.06 | .06 | −.02 | .77 | .60548 |
| 5. Per Capita in Dwelling Units | .01 | −.01 | .21 | .84 | .75127 |
| 6. Median Education | .46 | −.03 | .42 | −.04 | .39196 |
| 7. Highly Trained Labor Force | .13 | −.05 | .14 | .03 | .04168 |
| 8. Percent in Manufacturing | −.06 | .00 | −.96 | −.09 | .92646 |
| 9. Percent in Service Industry | .10 | .03 | .95 | .11 | .92531 |
| 10. Percent Managers, Proprietors, Officials in Labor Force | .73 | .01 | .47 | −.19 | .77836 |
| 11. Number Dun and Bradstreet Listings | −.03 | .93 | −.11 | .07 | .88584 |
| 12. Institutional Differentiation Scale | −.35 | .54 | .13 | −.26 | .49376 |
| 13. Medical Specialties Scale | .10 | .81 | .02 | .19 | .70996 |
| Cumulative Proportion of Total Variance Explained | .28 | .49 | .63 | .74 | |
| Eigenvalue | 3.67 | 2.70 | 1.86 | 1.36 | |

TABLE 5.4. Factor Analysis (Orthogonal Varimax Rotation) on Development Variables for 221 New York State Communities, 1960

| Development Measures | One Industrial Base | Two Structural Complexity | Three Domestic Ease | Four Socioeconomic Status | Communality |
|---|---|---|---|---|---|
| 1. Population Size | -.10 | .94 | -.05 | -.03 | .90754 |
| 2. Median Family Income | -.10 | .01 | .00 | .89 | .79793 |
| 3. Affluency-Poverty Ratio | .12 | .02 | .15 | .91 | .85956 |
| 4. Per Capita Flush Toilets | .02 | .04 | .95 | .05 | .90693 |
| 5. Per Capita in Dwelling Units | -.06 | -.01 | .92 | .13 | .87171 |
| 6. Median Education | .45 | -.03 | .20 | .53 | .52818 |
| 7. Highly Trained Labor Force | .17 | -.03 | .23 | .10 | .09339 |
| 8. Percent in Manufacturing | -.96 | -.01 | .02 | -.11 | .93767 |
| 9. Percent in Service Industry | .96 | .03 | -.04 | .13 | .93425 |
| 10. Percent Managers, Proprietors, Officials in Labor Force | .39 | -.03 | .06 | .82 | .83703 |
| 11. Number Dun and Bradstreet Listings | -.09 | .95 | -.07 | -.06 | .91772 |
| 12. Institutional Differentiation Scale | .23 | .48 | .20 | -.29 | .41683 |
| 13. Medical Specialties Scale | .21 | .75 | .12 | .13 | .63989 |
| Cumulative Proportion of Total Variance Explained | .29 | .50 | .65 | .77 | |
| Eigenvalue | 3.79 | 2.66 | 1.96 | 1.59 | |

is outside the scope of this chapter, but it is one of the many kinds of spin-offs readily apparent from comparative analysis using large social systems, such as communities, as units of analysis and observation.

Because the factors produced in any factor analysis are a function of the number and type of variables included in the original correlation matrix, as well as the type of rotation used in order to determine the constancy, or its lack, of the factors described here, another set of matrices was run for 1950 and 1960 which eliminated some of the possible overlapping variables. Thus, one variable in each of the couplets having the highest loadings on each factor in Tables 5.3 and 5.4 was eliminated, namely, affluency from the socioeconomic status factor, number of Dun and Bradstreet listings from the structural complexity factor, per capita flush toilets from the domestic ease factor, and percent in manufacturing from the industrial base factor. The new set of matrices based on nine rather than thirteen variables is given in Tables 5.5 and 5.6.

The four factors shown in Table 5.6, for the 1960 data, are virtually identical to the factors produced in Table 5.4, except that the size of the loadings on the variables with the highest loadings in Table 5.4 has decreased slightly and the loadings on the variables with more moderate loadings in Table 5.4 have now increased. Moreover, the factors maintain themselves in the same order in terms of amount of explained variance. Industrial base is still the strongest factor, followed in order by structural complexity, domestic ease—with education and a highly trained labor force making much stronger contributions to the factor—and socioeconomic status.

The factors produced in Table 5.5, however, show considerable variations from those presented in Table 5.3. The major difference is immediately noticeable in that four factors appear in Table 5.3 and only three factors appear in Table 5.5. A fourth factor, which is not included in Table 5.5 because the eigenvalue fell below 1.00 to .96, circumscribed the missing industrial base dimension, including percent in service with a .68 loading, median education with a .77 loading, and percent highly trained labor force with a .82 loading. The three factors which remain in Table 5.5, however, are the same as those in Table 5.3, namely, one each on socioeconomic status, structural complexity, and domestic ease. These three factors do not drop out, explain highly similar amounts of total variance compared to the factors in Table 5.3, and load high on the same variables as in the previous factors, with some of the more moderate loadings now becoming higher.

Two general conclusions may be drawn from these data: first, the appearance of clusters and orthogonally rotated factors conclusively demonstrates that there is no common factor behind the development measures; and, second, the nature of development measures consistently breaks into four clusters of variables, reflected in the

TABLE 5.5. Factor Analysis (Orthogonal Varimax Rotation) on Development Variables for 221 New York State Communities, 1950

| Development Measures | One Socioeconomic Status | Two Structural Complexity | Three Domestic Base | Communality |
|---|---|---|---|---|
| 1. Population Size | .03 | .79 | .06 | .63582 |
| 2. Median Family Income | .90 | −.04 | −.14 | .83525 |
| 3. Per Capita Dwelling Units | −.12 | −.01 | .91 | .84038 |
| 4. Median Education | .47 | −.02 | .02 | .22486 |
| 5. Highly Trained Labor Force | .03 | −.11 | −.15 | .03542 |
| 6. Percent in Service Industry | .13 | .12 | .47 | .25122 |
| 7. Percent Managers, Proprietors, Officials in Labor Force | .80 | .05 | .05 | .64602 |
| 8. Institutional Differentiation Scale | −.30 | .70 | −.27 | .65288 |
| 9. Medical Specialties Scale | .15 | .89 | .12 | .82016 |
| Cumulative Proportion of Total Variance Explained | .30 | .51 | .66 | |
| Eigenvalue | 2.69 | 1.93 | 1.28 | |

TABLE 5.6. Factor Analysis (Orthogonal Varimax Rotation) on Development Variables for 221 New York State Communities, 1960

| Development Measures | One Industrial Base | Two Structural Complexity | Three Domestic Ease | Four Socioeconomic Status | Communality |
|---|---|---|---|---|---|
| 1. Population Size | −.18 | .79 | −.05 | .05 | .66853 |
| 2. Median Family Income | −.01 | .01 | .16 | .92 | .87077 |
| 3. Per Capita Dwelling Units | −.14 | .07 | .83 | .05 | .71237 |
| 4. Median Education | .61 | −.04 | .46 | .48 | .81406 |
| 5. Highly Trained Labor Force | .27 | −.12 | .77 | .14 | .69673 |
| 6. Percent in Service Industry | .90 | .07 | −.01 | .05 | .81978 |
| 7. Percent Managers, Proprietors, Officials in Labor Force | .50 | .02 | .05 | .75 | .82208 |
| 8. Institutional Differentiation Scale | .18 | .68 | −.03 | −.41 | .66334 |
| 9. Medical Specialties Scale | .14 | .87 | .03 | .13 | .79738 |
| Cumulative Proportion of Total Variance Explained | .31 | .52 | .65 | .76 | |
| Eigenvalue | 2.81 | 1.90 | 1.15 | 1.01 | |

factors, for both years, 1950 and 1960. These four clusters are structural complexity, socioeconomic status, domestic base, and industrial base. That these factors emerge through orthogonal varimax rotations with varying numbers of measures strongly suggests that they will emerge consistently, even when additional measures are placed in the factor analyses.

It will be important, of course, that other variables to measure development be devised and included in future analyses; as well as that certain variables be treated as controls to discover whether these findings are valid for all types of communities, or actually differ from one type of community to another, such as Hadden and Borgatta (12) found in their analyses of a universe of larger United States cities.

The fact that the two intercorrelation and factor analytic matrices are so similar implies a high degree of correspondence between the values of measures as of 1950 and as of 1960. Since we had the same communities in both years, the measures were intercorrelated for the two years. Of the 13 development measures, five correlated at .90 or above, and four between .80 and .87, population size in 1950 correlated with population size in 1960 at .99, as did the two sets of Dun and Bradstreet measures.

The lowest correlations appear for the two domestic ease measures (.52 and .53), and in the proportion of the labor force employed in skilled or professional-technical occupations (.62). The association of the institutional differentiation scale for the two time periods is .72 and for the scale of medical specialties is .80.

Thus, the general picture is one of stability of the urban rankings except for housing and plumbing which, as noted earlier, stabilized in the ten-year period, and for the shift to skilled or professional work, which is a well-known trend.

A third perspective on the range and characteristics of development measures is provided by diachronic changes in the ten-year period from 1950 to 1960. Table 5.7 shows the intercorrelation of the various measures of change that were constructed. Methods of computing degree of change vary according to the nature of the variable. When absolute increases are computed, the percent of increase is also shown. In the case of ratios, the difference between ratios constitutes the measure of change, and in the case of the Guttman scales, we simply counted the number of steps in the change. It will be recalled that the same scale pattern held for both time periods, so the items, if not the intervals, are the same. Finally, as in most change measures, constants are added in order to eliminate minus numbers.

Table 5.7 contains many surprises. Given the independent clusters of growth measures cited up to this point, we did not expect the change measures to move together, but we were unprepared for the degree to which they did in fact diverge. For example, the rela-

TABLE 5.7. Intercorrelation of Selected Change Measures from 1950 to 1960 for 221 New York State Communities

| | Change 1950 to 1960 | | | | | | | | | | | | | |
|---|---|---|---|---|---|---|---|---|---|---|---|---|---|---|
| | 1 | 2 | 3 | 4 | 5 | 6 | 7 | 8 | 9 | 10 | 11 | 12 | 13 | 14 |
| 1. Population (percent increase) | | | | | | | | | | | | | | |
| 2. Population (absolute change) | .44 | | | | | | | | | | | | | |
| 3. Median Family Income (percent increase) | .16 | .09 | | | | | | | | | | | | |
| 4. Median Family Income (absolute change) | .34 | .31 | .44 | | | | | | | | | | | |
| 5. Affluency-Poverty Ratio | .29 | .18 | —.01 | .51 | | | | | | | | | | |
| 6. Per Capita Flush Toilets | .59 | .28 | —.17 | .25 | .22 | | | | | | | | | |
| 7. Per Capita in Dwelling Units | .65 | .23 | —.09 | .22 | .16 | .86 | | | | | | | | |
| 8. Median Education | .25 | .15 | .12 | .10 | —.07 | .15 | .15 | | | | | | | |
| 9. Highly Trained Labor Force | .14 | .04 | .15 | .15 | —.06 | .04 | .14 | .22 | | | | | | |
| 10. Percent in Manufacturing | .06 | —.05 | .08 | .03 | .01 | .19 | .25 | —.05 | .07 | | | | | |
| 11. Percent in Service Industry | —.05 | .04 | —.09 | —.06 | —.03 | —.19 | —.21 | .09 | —.01 | —.92 | | | | |
| 12. Percent Managers, Proprietors, Officials in Labor Force | .14 | .08 | .12 | .27 | .20 | .07 | .09 | .15 | .00 | .00 | .00 | | | |
| 13. Number Dun and Bradstreet Listings | —.08 | .01 | —.11 | —.01 | —.20 | .08 | .04 | .12 | .07 | —.06 | .08 | .03 | | |
| 14. Institutional Differentiation Scale | —.05 | .03 | —.12 | —.07 | —.25 | .10 | .08 | .14 | .06 | —.03 | .03 | .01 | .75 | |
| 15. Medical Specialties Scale | .13 | .01 | .18 | .04 | .17 | —.06 | .01 | —.10 | .02 | .01 | —.02 | —.07 | —.69 | —.63 |

tionship between change in median income and change in median education is both part of the socioeconomic status factor, and at best a relationship of .12. The number of Dun and Bradstreet listings, which strongly relates to population size in the structural complexity factor at the two points in time, does not change with population, as shown by the lack of relationships with percent increase in population (—.08) or the absolute increase (.01), or with diversity of medical specialties (.13). Even more extreme is the relationship between increase in institutional differentiation and medical specialties (—.63), and population change (—.05, .03), although these variables correlated highly with the structural complexity factors.

The most sensible correlations are those showing that as population increases, per capita flush toilets increase (.59, .28), as does per capita in dwelling units (.65, .23), and both these measures move together (.86). In addition, as expected, changes in percent in service industries correlate high and negatively with changes in percent in manufacturing (—.92). And, finally, as more businesses come into communities, they also diversify, so that an increase in institutional differentiation also appears (.75) in those communities experiencing the business growth.

But, given such results, one immediately asks the question, What happened? Several alternatives are possible. For instance, the technical procedures may be incorrect. The relationship between the percent increase and absolute increase of median income is only .44 and the same low association holds for percent increase and absolute change in population. Clearly, the method of computing changes has a great effect. Another problem may be the choice of correlation measure. Pearsonian r is misleading when applied to Guttman scales if the shape of the scale is not normal, and the same issue is debatable with respect to some other measures used in these tables. On the other hand, previous experience shows that one obtains essentially similar results with this statistic as one might with Spearmen's rho and, of course, it is much more convenient with respect to computer programs, particularly those for factor analysis. Still, measures of change introduce the problem of ordinal versus interval scales more directly. Treating the small increments of growth often present in the case of cities as equal intervals may seriously distort the actual trends.

It is also possible that certain "control" variables, such as city-suburb-metropolitan status, or distance to larger centers, would make the correlations conform more to our expectations.[3]

There is, however, one substantive fact that emerges from Table 5.7 which may hold regardless of technical deficiencies. Population,

[3] Some preliminary analyses indicate that "city status" does make a difference in these data just as it did for Hadden and Borgatta. These findings will be reported in subsequent papers.

which was related only to institutional differentiation measures in the 1950 and 1960 matrices, seems to be most relevant to change. The percentage increase in population, which gives the strongest relations with the other variables, correlates .34 with absolute increase in median income and .59 with the population/flush toilet ratio. On the other hand it is associated —.08 with the number of Dun and Bradstreet listings and .13 with increase in diversity of medical specialties. In short, it operates almost opposite to the way it functioned in the static situation. It does not go along with changes in institutional differentiation and it is related to an increase in median income. Since it is also a fact that middle size and small cities, especially suburbs, are the ones increasing fastest in population, they may in fact be increasing with respect to income too. One result of this is the ghettoization of larger cities (which are not increasing as fast in population) noted earlier. The strong positive correlation between population increase and the flush toilets and housing ratios also supports the decaying city interpretation.

Although it is not the purpose of this chapter to attempt to explain changes in any particular measures of growth, the various relationships between the state of development as of 1950 and the amount of change from 1950 to 1960 are helpful in understanding some issues in the nature of development. The central issue is to determine if development in certain directions is self-fulfilling, that is, if it is high on one measure at one point in time, will it continue to extend in this direction, or does it change toward other directions? To put it another way, "Do rich communities get richer while poor ones get poorer?" Or, are plateaus reached, resulting in new lines of development as Clark (2) helped us understand with regard to the relation of services to manufacturing?

Table 5.8 aids in resolving this issue by showing the correlations of our development measures as they were distributed in 1950 with their changes from 1950 to 1960. With regard to the income measures, median income in 1950 correlates .68 with absolute increase in income up to 1960 (although only —.04 with percent change in income), and .73 with change in the affluency ratio. Likewise, the affluency ratio for 1950 correlates .63 with changes in affluency and the MPO ratio also correlates .65 with changes in affluency. Thus, rich communities seem to be getting richer faster than poor communities are getting richer. Moreover, the extent of institutional complexity correlates .62 with changes in Dun and Bradstreet listings. Hence, communities with diverse businesses seem to attract even more businesses.

In addition, the level of education in 1950 relates .33 with changes in income and .46 with changes in affluency. But the level of education in 1950 is not associated (—.47) with change in educational level. This means, of course, that communities with high median education in 1950 changed relatively little (rather than negative-

TABLE 5.8. Relationship of Level Development in 1950 in 221 New York State Communities to Change during 1950–60

| Level of Development | 1 | 2 | 3 | 4 | 5 | 6 | 7 | 8 | 9 | 10 | 11 | 12 | 13 | 14 | 15 |
|---|---|---|---|---|---|---|---|---|---|---|---|---|---|---|---|
| | | | | Change Measures* | | | | | | | | | | | |
| Population Size | −.09 | .14 | −.08 | −.10 | −.05 | −.13 | −.18 | −.05 | −.10 | −.04 | .01 | −.08 | −.06 | .07 | −.06 |
| Median Family Income | .26 | .24 | −.04 | .68 | .73 | .27 | .16 | −.06 | −.01 | −.06 | .02 | .16 | −.20 | −.24 | .13 |
| Affluency-Poverty Ratio | .27 | .18 | −.10 | .58 | .63 | .31 | .19 | −.19 | −.09 | .00 | −.04 | .13 | −.30 | −.21 | .16 |
| Per Capita Flush Toilets | −.09 | .00 | .28 | .08 | .06 | −.28 | −.21 | .22 | .05 | .07 | −.12 | .05 | −.08 | .00 | .07 |
| Per Capita in Dwelling Units | −.07 | .01 | −.15 | −.07 | .10 | −.06 | −.04 | −.04 | −.07 | .05 | −.08 | .04 | −.05 | .02 | .03 |
| Median Education | .12 | .12 | .12 | .33 | .46 | .17 | .09 | −.47 | −.09 | .09 | −.13 | .10 | −.14 | .15 | −.14 |
| Highly Trained Labor Force | .30 | .15 | .20 | .35 | .18 | .34 | .25 | −.14 | −.26 | .05 | −.09 | .10 | −.09 | −.06 | .06 |
| Percent in Manufacturing | −.04 | −.04 | .09 | .03 | −.21 | −.11 | −.11 | .18 | .09 | −.44 | .41 | −.01 | .01 | −.01 | .01 |
| Percent in Service Industry | .05 | .05 | −.09 | −.01 | .23 | .12 | .10 | −.19 | −.13 | .40 | −.43 | .02 | −.03 | .00 | .00 |
| Percent Managers, Proprietors, Officials in Labor Force | .15 | .17 | −.01 | .39 | .64 | .15 | .07 | −.29 | −.06 | .08 | −.10 | −.18 | −.17 | −.20 | .17 |
| Number Dun and Bradstreet Listings | −.10 | .04 | −.08 | −.12 | −.07 | −.13 | −.18 | −.05 | −.10 | −.02 | .00 | −.09 | −.06 | −.07 | .08 |
| Institutional Differentiation Scale | −.27 | −.01 | −.11 | −.15 | −.17 | −.17 | −.22 | −.04 | −.11 | .00 | −.01 | −.10 | .62 | .50 | .39 |
| Medical Specialties Scale | −.12 | .18 | −.12 | −.04 | .07 | −.17 | −.27 | −.16 | −.10 | −.02 | −.03 | −.12 | .07 | .16 | −.16 |

*1. Population (percent increase)
2. Population (absolute change)
3. Median Family Income (percent increase)
4. Median Family Income (absolute change)
5. Affluency-Poverty Ratio
6. Per Capita Flush Toilets
7. Per Capita in Dwelling Units
8. Median Education
9. Highly Trained Labor Force
10. Percent in Manufacturing
11. Percent in Service Industry
12. Percent Managers, Proprietors, Officials in Labor Force
13. Number Dun and Bradstreet Listings
14. Institutional Differentiation Scale
15. Medical Specialties Scale

ly) to increase their educational level, whereas lower educated communities in 1950 generally upgraded their educational level over the ten-year period. This probably reflects the effectiveness of rural central school districts in giving nearly the whole population of New York State a high school education.

The main features of Table 5.8, however, are the discontinuities. By observing the diagonal, it can be observed that only the income measures correlate positively with their change counterparts. Although some are so low as to be considered zero, all other measures correlate negatively, and several of these measures reach considerable degrees of negative correlation. For example, the proportion of the labor force in manufacturing correlates —.44 with its change counterpart and .41 with change in service industries, as is expected from Clark and others' observations. But, more surprising, the proportion of the labor force in tertiary industries correlates —.43 with its counterpart, yet positively, .40, with change in percent in manufacturing. If this finding holds up in further analysis, it may indicate an important addition to Clark's observations. Not only do manufacturing centers tend to become service centers over time, but service centers over time also tend to become manufacturing centers.

Another of the high negative correlations is the relation of institutional differentiation with its counterpart, —.50. Although this may in part be a function of the scale itself, which does not adequately evaluate the very highly differentiated places, it surely also indicates that as the general system is developing, less differentiated places are becoming more differentiated institutionally.

Thus, with the exception of the income measures noted above, communities with a given high amount of development do *not* continue to grow *in that direction*. Of course, the information in this table gives no clues to the antecedents of changes in development measures. Nonetheless, the general point is clear: it cannot be assumed that communities move up or down development scales at a continuous rate. Cities do not grow steadily. But only further research, perhaps through path analysis, can indicate the trails actually followed in community growth and development.

## THE UNDERLYING ISSUES IN THE CHOICE OF A DEVELOPMENT MEASURE

Empirical analysis of variables, such as those just reviewed, can only illustrate the methodological and theoretical issues involved in the choice of measure for particular studies. In the last analysis the choice should be based on theoretical considerations, but an important belt of considerations lies between the conceptual scheme and the actual techniques of measurement. Sometime in the distant future these quasi-theoretical questions may be resolved, but in the present groping stage of work in development, they merit more intensive examination than is usually given them. They may be listed as follows:

## Aggregated Versus Structural Measures

The ready availability of census data has led to the widespread use of aggregated measures of development. Such measures most often use the central tendency of the values for the subunits (in most cases, people) of a system to stand for the level of the system itself. Median income is the foremost example. In contrast to such measures are those which attempt to measure the system *qua* system. These may be labeled *structural* because they are built up from attributes of subsystems within the system rather than simple aggregation of subunits. The two Guttman scales of institutional and medical differentiation are examples. These measures combine institutional characteristics of communities to yield an overall measure.

Another way to think about the difference between aggregated and structural measures is to see them as applying to two different system levels. Properly speaking, income applies to families, and the use of median income to characterize a city involves all the problems of skewed distributions. The distribution problems can sometimes be corrected, if by nothing more than a measure of variability, such as our affluency ratio attempted. But what cannot be corrected in the nature of the case is the fact that aggregated measures do not tap directly the state of the city as a social system. Only structural measures do that. However, this conceptual difference may only make a real difference depending upon researchers' theoretical interests. If an investigator attempts to explain why median income or some other such measure moves up or down, then he should certainly use that measure. But what happens in practice is that sociologists employ social theory designed for whole systems even when they are using aggregated measures. A fundamental problem of these differences is the theoretical linkage between systemic and subunit characteristics. Just how does institutional differentiation affect component subunits in a community?

Now it may be that an explanation of institutional differentiation, for example, can be extended to become an explanation of the shift in average income, but that is not obvious on the face of it. An initial problem is the lack of correlation, at least in the analysis presented here, of the structural and aggregative indicators. Even the assumption of isomorphism between levels of structural differentiation in a city and average level of families, as indicated perhaps by median income, involves many hidden differentiations. A more complicated linkage which predicts a decrease in median income with an increase in institutional differentiaton, as suggested by the ghetto generalization previously made, becomes a major enterprise.

Somewhere between the typical aggregated measure and the purely structural measure are measures such as the proportion of the labor force in service occupations. These may be labeled "quasi-structural." Here individuals are divided according to the type of place in which they work. In principle, indices of this sort should reflect their intermediate character. But the use of these measures with respect to cities and towns has important technical deficiencies. When the community is the unit of analysis, people may work in other communities, hence the characterization of industrial type may be misplaced. One can imagine that all employees of a typewriter manufacturing plant live in small communities some distance away and the town in which the factor is located is reported as completely service-oriented, because only the employees of local retail stores live there.

Another problem is that all white collar workers of the plant may live in a suburb, but because they are workers in a factory, they would be classified as manufacturing. Yet such a suburb would almost certainly have a different character from that in which the actual workmen lived. These problems are probably reduced as the size of community increases because, comparatively, workers are less likely to live outside its boundaries. On the other hand, since the trend toward suburbanization is so strong, measures such as these will be less and less relevant to certain areas.[4] It is hoped such "coding" errors are not systematic, hence only reduce the size of correlations rather than produce wholly spurious correlations because of uncontrolled conditions in data collection. Only closer control over data collection procedures can correct this source of error.

### Direct Versus Indirect Measures

Although little work has been done on the problem, it is generally acknowledged that some measures are more directly relevant to certain concepts than others. For example, the scale of institutional differentiation would appear to be a straightforward embodiment of the idea of division of labor between social organizations. In contrast, median income is much less directly related to a concept of increasing family well-being. Even if the emphasis is placed on consumption patterns, it does not necessarily follow that people spend their money on the same things. For instance, fluctuations in prices

[4] Allan Feldt's work (9, pp. 617–36) to establish boundaries for "community closure" to make units of analysis more comparable may move to resolve some of these final issues. But, his assumptions should be kept to a minimum or comparability may mean similarity.

stand between income and consumption, and thus there is always a degree of indirectness in using this measure. Another example of indirect measurement is the use of population size to stand for structural complexity. Clearly, some intervening organization of individuals, involving the assumption that a large number of people in a given place forces a diversity of roles, is built into this usage. Even if this is true, it is easy to imagine other outcomes of larger population, such as the segmentation of institutions. The multiplicity of drugstores and gas stations are standard examples. So the indirect method of measurement may lead one astray by overlooking potential intervening variables in the linkage of concepts to measures.

## Systemic Versus Sectoral Measures

The two Guttman scales used in the empirical analysis differ with respect to their generality. One tends to be a more systemic measure because its elements are taken from various institutions in a community, whereas the scale of medical specialties is obviously sectoral, that is, institutionally delimited. Similarly, the proportion of the labor force who are managers, officials, or proprietors is systemic in contrast to the proportion of the labor force in manufacturing. The systemic character of measures is of course always a matter of degree, but it is particularly important in development studies because of the inveterate tendency of investigators to distinguish things that are economic as opposed to those that are social. The presence of such a distinction usually signals the investigator's belief that economic changes are more worthy of explanation or that economic factors are more basic than are social variables. Not infrequently both assumptions are made.

Again we see that what begins as a methodological distinction rapidly merges with theory. We are prompted to ask whether a theory of social systems or a theory of institutional sectors is the proper goal. Although there is much talk in sociology about social systems, a careful scrutiny of variables in use suggests that a sectoral perspective is still dominant. Institutional categories, from a single sector, usually economic or political, may be used outright, or it turns out that the social system divides itself up into these sectors. It is the unconventional study which talks about social systems in terms of systemic dimensions over and above institutional categories.

## Operational Versus Conceptual Priority

Measures of development differ radically with respect to their operational or conceptual status. Some measures—and again population size and median income stand out—seem to fight conceptual interpretation. They are real in their own right, and there is great reluctance among otherwise well-trained social scientists to interpret them in the same way as, say, scores based on TAT stories.

When the concept and the operation are identical, however, suspicion is in order, because it is doubtful whether the theoretical homework has been done. Moreover, the demand on the part of social scientists for conceptual underpinnings of indicators is quite variable. It is less likely to be made by sociologists who were trained before World War II, because they came up through a period of intense empirical concern. Similarly, the applied worker is naturally less likely to be concerned about theoretical status. But beyond these dimensions of training there seems to operate a widespread acceptance of a kind of conventional wisdom that something like median income should not be questioned, whereas a scale of institutional differentiation must be theoretically defended. But if a theoretical justification is required of one variable, it should be required of all. At the very least, investigators should be aware when they attribute more importance to some measures than to others. The fact that certain measures are widely used does not constitute a theoretical justification.

## Local Versus Cross-Cultural Validity

Whether a measure is potentially applicable to cross-cultural situations is usually a matter of the abstraction of its supporting concept. The idea of institutional differentiation may be susceptible to abstraction so that communities anywhere in the world can be so rated. Obviously, the concept must be defined in such a way that any institutional pattern is potentially acceptable, and thus the emphasis is put on the diversity of whatever publicly organized structures exist.

Again, measures like population or income are difficult to place with respect to cross-cultural applicability because, although they have an apparent abstract quality, they are empirically intractable when one attempts to use them in different cultural situations. Is it, for instance, legitimate to think of individuals as equivalent whether they reside in an industrial or an agrarian society? The population size of Asian cities almost certainly means something different from that of European cities. The problem of equating income across national boundaries is even better known.

It is not required, of course, that investigators working in the United States use variables that are always applicable in foreign situations. But there are advantages in so doing. Comparative studies could be facilitated, and the results of analyses done in other countries would become relevant evidence in the solution of problems in the United States. But a more fundamental reason for using cross-culturally valid measures is that investigators are forced to abstract, forced to distinguish the generic from the particular. The analysis of domestic problems is thereby deepened.

## A STRATEGY FOR SOCIOLOGICAL STUDIES OF DEVELOPMENT

Given the foregoing review of measures, their empirical relationship for one sample of communities, and our analysis of what appear to be underlying methodological issues in the use of these measures, is it possible to define a clear line of attack for sociological studies of development? We answer with a cautious yes. Stated briefly and imperatively, such a course may be summarized as follows: choose a clearly delineated sample of units which constitute a stable system level. Establish a routine of data collection so that variables can be constructed at several points in time. Place special emphasis on structural variables, but include as many variables of development on which there is information. Compute measures of change over time and attempt to develop a time series as quickly as possible. Concentrate efforts at explanation on the structural dimensions, but attempt to take the other measures into account.

We arrive at this strategy by a number of routes. First, we are impressed by the relative simplicity and potential of the structural complexity dimension. The measures are easy to construct, they tap the system as a structure and they do so with broad coverage. They are direct, they are potentially usable on a cross-cultural basis, and they are theoretically relevant without being incomprehensible to applied social scientists. The question of theoretical relevance must be stressed because this chapter has deliberately side-stepped the great wealth of theoretical interpretations that could be supplied for what we have called simply structural complexity. Clearly this variable— whether viewed as a factor from factor analysis, or a Guttman scale, or some other ad hoc index—locks into a tradition as old as sociology itself. Insofar as sociology is concerned with the dynamics encompassing social organizations, it is surprising that sociologists seldom use aspects of organizations in building indices of their measures. On these bases it may not be too much to say that those variables fitting into the structural complexity factor are *the* sociological variables of development.

We are also led to emphasize structural complexity because of its contrast with most other measures reviewed above, particularly those based on census information. Almost all the relationships, especially the occasional negative associations, with the aggregated measures are striking and challenging. The divergence calls out for explanation and it would be a mistake to omit such measures from subsequent analysis. On the other hand, the independent status of structural complexity provides a vantage point, a new platform to be seized and exploited.

The proposed strategy enjoys study of a definite sample and computation of changes over time as an antidote to the vast amount of talk, otherwise known as theory-building, that is so unrelated to anything operational as to verge on the irresponsible. We are not suggesting that conceptual work stop. On the contrary, there is a pressing need for theoretical interpretations, for organized and abstracted statements that go beyond the neologisms, the vague insights and the warmed over generalizations that are continually reissued in the fancy dress of jargon. On the other hand, we do not consider it philistine to suggest that theorists attempt to explain phenomena that we may reasonably believe exist. The most abstract theoretical work in physics and chemistry typically begins with and returns to particular experiments or observations. There is no reason why social theory should not do so too.

A final consideration that leads to a concern with the comparative study of structural change in a readily managed sample is the realization that such a strategy could be reduplicated in different places and for different samples almost without limit. The communities of every state could be systematically monitored, and the possibilities for comparative study of counties, townships, and kindred units are equally attractive. It has often been remarked that a discipline surges ahead when it hits upon a feasible and heuristic paradigm of work. The rat experiment, the sociometric test, the standardization of techniques for studying social stratification, and, of course, the study of innovations in agricultural practices are well known. In all cases they mobilize energy, they release imagination, and they illuminate the empirical world. The comparative study of communities is similar to these work styles because it is easily organized into basic data and social accounting units, and these have almost immediate payoff.

## REFERENCES

1. Almond, Gabriel A., and Coleman, James A., eds. *The Politics of Developing Areas.* Princeton, N.J.: Princeton University Press, 1960.
2. Clark, Colin. *The Conditions of Economic Progress.* London: Macmillan, 1940.
3. Cutright, Phillip. "National Political Development: Its Measurement and Social Correlates." In *Politics and Social Life,* edited by Nelson W. Polsby, Robert A. Dentler, and Paul A. Smith. Boston: Houghton Mifflin Co., 1963.
4. Deutsch, Karl W., and Foltz, William J., eds. *Nation-Building.* New York: Atherton Press, 1963.

5. Duncan, Otis Dudley, and Reiss, Albert J. *Social Characteristics of Urban and Rural Communities, 1950.* New York: John Wiley & Sons, 1956.
6. ———. "Optimum Size of Cities." In *Cities and Society,* edited by Paul K. Hatt and Albert J. Reiss. Glencoe, Ill.: The Free Press, 1957.
7. Durkheim, Emile. *The Division of Labor in Society.* 1903. Reprint. Glencoe, Ill.: The Free Press, 1947.
8. Eisenstadt, S. N. "Initial Institutional Patterns of Political Modernization." In *Political Modernization,* edited by Claude Welch. Belmont, Calif.: Wadsworth Publishing Co., 1967.
9. Feldt, Allan G. "The Metropolitan Area Concept: An Evaluation of the 1950 SMSA's." *Journal of the American Statistical Association.* Vol. 30, 1965.
10. Friedmann, John. *Regional Development Policy: A Case Study of Venezuela.* Cambridge, Mass.: M.I.T. Press, 1966.
11. Goldberg, David. "The Fertility of Two Generation Urbanites." *Population Studies.* Vol. 12, 1959.
12. Hadden, Jeffrey K., and Borgatta, Edgar R. *American Cities: Their Social Characteristics.* Chicago: Rand McNally and Co., 1965.
13. Hawley, Amos H. "Community Power and Urban Renewal Success." *American Journal of Sociology* 68 (January 1963): 422–31. See also "Reply" to Bruce C. Straits. "Community Adoption and Implementation of Urban Renewal." *American Journal of Sociology* 71 (July 1965): 82–84.
14. Janowitz, Morris. *The Military in the Political Development of New Nations.* Chicago: University of Chicago Press, 1964.
15. Lerner, Daniel. *The Passing of Traditional Society.* Glencoe, Ill.: The Free Press, 1958.
16. McClelland, David. *The Achieving Society.* Princeton: Van Nostrand, 1961.
17. Perloff, Harvey S.; Dunn, Edgar S., Jr.; Lampard, Eric E.; and Muth, Richard F. *Regions, Resources and Economic Growth.* Baltimore: Johns Hopkins Press, 1960.
18. Sahlins, Marshall D., and Service, Elman R., eds. *Evolution and Culture* by Thomas G. Harding, et al. Ann Arbor: University of Michigan Press, 1960.
19. Smith, Adam. *An Inquiry into the Nature and Causes of the Wealth of Nations.* London, 1776.
20. Weber, Max. *The Protestant Ethic and the Spirit of Capitalism, 1920.* Reprint. New York: Charles Scribner's Sons, 1958.
21. White, Leslie. *The Science of Culture.* New York: Farrar, Straus and Cudahy, 1949.

# PART TWO
# SOCIOLOGICAL APPROACHES
# TO DOMESTIC DEVELOPMENT:
# IMPLEMENTING DEVELOPMENT

ONE OF THE PURPOSES of sociological theories of development is an input for the design of action strategies for the planning and achievement of development. It is characteristic of developmental change that future states are envisioned and means are selected for the achievement of such future conditions. Variation in both the future states possible and the means for achieving these states results in decision-makers having to select among alternatives, frequently without the benefit of some guiding conceptual framework. When such a framework is available, the problem of designing action strategies is not unlike the problem of stating operational measures for research purposes. In both situations the problem to be resolved involves the identification of empirical phenomena which correspond with the explanatory concepts employed.

The three chapters included in this section deal with the application of aspects of sociological theory to the design of strategies for development. In Chapter 6 Bertram Gross, who has had extensive experience with planning at the federal level, discusses twelve propositions regarding developmental planning derived from his experience. In Chapter 7 Harold Capener and Emory Brown present a general discussion of the characteristics of an applied sociology—the types of concepts and models required and the role of social science practitioners. In Chapter 8 Ronald Powers provides a detailed example of the use of sociological concepts and propositions in designing and initiating a multicounty development program.

## OVERVIEW OF THE CHAPTERS

### Development Strategies of the Federal Government

The chapter by Gross is a discussion of twelve propositions about development strategies at the national level that Gross derives from his intimate experience as a participant-observer within five different federal administrations.

There are two important themes that pervade the Gross discussion. First is the notion that domestic development deals with the transition from an "industrial to the postindustrial service society," the latest in a series of transitions from pastoral to agricultural societies and from agricultural to industrial societies. Second, developmental change, because it is guided or planned change, is concerned with the social power (authority and influence) involved in decision-making and is a form of social conflict, not an alternative to social conflict. It involves conflicts between those who believe in planning and those who do not, and conflict among planners themselves.

The propositions may be seen as summarizing his experience under each administration and presumably reflect both the general problems faced by that administration and the specific problems within the administration with which Gross was associated.

From the Roosevelt administration Gross proposes that strategies of development 1) are a form of social conflict, 2) are selective rather than comprehensive, and 3) in the American system are such that the President is the planner-in-chief. Experiences in the Truman administration suggest that 1) "domestic growth and foreign expansion" (e.g., the Marshall Plan) can be complementary and subsumed under the goal of "growthmanship," and 2) as with the F.D.R. administration segmental planning is more successful than attempts at comprehensive planning. From his experiences in the Eisen-

148

hower administration, which included work in the "preindustrial" countries, Gross derives two propositions: 1) institutions, and the values and beliefs inherent in them, are a crucial item to consider in development planning, and 2) development planning involves risk, so that a prerequisite for such planning is some level of wealth to offset this risk. In the Kennedy administration the problems of sustaining economic growth and managing its concomitant affluence were central. From these problems emerge two propositions: 1) Keynesian planning can be conservative, and 2) in a context of relative affluence "humanistic" goals of development tend to displace narrower economic goals. Finally, experience with the Johnson administration suggests that 1) feedback from some planning implementation may indicate that the planning is wrong and the program should be discontinued, 2) institutional constraints are as important in domestic development as in international development, and 3) planning is very much hindered by the existence of an intelligence gap (e.g., the lack of adequate social indicators).

## Strategies for Implementing Development

The chapter by Capener and Brown presents a number of ideas as background in considering the relationship between theory and strategy. For them strategy refers to a set of consciously planned activities intended to move from one structural state to some preferred state. They assert that development strategies must be more inclusive than any one discipline—in fact, they prefer strategies that are multiple in nature—so that sociological concepts are only one input into strategy design. Frequently the direct application of theory to action is hampered by the tendency for sociological theory to be descriptive rather than prescriptive. Applicability is also hazardous because of the variety of situational contexts that may surround the implementation of a strategy. The result is an urgent need for a "typology of treatment procedures."

Using a recent framework of Etzioni, the implications of sociological theory for action are viewed in the more general perspective of the relationships between societal knowledge and societal decision-makers. Knowledge is considered as an important independent variable in development which is subject to management.

To a great extent the successful application of sociological theory to development strategy is dependent on the role performance of the social science practitioner. The practitioner is likely to be most effective when he 1) works from a viable theoretical framework, 2) is familiar with the relevant body of knowledge, 3) recognizes dependent and independent variables, 4) looks for variables that can be manipulated within the constraints of goals and values held, 5) approaches such manipulation as a form of hypothesis testing, and 6) maintains appropriate objectivity with respect to the results. In summary, theory will be most applicable to action when applied by decision-makers who are well-grounded social scientists.

## Sociological Strategies in a Multicounty Development Program

In Chapter 8 Powers provides a detailed description of the process of operationalizing action strategy from sociological concepts and propositions.

The example used is a state extension service attempt to initiate activities in a multicounty territory designed to "increase total human satisfaction through a fuller use of resources." The program differs from direct-action programs in that the goals focus on the delivery of information to local decision-makers rather than the complete implementation of needed change activities. Broadly, the major components of this program involved organization (of the change agency and of local leaders), information generation (the collection of social indicators), and the delivery of this information. Strategy decisions were made within the following set of assumptions: 1) some form of local involvement was necessary, 2) program activities would be limited to information generation and delivery through the extension service staff, 3) minimal over-

150

lap with existing community development activities was required, and 4) the program territory should closely correspond to the functional economic area concept. Powers provides an overview of the action context and steps taken, a discussion of the models selected to guide program strategy and the criteria used for their selection, and a discussion of the manner in which these models were operationalized.

Two major conceptual frameworks were used to generate strategies: 1) Beal's social action construct,[1] and 2) Loomis's social system typology.[2] From these conceptual frameworks evolved an overall strategy designed to create a new area social system—the initial step being the creation of an area decision-making center operationalized as the area development leadership group.

A major point of the chapter is that the selection of sociological models for strategy-building may be constrained by characteristics of the change agency. Thus, a public agency such as the extension service might not consider a conflict model as an acceptable strategy component.

[1] George M. Beal, **How Does Social Change Occur?** RS-284. Ames: Iowa State University, Cooperative Extension Service, 1958.
[2] Charles P. Loomis, **Social Systems: Essays on Their Persistence and Change.** Princeton, N.J.: Van Nostrand Co., 1960.

# CHAPTER SIX

# LEARNING ABOUT
# PLANNED DEVELOPMENT

## BERTRAM M. GROSS

SOCIOLOGISTS have contributed to two major government documents issued within the last few years. Each of these documents is a classic in its own way. The first was the report of the President's Commission on Law Enforcement (7), which could not have been done without the most active participation of scores of sociologists. The second is the report of the National Advisory Commission on Civil Disorders (8), a report which will long be regarded as at least equal, if not superior, to the one on law enforcement. But I am afraid that the superiority of both of them will be more attested to by failure to act on them than by any sudden implementation in the near future.

To say something less complimentary about sociologists, I have met some rural sociologists in India with whom I associate the tragic failure of community development in that country. If I were pressed to indicate whether it was the ridiculous economic analysis of the reasons for underdevelopment in India, or the irrelevancy of the com-

I am indebted to Lambert Wenner for valuable assistance in editing this manuscript.

BERTRAM M. GROSS is Professor of Political Science and Director, Center for Urban Studies at Wayne State University. His wide academic and government experience has included serving as Executive Secretary for the Council of Economic Advisors to the President, 1946–1952, serving as a consultant on "social indicators" to the Secretary and Undersecretary of Health, Education and Welfare since 1966, and Director of the National Planning Studies Program, Maxwell Graduate School, Syracuse University. Recent publications include: **The State of the Nation: Social Systems Accounting** (London: Tavistock Publications, 1966; also included as Chapter 3 in Raymond A. Bauer, editor, **Social Indicators**, Cambridge: M.I.T. Press, 1966), editor of **Social Goals and Indicators for American Society (The Annals** 2 [May and September, 1967] Philadelphia: The American Academy of Political and Social Science), and editor, **A Great Society?** (New York: Basic Books, 1968).

munity development program for problems of agricultural growth, I really would have great difficulty in deciding which school most deserved the dunce's cap.

Perhaps you can tell from my language that I am not a true academician. In fact, as one who has been fully committed to the academic world only about ten or eleven years, I have come to report in quasi-academic terms on my own experiences as a participant observer in development planning over the last thirty years in federal housing, in wartime price control, in the Congress, in the Executive Office of the President, in local and regional planning in the United States, and in all sorts of places abroad. I like the participant observer approach. It is a technique that has been used by some of our best sociologists in studying small-scale institutions. When you talk about the big world of government and major efforts to guide social change, you must remember, of course, that there are many nonobserving participants (which, I am afraid, is the way I started out). There are also nonparticipating observers, which I am afraid is exactly what I am at the moment.

Now I shall smuggle into this presentation three additional concepts. One is social system transformation. The specific system model which I am using is developed in *The State of the Nation*. It also appears in the volume, *Social Indicators*. (1) This volume has become the bible of the new program to establish better social indicators in the federal government and to set up a Council of Social Advisors that would at least rival in importance the Council of Economic Advisors to the President and, perhaps, encompass its activities. However, the specific application of the social system model I have outlined and which is inherent in my chapter is one based on the historical process of change from pastoral to agricultural societies, from agricultural to industrialized societies and from the industrial to the postindustrial service society which, with great pain and agony, is now unfolding. Second, I shall also be talking in terms of power (or influence). When we refer to guided change or induced change, we are talking about strategies and tactics of people with power. You will find this unpleasant, although somewhat realistic, note introduced into the book as I write of the uses of power (or influence). Third, I shall refer to that strange and sometimes terrifying political institution called the United States Presidency. Since I do not believe in analyzing problems in terms of roles alone, but also of actors, I shall find myself referring to Presidents. In fact, I shall give you my report as a participant observer in guided development by trying to summarize some of the things I have learned on the firing line under five Presidents of the United States.

If I present twelve propositions concerning guided development that represent my own process of learning a little about life, I must add that for everything I learned I had to pay the price in at least a dozen errors. So, I shall be presenting a dozen propositions against the background of a gross of errors. I do not quite know how to estimate the things I have failed to learn, but will leave that to the reader. With new developments in medical technology, we all have many decades ahead of us, so I am less concerned with that and much more interested in the kinds of errors and kinds of learning you and I have ahead of us during the next thirty years.

## UNDER F.D.R.

### Planned Development a Form of Conflict

I first went to Washington thirty years ago when Franklin D. Roosevelt was still Dr. "New Deal," before he became Dr. "Win-the-War." Under Roosevelt the first thing I learned was that planned development is a form of social conflict, not an alternative to social conflict. It is a form of structured social conflict, of conducting campaigns against obstacles.

Somewhat later, when Poland was invaded, when the war clouds formed and we started to mobilize for the war, we went into our only seriously centralized economic planning period in United States history. Then I learned that the conflict was not only between the planners and those groups that opposed a program for planned change but one of conflicts among contending planners as well. Any who were in Washington in the days of the War Production Board and the Office of Price Administration and other wartime agencies will remember that planning was not the delightfully rational exercise that some of our decision theorists think or pretend it is. It was a very vigorous form of intragovernmental competition. All forms of this competitive planning, as I saw it in the peacetime of Roosevelt's first terms, or later during the wartime mobilization, were accompanied by what one would expect in any form of conflict, namely, strategies of bluff and deception.

It was at that time I learned that when you are presenting a good program (such as those I was involved in), you must always underestimate the outlay costs and overestimate the social benefits that will come. It is no criticism of the recent report on civil disorders that the authors of it (who were able to join unanimously on a policy of Negro-White integration together with enrichment of life in the ghetto areas, which is nonintegration) found their unanimity easier to support by merely referring to the fact that unprecedented funds would be required and avoided giving a single estimate as to what the costs would be.

## Strategic Planning Selective, Not Comprehensive

I learned something then which I have had to relearn in every period since: that strategic planning is always selective and can never be comprehensive. I must say that in many periods of my life, particularly when I was with the President's Council of Economic Advisors, I had lost track of this because we became interested in a comprehensive informational framework for the selection of strategic objectives. Now Franklin D. Roosevelt had some idea of what the Axis Powers were doing around the world, as provided to him by his Allied intelligence forces. But the strategy of winning World War II was the strategy of deciding neither to fight in the Pacific first nor to start the second front in France first, but to start strategically from Africa through Sicily to the Italian "soft underbelly" of Europe and then over the channel. This represented a set of global strategic decisions which were indispensable in preventing an overextension of the conflict that would have meant an even greater death of people throughout the world than there was. It meant saying "No, No, No" to General MacArthur and others who thought that the extension of American power in the Pacific was the first consideration, if not at least equal to the war in Europe.

This lesson, I might add, I learned again more recently while visiting underdeveloped countries. I found out that one could make a broad list of all the nice changes he would like to have, but the longer the list of genuine action programs, the less the possibility of breaking through at any single point. One of the most impressive formulations of the strategy of selective courses of development has been presented by Albert Hirschman in his two books, *The Strategy of Economic Development* and *Journeys toward Progress* (4, 5), both based upon the selective rather than the so-called balanced theory of economic development.

### The President as Planner-in-Chief

I have learned that in the American system the planner-in-chief is the President of the United States. Of course, the President is many men and the Presidency is in part institutionalized. But nevertheless the strategic initiative of the President has put him, perhaps for long before Roosevelt but unquestionably since Roosevelt, into the position of being the economic planner, the social planner, and the international planner.

This proposition—that the President is the planner-in-chief—was written into the Employment Act of 1946 (and I am very proud of the part I played in it). The President is to submit his annual program for "maximum employment, production, and purchasing power" to the Congress for whatever legislative action is needed, while the President himself may proceed with the equally arduous task of getting the governmental bureaucracy to do the things that he has the legal authority to tell them to do. The Employment Act was conceived and introduced by a bipartisan group. While Roosevelt was still alive the measure was gaining support and it was enacted during the first year of the Truman administration. I then had the good fortune to move from the senate committee working on it to the Executive Office of the President and became the first Executive Secretary of the Council of Economic Advisors.

## UNDER TRUMAN

As I review my experience during the Truman term I find two propositions to report on. The first is subject to considerable misinterpretation; I shall just plow ahead and let the sparks fly. Mr. Truman was saddled with a remarkably difficult problem. How would anyone like to try to fill F.D.R.'s shoes? He felt inadequate; he knew he did not have the support of the country. The problems abroad were fantastic; the domestic problems were extremely difficult. The advice he obtained from everybody, including my associates and me, was based upon the self-defeating prophecy (which was very successful) that there would be mass unemployment soon after the end of the war. By riding that self-defeating prophecy for all it was worth we made some contribution to developing a situation in which the big problem we had after the war was a serious inflation instead.

The Fair Deal developed as the domestic counterpart of the Truman foreign policy as expressed, first of all, in the Greek-Turkish aid program, subsequently in the Marshall Plan, and by giving the United Nations a political home in the United States. Some of this was possible through the good graces of Joseph Stalin, who may have been convinced that the American system was bound to collapse but certainly did everything anyone could have asked to conduct the affairs of the state of Russia in a way that would help us survive the test of postwar demobilization.

### Domestic Growth and Foreign Expansion Mutually Supporting

The first proposition I learned at that time was that domestic growth and foreign expansion may be mutually supporting developmental goals. In fact, I do not see how there would have been support in the United States for either the Greek-Turkish intervention or the Marshall Plan if the man from Independence, Missouri, had not also been the sponsor and author of the Fair Deal proposals which guaranteed him liberal (and even some measure of left-wing) support at the same time the right wing was pacified by his emerging foreign policy during the cold-war period. Growthmanship, economic growth as measured in GNP, either aggregate or per capita, was then developed as a major objective of national policy, for the first time in the Western world, by the Council of Economic Advisors. It was subsequently adopted first by the French, and then by other countries of Europe.

This growthmanship was oriented equally toward the initiation of a long series of domestic reforms, some of which have not yet been carried out, and the re-expansion of our military might in America and around the world. This theme has been subsequently developed by Professor Kuznets of Harvard University in his essays on economic growth, in which he extends this proposition as he reviews the entire nineteenth century and first half of the twentieth. He suggests that in the case of any large country, rapid economic growth has always been associated with foreign expansionism. (6, pp. 49, 51)

### Segmental Planning the Most Successful

The second proposition I learned during the Truman period is that segmental, specialized, confined planning in one area is usually much more successful than a plan for the coordination of a multitude of segmental developmental plans. It was at this time that I began my work as a planning commissioner across the Potomac River in Arlington, Virginia. Our planning commission had a so-called comprehensive plan for urban development. But the builders in the area had some very selective segmental plans for building high-rise apartments and for letting other people come in to foot the bill for the public services and transportation that would be necessary when that population came in. The builders succeeded. As a colleague on the planning commission told me when we were voting on a general land-use plan, "The real planning, Mr. Gross, is done where the money is. It's not here."

Actually this principle had been used by our Council of Economic Advisors itself in our planning at the national level. We conceived at that time of economic growth as something very, very comprehensive; nothing could be broader. In retrospect, I can think of few things narrower. One of the reasons we succeeded with the development of economic growth as a fundamental part of policy is that we did not pay much attention to the social aspects and social costs of growth. Our fiscal policies that were oriented toward the enlargement of the GNP turned out to be extremely segmental, leaving out of consideration all the problems of relative deprivation magnified by nonredistributing economic growth.

## UNDER EISENHOWER

During the Eisenhower administration (I shall try to make this a nonpartisan report), I had many opportunities to live and work in preindustrial countries embarking on ambitious developmental plans. In fact, at various times I found myself being labeled a foreign expert.

### Institutions and Values as Factors in Planned Development

It was under those conditions that I first found out that institutions, and the values and beliefs congealed in institutions, tend to become the most critical factors in guided development. The corollary of that proposition, by the way, is that technical aid and financial aid are a hopeless waste unless the recipients have the institutional capacity and the value and belief systems that allow them to use it and that they then know what to do with it. During this period I found that the most critical form of investment in development in preindustrial and presumably in industrializing countries is investment in the readjustment of old institutions or in the development of new ones.

Only much more recently have I learned that what I had thought was relevant only to the preindustrial societies may also be just as relevant to us.

I take as my text some of the findings of the report of the National Advisory Commission on Civil Disorders. The members of the commission ask themselves the question, "What has been the reaction in American cities and in Washington to the problems that have fired up in such a horrible form in the summer of 1967?" They report as follows: "Little basic change in the conditions underlying the outbreak of disorder has taken place. Actions to ameliorate Negro grievances have been limited and sporadic. With but few exceptions they have not significantly reduced tensions." I would add my suspicion that some of the efforts to reduce tensions, such as the previous civil rights laws and other ambitiously announced programs, have increased tensions by raising aspirations and expectations that will in practice be frustrated. The most significant reaction is the overreaction of preparations for the escalation of violence. In several cities—and you have read this in your papers, of course—the principal official response has been to equip the police with more sophisticated weapons. In several cities increasing polarization is evident with continuing breakdown of interracial communications and growth of white segregationist or black separatist groups. I mention this because it would be rather difficult to make a list of the three or four substantive development problems in the United States of America, and to keep off that list the question of urban development and redevelopment in the Negro ghettoes of our major American cities.

## "Start Planning by Being Wealthy"

Often in this strange capacity of being a foreign expert who came to various countries with a halo around his head—a halo based on the size of our per capita GNP—I learned that the secret of successful planning is to be born wealthy. This enables you to take greater risks without risking anything. And that, of course, is one of the principles of our free, competitive, private enterprise system. We can easily risk losing part of our tremendous heritage of the rich natural resources we found on this continent. We can easily risk losing some of our tax revenue. But frankly the opportunity to risk these things is much greater if you are born wealthy—and the risk by that token is much smaller.

Even in the so-called poor countries, there are differences of this type. I have a doctoral candidate who is preparing a remarkably perceptive participant observer analysis of the growth of CORDI-PLA (the Office of Central Planning and Coordination) in the Office of the President of Venezuela. Of all the countries of Latin America there is none other that has succeeded in establishing a serious or long-range economic and social development agency that could survive for two or three years in the very difficult Latin American atmosphere. But the Venezuelans have done it. So I ask myself, "Are they just smarter than the Chilians or the Mexicans or the Brazilians or the Argentinians or the Bolivians?" Are they just smarter? The answer is no! They have oil! They are selling it at a good price. They have money to spend. They can hire the experts. They can give them a good life. They can take great risks the other countries cannot take. Among the poor, they are the wealthy. The law of compound interest, I might say, has never been known to favor the poor.

## UNDER KENNEDY

Somehow or other the advantage of being born White or wealthy —but particularly both—brings me to the Kennedy period. I had turned into a professor by the time the professors came to Washington under Kennedy. I knew enough of them to know that in trying to carry out the Employment Act and to develop a policy of growth and significant economic and social development, the economic and social advisors of John F. Kennedy had great problems. It was not until more than two years after he was in office that he was willing to desert the conservative pre-Keynesian economics approach to the national budget and to fiscal policy. He finally did this when he made his first proposals, enthusiastically implemented by Lyndon Johnson, for tax cuts which succeeded in reinflating purchasing power and, along with some other things, helped put us on the continuous upward swing from that period until the present day.

## Keynesian Planning Can Be Conservative

It was then that I learned that Keynesian planning can be conservative. We now have two schools of Keynesianism. Conservative Keynesianism concentrates upon tax cuts which inflate the power of consumers to buy more automobiles, television sets, whisky, and similar marketplace goodies. The more progressive Keynesianism, advocated by both John K. Galbraith and Leon Keyserling, aims at achieving the same impact upon the economy and the same level of deficit financing through upping expenditures instead of reducing taxes. This distinction is tremendously important, but not so much with respect to specific fiscal policies. It is important because it illustrates the fact that people develop certain symbols of progress and, let us say, that the liberals in America thought of Keynes as a symbol of progress, whereas the conservatives thought of him as a bugaboo who married a Russian ballet dancer and whose ideas would lead us to fiscal ruin.

Well, both of these symbols are irrelevant today. The Chamber of Commerce and the National Association of Manufacturers are both led by conservative Keynesians. In fact, to be a little more specific, one of the reasons that Eisenhower and Humphrey, in the Department of the Treasury, were able to oppose deficit financing and Keynesian policy so much in their public statements is that they knew very well from the technical estimates that were provided them that they could rely upon the built-in operations of the existing tax laws to give them a whopping big Keynesian deficit during the Eisenhower administration—the biggest peacetime deficit up to that time. The point here is not fiscal policy; the point here rather is that the symbols that were relevant and that may have been significant to us in the 50s may have been irrelevant in the first half of the 60s, garbage in the last half of the 60s, and have no conceivable relationship to anything we can think about for the 1970s.

## Humanistic Development Goals

Under Kennedy, we (I say "we" because a group of my colleagues and I at Syracuse gave some serious thought to this) learned that in an age of increasing affluence, when everybody is touched somehow by the culture of affluence, the aims of development must become less economic, more social, and more humanistic. It was during the last year or so of the Kennedy period that more and more people around the country began to call for a new politics of affluence, a new set of goals for progress in America which would be much less oriented toward the minimum security ideals of the Bismarckian and Beveridge welfare states, would be completely disassociated from the recollections of the Great Depression from 1929 to 1939, and would be oriented toward the quality of life.

## UNDER L.B.J.

With the tragic death of President Kennedy and the succession of President Johnson, the concept of quality of life goals became an extremely important and a somewhat new part of American public policy. We conducted an interuniversity and interdepartmental inquiry on the subject at Syracuse University two years ago. We had the active participation of such distinguished scholars as Daniel Bell, Robin Williams, Kenneth Boulding, Peter Drucker, and many others. I am not advertising the resulting book, but I am excusing myself for not talking about the subject. I would like to point out that since the novel, *What Makes Sammy Run?*, this is one of the first books that has a question mark in the title. The title of the book is *A Great Society?* (3)

### Government Plans May Be Wrong

I suppose it was in the most recent years that I realized something about guided change which I knew all along but never wanted to face: namely, that government plans can be wrong. I had always tended to think that, well, a businessman could go wrong but that was a profit-and-loss situation and they "take their chances." But governments, I usually thought, tend to be wiser. Besides, there were always more social scientists around to be advisors to the government. Thus if anything is wrong with a governmental plan, it must be "unfeasibility." It must be just that it could not be implemented.

I shall never forget attending an international seminar on development in the summer of 1964 and having this question brought right to the forefront of discussion by a very great British economist, Peter Wiles, who has specialized in dissecting what he calls "the political economy of Communism." He did it the easy way by picking up one after another of the development plans in Russia and just making a case that they were wrong. They were wrong in Russian terms, wrongly conceived, wrongly executed, wrong from top to bottom.

It was then that I began to look around the world at some of the white elephants in underdeveloped countries, some of the ridiculous forms of wasting national and foreign resources in prestige activities that could only benefit the egos of a few people. It was then that I realized that one of the most important things in development planning in the preindustrial world and even in ours is to know how to stop a bad project. I tried to squirm out of this and say, "Well, the way to stop a project is to adjust it." That means it really was not bad; it was good, but it was not good enough; we could improve it. I have been pushed and pushed on this. I have had my eyes open in Latin America, in Asia, and in some parts of the United States and I have had to admit that sometimes the thing to do is not improve a project, just stop it, liquidate it, cut it out. If there is a building or something like that left standing, let it be there as a monument to man's rationality in stopping things that should not have been started. I would not have wanted to stop the Apollo Program in mid-air, but I do not think that John F. Kennedy would have turned over in his grave if, instead of putting a man on the moon by 1969, we had a few score of unmanned vehicles doing the 5 to 10 years of detailed automated research necessary to lay the basis for safer manned exploration of a later date.

## Institutional Change Difficult in the United States

I might say that with all of the new and fascinating work done at the Bureau of the Budget under the impetus of the "Whiz Kids" (who moved from the Rand Corporation to the office of the previous Secretary of Defense to the Bureau of the Budget to set up the new Planning—Programming—Budgeting System), there has been no reexamination of the costs and the social benefits of the manned moon-shot program and no serious examination of the program to move forward on supersonic civil air transport.

I have learned in these last few years that institutional change and the changes in the values and norms congealed in institutions may be much more difficult in the United States than in India, Korea, Venezuela, Kenya, and Uganda, naming only countries in which I have visited and studied development programs. Ours is a rapidly changing society but everything does not change, and while some things change very rapidly, other parts stay still. In contrast to the fantastic rates of technological change in America, all I can say is that some of our institutions are either standing still or moving rapidly backwards.

## Intelligence Gap Worse than Credibility Gap

My final proposition is the theme of the volumes of *The Annals: Social Goals and Indicators for American Society*. (2, vols. 371, 373) It is this: the so-called credibility gap is a very minor affair compared to the intelligence gap. The credibility gap assumes that the President knows, that he has reliable information which he is manipulating in the interest of the country or his party's political fortune, and that he is not revealing it. The intelligence gap occurs when he does not know. And I must say that all the authors in the various articles in the *Annals,* those dealing with values, crime and social breakdown, health and education, employment, art and culture, were amazed that as they began to develop their thesis they began to learn how horribly ignorant we have been. I am referring not only to those areas that have been seriously neglected in the past, such as information on values, culture, and art. I am also thinking of those areas where long and complex statistical series have been built up over the years. This is true of the misinformation that has continuously been used on crime and delinquency in the country; these are police reports limited to what people have reported to the police. As for information on education, the heads are not even counted properly, as you will find out if you read Wilbur Cohen's article—"Education and Learning"—on the uncounted areas in job training, on-the-job education, adult education, etc. (2) The situation is particularly criminal in the field of employment, an area where the economists have pretended to do the job well, but have rather abysmally failed. I must say that a few passing surveys to indicate what the picture might really be like were made by the Secretary's Office in the Department of Labor. You will find these figures set forth in the "Report of the U.S. Riot Commission." (8) They are rather startling because at the very time when the Council of Economic Advisors and the President's 1967 Economic Report had stated unemployment was going down and the conditions were very, very fine in such areas as Detroit and Newark and others, the truth of the matter is that things were getting much, much worse. There was an intelligence gap at the White House as big as that which was created back in those days (I was there) when Mr. Truman was told by General MacArthur that "those Chinese will never come south."

## FUTURE LEARNING

I have finished my twelve propositions. As I review the things I think I have learned during this period of participant observation in guided development, I am wondering about the future. Among other things, I am wondering what our presidents can learn. I suspect that learning is the first task of a President of the United States because the challenges that face us are rather unprecedented. They call for rather innovative adaptation to new situations.

The problem is also what we can learn. I, for one, would never say that intellectuals and university people and professors are qualified to advise political leaders on public policy just by virtue of their status as producers or packagers of certified knowledge. It seems to me that we all face tremendous challenges in developing our own abilities to understand the nature of change that is going on in the remarkably complex and interrelated world of today.

## REFERENCES

1. Bauer, Raymond A., ed. *Social Indicators.* Cambridge, Mass.: M.I.T. Press, 1966. Published separately as *The State of the Nation: Social Systems Accounting.* London: Tavistock Publications, 1966.
2. Gross, Bertram M., ed. *The Annals: Social Goals and Indicators for American Society.* 1967. Published in consolidated form as *Social Intelligence for America's Future.* Boston: Allyn and Bacon, 1969.
3. ———. *A Great Society?* New York: Basic Books, 1968.
4. Hirschman, Albert. *The Strategy of Economic Development.* New Haven: Yale University Press, 1960.
5. ———. *Journeys toward Progress.* New York. Twentieth Century Fund, 1963.
6. Kuznets, Simon. *Economic Growth and Structure, Selected Essays.* New York: Norton, 1965.
7. President's Commission on Law Enforcement. *The Challenge of Crime in a Free Society.* Washington, D.C.: U.S. Government Printing Office, 1967.
8. *Report of the National Advisory Commission on Civil Disorders.* New York: Bantam Books, 1968.

# CHAPTER SEVEN

# STRATEGIES FOR IMPLEMENTING DEVELOPMENT

## HAROLD R. CAPENER and EMORY J. BROWN

THIS CHAPTER assumes a general societal setting within which to explore strategies for implementing development. Both strategies and development as processes, of necessity, transcend single disciplinary lines, even though as Horowitz (20, pp. 427–28) points out, "customarily each social science discipline has a relative precise model of development." In explicating models and frames of reference we will, for purposes of illustration, draw upon specific examples of strategies and highlight their contextual relevance.

### DEVELOPMENT DEFINED

Development is the process of bringing about change in the societal structure under which institutions and organizations can effec-

Grateful acknowledgment is made of the invaluable bibliographic and editorial assistance of Miss Eleanor Cebotarev, a graduate student in the Department of Agricultural Economics and Rural Sociology at Pennsylvania State University, and Mrs. Jennie Farley, a graduate student in the Department of Rural Sociology at Cornell University.

HAROLD R. CAPENER is Professor and Head, Department of Rural Sociology at Cornell University. He holds the Ph.D. in rural sociology from Cornell University. He has worked with the Punjab Agricultural University in India and is currently involved in research dealing with the organization of multicounty development areas and with water resources development. Publications related to his chapter include: "The Rural People of Developing Countries, Their Attitudes and Levels of Education" (in **Agricultural Sciences for the Developing Nations:** American Association for the Advancement of Science, #76, 1964); **Comprehensive Regional Development** (Cornell Community and Resource Development Series, Bulletin #2, 1966); "Traditionalism and the Development of Human Resources" (**Civilisations,** Vol. XVIII, No. 4, 1968); **Alternative Organizational Models for District Development** (Final report submitted

tively cope with the environment and help bring about the desired values and goals of the members of society. Objectively, development may have a positive or negative connotation. Subjectively, development is thought of in a positive frame of reference and is the handiwork of conscious planned change. Bennis and others (4, pp. 208–11) refer to five categories that developmental models of change should contain. The first is a sense of direction, i.e., goal orientation or movement. The second is an identifiable state, stage, or level of development. The third is an observable form of progression or movement. The fourth is a set of forces or causal factors that produce growth or development. And the fifth is the potentiality or capability for change.

Different objects may be viewed as recipients of development strategy. These may be individuals, groups, organizations, institutions, and/or the society as a whole.

## STRATEGY DEFINED

By strategies is meant a set of consciously planned activities to facilitate the process of moving from one situational state to another within the framework of desired goals and values. Strategies may be aimed at particular levels in society and centered around particular goals and content areas. The goals and content areas are in turn related to other elements of the social system, such as levels of authority, statuses, and roles. Strategies may be planned at various levels, i.e., individuals, collectivities, institutions, and/or the society as a whole.

Planned strategic change thus occurs within spacial boundaries and when individuals or collectivities successfully expand their capacities to exercise controls over their environment they can be said to be developing. Mosca summed up this position when he said: "a nation, a civilization can, literally speaking, be immortal, providing it learns

to the Office of Economic Research for contract #7–35306, U.S. Department of Commerce, June, 1969, with Pierre Clavel and Barclay G. Jones); and **Regional Development: A Report of Project Research Findings** (Cornell Community and Resource Development Series, Bulletin #5, forthcoming in 1970).

**EMORY J. BROWN** is Professor of Rural Sociology and Assistant Director, Cooperative Extension Service at The Pennsylvania State University. He holds the Ph.D. in sociology from Michigan State University. His research has focused on analysis of the effectiveness of extension organizations and programs. Publications related to his chapter include: "Adapting to Resource Development" (**Journal of Cooperative Extension** 4 [Fall, 1966] pp. 169–78) and "The Professional Practitioner Role of Rural Soiologists" (**Rural Sociology** 32 [June, 1967] pp. 204–14).

how to transform itself continually without falling apart." (30, p. 462)

In incremental units, a global conscience about development is under formation. As Horowitz indicates, the developed countries as yet, however, have not achieved the kind of collective conscience needed to fully assist the less fortunate nations. (21, Preface, xi) Slowly, painfully, regions, areas, and nations do become more developed thanks to good strategies and even despite bad ones.

The processes of societal units moving along a continuum from traditional to transitional thence to modern are well documented in the literature. These processes reflect a pathway from relatively primitive, low-key minimum services to a highly developed pattern of modern interdependent services.

It was in relation to these processes of transition from a less complex society, as measured by social differentiation, to a highly complex society that Durkheim (10) referred in his theory of social evolution. Given a rise in population (moral density), a division of labor occurs leading to a higher degree of social differentiation which in turn contributes to the transition of a society from one of mechanistic solidarity to one of organic solidarity.

Auguste Comte (7) saw the development of a society passing through three distinct stages. The first stage addressed to the primitive or traditional society he called the stage of theocracy wherein all the mysteries of the world are explained by the supernatural presence of God. The first stage is eventually replaced by the second. Here the mystical religions give way to a more rational philosophy (metaphysical) whereby man's ability to reason establishes satisfactory explanations. This attempt at reasoning yields to the positivistic stage which is characterized by the wholesale adoption of scientific methods in both the physical and social world. Comte envisioned the physical and social scientists perfecting mechanisms of social engineering to enhance man and his world.

The dichotomy of gemeinschaft and gesellschaft as outlined by Tonnies (43) is descriptive of the quality and character of primary and secondary relationships of different types of societies at different points along a continuum.

One of the most viable contributions of sociological theory to modernization and change is that made by Max Weber. (46) His main contention was that the accumulation of material culture was an insufficient answer. The accumulation of capital was a necessary condition but that, in addition, there had to be a set of psychological variables, a value structure sufficient to create a climate for industrialization and a dynamic work ethic.

Ogburn (33) essentially paralleled Weber's thesis when he noted the disparity in the advancement of materialistic culture which is cumulative and the slow-moving pace of nonmaterial culture which is noncumulative and not readily transferable. This he called cultural lag or delayed modernization.

Other authors of grand strategy in societal development that must be noted for their significant contributions are Vilfredo Pareto (34) and his delineation of the concept of social system, Karl Marx (28) and his thesis of dialectical materialism, Arnold Toynbee (44) on a study of history, and Talcott Parsons's (37, pp. 2–6) general theory of social systems.

In his recent book, Nisbet (32) catches the contemporary significance of the thinking of some of these earlier writers, "Can anyone believe that Tonnies's typology of *Gemeinschaft* and *Gesellschaft*, Weber's vision of *rationalization*, Simmel's image of *metropolis* and Durkheim's perspective of *anomie*, came from logico-empirical analysis as this is understood today? Merely to ask the question is to know the answer. Plainly, these men were not working with finite and ordered problems in front of them. They were not problem-solving at all. Each was, with deep intuition, with profound imaginative grasp, reacting to the world around him, even as does the artist and, also like the artist, objectifying internal and only partly conscious, states of mind."

In reviewing strategies of development, one should not overlook the influence of early economic theorists such as Adam Smith (42), J. M. Keynes (23), and J. A. Schumpeter (39). The functioning of the economic system as a part of the larger social system is one of the crucial variables.

Barbara Ward (45, p. 118) succinctly describes the interplay of social and economic factors in the development of nations. She postulates the intertwining nature of four dynamic revolutions and their effects upon rich nations and poor nations. The first she mentions is the revolution of equality. Here the idea of man's equalness to other men and nations to other nations constituted a viable dream and a driving force for development. Second was the revolution of materialism. The development of material goods and services released man from the cycle of primitive needs and wants and gave impetus to the third revolution of science and technology, saving and capital investment which has propelled the Western nations into a position of unprecedented wealth. The fourth revolution is also one of consequence, namely, the rise of populations. In the Western nations, fortunately, the rise of populations largely paralleled the growing demand for a larger industrial labor force. Unfortunately, the reverse has been true in the developing nations. The forces behind these revolutionary developments were those generally outlined by Weber (46) in his speculation on the conditions related to modernization and the influence of the spirit of capitalism and the Protestant ethic.

## FROM TRADITIONAL TO MODERN

The early development period in the United States reflected the development pathway from local traditional to gradual modern. The early setting, of course, was local and relatively primitive. In such circumstances, the pilgrims looked to the members of their families, to the groups and organizations they formed. Their efforts in this period were largely of a private character. They made planning and development decisions in small group settings, i.e., town meetings.

The locality orientation was born of necessity in a hostile environment where the outer boundaries grudgingly gave way to penetration. Henry Adams (1, p. 1) wrote in 1800: "Even after two centuries of struggle the land was still untamed; forest covered every portion, except here and there a strip of cultivated soil; the minerals lay undisturbed in their rocky beds, and more than two-thirds of the people clung to the seaboard within fifty miles of tidewater, where alone the wants of civilized life could be supplied. . . . even Jefferson, usually a sanguine man, talked of a thousand years before the interior could be thoroughly settled."

Out of the great struggle for independence came a reaffirmation of the philosophy of rugged individualism with free expression in a frontier of wilderness. There was access to trade and commerce with Europe and a transplanted industrial revolution found resources, savings, and investments responsive to development efforts. Through private initiative and a free market economy, the young country grew in its wealth of material and human resources.

Colonial government was seen as an instrument to protect and secure the free enterprise system, not to dominate or unnecessarily intrude. The Jeffersonian philosophy prevailed, namely, that the best governed are those who are the least governed and the best form of government is that which is carried out closest to the people.

This pattern is reflective of an interesting contrast in developing strategies. The United States started with its emphasis on developing its human, material, and economic resources and not until much later emerged with a dominant government. Many of the developing nations located on the traditional end of the modernization scale are having to start with a dominant government with a focus on physical and natural resources and not until later will they emerge with an emphasis on human resources.

The gradual centralization of control mechanisms of parts of the society into the hands of decision- and policy-making units renders the social system more subject to planned development. Certain grand strategies begin to be focused to induce change from a national policy level. While these strategies do not have the name of national five-year plans, such as those formulated by the governments of certain developing countries, nevertheless the overall impact of these directional policies points toward nationally articulated goals and objectives. Examples are civil rights, the low-income audience, putting men on the moon, controlling inflation, renewing worn-out cities, aiding other developing nations, and trying to secure world peace.

## RELATIONSHIP BETWEEN SOCIOLOGY AND DEVELOPMENT

Sociologists have, by tradition, confined themselves to controlled observation and interpretation of what is, rather than of what should be. As Beers points out, "contemporary sociology can be more sure of itself when observing and analyzing than when advising on action or making recommendations." (3, p. 4) The reason for this prudence is well summed up by Gunnar Myrdal, who points out that "a worthwhile theory of development and underdevelopment, if it can ever be formulated, would have to be based on ideas distilled from the broadest empirical knowledge of social change in all its manifold aspects, acquired under the greatest freedom from tradition-bound predilections." (31, p. 235) Despite the fact that we lack such a theory, we still feel that the fruits of sociological research can be applied, with caution and forethought, to implementing development. That sociologists are providing information is illustrated by four recent books on "applied sociology." (16, 24, 40, 48)

The purpose of sociology as a science is to describe and explain the nature of social change in all its manifestations. Theories of social change generally specify conditions which are associated with changes in society or that give rise to changes. While theorists are not primarily concerned with practical benefits or utility, still the validity of the theory must be empirically tested out in propositions.

It is possible, therefore, to identify some of the major variables which each theorist presumes explain some of the variance in the change process. While in many cases these factors or conditions associated with change may not be causative, we can use the ideas as hypotheses in the construction of practice theory for the practitioner.

The practitioner needs not only to select out variables which are predictive but also must identify those which he can control in order to guide change in the desired direction to accomplish proposed goals. We are interested at this point in identifying some of these major variables as perceived by theorists in order to formulate strategies for inducing change. The ideal is to identify the factor or factors which explain most of the variance. If the strategist knows the direction, the rate of change which will occur without intervention, and the sources of these changes, he has considerable knowledge with which to decide strategy for altering the changes in line with his goals.

A complete practice theory, according to Greenwood (17, pp. 78–79), would develop a typology of treatment procedures. What would be needed would be a series of generalizing propositions to describe operationally the stages in the treatment indicating when the treatment is appropriate and specifying the criteria whereby success or failure of the treatment may be determined. Typologies are needed for both diagnostic analysis and treatment. Each type of diagnosis will contain implications for certain kinds of treatment.

## STRUCTURAL FUNCTIONAL THEORIES OF SOCIAL CHANGE

According to Parsons (35, pp. 481–525), structural change occurs after disturbances within the system, or its environment, are sufficient to overcome the forces of equilibrium. As strategies, he suggests an analysis of the vested interest complex in the system and the principal set of forces which support maintenance of equilibrium of the system. The next step would be to impose strain on one or more of these stabilizing forces, thereby creating change. Then there is the need to develop a mechanism for coping with the strain, such as providing new alternative definitions of the situation, enlist allies within the social system itself who are on the side of the change in the desired direction, and also allow for rationalizations which permit people to deny that conflict actually exists. (36)

Boskoff (6, pp. 231–32) indicates that the most sensitive phase in the process of social change is one concerned with innovation and with factors affecting legitimation of these innovations. He suggests the following conditions under which there is a greater probability of innovation: 1) if there is success with pattern maintenance and tension management, 2) if the interaction in the system is diffuse and flexible, 3) if there is two-way communication provided, 4) if control mechanisms are indirect, 5) if individual elites are recruited on criteria of achievement, and 6) if institutional elites are relatively permeable.

## MODERNIZATION THEORIES OF SOCIAL CHANGE

Lerner (25, p. 346) feels economic growth is likely to occur under those conditions where individual efforts are associated with rewards. If this does not occur, then the rising levels of expectations become instead rising levels of frustration which perpetuate the cycle of poverty.

The communication process is a key link between effort and reward. Mass media become the major instrument of social change by socializing traditionally oriented individuals to become modernized. The consequences are new aspirations to the people which may produce frustrations when the expectations are not met. His basic strategy is to develop a moving equilibrium between the new aspirations created by mass media and the possibilities of achievement within a society, merely by manipulating the type and content of mass media. Exposure to mass media ought to be controlled so that enough new desires and aspirations are created to provide the forces needed for a self-sustaining growth without leading to frustrations and dissatisfactions created by unrealistic expectations.

Smelser (41, ch. 5) illustrates the historical appearance of dissatisfaction with industrial production as the beginning of a sequence of structural differentiation of roles. Also, under specific pressures, the family may become inadequate in performing its defined functions. Dissatisfaction then occurs. Gradually new ideas are introduced and accepted and new units of social organization are developed. Dissatisfactions then trigger sequences of differentiation and change.

Differentiation represents a primary process of social change in the view of Eisenstadt. (11, Introduction) It takes place in stages, cycles, or trends. Sources of social change are ecological, demographic, and technological.

The center control mechanisms of society are the crucial ones for converting social change into modernization. The center core must constantly react to changes which means increasing differentiation created by ecological and demographic factors, technological and economic factors, political factors, broad cultural changes, and the creation of organizational subgroups. Conditions for successful modernization, according to Eisenstadt (11), are: 1) strong centers guided by innovating elites who are effective in creating new viable and flexible institutions; 2) structural autonomy of basic institutional spheres which means compartmentalization, which is necessary for the cultural order to develop new symbols for collective identification and legitimation of structural changes and to crystallize new organizational nuclei without disrupting the whole system; and 3) flexibility of social strata to provide opportunity for social mobility.

## CONFLICT THEORY IN SOCIAL CHANGE

Dahrendorf (8, pp. 232–34; 9) has a social conflict model which assumes that social conflict is widely prevalent in society, that every element in society contributes to its change, and that every society rests on constraint of some members by some others. Conflict in groups emerges out of the authority or superordinate relations of groups which prevail within certain units of the social organization. The conflict among interest groups leads to change in the structure of social relations in question through changes in the dominant relationships. Factors which contribute to emergence of interest groups are 1) the possibility of communication among the members of quasi groups so that recruitment is assured; 2) political conditions permitting freedom of organization and coalition; and 3) access to technical resources, that is, the organization must have material resources, a leader, and an ideology. Conditions leading to various forms of conflict are 1) social mobility of individuals or families and 2) presence of effective mechanisms of conflict regulation. Conditions influencing the direction of change are 1) the capacity of rulers to stay in power and 2) the pressure potential of the dominant interest group. Hence, the major idea for strategy, emerging from the conflict model, would be the formation of interest groups which requires effective communication processes, an atmosphere of political freedom to organize, and access to the technical means of resources needed to establish an organization such as material resources, leadership, and ideology.

## THE PRACTITIONER IN DEVELOPMENT

The concepts used by theorists to understand social change should have utility for building a practitioner model. (4, pp. 201–14) We need a bridge to demonstrate how concepts of theory are useful to the practitioner. The theories of social change are cast in generalizations relevant to many cases. The practitioner deals with a specific case, hence, the practitioner reduces from scientific generalization whatever is useful for specific cases. It is suggested that scientific generalizations have most utility in formulating and criticizing, or revising, diagnostic orientation toward specific cases.

## THE INTERVENTIONIST IN DEVELOPMENT

Strategies of development and change assume that man can control or change his environment and that the rate and direction of change can be influenced. Two modes of analysis are identified by Feuer and others. (14, pp. 191–208) One is the interventionist. This is a role where man can intervene in social situations to change conditions, determine directions, and alter trends in social change. The interventionist's model includes laws which permit the strategist to intervene and alter the existing state in order to effect states which otherwise would not have occurred. Thus, ends or goals are achieved which would not ordinarily be expected to happen. Although the core ideas of interventionism may not yet be tested propositions, as long as they are not refuted they can serve as an action guide for the social change agents.

The interventionist's model seeks independent variables which are accessible as entry points for the interventionist. He manipulates these variables to obtain a certain change. It is these accessible variables which we search for in building a strategy model.

The second mode is the necessitarian. This one holds that man cannot change the evolutionary trends of society. It is a fatalistic view that ascribes change only to the hands of providence.

## DEVELOPMENT INSIDE VERSUS OUTSIDE THE SYSTEM

Zurcher and Key (49) describe a comparative strategy for effecting social change among low-income groups. In this analysis a comparison is drawn between the overlap OEO model and the Alinsky model. These two models illustrate two different locations of the change agent. The OEO model attempts to work within the system while the Alinsky model works from outside the system. Other elements in strategy are illustrated by these two models. The Alinsky model fits best in communities where militant direct action gains appeal and receptivity among the active local poor. The OEO model is adapted to communities where poor individuals are rather complacent, hence the strategy model must fit or build upon the culture and social organization of the community. The Alinsky model postulates that planned and open conflict between the poor and some enemies of the nonpoor will build self-esteem and confidence because of their awareness of newly discovered powers. The tactics of Alinsky are opportunistic. The OEO model assumes that self-esteem and confidence will grow among the poor as they expand their social roles by active participation in the OEO organizational complex. In the OEO model the poor people work cooperatively with the nonpoor and the conflict that may result as a by-product is extraneous to the social change process of problem solution. The poor, however, have more to gain by working within the system. Both models build on organization of the poor in neighborhoods.

The Alinsky model has no commitments to the establishment. The OEO model originates from above and attempts to build expertise among participants so they can increase their control and power as they become more expert. It is assumed that the OEO model will result in greater stability and a more permanent social change. The implication of comparing these two strategies is that any change strategy is contingent upon the type of community in which it is being implemented. Also, the strategy depends on whether the social change agent comes from within the system or from without. Another variable is whether strategy is imposed from a higher level or a lower one. It is also evident that the values of the change agent are an influencing factor in choice of strategy.

Adequate knowledge is not yet available to cite with any degree of precision the probable outcomes of given strategies. The responses of client groups or target systems are, of course, greatly varied. Four ways in which societal problems can be approached are identified by Kallen, Miller, and Daniels. (22, p. 235) They point out: 1) efforts can be aimed at alleviating symptoms without getting at basic causes, 2) attempts can be focused on changing the organizational institution which is the source of the problem, 3) efforts can be aimed at a major structural transformation and a set of interdependent systems, and 4) pressures can be increased on the system even though no clear solution is perceived. These patterns arise from different structural situations. Each pattern is associated with change agents from different locations in society.

## TOWARD AN ACTION FRAMEWORK FOR DEVELOPMENT

A recent macro-analytic framework for societal development is that explicated by Etzioni in his book *The Active Society*. (13, pp. 652–54) Etzioni identifies three main variables that are set in a relationship one to another and that comprise the main elements of an active society. These at a simple level are 1) a self-conscious and knowing actor, 2) one or more goals he is committed to realize, and 3) access to levers (or power) that allows resetting of the social code. At the more complex level, the three elements are an active base of societal knowledge, a conscientious level of societal control mechanisms, and a concerned and active societal unit (Figure 7.1).

The explosion of knowledge at the societal level is a phenomenon of great magnitude in terms of potential influence on change and development. The openness and accessibility of certain knowledge both to the masses and to the elites serve to mold and shape opinions and value orientations. The knowledge flow through the mass media not only provides information about the social, economic, and political environments, it tends also to provide a meaning. (13, p. 136) This meaning is internalized and serves as a general guide for the action of the average citizen. The elitist leader is given considerable leeway to act within broad limits of the citizen's norms and interests. Only when the leadership noticeably swerves out of bounds does the active citizen raise objection and it is under these circumstances of significant shift in social change strategies that the elitist must inform the constituency and determine their support before proceeding too far. (13, p. 164)

Knowledge is a powerful source of public influence. It can be used to highlight issues, mold opinions, shape relations, allocate priorities, and commit institutional resources. The relationship to knowledge and its uses is of importance between the knowledge builders (scientists) and the elites. The scientists generally are engaged in building up bodies of knowledge using a model geared to fine toler-

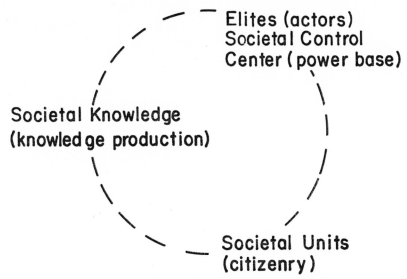

Elites (actors)
Societal Control
Center (power base)

Societal Knowledge
(knowledge production)

Societal Units
(citizenry)

FIG. 7.1. The main elements of an active society.

ance levels of validity and reliability. (The .01 percent and the .05 percent levels serve as the standard.) Much of this science knowledge is not available, known, or seen as being useful to the elitist decision maker. His approach to knowledge is more randomly organized, incremental in character, and, in pragmatic terms, is a mixture of facts and value judgments. (13, p. 137)

The viability of the general model postulated by Etzioni[2] lies in the functional interrelatedness and operational linkage between and among the three sectors. To the extent that information flows can usefully proceed clockwise, the society will be partly engaged (Figure 7.2). To the extent that information flows go in both clockwise and counterclockwise directions, the society is more apt to be fully engaged as an active society (Figure 7.3).

Where breakdowns and blockages occur between and among the linkages, each sector is rendered less effective in roles and functions. The problems arise then of citizens who are either complacent or if active find thin ties or connections through which to channel their participation.

Decision makers not structurally tied to their constituents lack

[2] The authors' interpretation of Etzioni's thesis obtained from a lecture and diagram presented by Professor Etzioni at Cornell University, Ives Hall, May 6, 1968. (13)

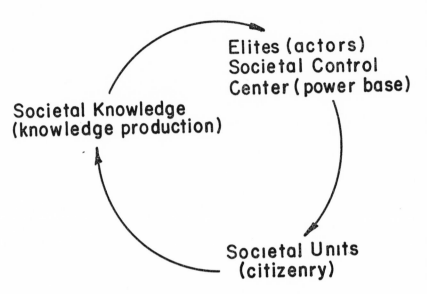

Elites (actors)
Societal Control
Center (power base)

Societal Knowledge
(knowledge production)

Societal Units
(citizenry)

FIG. 7.2.   Clockwise information flows.

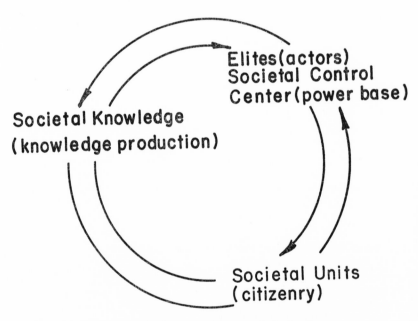

Elites (actors)
Societal Control
Center (power base)

Societal Knowledge
(knowledge production)

Societal Units
(citizenry)

FIG. 7.3.   Clockwise and counterclockwise flows.

sensitivity to reality and acceptance limits. The knowledge production proceeds in isolation without sufficient reference to the environment of which it is a part.

Etzioni (13, pp. 1–16) defines the active society as:

1. One that is master of itself.
2. A society in which the collective individual is aware, committed and potent.
3. The exploration of a society that knows itself, is committed to moving toward a fuller realization of its values, that commands the levers such transformation requires, and is able to set limits on its capacity for self alteration.
4. A society with strong institutions and with viable control mechanisms to achieve consensus.
5. The rise of new groups from out of passivity, the spread of consciousness, the expansion of social options, the growth in membership bound by a contract, and most gradually we shall see a decline in the emphasis on material wealth in favor of increased symbolization.
6. Members who are active can change the societal structure, advance the general will, and, in turn, rely on the changed structure in advancing themselves.
7. In the process of societal activation not only do more people gain a share in the society, therefore reconstituting the structure, but the membership themselves are transformed; they advance along with the society that they are changing. The connecting links are not only between the rising new groups and the establishment but between the leaders of yesterday and tomorrow.

With respect to the traditionally separated roles of the intellectual (scientist) and the activist (practitioner), Etzioni says (13, p. 9), "a study of societies as well as a study of the regulation of scientific endeavor can no longer be treated as an isolated subject or as exploration of detached activities. The intensified effect of the natural and social sciences on society must find a corollary in an intensified study of societal guidance if either science or society is to continue to evolve."

## THE ROLE OF SOCIAL SCIENCE IN DEVELOPMENT

The fact is inescapable that the social science disciplines in general, and sociology in particular, are being pushed onto "center stage" with societal expectations not only for greater understanding of, but for relevant assistance in, the resolution of overburdening societal problems.

The perplexing problem with regard to societal development is that many of the ingredients are available, i.e., knowledge, institutions, leaders, and participants. The dilemma is to put them together in the right combinations. An analogy may be drawn from recently postulated efficiencies gained in agricultural development. Here the concept of a package of tightly integrated practices in the right combinations with the right sequence of timing has produced promising results. Until this integrated strategy was formulated the separated roles of quality seed, appropriate fertilizer, proper cultural practices, and essential credit could not by themselves trigger a breakthrough.

The strategy for societal development calls for a similar right combination of variables with predictable or testable outcomes. Etzioni (13, p. 15) correctly identifies that "man cannot reweave anew the normative fabric of society each morning; institutionalization is both necessary and inevitable. Along with the requisites of structure and norms is the need for purpose, goals, decision making, guidance control mechanisms and participation."

With the new aspirations for the social sciences to contribute to more rational development, there is varied optimism about our ability to alter and change institutional structures in our society. Striking examples of institutional structural changes attempted at the international, national, regional, and local levels are numerous: the NATO Alliance, the United Nations, the Civil Rights Act, the Economic Opportunity Act, the Tennessee Valley Authority, the Appalachian Commission, the consolidation of local school districts, and the integration of housing districts.

Success in effecting meaningful change in these structural areas varies considerably depending upon the complexities of the issues and environments. The knowledge, experience, and skills associated with affecting such change is laden with social, political, and economic implications. The worth of such knowledge, experience, and skills, therefore, is potentially a great source of social power. The appropriate use of such power to guide societal development is the challenge of social scientists.

## THE ROLE OF THE SOCIAL SCIENCE PRACTITIONER

The social science practitioner is likely to be most effective when he is 1) proceeding from a viable theoretical framework, 2) familiar with the relevant body of knowledge, 3) cognizant of dependent and independent variables, 4) searching for the independent variables that may be manipulated to bring about desired change compatible with shared values and goals, 5) aware that his attempts to effect such manipulations constitute experimentation or proposition testing, and 6) maintaining appropriate objectivity with respect to the results. This is the type of role that characterizes a professional scientist practicing or applying the fruits of his discipline.

The social science practitioner is likely to be least effective when 1) he has no conscious theoretical frame of reference, 2) he is unaffected by research-related knowledge and experience, 3) his activities are guided more by habits and gimmicks than by insight and analysis, and 4) the quality of results are measured more by how clients feel than by objective assessment of overall change or development achieved. In this role the social scientist is functioning less like a professional and more like a para-professional.

In this chapter the authors have attempted to illustrate the wide array of theories and frames of reference from which strategies of development can be derived. The professional practitioner has an extensive arsenal of separate strategies from which to choose in implementing development. In social, economic, and political development, as in agricultural development, the single strategy has less viability than well-coordinated and timely multiple strategies. Thus, the benefit can be understood of utilizing the analysis and action components that derive from such theories as social systems (27, 35), social action (2, pp. 233–64), diffusion and adoption (26, 38), reference groups (12), communication (5), conflict (9), tension management (29), policy planning (19), political unity (47, pp. 150–66), social integration (15, pp. 167–88), and national planning (18, pp. 7–20).

Development strategies are yet in formative stages, requiring further codification, testing, and specification of conditions for differential success. Since development is a product of social innovation, the shape of our future lies in our capacities to establish necessary conditions for self-renewal and social renewal; to set societal goals and establish guidance and control mechanisms to achieve them.

## REFERENCES

1. Adams, Henry. *The United States in 1800*. Ithaca, N.Y.: Cornell University Press, 1959.
2. Beal, George M. "Social Action: Instigated Social Change in Larger Social Systems." In *Our Changing Rural Society: Perspectives and Trends*, edited by James H. Copp. Ames: Iowa State University Press, 1964.
3. Beers, Howard W. *Application of Sociology in Development Programs*. New York: The Agricultural Development Council, 1963.
4. Bennis, Warren G., Benne, Kenneth A., and Chin, Robert, eds. *The Planning of Change*. New York: Holt, Rinehart and Winston, 1964.
5. Berlo, David K. *The Process of Communication: An Introduction to Theory and Practice*. New York: Holt, Rinehart and Winston, 1963.
6. Boskoff, Alvin. "Functional Analysis as a Source of Theoretical Repertory and Research Tasks in the Study of Social Change." In *Explorations in Social Change*, edited by George Zollachan and Walter Hirsch. Boston: Houghton Mifflin Co., 1964.

7. Comte, Auguste. *The Founder of Sociology*. Translated by F. S. Marvin New York: John Wiley and Sons, Inc., 1937.
8. Dahrendorf, Ralf. *Class and Class Conflict in Industrial Society*. Stanford, Calif.: Stanford University Press, 1959.
9. ———. "Toward a Theory of Social Conflict." *Conflict Resolution* 2 (June 1958): 170–83.
10. Durkheim, Emile. *Suicide: A Study in Sociology*. Translated by John A. Spaulding and George Simpson. Edited with an introduction by George Simpson. Glencoe, Ill.: The Free Press, 1951.
11. Eisenstadt, S. N. *Comparative Perspectives on Social Change*. Boston: Little, Brown and Co., 1968.
12. ———. "Reference Group Behavior and Social Integration: An Exploratory Study." *American Sociological Review* 19 (April 1954): 175–85.
13. Etzioni, Amitai. *The Active Society: A Theory of Societal and Political Processes*. New York: The Free Press, 1968.
14. Feuer, Lewis S. "Causality in the Social Sciences." In *Cause and Effect*, Hayden colloquium of scientific method and concepts, edited by Daniel Lerner. New York: The Free Press, 1965.
15. Geertz, Clifford. "The Integrative Revolution: Primordial Sentiments and Civil Politics in the New States." In *Political Modernization*, edited by Claude E. Welch, Jr. Belmont, Calif.: Wadsworth Publishing Co., 1967.
16. Gouldner, Alvin W., and Miller, S. M., eds. *Applied Sociology*. New York: The Free Press, 1965.
17. Greenwood, Ernest L. "The Practice of Science and the Science of Practice." In *The Planning of Change*, edited by Warren G. Bennis, Kenneth A. Benne, and Robert Chin. New York: Holt, Rinehart and Winston, 1964.
18. Gross, Bertram M. "The Great Vista: National Planning Research." *Social Sciences Information, International Social Science Council* 4. Paris: Mouton and Co., 1965.
19. Hirschmann, Albert O., and Lindblom, Charles E. "Economic Development, Research and Development, Policy Making: Some Converging Views." Revised version of paper no. P–1982. Santa Monica, Calif.: The Rand Corp., 1960.
20. Horowitz, Irving. "The Search for a Development Ideal: Alternative Models and Their Implications." *Sociological Quarterly* 8 (1967): 427–28.
21. ———. *Three Worlds of Development*. New York: Oxford University Press, 1966.
22. Kallen, David; Miller, Dorothy; and Daniels, Arlene. "Sociology, Social Work and Social Problems." *American Sociologist* 3 (August 1968): 235.
23. Keynes, John Maynard. *Monetary Reform*. New York: Harcourt, Brace and Co., 1924.
24. Lazarsfeld, Paul F., Sewell, William H., and Wilensky, Harold L., eds. *The Uses of Sociology*. New York: Basic Books, 1967.
25. Lerner, Daniel. "Toward a Communication Theory of Modernization: A Set of Considerations." In *Communication in Political Development*, edited by Lucien Pye. Princeton, N.J.: Princeton University Press, 1963.
26. Lionberger, Herbert F. *Adoption of New Ideas and Practices*. Ames: Iowa State University Press, 1960.
27. Loomis, Charles P. *Social Systems*. Princeton, N.J.: D. Van Nostrand Co., 1960.
28. Marx, Karl, and Engels, Frederick. *The Communist Manifesto*, edited by Samuel H. Beer. New York: Appleton-Century-Crofts, 1955.
29. Moore, Wilbert E. *Social Change*. Englewood Cliffs, N.J.: Prentice-Hall, 1963.

30. Mosca, Gaetano. *The Ruling Class.* New York: McGraw-Hill Book Co., 1939.
31. Myrdal, Gunnar. *Value in Social Theory.* New York: Harper, 1958.
32. Nisbet, Robert A. *The Sociological Tradition.* New York: Basic Books, 1966.
33. Ogburn, William F. *Social Change.* New York: The Viking Press, 1950.
34. Pareto, Vifredo. *The Mind and Society,* edited by Arthur Livingston. Translated by Andrew Bongiorno and Arthur Livingston. New York: Harcourt, Brace and Co., 1935.
35. Parsons, Talcott. *The Social System.* Glencoe, Ill.: The Free Press, 1951.
36. Parsons, Talcott; Shils, Edward; and Olds, James. "Values, Motives and Systems of Action." In *Toward a General Theory of Action,* edited by Talcott Parsons and Edward A. Shils. Part II. Cambridge, Mass.: Harvard University Press, 1951.
37. Parsons, Talcott, and Smelser, Neil J. *Economy and Society.* Glencoe, Ill.: The Free Press, 1956.
38. Rogers, Everett M. *Diffusion of Innovations.* New York: The Free Press of Glencoe, 1962.
39. Schumpeter, J. A. *Capitalism, Socialism, and Democracy.* 2nd ed. New York: Harper and Bros., 1947.
40. Shostak, Arthur B., ed. *Sociology in Action.* Homewood, Ill.: The Dorsey Press, 1966.
41. Smelser, Neil. *The Sociology of Economic Life.* Englewood Cliffs, N.J.: Prentice-Hall, 1963.
42. Smith, Adam. *An Inquiry into the Nature and Causes of Wealth of Nations,* edited by Edward Cannan. New York: The Modern Library, 1937.
43. Tonnies, Ferdinand. *Community and Society.* Translated and edited by Charles P. Loomis. East Lansing: Michigan State University Press, 1957.
44. Toynbee, Arnold J. *A Study of History.* Abridgement of volumes 1–6 by D. C. Somervell. New York: Oxford University Press, 1947.
45. Ward, Barbara. *The Rich Nations and the Poor Nations.* New York: W. W. Norton and Co., 1962.
46. Weber, Max. *The Protestant Ethic and the Spirit of Capitalism.* Translated by Talcott Parsons. New York: Charles Scribner's Sons, 1958.
47. Weiner, Myron. "Political Integration and Political Development." In *Political Modernization,* edited by Claude E. Welch, Jr. Belmont, Calif.: Wadsworth Publishing Co., 1967.
48. Zetterberg, Hans. *Social Theory and Social Practice.* New York: The Bedminster Press, 1962.
49. Zurcher, Louis A., and Key, William H. "The Overlap Model: A Comparison of Strategies for Social Change." *Sociological Quarterly* 9 (Winter 1968): 85–96.

# CHAPTER EIGHT

# SOCIOLOGICAL STRATEGIES IN A MULTICOUNTY DEVELOPMENT PROGRAM: A CASE IN SOCIOLOGING

## RONALD C. POWERS

MANY DOMESTIC social and economic development projects and programs could have been chosen to reveal the extent and fidelity with which sociological theories, frames of reference, and/or models are being used by those sociologists faced with problematic development situations which will not wait for further refinements in sociological theory. The type of development effort presented here represents a type of development where neither the ends nor the means are like those in such "direct-action" examples as getting new industry for a town or securing voter registration in the ghetto. The importance of such differences, as well as an attempt to classify them, are discussed later in the chapter.

An extensive literature review of the theories of change and the like would be redundant at this point and would probably generate more heat than light. As others have said during the last decade, sociology has an abundance of theories of change ("noun" theories if

**RONALD C. POWERS** is Professor and Head, Department of Family Environment and Professor of Sociology at Iowa State University. He holds the Ph.D. in rural sociology from Iowa State University. He has served as an extension sociologist at Iowa State University and as Visiting Professor in Community and Resource Development at Colorado State University, University of Arizona, University of Florida, and the University of Saskatchewan. Publications related to his chapter include: **Social Action and Interaction in Program Planning** (Ames: Iowa State University Press, 1966) and "Power Actors and Social Change: Part I and II" (**Journal of Cooperative Extension 5** [Fall and Winter, 1967]).

you please) but few theories of changing ("verb" theories). It is the latter that are particularly needed by the change agent (or alternatively the policy maker, program operator, program developer, and the like). This is particularly true since many of the general theories of change focus on independent variables not accessible to control by the change agent. As an example, the identification of industrialization and/or urbanization as a major variable in bringing about a population explosion is of little practical use or comfort to the change agent attempting to control population growth rates. Etiology, the science of causes, is an important background for an instigator of change, but it is often inadequate to the task of forecasting the means of problem solution. To stress it yet another way, the present state of sociology does not provide the base for training in the science of changing.

The change agent needs models which move his possibilities for effecting his objectives from chance to some predicted probability level. Parenthetically it might be noted that the acceptable probability level is nowhere near that usually required by the researcher investigating relationships between variables. The change agent also needs models which identify variables subject to some degree of control and which will provide cues to a general strategy for his actions re: the target system(s). Moreover, the models most useful to the change agent must be those that can be conceptually coupled with each other to simplify and order the complexities encountered in the problematic situation of social and economic development.

An instigator of change should be a multidisciplinarian and adept at eclecticism. Consequently, while the central concern in this chapter is with sociological models, reference will be made to social psychological and psychological models as well. While discipline "boundary maintenance" may be stimulating to some it is a bore to the applied social scientist and a barrier to useful analysis and strategy development.

The primary objective of this chapter is to present an example of the "sociologing" used in a concrete case of social and economic development initiated by the extension service of Iowa State University. In so doing, I wish to direct particular attention to the following aspects:

1. The basic postulates of the problematic situation in which the effort was initiated.
2. The theoretical frames of reference used to guide the analysis and the selection of strategies.
3. The manner in which the frameworks were operationalized.
4. The data being accumulated to judge the effectiveness of the process.
5. The extent to which the objectives of the change agent and the target system(s) are being achieved.

Thus this chapter will have one of the few public confessions of the sociological models being used in social and economic development and the manner in which they have been used. This should provide the discussants, listeners, and readers alike the opportunity to assess the appropriateness of the choices in the selection of models and to further assess the fidelity with which the models were used by the change agents.

## DIMENSIONS OF DEVELOPMENT

A definition of development—as used in this chapter—may be helpful in evaluating the ends and means chosen by the change agent in the case to be presented. The definition does not attempt to resolve all the arguments that have taken place regarding such terms as progress, program, movement, process, equilibrium, growth, quality of life, human satisfaction, and the like. It is not that these arguments are unimportant, but the applied sociologists (or any social scientist who finds himself in the position of instigating change) find it more important to establish a frame of meaning with the layman than with his academic peers—thus the definition chosen reflects this concern. Moreover, the change-instigating system usually sets the parameters to be included in social and economic development.

The general statement of the development objective which guided our efforts was "to increase total human satisfaction through a fuller use of resources." Though this was without question a platitude, perhaps even the preamble to political slogans such as "the great society" or "the war on poverty," it was a starting point from which to develop a framework which could be used to organize the situational data and establish a convergence of interest and understanding with the target system. The general framework used in Iowa has been the imbalance model seen in Table 8.1.

The objectives of the target system were the correction of the imbalances. The objectives of the change agent (in brief) were to generate and deliver information which allows the target system to assess the magnitude of the problem, assign a priority, and initiate appropriate actions. Implicit is the involvement of the people in the target systems, and therefore the creation of new and appropriate social machinery. To the extent that the actions required to correct the imbalances involve more than one social system (organization, community, county)—this usually means the creation of a new social system to receive, evaluate, and act on the information. The action may be concerted by individuals or subgroups in the development arena.

Implicit in the acceptance of the imbalances in Table 8.1 as a conception of the development objectives is the notion that develop-

TABLE 8.1. Imbalance Model: Imbalances in Structural and Human Resource Use

| IMBALANCES | EXAMPLES |
|---|---|
| I. STRUCTURAL | |
| A. Production | 1. Agriculture—inappropriate labor-to-capital ratios. |
| | 2. Manufacturing—imbalance between job opportunities, types of training, and new entrants to labor force. |
| B. Services | 1. Retail trade—number and location of many retail stores out of balance with number, location, and demand of customers. |
| | 2. Health—number and location of clinics, hospitals, specialists, and senior-citizen housing facilities out of balance with number, location, and health problems of people. |
| C. Institutions | 1. Church—number, location, and program quality of churches not balanced with number, location, and needs of members. |
| | 2. School—number, location, and curriculum not balanced with number, location, and needed training of students. |
| | 3. Government—structure, operation, and location of government facilities lagging behind technology of record keeping, movement of people, and improved transportation and communication. |
| II. HUMAN | |
| A. Skills and abilities | 1. Adults with skills that are in declining occupations. |
| | 2. Young people not being trained for emerging occupational demand structure. |
| B. Attitudes | 1. Tendency to believe that individual and community are helpless in face of changes. |
| | 2. Tendency to resist change without analyzing possible gains. |
| C. Information | 1. Lack of information to make sound individual decisions about resource use. |
| | 2. Lack of information to make sound group decisions about resource use. |

NOTE: Basic source of this framework taken from Eber Eldridge, *Imbalances in Rural America*. Ames, Iowa: Iowa State University, Cooperative Extension Service, Area 2, April, 1963.

ment will need to be operationalized at a level of social organization and complexity beyond the single community center—and for that matter—the single Iowa county.

Since this chapter is to discuss the strategies used in a development effort and to show the sociological models used in those strategies, it seems important to digress for a brief time for a general discussion of strategies and the specifics of the ones used in the case central to this chapter.

## STRATEGIES OF DEVELOPMENT

What one chooses to delineate as strategies of development depends in large part on the position or point of view of the person making the delineation, and, of course, the definition of development assumed. A brief comment is in order about the kinds of strategies available since it is argued here that the strategies available to a change agent within the extension division of a public-supported university, such as Iowa State University, are necessarily different from the choice of strategies by a change agent in a "line agency" supported either by public or private funds. If the ends and the means of the program initiator within an organization such as the extension service of a land-grant university are different from the ends and means of other kinds of change agents, it is likely that this difference will have an impact on the sociological models imported to analyze, design, and implement purposive development. For example, with several implicit assumptions, I would argue that it is highly unlikely that a program developer from a public institution could (or should) use the Saul Alinsky model of social action (rebellion?) in an attempt to aid in the development of an urban area. As a recognition of the basic value system attendant to a land-grant university such as this, however, a strategy approaching his model might be acceptable if the action was directed toward the extension of electricity or telephone lines into remote rural areas.

If one thinks of the means for instigating development (some actual reallocation of resources), the strategy might be a choice or combination of public and private investment. Such strategies are direct action oriented and usually require taxing or fund-raising activity.

Another delineation of strategies would be the choice as to the different levels of society which could or should be involved in instigating change. These levels could range from the local to the national with combinations as a distinct possibility. Moreover the combinations could involve mixtures of both public and private as in the case of various cost-sharing arrangements.

If one views organizations external to the development area being considered, then strategies may also be viewed in the context of hierarchial organization, both public and private, which have rather specific objectives and are usually quite action oriented. Alternatively there are primarily autonomous organizations, both public and private, which have specific objectives and are action oriented as well. Examples of the first would include Farmers Home Administration, Employment Securities Commission, or the American Heart Fund. Examples of the second include industrial development corporations, hospital boards, and city councils.

All these strategies are characterized by direct action with a heavy emphasis on projects. In addition the change agent often comes with problem "answers," i.e., he assumes or attempts to impose the values and attitudes necessary for the project to succeed.

It should be fairly obvious that certain models of social action and social systems are applicable to any of the above approaches—and to that extent the models have a general utility. But the ends and means of the change-instigating system itself do have an impact on the manner in which any of the action or system models used in changing come to be operationalized.

Thus, in the case at hand, one can ask where the extension service of a land-grant university fits in the strategies just outlined. There is a combination of both public and private funds, the levels from which support is drawn include local to national, and there are some "line" aspects to the organization—though the proclamation of autonomy is often heard. Since it is reasonably accurate to describe the university and its extension service as semiautonomous, it can take a posture toward development which is more planning oriented than action oriented and which includes broad as well as specific objectives. Within this context the university's objectives may be quite different from the objectives of the target systems to which it relates in development.

The university development thrust may be based on the generation and delivery of technical coefficients for alternative actions (or inaction) whereas the target system concentrates on a choice of actions (sometimes the first acceptable action rather than a rational consideration of the known alternatives).

Operating with a planning orientation as outlined above is intended to suggest that the concern is with more than action with single objects or social institutions. Planning involves deliberate regulation and intelligent mastery of the relationships between several objects and institutions. The conceived difference that the imposition of the extension service into the social and economic development process makes, might be illustrated by outlining the general steps of development that are in existence in any community or area and then indicating extension's primary role which is derived from the ends and means of the university, including an education and planning orientation along with a policy of nonadvocacy in controversial issue areas.

Though oversimplified, the typical development strategy being used by communities, organizations, and institutions is as follows:

1. Awareness of the need, definition of the situation, and tentative selection of project objectives.
2. Some form of organization—likely committees—and analysis of the situation.
3. Analysis of alternatives until the first acceptable alternative is reached.
4. Gaining of support and participation by the necessary target systems.
5. Completion of action and observation of results.

The variation in these steps may be considerable depending upon the pool of social action skills and knowledge, amount and kind of external expertise brought to bear on the problem, and the like.

The basic assumption behind the choice of strategy used in the case to be presented here was that local people could and should make their own decisions about whether they wished to change toward a situation of balance. Furthermore, the local people were to be the ones to take action, not the university. Thus, the extension service of the university was to provide the necessary information for making decisions, to organize the information-giving processes in such a way that the information could and would have maximum coverage, and to use its knowledge of social action process and organization in assisting the people to organize in an effective manner to receive, evaluate, and, if desired, act on the basis of this information. In short, the university through its extension staff was not to opt for priorities on needs, opt for particular solutions, or to be the prime mover in any projects that might be selected.

Such a posture can and does create tension for the target systems as well as for the program operators within the change-instigating system itself. The objectives of the extension service in this framework are quite intangible. For example, how does one measure the results from an information and educational program presented to 100 people in an area regarding the impact of technology on churches as compared to measuring the results from a fund-raising campaign to build a recreation facility? The connection between information and educational efforts and the correction of imbalances may seem remote to the local staff member as well as to the local leader. Because of this, there is a general tendency for any social machinery that is created (as well as existing groups) to displace such intangible goals as education and information with tangible goals such as brochures, highway signs, and fund raising. (15)

The raising of money for a new industry may be quite appropriate for the achievement of development objectives of local people (for example more jobs, increased per capita income, increased retail trade, and the like), but it was not the primary objective assumed by the social and economic development change agents in the case to be presented.

It should be explicitly pointed out that while I have used the term extension service and have defined the posture of this system to social and economic development in general terms, it would be more nearly correct to label this as the posture of one extension service in its program of social and economic development. This is true because each university and its off-campus component have a history which either supports or rejects the choice of certain strategies of change. Even within a single university's extension service there will be differences in strategies chosen, depending upon the subsystem and on whether its objectives are so universally accepted by the target audience that there is little, if any, concern as to the neutrality and nonadvocacy actions of the change agents.

A lively controversy exists as to whether the university actually makes any contribution to social and economic development by following the practices I have described. Many would argue that you have to get directly involved in the projects per se. The question of whether there is need for a professional "doer" in community development is related but separate from whether a university should be in that role.

I do not mean to imply that the prior mode of operations by an organization prevents it from a "jump-shift" in strategy. To do so, however, requires extreme attention to make the distinction between the old and the new "come through," rather than justifying the new program in terms of an old or existing program. The tendency for lower echelon staff in an organization to justify new efforts on the basis of past efforts has implication for the kind and amount of in-service training necessary when an organization attempts a jump-shift in strategy.

To give empirical content to this and other points, let me give the scenario for the effort I have chosen to present and move to the discussion of the sociological models which were used and the manner in which they were used.

## SCENARIO

Seminars in 1960 and 1961 on the campus at Iowa State University involved representatives from several disciplines in a discussion of how the extension service should attempt to assist in community adjustment to the change caused by rapid adoption of technology in agriculture. A primary result of these seminars was to suggest that a special thrust be given to social and economic development on a large enough geographic (and hence social and economic) base (5) that enough resources would be available to correct some of the major imbalances suggested in Table 8.1. This led to the formation of a core group located at the university to develop the strategy for initiating social and economic development programs which, because of their focus on a geographic area larger than a single county, came to be known as area development.

The core group was made up of sociologists, economists, extension administrators, information specialists, and community-planning specialists. They were charged with the responsibility for initiating extension social and economic development programs on an area basis which would include eight to ten counties, with 60 to 90 towns, and a total population ranging from 80,000 to 175,000. The first area program was initiated in 1961 in southeast central Iowa and has come to be known as TENCO. Key assumptions guiding the formulation of strategy were as follows:

1. Some form of local involvement (an organizational structure) was assumed as necessary.
2. The program was to be confined to the generation and delivery of information.
3. A minimum of extension staff would be used in projects such as getting new industry, recreation facilities, and the like.
4. There was to be no usurpation of roles previously defined for government and private agencies concerned with community development.
5. The organization, generation, and delivery of information were to occur through the hierarchially arranged extension service which included state specialists located at the university, an area development agent assigned to the area, and the several county extension staffs.
6. The delineation of the geographic area was to correspond as closely as possible to the functional economic area concept developed by Fox.

In 1967 there were four multicounty areas in Iowa with social and economic development programs. That is, there was an extension leader for area development in the area, at least an economic base and population study of the area, some organization of local people on an area basis, and some area-wide information and educational activities.

The first area, TENCO, was initiated in 1961; the second, NIAD, was initiated in 1963. MIDCREST, the third area, was initiated in 1965 and the fourth area, centering around Fort Dodge, was initiated in 1966. There are many similarities in the strategies used in these four areas. There are also some very significant differences. These differences grew out of resource constraints, changes in extension personnel, differing philosophies of area extension personnel, and judgments about the effectiveness of strategies used in preceding areas. As is characteristic of programs that are "happening," as opposed to those that have "happened," it is difficult to get an on-the-spot analysis of variance which identifies the critical variables that can be controlled.

It is my intent to use the third geographic area—MIDCREST—as the referent for the rest of this discussion. I believe, but cannot completely demonstrate, that MIDCREST to date has been the most successful in achieving the objectives of the program developers (though this may not be the most effective route to social and economic development). It is also the area in which I was personally most involved and can offer for consideration those unsophisticated things called insights, hunches, hindsights, and/or gut-level theories.

Following the discussion of the models used and the manner of application in the MIDCREST area, I shall discuss the variations from the procedures in the other areas and provide some judgment as to the most effective strategy.

MIDCREST is an eight-county area in southwest central Iowa. Creston, a city of about 7,500, is centrally located, but generally not a fourth order (wholesale) city. Residents in the western half go to the Council Bluffs-Omaha area for specialized items such as medical treatment, discount buying, recreation, and the like. The people in the eastern half go to Des Moines. The total population is about 80,000 and has been declining continuously for more than 20 years. The smallest county—Adams—has less than 8,000 people. About 20 percent of the population is over 65 years of age. The average family income in 1960 was about $5,000. There are only three towns over 2,500 in the area.

Following is a brief chronological listing of events from time of the initiation of the social and economic development effort in MIDCREST until 1967.

MARCH 1964

Three key leaders from the MIDCREST area requested the state extension administration to initiate an area development project in the eight counties.

MAY 1964

The decision was made by extension to initiate an area program. Specialists initiated data collection and analysis for economic base and population studies of the area. It was decided that the extension staff in the area would take a graduate course on economic growth and development. Special sessions on the role and identification of the community power structure were included in the course.

FALL 1964

The graduate course was initiated for all staff in the area. Strategy was developed for initiating the program with area residents.

JANUARY 1965

An area meeting was held with members of the eight county extension councils (a legally elected body) in each county responsible for extension to discuss the concept of social and economic development and the general procedure we expected to use.

County extension staff—using the procedure discussed in the fall of 1964—identified 15 to 23 key leaders in each county.

MARCH 1965

The Extension Sociologist and an Extension Economist met with the key leaders in each county to outline the anticipated extension program in social and economic development for the area. Leaders were asked to attend six two-hour sessions before beginning any planning or identification of problem priorities. They were given the option of participating in the series of meetings or refusing. Every county decided to become involved in this program which later became known as the Seminar Six program.

MAY–SEPTEMBER 1965

The Seminar Six program was carried through to completion with six meetings held in each county. There were a total of 106 participants.

OCTOBER 1965

An area-wide meeting of the Seminar Six participants was held to summarize what had been accomplished. Suggestions for next steps were presented. A proposal was made to form an area-wide organization to be known as the area development leadership group (ADLG).

OCTOBER–DECEMBER 1965

Two or three additional meetings were held by each county group to firm up the identification of problems in their respective counties. The problems were identified in two categories. One set of problems were those which required information and education inputs by the extension service. The second set were those which were subject to direct action by the area residents. Discussion forms using the imbalances listed in Figure 8.1 were used to facilitate problem identification.

JANUARY 1966

The organizational meeting of the ADLG was held. Forty-eight of 106 Seminar Six participants were selected to be members of this group. Only one did not agree to serve.

MARCH 1966

The second meeting of the ADLG was held. They began to move toward assignment of priorities to problems and sorting out those to which extension could make a contribution through information and educational programs. Continued effort was devoted to developing an understanding of the role of extension in social and economic development. An effort was also made to clarify the difference between extension's objectives and the objectives of the area residents.

SEPTEMBER 1966–PRESENT

Periodic meetings of the area development leadership group

have been held. Several area-wide information and education efforts have been initiated, completed, and/or are in process. Included would be a program for local government officials based on a study of local government by staff members at the university, a program for key women leaders in the area to look at the impact of social and economic change on the family, and the initiation of a program for church clergy and lay leaders to assess the impact of change on the church.

MAY 1967

A survey of all the ADLG members to determine the extent to which the objectives of the extension service were being realized, particularly in regard to the creation of the ADLG.

## SOCIOLOGIST'S TASK

Having glimpsed the chronological set of events constituting the major steps in the MIDCREST social and economic development process, I now propose to step back and ask what is the task of the sociologist who enters the "play" at the stage where the geographic area has been determined and the basic posture of the extension service as a change agency has been defined—i.e., it is a *given*.

The general objectives of the development activity being described were organization, information generation, delivery, and insuring the "use" of the information. Sociologists in this situation began "sociologing" by asking the following questions with regard to their repertoire of models, frames of reference, and concepts:

1. What can be used as a framework for the overall process, keeping in mind that the process will involve several levels of social organization in an arbitrarily defined (i.e., quasi) social and economic drainage basin of substantial complexity?
2. What can be used to guide the analysis of the existing and changing situation within the area?
3. What can be used to predict the actions and combinations or sequence of actions potentially most effective in achieving the program's objectives?
4. What can be used to guide the operationalization of each episode of social action to be initiated by the change agency?

## MODELS TO CHOOSE FROM

Beauty, it is said, "is in the eye of the beholder." The utility of a sociological model likely is in the "mind of the user." Thus one of the criteria for selecting models is the extent to which it brings a certain amount of *Verstehen* to the user. Other criteria which are relevant include

1. The extent to which key independent variables are subject to control or accessibility by the change agent.
2. The extent to which the dependent variables are reasonably predictable.
3. The extent to which the model can be adapted to different levels of phenomena.
4. The extent to which the model can be useful for both process and content.
5. The extent to which it is applicable to the problems and processes perceivable by the layman and can be used in communicating with him.

Since the confronting problem was one involving vertically oriented, closed and open, and formal and informal social systems within which it was the intent to instigate social actions, it was reasonable to begin by looking toward the social systems and social action models in sociology. Systems models seemed particularly appropriate since they make the program developer cognizant that 1) the change or treatment of one variable may yield unintended consequences on another part of the system, 2) changes in any one variable may be brought about by indirect actions as well as direct, and 3) there are multiple possibilities of intervention with respect to a single problem.

Social action models provided insight into the arena of action, the actors involved, and the sequence of steps considered necessary to effective action.

An overall criterion for the selection of models in the development concept we were using was to choose models that were close to a "theory of changing" as contrasted to a "theory of change." The latter is often retrospective in orientation as well as concerting on variables not accessible to control of the program developer. For a general discussion supporting the systems models and social action models see Chin (4), Gouldner (6), and McKinney (12).

The primary sociological models chosen for the task of analysis and strategy in the social and economic development in Iowa were those of Beal (2) and Loomis (10). Models from psychology and social psychology were often used in conjunction with the master processes of Loomis's model and in the action steps of Beal's social action construct. For example, Maslow's (11) hierarchy of needs was useful in outlining the strategy for involving individuals in a new social system (the ADLG). Similarly the work of Krech, Crutchfield, and Ballachey (7) on attitude formation and change was particularly useful in outlining the information process. Likewise research from group dynamics was applied in the meetings in the seating of the people and the location of change agents in the group. Thus at the orientation meetings in March of 1965, the sociologists and economists were careful to sit at different sides of a square or round table arrangement rather than both at one "end." Moreover, when the ADLG group began to meet there was a deliberate change in the seating arrangement each time so that interaction would develop between people from different parts of the geographic area.

As suggested before, the effective program developer or change agent is not a pure disciplinarian, but rather a multidisciplinarian, or perhaps more precisely, an effective eclectic.

We approached the overall process through the social action construct (see Figure 8.1). This indicated a need for the analysis of the arena in which we were going to work, that is, the multicounty area and its several subsystems. It also indicated the need to identify the power actors or legitimizers in the area.

To do the analysis of the total arena of action and its subsystems as well as the identification of power actors in the system, it was decided to operationalize the elements and processes in the Loomis system model.

## LOOMIS MODEL AND ITS APPLICATION

Table 8.2 is a brief summary of the PAS (processually articulated structural) model of Loomis. The following material is an attempt to show the manner in which the elements and processes were used in a social reconnaissance of the MIDCREST area, that is, Steps 1 and 4 in the Beal model.

Starting with the conditions:

*Territoriality.* The county lines of MIDCREST defined the territoriality with which we are concerned.

*Time.* There is a tendency to say the time is constant when considering change, but not because it makes a difference at what time the change agent attempts to initiate change. In the area under question, time was an important variable. The fact was significant that some members of the area were aware of the possibilities for social and economic development and had in fact requested it. Looked at from another point of view, however, if one could hypothesize that the seeds of an area social system (that is, area interaction, but not area identification by the people) were present, but not yet germinated, the initiation of area projects too early (before the people understood the area concept for example) could mean that the subsystems (in this case counties and/or towns) would expend additional efforts at boundary maintenance rather than working toward systemic linkage of the systems subordinate to the area.

198

GENERAL SOCIAL SYSTEM

Sub Systems

Prior Social Situation

1  2  3  4  5  6  7  8  9  10  11  12  13  14  15  16  17  18

(SOCIAL SYSTEM BOUNDARY)

Extra system influence

Professional living in system & representing outside system

Convergence of interest(s). Original formalization of definition of need & tentative goals and means. Enough agreement on need for motivation to action.

Those inside system

Problem or Situation

Evaluation
Decision
Planning
Action

Evaluation

6 — Delineation of relevant social systems

7 — Initiating Sets No. 1 . . . . n

9 — Legitimation by relevant key people or groups; consulting; "sounding board"

12 — Diffusion Sets No. 1 . . . . n (May differ from initiating sets)

14 — Definition of need by relevant more general target systems, informal groups, general public, etc.-becomes the 'peoples' problem

16 — Commitment to action

18 — Goals Setting up more formal, generally agreed upon goals and objectives

Evaluation

Alternative Course

CONTINUING PROCESSES AND CONSIDERATIONS

A. Probability of formal structure for action increases as actions steps progress ————
B. Continuity of organization is not generalizable. The original convergence set may continue as major actor, may add or drop members, or may withdraw from program as action steps progress ————
C. Research and analysis of social and physical situation, though varying in kind and depth, is necessary at all stages ————
D. Resources must be found, motivated and organized at all stages ————
E. Finding and setting up social situations out of which leadership and social action may evolve at all stages ————
F. Social action may be stopped or reoriented at any stage on the continuum ————

(SOCIAL SYSTEM BOUNDARY)

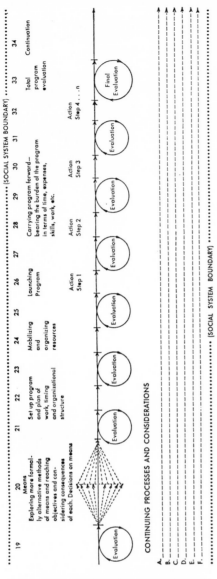

The construct presented here is the conceptualization of George M. Beal, Department of Economics and Sociology, Iowa State University, that has evolved out of participation in and analysis of social action programs, reading and discussion with action people and sociologists. In terms of actual documentation the following works have been knowingly drawn upon: (1) Beal, George M. How to get community acceptance and participation for an activity in tuberculosis control. Paper presented to National Tuberculosis Association, Washington, D.C. April 1950. (2) Beal, George M. Organizing for social change. Iowa extension social science refresher course. Iowa Extension Service, Ames. January 1950. (3) Brown, Ida Stewart. Working toward goals. Adult Education 1:13-20. 1952. (4) Green, James W. and Mayo, Selz C. A framework for research in the actions of community groups. Social Forces 31:320-327. 1953. (5) Holland, John. Mass Communication Seminar. (Personal notes taken from Holland presentation.) Iowa State College, Ames. May 1952. (6) Miller, Paul. Community health action. Michigan State College Press. East Lansing. 1953. (7) Miller, Paul. Decision making within community organization. Rural Soc. 17:153-161. 1952. (8) National Education Association, National Training Laboratory in Group Development. Bul. No. 3. National Education Association, Washington, D.C. 1948. (9) Sanders, Irwin T. Making good communities better. University of Kentucky Press, Lexington. 1950. (10) Sower, Christopher, et. al. Community involvement. Free Press, Glencoe, Illinois. 1957. (11) American Association of Land-Grant Colleges, George Beal and Joe Bohlen. The group process, Instructor's guide, communication training program. National Project in Agricultural Communications. East Lansing. 1956. (12) Reports of the Sub-committee on Social Action, North Central Rural Sociology Committee, sponsored jointly by the North Central Agricultural Experiment Stations and the Farm Foundation. 1956-1962.

FIG. 8.1. A construct of social action.

TABLE 8.2. Processually Articulated Structural Model (PAS); Elements, Processes, and Conditions of Action of Social Systems

| Processes | Structural-Functional Categories | Elements |
|---|---|---|
| (1) Cognitive mapping & validation | Knowing | Belief (knowledge) |
| (2) Tension management & communication of sentiment | Feeling | Sentiment |
| (3) Goal attaining and concomitant "latent" activity as process | Achieving | End, goal or objective |
| (4) Evaluation | Norming, standardizing, patterning | Norm |
| (5) Status-role performance | Dividing the functions | Status role (position) |
| (6) Evaluation of actors & allocation of status roles | Ranking | Rank |
| (7) Decision making & its initiation into action | Controlling | Power |
| (8) Application of sanctions | Sanctioning | Sanction |
| (9) Utilization of facilities | Facilitation | Facility |

| Comprehensive or Master Processes | | |
|---|---|---|
| 1) Communication | 3) Systemic linkage | 5) Socialization |
| 2) Boundary maintenance | 4) Institutionalization | 6) Social control |

| Conditions of Social Action | | |
|---|---|---|
| 1) Territoriality | 2) Time | 3) Size |

Reproduced from Charles P. Loomis and Zona K. Loomis. *Modern Social Theories,* p. 5. Princeton, N.J.: D. Van Nostrand Co., Inc., 1961.

*Size.* The question of size relates to the elements and all the master processes; particularly it would seem, communication and social control. Other human experience would not negate the possibility of finding or developing a social system within the area because of size. The number of people (80,000) is not overwhelming, but there are problems when considering the number of subsystems and the 7,200 square miles they are located in. Many planners are asking for an optimum size figure for population centers. Though no answer is yet available, there is a suggestion that 300,000 people may be an optimum size.

To make the analysis of a system as complex as an area manageable using the processes and elements of the Loomis model, it is necessary to define the objectives of the change agent. Without such definition there is no effective means of limiting the scope of inquiry. The primary objective of the change agent, as has been stated before, was to generate, develop, and deliver information and to do this through some form of social machinery to be created for the entire multicounty area. A basic premise was that some type of area social system needed to be developed—if it did not already exist. It is within this context that preliminary analysis was approached. Let us look first at the master processes within the context of the total area:

*Communication.* Mass media channels did exist which were nearly coterminous with the area. Thus there were mass media mechanisms available for transmitting knowledge, information, decisions, and the like. Additional communication channels also existed between subsystems (population centers, formal groups, and institutions). Field personnel for public and private agencies were located in several of the population centers of the area and had their central office in one of the county seat towns. In addition, there were associations of clergy, school administrators, businessmen, women's clubs, and the like, which provided several formal and informal channels of communication. Few of these were exactly coterminous with the area. If our analysis had been an attempt to determine whether or not a social system actually existed which was coterminous with the eight counties we would have needed to be more refined. What we were seeking at this point was the extent to which there were available communication channels that cut across the area, even though they were not now being used for sending area messages.

*Boundary maintenance.* Prior to the initiation of the social and economic development effort in MIDCREST there was little evidence of boundary maintenance activity relative to that area. No common name was used for the area. There were some recently formed social systems for community action programs and the like, which did not correspond to all eight counties, but did cover a major portion of the area. An observation of the data would suggest that there were a commonality of problems, a rudimentary level of economic interaction, and a common social and cultural heritage. This suggested bases around which boundary maintenance could be developed.

*Systemic linkage.* As indicated in the preceding paragraph, some systemic linkage had occurred between subsystems in the area prior to the development project, but not between the total network of subsystems covering the entire area. In the reorganization of schools and the building of hospitals one could observe past unfreezing of boundary maintenance and the subsequent freezing of new boundaries. Whether or not these actions would be an impediment to a new proposal requiring broader scale systemic linkage was unknown. (A research question: Is one "giant" step possible or must one take three "baby" steps in achieving social change?)

*Socialization.* The available communication channels for the area suggested a potential instrument for socializing the members relative to an area social system and to a social and economic development program. There was little evidence prior to the advent of the program however, that they were being used for this purpose. The fact that people were psychologically identified with one population center, despite their multicenter social and economic interaction pattern, indicated that little area socialization was occurring.

*Social control.* There was no formal or legal mechanism for exercising social control in the total area. Furthermore, as will be indicated in the discussion of the element of power, there was no concerted social power structure for the area. This observation suggested that while there was interaction in the area, it was not regulated by any cognate social control mechanism for the area, thus any suggested changes or implication that the people should act on an area basis would demand a development of effective area social control mechanisms.

*Institutionalization.* That institutionalized practices existed within the area was not in doubt. However, there did not seem to be any evidence that there were institutionalized practices coterminous with the area. It was the institutionalization of various practices within the subsystems of the area which were a major barrier to the implementation of an area social system.

Briefly, the elements were utilized in the analysis as follows:

*Beliefs.* It was readily apparent that the people in the area within their subsystems believed that new industry was necessary, population out-migration should cease, job opportunities must be created, and that vocational-technical training was necessary. There was less expression of belief that a deliberate planning and education program was a necessary prerequisite for development. There were beliefs that could impede the creation of a manifest area social system. As one example, localism at both the community and county level was very predominant.

*Sentiment.* The concern here was how strong the people felt about those beliefs which could both impede and facilitate area activity. Strong emotions were attached to local control, creation of new jobs, and increased income.

*Ends.* The question was whether there were ends or objectives that could be identified as conscious aspects of the area. The objectives for many of the subsystems were the same as one would expect to be necessary for area development. As is so often the case however, agreement on objectives is frequently easier than agreement on means. And the area concept itself was a means.

*Norms.* Since there were no objectives for the area as a system, one would not expect to find norms associated with the area. If the area had been a natural sociological and cultural area, one might have reasonably expected to find norms associated with the area. In states less homogenous than Iowa, one could expect to find distinct cultural areas. While there is some reason to believe that there is a distinction in the norms of people in southern Iowa from northern Iowa it could not be used to differentiate between the counties in MIDCREST and those which were adjacent to it.

*Status roles.* Change agents for organizations and agencies covering the major part of MIDCREST as well as managers and owners of industrial firms which cover most of the area, constituted status roles on an area level. Again however, they were not coterminous with the area in question and therefore did not constitute any formal or informal area influence structure.

*Power.* A social power structure for the area was not observable. Most studies to date indicate that social power is clustered around community centers and/or organizations. Analysis of the community power structures in MIDCREST verified this finding. Thus there was no area level power structure that could be sought out for legitimizing the area program. (This is one reason an area group was formed.)

*Ranking.* That there was a class structure within the area is tautological. But there was no evidence of people being evaluated in terms of their worth to the area as a system.

*Sanctions.* Since there were no apparent norms for the area, one would not expect to find sanctions. In general norms give rise to sanctions, rather than the other way around, except in those cases where the sanctions of a larger social system can force new norms in a subsystem.

*Facilities (means).* Means—people, organization, communication media, permissive legislation, and the like—existed in the area. It was the assessment of the means in the area which further suggested that an area social system could be contrived for the purposes of social and economic development activity.

What I have tried to do is to represent in brief form how one can use the elements and processes of the Loomis model. It is obvious that extensive research efforts could be instigated within any geographic area to determine the extent to which the processes are coterminous with the delineated area and the manner in which the elements are articulated. Enough work has been done that if one conceived the ideal system for development, he should be able to formulate questions for each element and process, such as Beal has done with the social action process in identifying the conditions to be met for each step in the process.

After the Loomis model had been used for assessing the social situation, the next task was to set forth the strategy to be used in initiating the extension efforts. Looking to the Beal model of social action suggested the need for identifying the key leaders within the area and to move toward some kind of organizational structure which would provide the mechanism for the change agent to communicate the concept of area development.[1]

As indicated earlier, this led to the identification of community power actors in the communities within the area. As a practical consideration, the extension staff members were not asked to interview people in communities of less than 500. In all those communities above 500, they used the procedure outlined in a previous publication on identifying the community power structure. (14)

Having identified the key power actors in each county, we moved to the creation of *new* county and area social systems. Recognizing that we were attempting to initiate a new concept and new systems, we took our strategy cues from research on social action and interaction in program planning committees. (2) Our analysis of the area and the beliefs of the people suggested that it would be unwise to

---

[1] Without going into detail, the significance of the social action model is best realized by recognizing its multiphasic use. That is, the overall task was conceived within the social action construct. The instigation of staff training and participation was also conceived in the framework. Each of the educational efforts which followed was also operationalized through the steps of the social action construct.

attempt to move to area-wide activity as our first order of business. Therefore a critical decision was made to first involve the people within the context of their counties to obtain an understanding of the social and economic system in which they lived and to then attempt to involve them on an area-wide basis when they had the background for assessing the extent to which it was logical that this set of counties attempt to operate for certain development purposes at an area level. The evidence from the program-planning research indicated that the most effective planning groups (which were essentially what we were forming) were those groups which had a complete understanding of the system elements of beliefs, ends, and means. Moreover, the role of background information in effective planning was identified. The primary finding suggested that the usual technique of giving a "convulsion of facts and figures" at the first meeting of a new group was not an effective means of gaining understanding of the social and economic system to which the group would be addressing their attention. In short, this procedure did not facilitate using background data in the decision-making process.

These considerations led us to approach the key influential leaders in each county using the model outlined in Table 8.3. (13) Our first meeting (March 1965) was addressed to Stage II in Table 8.3. Seminar Six constituted Stage III. Thus we fused the need for background information to the process of group formation.

The essential interpretation of the Loomis model for the creation of these county groups was that the change agent initiating a new committee has the responsibility for identifying the objectives, means, beliefs, and some of the norms, sanctions, and the like. To do otherwise is to submit to a confused application of the grass roots philosophy which expects the collection of individuals to "know" the group's objectives.

The specific manner in which the Loomis model can also be used to devise the strategy for an orientation meeting (Stage II of Table 8.3) of a new social system is depicted in Table 8.4. In this framework, each element and process can be systematically accounted for. The first task is to ascertain the present state of the element in the collection of people to be formed into the new social system. Then a statement of the desired state of the element is needed. Following this, the content of the message needed to achieve the change can be determined. Taking beliefs as one example we note the beliefs that the people have that are relevant to the purposes we have in mind. If it is social and economic development, this covers a wide range. If the committee is determining what forms of social recreation should be initiated, the range may be less.

In developing a new social system, major emphasis is given to the elements: beliefs, ends, power, norms, sanctions, needs. The elements of sentiment, ranking, and status roles become articulated

TABLE 8.3. Flow Model: Background Information and the Flow of the Planning Process

---

STAGE I: *Committee Selection*
1. Identify the key influentials in each community.
2. Determine size of committee—usually enough to insure attendance of 12 to each 15 each time.
3. Select from influentials to obtain representativeness of communities, occupations, institutions, etc.
4. Obtain approval from governing or advisory board if there is one.

STAGE II: *Committee Orientation*
1. Present and discuss committee purposes, means of operation, and extent of responsibility.
2. Delay selection of officers until end of Stage III.
3. Discuss proposed means and content for Stage III.
4. Establish schedule for Stage III.

STAGE III: *Examination of Situation*
1. Series of seminar-type sessions on community change, economic growth, imbalances in situation, and process of social action for change.
2. Sources of data including census reports, agency reports, popularized research reports, and current studies of the area.

STAGE IV: *Identification of Problems (Needs)*
1. Situation is continually examined and comparisons made between *what is and what ought to (could or should) be.* The gaps represent problems or needs.
2. More specific data are added to those presented in Stage III.
3. *What ought to be* is determined from research and value judgments of the committee and extension staff.
4. Some problems may be subjected to further study.
5. Sources of data are the same as in previous stage.

STAGE V: *Determination of Failure Elements*
1. Indicate the likely *human or structural imbalances* causing the problem.
2. Sort problems into those that could be addressed by extension and those which need to be approached through social action of other groups and agencies.
3. Add data from social science research. In some cases additional study will be necessary.

STAGE VI: *Selection of Priorities*
1. Problems to be addressed by extension are ordered by priority.
2. Sources of data include review of current programs, available resources, and state or area priorities.

---

NOTE: The amount of data, increased over time, is brought to bear when needed, and moves from general to specific.

through the interaction of the people. Certain decisions about the timing of meetings, place of meetings, replacement of members, and the like, can be the initiative of the members. This helps to realize an effective mix of involvement by the people and the change agent.

Returning to the chronological set of events for MIDCREST, it will be noted that once the series of meetings had been held in each of the counties, there was an area-wide meeting of all the participants in the Seminar Six series. This was the initiation of an area-wide social system. Through discussion and interaction of the people themselves, reflecting their own county discussions, it became obvious

TABLE 8.4. Paradigm for Using Social System Model to Create New Social Systems

| Element | Previous state | Desired state | Content of message |
|---|---|---|---|
| Belief 1 . . . | Action more important than planning | Planning should precede action | Experiences of business, farms, military in planning before action |
| Belief 2 . . . . . . | Each population center should grow | Population centers need to adjust to needed function | Information about dev. of community, great changes affecting comm., actual data concerning people's patterns of economic behavior |
| Belief n | | | |
| Objective 1 . . . | | | |
| Objective n | | | |
| Norm 1 . . . | | | |
| Norm n . . . | | | |
| Element ijl . . . | | | |
| Element ijn | | | |

to them that there was a commonality in problems and a possibility of linking the subsystems in the area. Subsequent activities were aimed at bringing about the rudimentary elements of an area-wide social system, that is, the area development leadership group (ADLG). For our objectives, linking for education and information was all that was immediately necessary. Another major reason for forming the ADLG was to systematize routes of access to local communities by the area development agent so that a second wave of education and information could be initiated. The ADLG was an initiating set, legitimizer, and diffusion set within the context of Beal's model. If one takes the position of an actionist, then this is a possible means to formal linking and even merging of two systems (say, school districts) into one.

The same framework outlined for use with the county groups in Table 8.4 was applied in developing the content of early meetings with the area development leadership group.

In review it can be noted that decisions were made about numbers of people, numbers of meetings, place of meetings, content of meetings, and many other things by operationalizing our knowledge and impressions within the context of the system model, the social action construct, and those other assorted models of human behavior which seemed to fit. We do not have an objective basis to conclude that our objectives in social and economic development could not have been achieved by using other sociological models to guide our thinking. Nor can we objectively compare the manner in which we operationalized them. We are able, in a rudimentary fashion, to state that we achieved our objectives reasonably well. This conclusion is based on the research findings of a study focusing on the 48 people who participated in the area development leadership group. (8) Throughout the entire process we were careful to write down our objectives, our means of operation, and the like. As a consequence, we were able to administer a questionnaire to these people to assess their knowledge and understanding of the elements which we believed to be important. We found their understanding and knowledge to be rather good and in the hypothesized direction. We found their understanding to be significantly higher than the level of knowledge and understanding by the people in our original program-planning research, where the Loomis model and the procedures outlined in Tables 8.3 and 8.4 were not used. It is obvious that we cannot conclude that the difference is due solely to the deliberate strategy which we used. More importantly, at this point we have no way of knowing whether the eventual social and economic development outcomes in the area will be any better than if we had not used this procedure, or indeed if we had not been there at all.

As a person who was at least partially responsible for coming up (or in army jargon, "doing something even if it's wrong") with the strategy for the program in social and economic development, I believe that one of the real needs in sociological research relevant to development is in the investigation of purposely different strategies used by a change agency such as the extension service. The data to assess the accomplishment of objectives for all of the systems involved are desperately needed to raise future choices of strategies above an "art" form.

## A WORD ABOUT THE OTHER AREAS

In the first two geographic areas the procedure was to involve the staff in the same graduate course on economic growth and development and to have them identify the power actors in their respective counties. In TENCO about 60 of these leaders were brought together on an area basis for a meeting at which the general concept of social and economic development was outlined and they were asked whether they wished to participate. They indicated that they did and a steering committee for the area was formed by obtaining a representative from each of the ten counties. Within a short time there were four subcommittees of ten members each formed in the areas of industry, agriculture, recreation, and education. In NIAD, the second area, after the power actors had been identified there was a meeting in 18 of the major communities within the nine-county area to visit with the power actors in their own environment about the general concept of development. This was followed by an area-wide meeting attended by some 200 people at which the concept was reviewed and they were asked to indicate whether they wished to participate. They agreed and an executive committee was formed of some 27 people. This increased number was based on experiences with committees of 10 in TENCO. The executive committee developed four committees (identical to TENCO) with 27 members each. In both of these areas economic base studies and population studies were made available, as well as studies in education, local government, recreation, and the like. In neither case was there an extended series of meetings (such as Seminar Six) held at the county or area level prior to the formation of the area group and its subcommittees. Two outcomes from this procedure led us to the change that I have described in detail for the MIDCREST area. The first was that the area agent became very much involved in social machinery maintenance and was more of an executive secretary for committees than an educator, which was to be his primary objective. The second was the difficulty committee members had in identifying their objectives and means of operation. In short they did not have an understanding of the social and economic system in which they were living, nor did they fully understand the objectives and means of the new groups (i.e., committees) which were formed. In the main, they wanted to move in direct action—and did in the development of brochures on industry and recreation. In both of these areas, programs analogous to the Seminar Six series were held from three to four years after the initiation of the area program. Though useful as an education effort at any time, it is unlikely that this timing of creating basic understanding will serve the same purpose as it did in the MIDCREST area.

Several other deviations were also operative because of problems entirely within the context of the change agency itself. The problems of initiating a new program within a bureaucracy would be worthy of a separate paper.

## SUMMARY

To move from the general models used in the case of social and economic development discussed here to the presentation of the empirical case is laborious, tedious, and sometimes a seeming collection of picayunish differences. It also rests on some rather basic assumptions about the nature of the system initiating the program and the target system. The most important test of any model, given one's objectives, is whether it works and whether it works better than some other model. As an assessment and indictment of the state of the applied social sciences, we cannot answer that question with any certainty.

The reader will have noted an absence of such community development models as those of Biddle and Biddle (3) and Lippitt, Watson, and Westley. (9) Both of these, and others provide useful cues to social and economic development, but their major utility is at a relatively simple level of social organization, say a single community center as contrasted to the complex social system described in this chapter. Perhaps it is a fundamental weakness of the sociological tool kit that theories have been developed either for society or for reasonably small well-defined groups, organizations, and communities but not for this intermediate level in which an articulated social system does not exist a priori.

This chapter focused on two models which had multiple uses in the instigation of social and economic development efforts. The sociologists involved in this process drew from the sum of their training in sociology, psychology, and economics at all times however, and as such "used" many models and findings of human behavior. It is difficult, if not impossible, to identify the exact manner and exact time at which each of the models was applied. The essential point seems to be that even though sociological models which can readily be operationalized for development are scarce, we felt it more productive to be "sociologing" with what models we had than to be switching to a series of recipes and guidelines derived from a collection of "success" stories.

## REFERENCES

1. Beal, George M. *How Does Social Change Occur?* RS–284. Ames: Iowa State University, Cooperative Extension Service, 1958.
2. ———. *Social Action and Interaction in Program Planning.* Ames: Iowa State University Press, 1966.
3. Biddle, William W., and Biddle, L. J. *The Community Development Process.* New York: Holt, Rinehart and Winston, 1965.
4. Chin, Robert. "The Utility of System Model and Developmental Models for Practitioners." In *The Planning of Change,* edited by Warren G.

Bennis, Kenneth A. Benne, and Robert Chin. New York: Holt, Rinehart and Winston, 1962.

5. Fox, Karl A., and Kumor, T. Krishna. *Delineating Functional Economic Areas for Development Programs.* Mimeographed. Ames: Iowa State University, Department of Economics, 1964.

6. Gouldner, Alvin. "Theoretical Requirements of the Applied Social Scientists." In *The Planning of Change,* edited by Warren G. Bennis, Kenneth A. Benne, and Robert Chin. New York: Holt, Rinehart and Winston, 1962.

7. Krech, D.; Crutchfield, R.; and Bellachey, E. *Individual in Society.* New York: McGraw-Hill, 1962.

8. Lind, Marvin. "Social Interaction and Personal and Social Characteristics of the Members of an Area Development Leadership Group." Ph.D. dissertation, Iowa State University, 1967.

9. Lippitt, Ronald; Watson, Jeanne; and Westley, Bruce. *The Dynamics of Planned Change.* New York: Harcourt, Brace and World, 1958.

10. Loomis, Charles P. *Social Systems: Essays on Their Persistence and Change.* Princeton, N.J.: D. Van Nostrand Co., 1960.

11. Maslow, A. H. *Motivation and Personality.* New York: Harper and Bros., 1954.

12. McKinney, John C. *Constructive Typology and Social Theory.* New York: Appleton-Century-Crofts, 1966.

13. Powers, Ronald C. "Background Information in Planning." *Journal of Cooperative Extension* 1 (Spring 1966): 11–23.

14. ———. *Identifying the Community Power Structure.* Soc.-18. Ames: Iowa State University, Cooperative Extension Service, 1965.

15. Warner, Keith W., and Havens, A. Eugene. "Goal Displacement and the Intangibility of Organizational Goals." *Administrative Science Quarterly* 12 (March 1968): 539–55.

PART THREE

# THE PARTICIPATION OF MAJOR INSTITUTIONS IN DOMESTIC DEVELOPMENT

THEORIES of development are explicated into strategies of development and finally are implemented by some agency, organization, or set of such. As the chapter by Powers indicates, the choice of a development strategy is influenced by certain characteristics of the implementing agency. The chapters in this section illustrate that organizational patterns of the implementing agency are also a constraint on the effectiveness of strategy implementation. As Ratchford indicates in his chapter, for the university to effectively perform its development roles a number of organizational adjustments will be required.

In this section the development roles of three major sectors of society are discussed; the private sector, the university, and government. These are not the only societal sectors that implement development, although together they account for the vast majority of such activities.

Chapter 9 illustrates some of the diversity of development activities possible within the private sector. It also calls attention to the heterogeneity of firms within the private sector and their varying concern with development implementation. Chapters 10 and 11 deal with the provocative question of whether government and the university with their present patterns of goals and structures can effectively be the carriers of planned change.

211

## OVERVIEW OF THE CHAPTERS

### The Private Sector in Development

Chapter 9 was originally prepared by Randall T. Klemme as a banquet address. It has been included in the book because of the relevance of the private sector to development. The chapter provides the reader with an example of the variety of development efforts engaged in by just one corporation and a commentary on the "emerging concept, on the part of business, of its social responsibility."

Klemme's comments touch on the role of business in both the preindustrial and postindustrial development context. To illustrate the role of business in a developing society he refers to the case of Puerto Rico to illustrate his generalization that economic development is a prerequisite of social development, and economic development proceeds in a context of opportunity for profits.

The roles of business in the postindustrial society are categorized into three development areas: 1) self-serving activities such as efforts to expand industry, 2) conforming activities in which business performs the duties of a good citizen, such as contributing money to colleges and serving on advisory boards, and 3) innovative activities.

The innovative activities of Klemme's corporation indicate the wide spectrum of activities possible within the private sector: the collection of art to record and add to the cultural base of an area; the training of unemployables; the creation of a research center for projecting social, political, economic, and technological trends.

Understanding the role of the private sector in development requires a recognition that "you can't lump business into one homogeneous mass anymore." Two major segments of the contemporary private sector are the mega-corporation (Galbraith's industrial system) and small business. These segments each possess distinctive characteristics which will influence their role performance in development activities. The mega-corporation's emphasis on long-range growth versus the small business concern with short-run profits illustrates that these segments of the private sector may hold different perspectives of social responsibility.

## Role of University in Development

In Chapter 10 Brice Ratchford discusses the role of the university in achieving development from the perspective of his experience with the past, present, and emerging activities of the land-grant university. He suggests that the land-grant university, in its efforts to develop the agricultural sector, produced two organizational innovations that may find their counterparts in organizing for development in other sectors: the experiment station for the production of new knowledge and the cooperative extension service for the specification and dissemination of this new knowledge.

Ratchford proposes five general development roles to be performed by the university: 1) developing and interpreting new knowledge, including consideration of the consequences or impacts of the new knowledge, 2) delivering the knowledge to relevant clienteles, 3) providing this information to organizations (as a special clientele type), 4) performing a linking role between available resources and action groups needing such resources and 5) delivering information to a variety of decision-making units so as to coordinate decisions at different levels. Ratchford emphasizes that historically the extension service has thought of individual decision-makers as its target audience. He suggests that formal groups, units of government, and other group decision-making units should receive increased emphasis in future development activities of the extension service.

The performance of these roles will require a variety of adjustments in current university structures and functions. Four major prerequisites for performing the development roles are as follows: 1) adjustments in university goals so that development activities are given reward at least equal to other "missions of the university," 2) adjustments in the organizational pattern of the university, for example, the establishment of regional centers within a state, 3) securing resources for research and extension activities, and 4) developing relations with other universities, government agencies, and businesses involved in development research and extension.

### Federalism and Domestic Development

In Chapter 11 Paul Miller, writing at the time when he served as the Assistant Secretary for Education in HEW, discusses the federal system of government as an institution for achieving development. The government is a major participant in development with over 200 programs that approximate the development category. He poses the general question of whether the federal government can effectively plan and implement development programs, given the past and present problem of interrelationships 1) between levels of government—federal, state, and local, and 2) between the special interest departments of government.

Miller discusses some of the current forms of "creative federalism" which are attempts to create new ties between the federal government and both its states and its cities; and the new patterns of interaction among the states and among the metropolitan areas. These interrelations are of paramount importance to development questions such as: Who should make what kinds of planning decisions? Who should provide the needed resources? What controls should accompany the allocation of resources? Who should implement the programs?

The author also identifies the "management muddle" which exists at all levels of government, but especially at the middle management level, as an important constraint on the implementation of development. Without the coordination of the legion of categorical government programs, the impact of both the individual and the cumulative effort is reduced.

The government, as might be expected, is seen as responding to problem crises. This means that many programs are geared to problems: more accurately their symptoms rather than their causes. In many cases, the news media stimulate unrealistic expectations of the possible achievements of such government programs.

Miller indicates that from the federal perspective "development appears more and more to be an exercise in equalization of opportunity and the delivery of services." To correct this problem of the distribution of opportunity, the federal government has attempted to perform a redistribution role through the channeling of resources to the states and metropolitan areas.

As indications of positive approaches to the implementation of development, Miller cites the efforts at regional programming, efforts to strengthen the posture of states and municipalities, increased efforts in statewide planning, and increased state interest in social and economic development.

# ROLE OF THE PRIVATE SECTOR IN DEVELOPMENT

## RANDALL T. KLEMME

WE ARE IN THE PROGRESS of rapid social and technological change; we are in the process of changing the role of social institutions in this country. I would say that the conflict, the tension, or the crisis which is affecting the private sector can be characterized by contrasting James Burnham's *Managerial Revolution* (2) with Andrew Hacker's *The Corporation Take-Over* (6) or, from the standpoint of society as a whole, Alexander Clifford's *Enter Citizens* (3) with Ortega's *Revolt of the Masses*. (8)

I believe social development is gradual, purposive, and goal oriented. Social change is the result of social dynamics, planned or unplanned. The subject is purposive, planned, and goal oriented; development is not a random activity. Therefore, in a free society it seems to me the purposive nature is shaped by consensus of individuals and institutions having unique, and often pluralistic, value systems. We are considering the means to the end of society's systems of values. The process is essentially normative since the value system contains metaphysical absolutes.

How do you judge social change and social development? A system of ethics will determine if the choice of development decisions is right. Social development can come only from within, and I am not speaking in the Parsonsian sense. It cannot be imposed from

**RANDALL T. KLEMME** is Vice-president and Corporate Economist with Northern Natural Gas Company and Adjunct Professor of Economics, University of Nebraska at Omaha. He holds the Ph.D. in agricultural economics from Iowa State University. He has been a member of the graduate faculty at the University of Karachi, Pakistan. Publications related to his chapter include: "The Role of Private Enterprise in the Implementation of Progress of Regional Development" (presented at Congres International d'Economics Regionale, Onstend, Belgium, 1958) and "NEMBA: A Case Study of Private Enterprise as the Initiator of Regional Economic Development" (presented at Third International Congress of Regional Economics, Rome, 1965).

the outside. This is why I do not fear coercion. I believe totalitarian control is reached when reason ultimately counsels the acceptance of totalitarian goals. I would remind you that this decision of acceptance is made in the minds of individuals within that totalitarian society.

I think that to the most casual reader it is clear that within the private sector we are becoming deeply involved at the community, the regional, and the state level in the field of development. And I might point out, from the private sector standpoint, that while the exogenous exigencies of the problem are economic, there is still a deep concern with social development as well. Almost every day you read about the further involvement of firms within the private sector in the field of social development. In Roxbury and Danbury, Massachusetts, the private sector is moving forward to redevelop a large section of their blighted ghetto area. Our friends at the Boston Gas Company are deeply involved in this activity. In Omaha we have placed a quarter of a million dollars into a nonprofit corporation to work on the redevelopment of housing in the ghetto area. We realize that this is not an ultimate answer to the ghetto problem, but at least this money is a start toward improving the quality of living in these areas.

You read of the involvement of American industry in such things as the Job Corps and the training of the hard core of the unemployed. The names are familiar: Litton, Burroughs, and I.B.M. Even we, Northern Natural Gas, operated a Job Corps in Lincoln, Nebraska. Let me say that the Job Corps project was an interesting experience for us. For a long time we have taken the ideological position that the private sector can do certain jobs better than the public sector. We learned that while we believe we did this job better, it was not easy. In the public sector the publics are more divergent, multifaceted, as in our own industrial activity. Corporately, our support of art and culture, and our work in the implementation of regional development groups like the Upper Midwest Research Council, are further evidence of corporate involvement in social and economic development.

I think one of the best examples of private sector involvement is to be found in Puerto Rico. Here we have a classic case which illustrates what we are trying to get done now in Omaha and elsewhere in the ghetto areas of this country. Puerto Rico, in 1930, was a ghetto with heavy out-migration. The government of Puerto Rico realized that it would have to do something to correct this. Under the leadership of Rexford Tugwell, the government, between 1940 and 1947, made an investment of 22 or 23 million dollars and actually operated the industries. They created 2,000 jobs when their goal was 100,000. In 1947 Beardsley Ruml went to Puerto Rico and began to work with the government of Puerto Rico in developing a new program. Today there are 2,400 industrial plants, 125,000 jobs, and 31 vocational and technical training institutes on the island. I am told that out-migration has virtually stopped and in-migration of Puerto Ricans back from New York City has begun. What was the basic philosophy of the Puerto Rican plan? Very simply, it was profits-tax concessions and financing which allowed industrial firms moving into Puerto Rico to make as high as 40 to 45 percent profit. Now it may be difficult for many of us to rationalize workers earning something less than 25c an hour when the manufacturer is making 40 percent profit. However, Adam Smith answered this problem. In any developing area, exploitation of some type is necessary as a first step toward capital formation.

One of the basic problems faced in Pakistan and India was that most of the educated civil servants of these countries, educated in Oxford, Cambridge, or the London School (most of them Fabian socialists in their outlook) could not equate the twentieth century conditions in the United States and England with a situation of high profits necessary to achieve high rates of capital formation in their own country. The point that I am trying to make is that the forerunner of social development of Puerto Rico was economic development, and the motive for economic development was profits.

To return to the matter of private sector involvement, I believe you can divide our development activities into three areas: those which are 1) self-serving, 2) conforming, and 3) innovative. Much of what we do is self-serving. To illustrate this (not to presume to speak for other companies in the private sector) let me do so in terms of my own company. We have one of the largest area development staffs of any utility company in the country. Our group consists of nearly 30 people and we spend nearly a million dollars a year in these activities. Our program at Northern Natural Gas rests upon four major areas. The first of these is basic economic research. As a matter of fact we began our activities in area development by first assembling a research staff in order to determine the character of our region, its needs, and its potentialities. The second program, in order of development, covers those activities related to what might be termed "community development." Here we were concerned with the quality of living in the communities of this region since we recognized that many of them have very little chance for industrial growth and expansion. Our third major area dealt with activities designed to assist the existing industries of the region to expand. A much overlooked parameter of this problem is that for most areas 85 percent of industrial growth arises out of expansion of existing firms. Finally, we pursued the problem of new industry promotion which seeks to locate or relocate major firms and branch operations in our market area.

You would be correct in assuming that a corporation of our size would not continue to make this level of expenditure if it did not produce returns. We know that this program has produced both economic and social returns for the region that we have served. Perhaps the most important result of our activities has been to check the out-migration of certain industries from this region. Of course we have assisted in bringing new industries into the area as well.

We have also worked in other areas. We were one of the sponsors of the Upper Midwest Research and Development Council, which was carried on by the University of Minnesota. Waldo Wegner's activity at Iowa State University is an outgrowth of the activities that we undertook with Iowa Power and Light to set up a scientific center. These are evidences of enlightened self-interest—so-called since they do serve our own interest.

We have other activities that I call conforming. This is largely our philanthropy. We contribute not only money to colleges and universities but, more importantly, we contribute manpower and time to such groups as the United Community Services, hospital and college boards, the Urban League, civil rights movement, advisory boards to government, education, and churches. But in this respect we are conforming to good citizenship. This really does not represent anything that is new.

In the innovative field, however, we do feel that we are moving in certain directions that are important. Let me list three. First, we are a patron of art. Several years ago some 500 paintings by a Swiss painter, Karl Bodmer, came to light in a castle in Germany. Prince Maximilian of Neu Wied was one of the first natural scientists to travel up the Missouri River. He had with him Karl Bodmer to paint the conditions of the Indians and the Northern Plains as they existed in the 1830s. As you may know, the stylized dated painting of later artists, like Miller and Russell and others, tended to idealize the Indians. These pictures of Bodmer showed the Indian as he was —underfed, undernourished, and diseased. There is artistic credit to the painter that he painted things as they actually were. We also acquired the Prince's Journals for our archives (which are even more important in the long run) to describe the ecology of the area. Since that time we have added to this a collection of 113 watercolors of Alfred Jacob Miller and (most recently) a collection of 86 Russell, Miller, Herd, and other painters of the West. From one standpoint you can say this does not represent very much of a contribution on our part because art collections have a habit of increasing in value, and this is true. Yet on the other hand, we feel that material dealing with the culture and history of our area should be located here to be used by scholars. We bought these works because we felt in so doing we at least were contributing something to our area's historical past. Other companies make their contribution to the art culture in other ways.

From my point of view, an even more important activity was our creation two years ago of a subsidiary company. We call it

"Northern Systems." In some respects this is an outgrowth of some thinking that was done by our then Board Chairman, John Merriam. (Merriam's father, Charles Merriam, was the eminent political scientist at the University of Chicago.) Merriam, in the middle 1960s, conceived the idea that the private sector has direct responsibility for the problem of unemployment and unemployables. We are the ones who create jobs; we are the ones who terminate jobs. Therefore, rather than turnng this problem over to the government, John Merriam proposed, at a meeting of the Committee for Economic Development in New York City in 1965, the creation of "learning pools" within industry, where American industry (out of its own resources) would take on hard core or unemployed people, train them in new skills, and pay them until such time as their skills enabled them to go out into private industry on their own. This idea has been heavily borrowed by the recently created "National Alliance of Businessmen" headed by Henry Ford II. Northern Systems is also conducting training activities in Washington, D.C., Detroit, Houston, and Los Angeles. We have learned a great deal about these problems and we realize that social adjustment of these people is the first thing that has to be undertaken. While we are not making much profit in this area, we do believe that we are making a contribution toward a start on the road to the solution to one of the most traumatic social problems that we face in the country.

Our third innovative activity is very close to my heart. It is the center which we created just last year for the study of environmental analysis and technology forecasting. This activity reports directly to me. Here we are trying to identify, as Herman Kahn did, the broad social, political, economic, and technological trends to the year 2000. In this activity we will draw very heavily upon the resources of the colleges and universities in our region. We hope eventually to be able to bring to this study projections that are meaningful in terms of alternatives for the future. The basic problem is that we are a billion-dollar corporation, that our cash flows are large and their wise use is of utmost importance. We realize the solution to the problem that we look at today is not altogether economic. If it is true that we are moving into a postindustrial society, what does this mean in terms of opportunities and constraints? What does this mean in terms of problems? It is conceivable that by the year 2000 our Northern Systems, working in the field of education and seeking to implement social change, may be the most important arm of Northern Natural Gas.

Again, why all of this activity in the private sector? It is founded on the emerging concept, on the part of business, of its social responsibility. Arjay Miller of the Ford Motor Company has said, "The new attitude that I think business should assume in recognizing its responsibilities to society—the traditional view that corporation management is responsible solely to its shareholders—must be enlarged. I think that we, in management, cannot discharge our long run responsibilities to shareholders unless we behave responsibly with regard to customers, employees, government, education, and the press."

My own Board Chairman, W. A. Strauss, last year said, "Today's manager does not believe his contract with the owners limits him to the narrow interpretation of short-term profit maximization. He does not believe the sole business of business is profits. Nor does he believe his sole responsibility is to the stockholder. He believes that both he and his company have responsibilities to the society that allowed the corporation to develop and which sustains the environment in which it operates. It is the scope and nature of these responsibilities that are of concern to the modern businessman."

How do these business leaders interpret socially responsible action? Arjay Miller says, "The businessman must take a broader-than-business view of our environment and be prepared to bring comprehensive and sound solutions before pressure reaches a boiling point." To this W. A. Strauss said, "all volitional activities engaged in by a corporation in which the welfare of society is the overriding criteria" and further, "This definition places the concern for social welfare in its proper perspective within the framework of the profit-motivated free enterprise system."

One of the most important concepts is that business and its self-image are changing. Many businessmen today still follow the free-market ideology of the nineteenth century in their public utterances. I know also that the business community, by and large, goes around with a persecution complex because for years they have felt that the world that they desired, and desired to emulate, was opposed to them. I can go back to Plato's men of metal. The merchant was the man of brass. In Saint Augustine's *City of God,* in the Manichaeists' philosophy, and that of the Stoics, the natural law concepts of profits and usury, are all points in case. Even Adam Smith had a very low regard for businessmen, if you will remember. Only the Mercantilists and the Cameralists, and later Ricardo and the classical economist, gave businessmen a position of esteem. Now the Lockean principles, with emphasis on property and self-interest, became a free market ideology under Ricardo and the classical economist replete with the wage-fund theory and class conflict. This concept of the business community, I believe, has to be changed. John Kenneth Galbraith, in his *New Industrial State* (5), comes closer to this, in my judgment, than any modern institutionalist in describing the situation. While I do not agree with all that Galbraith says, he is closer to the concept of what business sees in itself today.

We have, as always, a taxonomic problem. While Berle and Means (1) in the 1930s were concerned with corporate concentration, a shift had already been noted by James Burnham (2), and this shift was well underway. Business is being reclassified today. You cannot lump business into one homogeneous mass anymore. On one hand I would say there is the mega-corporation, those large corporations, few in number but constituting more than half of the productive capacity of the nation. On the other hand there are the thousands of small businesses. They, too, have distinguishing characteristics which are important in your analysis of both social development and economic development. First of all, the mega-corporation is not proprietary—it is managerial. The mega-corporation does not operate in a competitive market—it operates in a monopolistically competitive situation. The drive of the small firm is price competition—the drive in the mega-corporation is nonprice competition. Even the profit goals are different. Small business seeks to maximize short-run profits as a means of survival—the mega-corporation's goals are long-run growth, not short-term profit maximumization. There is need, it seems to me, for a complete new body of thought with respect to the mega-corporation as contrasted with the traditional concept of business. It is no more meaningful to compare the mega-corporation to the corner drug store than it is to compare a university scholar to a garbage collector on the basis that both are men.

I would like to refer briefly to the matter of legitimacy of the social orientation of the mega-corporation. I believe the mega-corporation has become a social institution in the Western world. People like Hacker in *The Corporation Take-Over* (6), Mason in *The Corporation in Modern Society* (7), and Eells in *The Meaning of Modern Business* (4) all have failed to see what John Galbraith demonstrates in his *New Industrial State* (5)—that power flows to the scarce factor. The scarce factor today is intelligent management, and intelligent management is created by the university. The university, the state, and the church are institutions which were created by society to fulfill certain needs. They exist on the basis of the consent of society, tacit or overt. In like manner the mega-corporation is a creation of society. I do not fear with Galbraith that society is going to fall under the spell of the technostructure of the new industrial society, because from time to time fears have been expressed about each of these institutions assuming complete control. The nineteenth century socialists called the church "the opiate of the working classes." The John Birchers today call the state the "wreckers of morals" because of the excessive paternalism. I do not agree with many of my university colleagues who call the mega-corporation the "panderer to the venal," nor do I agree with many in industry who accuse the university of the "subversion of youth" and suggest a cup of hemlock for many of my university colleagues. Being an Aristotelian, and I hope a true Lockean liberal, I have faith that society will find a way to accommodate. I recognize that from time to time certain of these institutions have achieved roles of dominance. The universities, the state, the church, and the corporation are, in my mind, equals as social institutions. I do not accept the view that any of these is the "first among equals."

Finally, what is the approach of the private sector in this field of social development? I think it is best described by a general systems approach. We have learned to work with many different publics. We know that we must know the value system of the publics with which we work. We know that to effect change we are going to have to use education and demonstration. We are going to seek integration of social institutions in the short run, but we are constantly seeking innovations to meet the continuing change which is part of the dynamics of any system. We are going to be constantly evaluating the opportunities for change. Thus we will legitimately serve society—and in so doing we will serve ourselves.

## REFERENCES

1. Berle, Adolf A., and Means, Gardiner C. *The Modern Corporation and Private Property*. Rev. ed. New York: Harcourt, Brace and World, 1968.
2. Burnham, James. *The Managerial Revolution*. New York: The John Day Co., 1941.
3. Clifford, Alexander. *Enter Citizens*. London: Evans Bros. Press, 1950.
4. Eells, Richard S. P. *The Meaning of Modern Business: An Introduction to the Philosophy of Large Corporate Enterprise*. New York: Columbia University Press, 1960.
5. Galbraith, John K. *The New Industrial State*. Boston: Houghton Mifflin Co., 1967.
6. Hacker, Andrew, *The Corporation Take-Over*. New York: Harper and Row, 1964.
7. Mason, Edward S., ed. *The Corporation in Modern Society*. Cambridge, Mass.: Harvard University Press, 1960.
8. Ortega y Gasset, José. *The Revolt of the Masses*. Translated from Spanish. New York: W. W. Norton and Co., 1932.

# CHAPTER TEN

# ROLE OF THE UNIVERSITY
# IN DEVELOPMENT

## C. B. RATCHFORD

DEVELOPMENT tends to be considered in modern and popular usage as synonymous with growth measured in terms such as income, population, employment, etc., and "rapid" development means "rapid" growth. As a generalization, and particularly when applied to a nation, such a meaning has some validity. It is an unsuitable concept, however, when relatively small geographic areas or individual decision-making units are involved. There are some areas that will decline by all economic measures in spite of whatever reasonable efforts are made to promote growth. Further, some individual decision-making units may find it highly desirable or necessary to contract rather than grow. A university, with its concern being for people, cannot work without reservation for development which is defined as growth.

For purposes of this chapter, development is defined as (rapid) achievement of realistic goals. Personal development for its own sake is excluded. For many private decision-making units and geographic areas, this definition may well mean growth in economic terms. For the dying town, however, it may mean a rapid demise with the lowest economic and social costs.

Development in any area is the sum of the results of the implementation of decisions made by individuals, firms, organizations, and the public sector of the area; but it is also the result of decisions made

**C. BRICE RATCHFORD** is Vice-president for Extension at the University of Missouri. He holds the Ph.D. from Duke University. He has been a long-time participant in extension programs at North Carolina State University and the University of Missouri. Publications related to his chapter include: "Role of State and Land-Grant University Extension Services in Eliminating Rural Poverty" (Columbia: University of Missouri Extension Division, MP 73, 1967) and "The Public Service Role of the Modern University" (**The College and Its Community—A Conference on Purpose and Direction in the Education of Adults,** Boston: The Center for the Study of Liberal Education for Adults, Boston University, Occasional Papers No. 16).

by similar groups in the nation and throughout the world. The increasing number of substitute products and improved communications and transportation, all the result of new technology, have reduced the isolation of any particular area or region. Development in one area or region may favorably or adversely influence areas or regions on the other side of the country. The influence of the public sector on economic and social development is increasing rapidly and becomes an important new dimension as compared to earlier years when development of an area or regions was largely in the hands of private decision-making units.

## HISTORICAL ROLE OF THE UNIVERSITY IN DEVELOPMENT[1]

All universities have contributed to development through enlarging the human capital supply and expanding the stock of knowledge by the training of the regularly matriculated students and the scholarly research of the faculty and students.

The land-grant university introduced a new dimension; it made development in at least one area—agriculture—a major objective. The agricultural experiment station and cooperative extension service were created as developmental instruments for agricultural and rural sectors. Both were established to help solve immediate problems—such as insect damage—and to make farming and rural life more satisfying and profitable. These institutions have been fantastically successful, although some of the benefits have not been distributed as the originators of the instruments assumed. While farmers and rural people have benefited in many ways, the public has received most of the income benefits.[2]

The experiment stations have a significance to development, not only for the new knowledge generated but also for new processes perfected for finding new knowledge.

Less than a century ago, most new knowledge was the result of an individual scientist pursuing his scholarly research, usually at a university or hospital, or an individual who was called an inventor. The inventors of the spinning jenny, the steamboat, the cotton gin, the reaper, and airplane were seldom trained scientists, but rather were innovative skilled craftsmen.

The experiment stations pioneered a new pattern. The federal

---

[1] An excellent and comprehensive discussion of this subject is contained in a speech by Paul Miller, *The Agricultural Colleges of the U.S., Paradoxical Servants of Change,* which was given at the annual meeting of the American Association of Land-Grant Colleges and Universities, Kansas City, Missouri, 1961.

[2] This point is made by Heady and many other economists. These results occur because of the inelasticity of demand for most farm products. These strict economic analyses have tended to overlook other real benefits farmers *have* secured: less physical effort, less risk from natural hazards, greater self-respect and dignity.

government and the universities cooperating established the machinery for systematically uncovering new basic knowledge, and for developing products and practices from this that the ordinary farmer or consumer could use. It is comparatively recent that industry became a partner— serving in the role of turning basic knowledge into useful products and services.

A similar pattern for other fields did not emerge until World War II, with the possible exception of health sciences. The federal government made massive investments in basic and applied research during World War II, and scientists from the government, universities, and industry contributed together under a variety of arrangements. The jet planes, rockets, and the "A" bomb demonstrated the productivity of such an approach.

Some half century after the land-grant colleges were established and a quarter century after the founding of the experiment stations, it was found that farmers and rural people did not have ready access to and were not making extensive use of the college and the experiment station. This resulted in the establishment of the Cooperative Extension Service, an organization that has developed into the largest adult education program in the world and is further unique by being the first adult education agency directed specifically to bringing about economic and social development. The role of cooperative extension has been described in many ways, but I like to think of it having served from its beginning as a vehicle for continuing dialogue of a significant nature between the university and rural people. The dialogue provided farmers with information, skills, and motivation which led to many types of development. The "feedback" from farmers led to changes in the university, brought it support and made it an even more effective developmental tool.

Other university adult education programs directed to development have been slow to develop. A number of universities developed fairly comprehensive general extension programs; but the primary goal was the development of the individual, and the main approach was extending regular university academic programs to students off campus or to those coming on campus at unusual hours, i.e., the evening. There are several notable exceptions to the above generalization. A few universities have conducted extensive training programs for the public sector for many years; a handful have taken seriously the education of organized labor; and several have developed programs for transferring technology to industry. The failure to develop general extension programs directed to development is due to the universities either not perceiving a role in development or not being equipped to serve in such a role.

For purposes of this chapter, the results of these developmental efforts on the university are more significant than "end" results. In most colleges of agriculture, the resident teaching budget and staff are smaller than either the experiment station or extension budgets and staff. The addition of these arms has made the college of agriculture different from all other colleges.[3] The main point being made is that the same staffing pattern may well prevail throughout the university if the total university becomes an instrument dedicated to development.

Several generalizations may be made about university developmental efforts to date, recognizing that there are exceptions which serve only to prove the rule.

1. A large percentage of the total effort has been, and continues to be, directed to agriculture and rural people.
2. In all fields—not just agriculture—a very large percentage of the effort has been directed to nonmetropolitan areas. Most land-grant universities have respectable development efforts in engineering, government, and community development. In general, these have an even larger nonmetropolitan orientation than the agricultural program.
3. Technology has received major attention. With the exception of the programs for family and youth, relatively little attention has gone to social concerns and, until recently, little emphasis was given to economics and management. The heavy emphasis on technology resulted, at times, in more interest and concern in swine and corn than people.
4. The clientele was almost entirely individual decision-making units in the private sector. Aggregative effects and the public decision-making units were largely ignored.

The experiences of the past show that the university can, through planned programs of research and extension, be a powerful force in development, in at least some areas. Valuable lessons have been learned about what to do as well as things to avoid.

## THE ROLE OF THE UNIVERSITY IN DEVELOPMENT[4]

It is not a proper role of the university to make decisions for people or organizations. Neither should it serve as an instrument of

---

[3] In spite of pride in the developmental arms which have proven their value for over a half a century, the college of agriculture is at times apologetic about the situation, feeling compelled to say that the main justification for these programs is to enhance the resident teaching programs. This point is made here because it has relevance to a later section of the chapter.

[4] An excellent discussion of this subject may be found in a bulletin titled, *The University at the Service of Society*, The Carnegie Foundation for the Advancement of Teaching, 589 Fifth Avenue, N.Y., N.Y. Also see John W. Gardner, "Universities as Designers of the Future," *Educational Record*, Fall, 1967.

direct economic or social action.[5] It can be a vital force, however, in bringing about action on the part of individuals, firms, organizations, and institutions in three major ways:

1. New knowledge, either to mankind or to a particular individual, gives a new set of alternatives and hence becomes a very important motivator of change.
2. Attitudes in an affluent, developed society may well be the major determinant of the amount and type of development, and education is a major force in changing attitudes.
3. Values are a large factor in development, and knowledge new to an individual and broadening to the mind (one concept of education) often results in changed values. A critical question (which is discussed later) is the extent to which the university deliberately sets out either to influence values or to make value judgments and disseminate these to society.

Here are some of the positive ways that a university can help bring about development.

### Developer and Interpreter of New Knowledge

New technology is the most important single motivator of development. Universities have demonstrated that research conducted either as part of a graduate program or independent of the teaching programs is very productive of new technology in many fields. Because of the capability of universities, an increasing number of governmental agencies and industries are turning to the universities for research. The universities are learning how to interact productively with either or both government and industry in developing new technology.

The impact of new technology is usually not restricted to the manufacturer who converts new knowledge into a product for those who use it. As an example, the automobile has changed the public sector completely; consider the investment in roads, traffic control devices, and patrolmen. It created a new business—casualty insurance. The "A" and "H" bombs have affected the policies of the world. The supersonic plane will profoundly affect the social situation of the world. These are but a few of hundreds of examples that could be given.

The examples indicate that a major gap in the total informational picture is the impact of technology on society. Firms evaluate technology in terms of profit potential and federal agencies from the

---

[5] This point is discussed by Chancellor Roger Heyns of the University of California at Berkeley in *College and University Business,* 1967, p. 47.

standpoint of their mission—i.e., effectiveness in defense or delivering the mail. Most of the aggregative evaluations that are available have been done by economists and sociologists and apply to agriculture, and here most of the studies have been "after the fact." The brain power and computers are available for evaluating within fairly narrow ranges the consequences of possible courses of public action and new technology on the total country as well as on its several parts in terms of economic, social, or political goals. Such an evaluation system will cost a great deal when compared to present budgets for such work, but the cost is very small in relation to expenditures for development of new technology or the expenditures by the public sector to achieve certain social or political goals. Such evaluation must be undertaken by the public sector; and a partnership effort of the federal government and universities can be most effective. The universities with their objectivity are ideally suited to make such appraisals; but the federal government probably must serve as the major collector of the raw data. Since the public sector is the major investor in uncovering new technology, the major force behind policies and programs to achieve social goals, and the residual force to solve problems created by others, it is desirable for government policy makers and the public, whom the policy makers represent, to have such evaluations.

While new technology is the major dynamic force leading to development, there are other types of information that are relevant. Without intending to be exhaustive, here are a few of the more important areas.

The technology is adapted within an economic setting. The developmental decisions will be improved if those making the decisions understand and can use the tools of economic analysis and have available economic data relating to both the short and long run. New economic analysis tools are needed to make it possible for decision-making units to effectively make use of computers.

Far too little is known about the decision-making processes, particularly in large organizations and in the public sector. Universities have recognized for years the necessity of involving faculty in decision-making, and some research in the behavioral sciences is indicating that the same principle applies in business and social areas.

Institutions and governmental units will be increasingly important to development. Too little is known about the operation of such units and there is practically no information which would enable people to develop and appraise alternative organizational arrangements.

Motivation of people is obviously important to achieving development. Except for the field of education, very little is known about basic motivators of people, particularly as they relate to economic and social concerns.

Education can be a developmental force within itself and certainly the results of education are important to development. There has been a relatively small investment in discovering more about the teaching-learning processes, particularly as they relate to alternative systems of education for adults. The research input in the broad field of continuing education or adult education is ridiculously small.

## Conducting an Extension-type Educational Program

New information is useless from a developmental point of view until put to use by decision-making units. The majority of most clientele groups will not actively seek out new information, which means that an aggressive educational program must be conducted if the research results are to be used.

The lessons learned from over fifty years of cooperative extension and other university extension programs directed to development indicate that the educational program must do more than simply transmit new knowledge. The additional components include elements of salesmanship, motivation, and perhaps most important, making the new information relevant to the problems and goals of decision-making units.

There is not complete transferability of methods and approaches between program areas—such as agriculture and medicine—and clientele groups—such as rural and urban homemakers. It does seem that regardless of the subject or clientele the best way for the university to accomplish its developmental educational objectives is to establish a continuous dialogue between university personnel and the clientele. "Dialogue" means a two-way flow of information. Obviously as its part of the dialogue, the university provides education; the other side or "feedback" indicates still another function of extension—namely, letting the university know of problems and gaps in information. This information should help the university make its research and resident teaching programs more valuable.

It was mentioned previously that one of the main tasks of extension is to make information relevant, and this can be accomplished only if the goals and problems of the audience or clientele are well known to the educator. This strengthens the argument for the basic philosophical approach being the establishing of a continuing dialogue.

Recognizing that there are many differences in details, at a generalized level the jobs of university extension with all types of clientele are identical. These are:

1. Disseminating information new to mankind or new to the particular decision-making unit.
2. Helping the decision-making unit see how the information will

help achieve its goals. This is a crucial point; all people have information stored in the brain which is not being put to use because its relevance for solving their problems and for reaching their goals is not recognized.

3. Suggesting alternative goals for the decision-making units. Goals grow out of the aspirations and knowledge of the decision-making units, and an analysis of possibilities often leads to a change of goals.

4. Indicating decisions that should be faced up to and decided on a positive basis. Decisions are made either through a positive choice or by doing nothing. Public bodies are particularly prone to the latter, but it is an accident if decisions made through default are the best that are possible.

5. Providing information that helps decision-making units become more adept at using the skills and processes which lead to sound decisions. The decision-making process is the same in principle for all units. Only the more sophisticated units in either the public or private sector consistently follow the best methods.

6. Providing information that will help the decision-making units evaluate the economic and social impact of a particular course of action. This is somewhat related to 2 above, but goes further and helps the units know the effects after the decision is implemented.

## Work with Organizations

Organizations could have been considered as just another type of decision-making unit, but they are pulled out for special consideration because they are becoming increasingly important as forces in economic and social development. The university can play a unique role with such decision-making units. Organizations influence development through their own actions and through their influence on the public sector. Organizations may be classified into three types:

1. Those whose primary purpose is enhancing the welfare of its members, examples being the farm organizations, labor unions, and trade associations.

2. Those whose primary purpose is social or public development, examples being the voluntary social welfare associations and United Funds.

3. The semipublic organizations, such as economic development corporations, and community action agencies administering the Economic Opportunity Act.

Many of the organizations perform several roles. A labor union may take steps to bring about economic or social development of an area which is only indirectly related to the welfare of its members. The National Association of Soil and Water Conservation Districts has as a primary goal promotion of conservation, but also serves as a lobbying group for several federal agencies.

The university can make existing organizations more effective in much the same way it assists other decision-making units. The organizations need new knowledge, an appraisal of consequences of alternative courses of action of new knowledge on goals and alternative goals, how to use the social action processes, and the impact of their decisions on the other parts of the economy and society.

There are at least two additional roles, however, that the university can play. First, it can serve as a critic or evaluator for members and the general public. This becomes increasingly important as the power of organizations increases. This role may often prove to be unpopular with certain organizations, but perhaps this only strengthens the need for the university to be involved in such a manner. Second, the university can guide the development of new organizations. There is a great proliferation of organizations and each new program or problem tends to create a new one. Old ones seldom die, although they may become ineffective. As part of its continuing analysis and appraisal of the situation, the university can help people decide whether a new organization is necessary, or whether some existing organization can modify its purposes to handle the immediate need.

## Implementation of Action

The university is usually not considered to have a role in the implementation of decisions by the various units. There is a role that is proper as the experience of cooperative extension has demonstrated. A very useful role, and one that requires relatively little time, is acquainting decision-making units with aids that they may secure to implement decisions. As examples, a farmer may be told of possible sources of credit, or a town of the possibilities of federal grants to pay part of the cost of a project. Increasingly, there is expertise available from many sources to individuals, firms, and public bodies, either for free or a modest fee. This should be called to the attention of the decision-making units as they implement decisions.

A second relevant role is to serve as a "prodder." The simple question "How are you coming along with your plans?" may be a very powerful stimulator to a unit moving ahead.

A third proper role is providing information that will help decision-making units constantly reevaluate goals and consequences of alternative courses of action. Usually there are many points during the implementation process where adjustments can be made with minimum costs that would produce more desirable results. There is a tendency, particularly on the part of the public sector and its organizations, to pursue a goal long after it becomes irrelevant or less effective than another goal that might be achieved with the same resources.

### Providing Information That Will Help Harmonize Decisions at the Several Levels

There are many examples of decision-making units working at complete odds with each other. Some of this is unavoidable, particularly between the public and private sectors, but much of it is unnecessary. There are also many examples of directly conflicting actions within the public sector, sometimes between different levels of government, but often by the same governmental unit.

Much of this is the result of the several decision-making units not knowing what others are doing or not recognizing that by a minor shift in goals, efforts could be harmonized. The university cannot and should not tell any decision-making unit what to do. It can serve in a harmonizing role, however, by indicating the points at which conflicting action is taking place and suggesting alternatives which would result in a harmonizing of efforts. This is really a special case of the evaluation of the impact of decisions that was mentioned in the section labeled, "Developer and Interpreter of New Knowledge." Information needed to accomplish this role would be forthcoming from the evaluations it was suggested that the university should perform in connection with the federal government.[6] It is recognized that there can never be complete harmonizing of decisions in a dynamic economic, social, and political system. The only point that is being made is that conflicts which result from lack of knowledge and lack of consideration of alternatives should be publicized for the consideration and action of the decision-making unit.

### Role of the University in Expressing Value Judgments

The question which has been avoided is whether the university passes value judgments on issues. For ease in exposition, the term "university" has been used throughout this chapter. The university is not a simple institution; it basically is a faculty. The faculty mem-

---

[6] Parenthetically, it must be mentioned that the university is not always internally consistent; in fact, it is full of conflicts. These should be uncovered and publicized by the university itself and by the clientele the university serves. The university should respond by becoming as internally consistent as is possible.

bers hold many diverse political, social, economic, and ethical views. Any university permits a faculty member to express his views to his students and the public. Universities generally take the stand that being a university employee should deprive no employee of any of his basic rights as a citizen. This leaves the faculty member with a right and perhaps a responsibility as a citizen to express his views on any subject.

In exercising this right, the faculty member has a very serious responsibility. He should make it clear that he speaks as a citizen and not as a representative of the university. A more subtle point relates to the posture assumed as an individual. Almost every university faculty member is an authority in some field; but none is an authority in all fields. When speaking in his field, the faculty member might well expect that more credence be given to his views than to those of any ordinary citizen; when out of his field, he has no greater insight than any educated citizen.

No university is likely to call faculty meetings to determine a stand on matters which are extraneous to the internal operations of the university. It would be inappropriate to do so, in my opinion. This is in the same category as groups of students or faculty members trying through concerted action to force their views on others. This is as much in conflict with the principle of free speech as some administrator trying to tell the faculty what it can and cannot say.[7]

## Clientele Important to Development[8]

There are several groups in society which play a crucial role in development. It is to these groups that the university beams its development efforts. A group obviously important is the *private entrepreneurs*, including the farmers, businessmen, and industrialists. Decisions of this group influence employment, income (total and distribution), location of economic activity, use of natural resources and social goals. Out of this group come many of the leaders who individually and through the various associations and organizations become a major force in influencing actions of the public sector in economic and social matters.

*Professionals*, which include teachers, engineers, doctors, lawyers, social workers, and many others, are important in development for several reasons. The relative number and quality of such people in a given location are important to development. Again their influence extends beyond their individual contributions, for they often are major forces in influencing decisions of organizations and the public sector.

[7] See *The University at the Service of Society* cited in footnote 4.

[8] Organizations are an important clientele group, but were treated separately.

The *family* continues to be a basic institution in major segments of the society. The family as a major spending unit has an effect on resource allocation; but from a developmental standpoint, the values which are required as part of a family may be more significant. As an example, mobility is important to development and this is closely related to values acquired from and related to the family.

The *public sector,* as mentioned several times and repeated again deliberately for emphasis, is becoming the major force in the achievement of social goals, and is of increasing importance in the economic sphere. The public sector at first glance appears as an intangible, amorphous body; but on closer scrutiny, it breaks down to a number of very human citizens.

All *citizens* or the *general public* are not usually a major direct force in development, but are a major indirect force through their effect on the public sector. Elections can and do change the role of government in development. Many issues, particularly at the local level, require a referendum, and here citizens have a more direct voice.

Every decision-making unit in the country can be grouped into one or several of the major clientele categories just listed. This "laundry list" should not lead to the conclusion that the university should be the main research and development arm for all of these units at any given time. More will be said on this subject when priorities are discussed in the next section.

## HOW THE UNIVERSITY CAN BECOME AN EFFECTIVE INSTRUMENT FOR DEVELOPMENT

Each university can decide whether it will become an active and positive instrument in development. If it chooses to become such, there are several things it must do and others that will help make it an effective instrument.

### Securing Commitment

An absolutely essential step is the university accepting "helping development" as a relevant role; without this commitment, any role that it plays in bringing about development will be an accident. The role must be given the same importance as other missions of the university. This does not mean that other roles are relegated to secondary places, but it does mean that there must be a reasonable allocation of resources between the missions. The university that accepts development as a relevant role only when it has fully achieved its objectives in other program areas will never become an instrument for development. There are those who argue that serving in a developmental role will take resources from other roles and make it a second-class institution in all respects. This is theoretically possible, but the experience of agricultural colleges and selected colleges which have moved ahead as development arms seems to indicate that there is likely to be a strengthening, rather than a weakening, of other roles if the university does become effective as an instrument for development.

Securing the commitment is difficult because it must be made by the governing board, the administration, and the faculty. Getting faculty commitment is extremely difficult and some evidence of this lies in the lack of complete commitment within agricultural colleges after a hundred years of tradition. Faculties which have had no experience in development work, and which tend to be afraid of anything which threatens the status quo, will have real difficulty in reaching the necessary commitment.

The commitment cannot be secured overnight and many techniques must be used. Some of these include exposing the faculty to outside consultants in their own field who do understand and believe in the developmental role of the university, employing new faculty members who do have the commitment, long-range planning with the objective of bringing relevance of the university to the modern society, visitations to other universities which are doing developmental work, and at selected times and places "buying" the faculty. This is accomplished by buying released time for special developmental projects, special travel funds for those doing such work, etc.

A necessary condition for securing the commitment is an adjustment in the reward systems. Activities of faculty members leading to development must count as much as excellence in classroom teaching and scholarly publications toward promotion, salary adjustments, committee assignments, etc. Perhaps a more difficult problem is changing the value system within the academic disciplines on a national and international level. Stature among peers is often of greater importance to individuals than their standing within their own university. The primary means at present of securing stature among one's peers in the same discipline is scholarly publications. The values can be changed, and the faculty working in developmental efforts needs to have time to contribute to the scholarly publications.

## Organizing to Do the Job

Organizational structure and administrative policies are tools to accomplish the objectives of the organization. There is nothing sacred about any particular organization framework. Clear goals, commitment to the goals, and good communications are the real keys to success.

Regardless of the particular organizational structure, it is clear that several conditions need to be met if the university is to be an effective development force. Practically every discipline within a comprehensive university has a useful role to play in development. This is true even if the university chooses to work with only a segment of the population, for example, rural people, or at a single development goal, for example, economic development.

There must be competent faculty members who are interested in development functions and who have time to devote to the work. When there is a large number of decision-making units of a particular type that are not highly mobile, generalists are needed to serve in somewhat the role that the traditional county agent performed for agriculture. If some sort of generalist working in the field is used, he must be backed up by highly trained specialists.

The most significant developmental problems require a team of people representing several disciplines. The makeup of the teams needs to vary from problem to problem.

The entire job cannot be done on campus. There are inadequate facilities to house staff and to serve the clientele. Of more importance, many of the people who need to be reached will not or cannot come to the campus. Further, if one of the stated roles of providing continuous dialogue between the university faculty and the decision-making units is to be met, much of it must take place on the home grounds of the target decision-making units.

This situation suggests that a number of regional centers are needed. These would be staffed by personnel who do direct teaching with clientele, do some research, and serve as the primary interface of the university with decision-making units. The county-based operations of cooperative extension could gradually be brought into the regional centers. Perhaps these centers could be used by several universities and with the advent of community colleges in many areas, consideration should be given to these being the location for regional centers.

Given these requirements, how does a university organize itself to accomplish the task? It seems fairly clear that there must be direction and coordination at the very top level. No one school or college within the university can harness the expertise of all disciplines. Each faculty member, school, college, or division going its own way, oblivious to what others are doing, also will not accomplish the job.

Most universities realize that they are not organized properly to achieve the developmental role, and a great deal of experimentation is underway. A number of universities are designating vice-presidents to give the necessary direction and coordination. Within this basic framework there are many variations. At the University of Wisconsin, extension has been organized in effect as a separate campus. At the University of Missouri, efforts have been made to build extension into every academic department. At North Carolina State University, each college has been encouraged to develop its own extension program; but there is an administrator at the top level responsible for coordination. No one is sure of the best pattern, and likely what is best for one situation is not best for another.

The same sort of experimentation is taking place in research. In addition to top level coordination, universities have organized a series of institutions or centers; and some have established separate corporations to accomplish certain research tasks. Again, no clear, best pattern has emerged.

A problem which is only beginning to be grappled with is the merging or coordinating of the research and extension functions. Both are needed in development work and, increasingly, there is no clean line between the two. Some universities are trying to handle this situation by having one vice-president in charge of academic affairs, which includes regular curricula and faculty research, and another vice-president for public service which includes organized research programs and extension.

The only point that is clear at this time is that further innovation is needed and it is far too early to be selecting any organizational structure as "best."

## Securing Resources

It may seem surprising that this is not at the top of the list of the requirements. It is not because resources will come with the commitment and the ability to do the job. There has been a rapid increase in funding possibilities at the federal level. Almost every agency of the federal government has some funds for research, and most of these look to universities to perform part of it. Many of the arrangements for federal agencies working with universities are cumbersome and time-consuming for both the agency and the universities. Further, a high percentage of the research funds are mission oriented. In spite of the difficulties, much of the research required is consistent with the interest of the university and has a direct relationship to the development of the geographic area the university chooses to serve.

Much the same picture exists in extension. Most of the federal agencies have either a recognized extension program or are willing to invest funds in continuing education of its own staff. As an example, the Post Office Department just announced a massive training program for its employees, and the Department of Justice has funds for retraining its own people and also for training all types of law enforcement personnel.

State governments are showing increased willingness to devote funds to research and education in program areas which show promise of bringing about development. Fees and user charges can be an important source of revenue, particularly for some types of research and extension activities. Many units in the public sector—cities, counties, planning commissions, etc.—are indicating a willingness to pay at least part of the cost of applied research and extension work.

## Relations with Other Universities, Government, and Private Business

Until fairly recently, few universities that were not publicly supported were active in a developmental role. This picture is changing rapidly and private universities are very much involved in research and extension. The community colleges which are emerging in all parts of the nation will be important and viable instruments for extension and possibly some research.

Governments, and particularly the federal government, have become much more active in conducting research and extension-type programs. The federal establishment has built a tremendous in-house research capability which at times comes into conflict with the interests of the university. The federal government also conducts directly a number of educational programs, some of the more notable being the spin-off programs of AEC and NASA, the clearing house operation of the Department of Commerce, and the training programs of the Small Business Administration.

One approach which is being used to implement the concept of creative federalism is to have a state agency, which in effect serves as a broker for a federal agency. Because of this situation the state government, even if it does not increase its resources for research and extension, is playing a more active role. The comparatively short experience with this vehicle indicates that it will result in many changes in allocation of funds and operations.

The private sector is becoming more active in research and extension. There has been a sharp increase in the number of companies established to do research or training. Industry has been in the educational field for many years, but the primary objective was to increase sales. A very new phenomenon is a private firm in the business of continuing education for profit. To date, most of their work has been funded by the federal establishment, but resources are being invested in learning how to use the new educational hardware and make a profit from educational programs.

These developments necessitate the land-grant and public universities reassessing their role and perhaps changing their posture on some of these matters. The relations of the universities with the federal establishment and with state government are so complex that no attempt will be made to discuss these in this chapter. It does seem fairly clear that the state and land-grant university must assume a positive role with other institutions of higher education. We should assist them to become more effective in their research and extension programs. This can be done through consultation, training staff, providing expertise, interchange of staff and, perhaps on occasion, subcontracting work to them.

The university must also take a positive role toward the private sector. It can train the personnel of the private research and educational firms, provide expertise, and generally stay in a noncompetitive role. The university does have some responsibility to assess the quality of the work of the private sector, to use this information to guide its own course of action, and to provide basic information for the general public and governmental agencies.

## Some Additional Considerations

Increasing the flexibility in use of staff would be a major step in increasing the potential of the university for development work. This can be accomplished through changes in assignments—that is, periodically switching from research to extension to resident teaching or to different combinations of these functions. This would make it possible to have staff members available for developmental work at a particular time and should partially solve the problem of second-class citizenship status for those involved in applied research and extension. As indicated earlier, teams of people are needed in much developmental work and the composition of the teams needs to change with each problem. One of the reasons universities established institutes or centers was to get an interdisciplinary approach, but centers become institutionalized and rigid in their structure, and a new institute or center has to be established to secure the team needed for a new problem. Increased flexibility in assignments would make it easier to secure teams of faculty and also to change the composition of the teams over time. There should also be an increase in sharing staff between universities for short-term and/or special assignments. Certain individuals on short-term assignment could be immensely helpful to a particular region or a particular university that was organizing itself to do a particular developmental task.

One obvious way of increasing flexibility is the ability and willingness to redirect resources, and the top administrator must accept responsibility for achieving this. The different units—that is, the academic departments and divisions—will do some redirecting, but it will be within a restricted framework.

Establishing priorities is an essential step. Even the largest and most comprehensive universities cannot do all things for all people, even those things which are clearly classified as being of university level. It will undoubtedly be better for the university to do an acceptable or excellent job with some clientele group, program area, or geographic area than to scatter its shots.

Priority should be established after careful study of needs and possibilities and consideration of the opinions and thoughts of potential clientele and how these relate to the goals and strengths of the university. The university must resist setting priorities because of the availability of funds in a particular field. Simply following funding that might be easily available at a given time will lead to useless meandering and a loss of morale and confidence of the faculty.

More cooperation and division of labor among universities, both within the state and between states, will strengthen the developmental capability of the total university community.

The major metropolitan areas will be increasingly important from the standpoint of both people and problems. No university has yet learned how to carry out an effective developmental role in a major metropolitan area. The large city is an extremely complex entity and differs in many ways from the more familiar rural scene or underdeveloped foreign country.[9] If the university is to be important in development in the future, it has no alternative to giving major emphasis to the cities. As a first essential step to success, the university must understand thoroughly the metropolitan community, its people, institutions, problems, and opportunities. Without doing this, the university will be in the position of the well-intentioned but uninformed do-gooder.

It has been mentioned several times that one of the main techniques for the university's being effective in development is to establish a continuing dialogue with the decision-making units. Dialogue means the university *listening* and modifying its efforts as well as *telling* decision-making units. While there should be full involvement of clientele, ownership and direction of the programs must not be turned over to the clientele. This has happened infrequently in certain cooperative extension programs and these experiences show the necessity of the university maintaining control of the programs, setting its own priorities, and determining what it tells decision-making units through the dialogue processes.

There are many possibilities for the university securing multiplier effects from its own staff. Both cooperative and general extension have had enough experience to demonstrate that it can be done, but the possibilities have not been fully exploited. There is expertise outside the university in all parts of the country which could be used in educational programs either for free or for a very modest cost. A major objective of the university is retraining professionals. Why not use the professionals who keep up to date as teachers for their peers?

[9] Paul A. Miller, "Additional Remarks on the University Service," a speech given to the 81st Meeting of the ASULGC.

General extension has developed to a fairly high degree the concept of educational programmer. Some cooperative extension workers have been quite expert in the process, but have not used the name. These staff members are experts at getting together clientele and a teacher and building a meaningful educational program.

An exciting concept, new in many fields, is the use of subprofessionals. It is now evident that many roles traditionally performed by the teacher or researcher can be turned over to a subprofessional or paraprofessional who may actually be more effective in doing the specific job than the professional teacher or researcher. Several paraprofessionals can usually be employed for the price of a single professional. In many fields, a single professional can train and supervise ten to twenty subprofessionals. More resources need to go into this category of employee.

The university must be willing and even anxious to turn loose certain developmental tasks as other agencies of government or private business acquire the capability of doing the task, thus freeing resources for new possibilities.

The explosion of technology in the communications field parallels that in other fields. Radio and television are now well established, but their potential as educational media remains largely untapped. The tele-lecture and electro-writer have been demonstrated as effective in many situations. Programmed instruction, the so-called teaching machines, and interface with the computer have also been available for some time, but are still not widely used. Some resources should go into learning how these machines and techniques can stretch scarce faculty resources. A possibility which should be tried is a self-learning center which would be equipped with a number of self-instructional possibilities. The center should stay open seven days a week, 24 hours a day. This is no more than an elaboration upon the concept of a library.

# CHAPTER ELEVEN

# FEDERALISM AND DOMESTIC DEVELOPMENT

## PAUL A. MILLER

TALKING ABOUT the role of government—in development, or anything else—presents very special problems today because of the unprecedented rate and scope of change prevailing in our time. What was true of the federal government's relations with the states last year may be of merely historical interest next week; the pattern for dividing responsibilities among the executive, legislative, and judicial branches is as variable as the nature of the responsibilities themselves.

This extraordinary mutability confronts us both at home and in the international community. All kinds of shifts are taking place in the world power structure. Power itself takes on new connotations as we see millions die in technological war while another manifestation of governmental power saves millions more through technological medicine.

And, as we scrutinize it from vantage points near enough to the centers of authority to see some of what goes on there, we are also aware of the limitations of power. I cannot help remembering President Kennedy's comment that his greatest surprise on coming to the presidency was to find out how many situations he could not do anything about.

There are indeed limits to what any one person can do, no mat-

PAUL A. MILLER is President, Rochester Institute of Technology at Rochester, N. Y. At the time his chapter was written he was Assistant Secretary for Education of the Department of Health, Education and Welfare. He has served as the director of rural development programs at Michigan State University and has worked in South America and East Africa. Publications related to his chapter include: "New Missions for Old Programs: A University-Wide Approach to Continuing Education" (**Journal of Higher Education 35** [November, 1964] pp. 450–58) and "Poverty Amidst Affluence: An Overall View of Poverty in Contemporary American Society" (**Working with Low-Income Families,** Proceedings of the American Home Economics Association Workshop, University of Chicago, March 15–19, 1965).

ter what his position. And always the unanswered questions about the *nature* of power in society remain. Today we see uncontrolled eruptions of social force all around us, power which has not been channeled for constructive use and, instead, breaks out in meaningless or destructive ways. Can we harness the human energy this represents and make it work for human betterment? This is the central issue of our time.

In one of the lectures he made at the University of Virginia in 1940, Carl Becker described it in terms of grim alternatives. He said, "Can the flagrant inequality of possessions and of opportunity now existing in democratic societies be corrected by the democratic method? If it cannot be so corrected, the resulting discontent and confusion will be certain, sooner or later, to issue in some form of revolutionary or military dictatorship. This, then, is the dilemma which confronts democratic societies: to solve the economic problem by the democratic method, or to cease to be democratic societies."

In government as well as outside, this issue, and how the federal system can relate to it, is an overriding concern. Federal ties with the states, and the growing needs of cities and metropolitan areas are subjects without equal now increasingly discussed by the departments of the executive branch. President Johnson has contributed a new concept to these discussions in the term "creative federalism."

Of course, it is not only between the federal government and the states that one finds new relationships; among the states too, new alignments and new patterns of interaction are arising. The nation-wide education compact among the governors is one such lateral entente. Then too, springing from the new concentration on city problems are many new structures like the Urban Coalition.

The aliveness of federalism as an issue is further apparent in popular debate over the disbursement of federal funds to the states and municipalities. There is constant talk in Washington about proposals like the Howard Pechman plan, and the possibility of moving the surplus of federal taxes "en bloc" to the states and municipalities. I would say that the sharpest debates about education that I have had anything to do with have been about how the states may transfer funds to municipal school districts and local government units, and what becomes of power and control when that happens. Every piece of new legislation being drafted these days reflects an awareness of these fluidities.

A case in point was the great struggle that went on over Title III of the Elementary and Secondary Education Act. There was sharp controversy over whether innovations within the educational system could best be stimulated from Washington or carried out by the local school districts or the state commissioners. A similar situation arose in connection with the poverty programs in the Congress last year. Who would operate the Community Action Programs? Should

Washington have the final word, or should authority be localized in the cities? In yet another area—science and technology—we find Congress preoccupied with the same sort of thing. There are uncertainties about the distribution of competence throughout the country, and about regional balances in public expenditures.

Meanwhile, traditional federalism is being further altered by the introduction of regional authorities such as the Appalachian Regional Commission. Nor is it only the forms of federalism that are being altered; what goes on in the system is also changing. Equality of opportunity, civil rights, poverty, environmental quality, consumer protection—there is a whole new vocabulary to express the concerns of the federal complex as we think of them today.

It is interesting to note that Article I, Section 8 of the Constitution in which the powers of the national government are set forth has nothing to say about many of the vital citizen needs that now dominate the domestic political agenda. The Tenth Amendment which elaborates the powers of the states is also noncommittal. In fact, such matters as education, welfare, public health, and highways are nowhere mentioned in the United States Constitution. As the federal system has grown up, it has been assumed that these are within the province of the states, under the concept of residual powers.

A second point of legal and historical significance is the fact that unlike the federal-state relationship, the state-local relationship is not one between sovereign governments. Indeed, local governments are, by law, creatures of the state governments. This was formalized in 1868 by Justice Dillon of the Iowa Supreme Court when he ruled that municipal corporations owe their origin to, and derive their powers and rights wholly from, the legislature. Said Justice Dillon of the legislature: "It breathes into them the breath of life, without which they cannot exist. As it creates, so it may destroy. As it may destroy, it may abridge and control."

The relationship between the federal government and the states has never been this clearcut. Uncertainty over the boundaries of power between the two threatened the Union repeatedly between 1781 and 1788. There was a time when the states were so jealous of their prerogatives that the federal expenses were allocated to the states and paid within them. The new Constitution of 1788, of course, gave the federal government power to levy and collect taxes, but the states remained strong and obstreperous in their relations with national authority until the Civil War gave the sanction of successful power to the idea that the Union was more than a confederation of states.

After the Civil War, the states were weak, and yet the federal government was not what we would think of today as strong. It was local governments that took care of the civil functions. In 1900, localities spent more than state and federal governments together on such matters as health, education, highways, and other similar functions.

The figures involved in 1900 contrast strikingly with the magnitude of expenditures we expect today. The total spent for the civil functions in 1900 was a mere $1.2 billion, of which 71 percent came from local governments, a little more than 18 percent from the federal sector, and a little less than 11 percent from the states. The sum of these contributions represented about 6 percent of the gross national product as compared with the 17 percent we now spend for domestic public needs.

This was the general pattern even after World War I and the introduction of the federal income tax. It took the depression of the 1930s to raise the federal contribution to the domestic needs of the nation. By 1938, however, it was up to 35 percent and there was much talk of the impotence of the state governments in dealing with social and economic development. No one was particularly worried about federal control of local activities at this time; most of the money came to the states in the form of grants, with no strings, and with none of the guidelines typical of current practice. It was outright federal support for local people acting on the local level.

World War II was another watershed of change. By 1946, state and local governments were spending $11 billion for public needs— and with a $16 million debt. Twenty years later—in 1966—state and local governments were spending $84 billion with a $100 billion debt. In 1946, federal spending to help the states on civil functions was less than a billion dollars. By 1966, it had grown to $14 billion—a figure which covers only the federal contribution to states, counties, and school districts and includes none of the direct expenditures of federal agencies for activities of their own.

Estimates are that in the next few years, state and local spending will go to $120 billion. Startlingly enough, estimates on the federal side are almost as great. Given an end to the war and the carrying out of plans now being made, it is quite possible that by 1971, for the first time in history, fully half of the support for state and local civil functions will come from the federal government.

Government personnel figures show another side of the picture. Between 1946 and 1966, state and local public employment almost tripled, going from about three million workers to eight. In the same twenty-year period, federal employment declined slightly.

All this indicates, among other things, the remarkable flexibility of the federal system in emergencies. Clearly, the federal system has had to be flexible to survive some of the changes that have come about since it was instituted. The shift in rural-urban ratios is a case in point. When the Constitution was written, only 5 percent of the

American people were urban; by 1900, the figure was 40 percent; today, of course, the fully rural sector has dwindled substantially beyond that.

## NONRESULTS FROM NONSYSTEMS

The federal system has indeed survived changes of this kind, but not without a pile-up of anachronisms and organizational inefficiencies. We are trying to deal with the problems of an urbanized society through institutions developed for an agrarian one—institutions patched and extended and redirected to form a makeshift pattern of what General Gavin, in his recent book on the urban crisis, calls "nonsystems."

The capacity of these nonsystems for nonresults is the source of new pressures and tensions within the federal system. As the nation moves to solutions to the problems of its stricken cities, there is great interest in strengthening state and local governments. There is also considerable anxiety about the encroachments of federal power.

Meanwhile, the growth of big government at every level is a continuing fact of life in America. Since World War II, the number of federally sponsored programs within what might be called the development category has reached the 200 mark, and the number of departments and agencies involved is above 20.

I think all three levels of government within the federal system are going to continue to enlarge their spheres of responsibility. At the same time, it is likely that the revenue problems of the state and local governments will bring about an overhaul of the entire structure of fiscal responsibility for local services.

No matter who pays, however, the effectiveness of government programs on any level will depend on cutting through what some call the "management muddle." It is a reference to, first of all, a hardening of institutional blocs concerned with one kind of function at the federal level. Middle management has a way of becoming absorbed in the narrow interests of a particular office or bureau, and it may ignore the broader issues of nation, state government, and even the department where it operates.

The Department of Health, Education and Welfare is trying to coordinate and bring coherence to the scattered and disparate units representing health, education, and welfare activities. The problem is one of communication at middle management levels, and also one of relating policy decisions to an overall standard in the face of shifting leadership up and down the line.

The same kind of thing happens on the state level. The prevalence of categorical aid programs encourages the development of narrow and separate streams of institutional communication between state and federal levels of government. Local health, agriculture, or highway administration units keep in close touch with the federal agencies that nourish their budgets, but have less to do with each other, or with the rest of the federal structure.

Who is responsible? In this situation, as in so many others where things go wrong with a vast complex of people, institutions, and functions, everyone is to blame, and no one: Congress has fostered the trend by stressing categorical legislation; administrators have smoothed the way by settling so readily into comfortable special-interest grooves; upper leadership has sanctioned it by failing to insist that different kinds of activities be coordinated for the further-ance of overall objectives. Yet no one is really accountable for the development of these insularities in organization because the inter-play of so many forces has made it virtually inevitable.

Governmental effectiveness at all levels is also retarded by certain archaic constitutional and legal strictures. In all too many parts of the country, personnel systems oriented to nineteenth-century style patronage keep the caliber of state and local administration from rapid improvement.

Reform in this area would solve some of the manpower problems now producing stresses within the federal system, but by no means all. Shortages of people trained in human servicing occupations are now at crisis proportions throughout the nation. We started school last fall in the United States with about 200,000 teaching positions vacant. As for doctors, we find ourselves actually dependent on the developing countries for a supply of physicians—a supply which re-mains inadequate even with the employment of large numbers—16 percent of the total—of foreign-trained doctors.

The failure to provide needed personnel transcends the classic professional categories; it is also a failure to develop new occupa-tional specializations. While technical occupations—pharmacy, for example—elaborate their training requirements in an effort to climb the professional hierarchy, new situations cry out for new types of personnel and no one supplies them. Agronomists are hired and sent to special institutes that try to transform them into community de-velopment experts, but too little is done about training community developers in the first place.

A recent report by the Organization for Economic Cooperation and Development points out that the United States has so oriented its research and development facilities to technological development that manpower problems might make it impossible to move in another direction—there simply would not be enough people capable of doing other kinds of research and development.

Other manpower imbalances arise from categorical support for the preparation of specialists in new fields without regard to the broad sweep of manpower needs nationally. Thus, oceanography is currently in vogue; all sorts of institutions, coastal and inland, have responded to the lure of available grant money and developed an interest in this field.

Every pressure on the federal system is, I think, the greater because of a national tendency, born of the mass media, to overemphasize policies geared to problems and to underemphasize those geared to solutions. Infinite streams of unrelated messages, highlighting the bizarre, dramatizing deficiencies and hopes, set up frequently unrealistic expectations about what is feasible and, consequently, distort judgments about what should be tried.

Rushing from sensation to sensation and from novelty to novelty, the mass media constantly widen the gulf between patterns of desire and patterns of reasonable expectation. Government, on its side, can do little to counterbalance the shallow faddism that goes with this, for it is itself handicapped by the absence of the kind of memory system that would enable it to digest past experience and relate it to present problems.

Knowledge exists in vast quantities, but—perhaps particularly with regard to development—we have not worked out the systems to correlate and codify it so that we can weigh the options of new policies in a meaningful way. Universities have taken only a few tentative steps in the direction of using technology to tame the increasingly unwieldy mass of collected information.

Meanwhile, big science and technology exert their peculiar pressures on frail community institutions at increasingly local levels. Everywhere there are gaps and inadequate institutional structures. The property tax is insufficient for the burdens placed upon it. Few models of metropolitan community development exist; these are not yet evaluated. Regional groupings are being established without regional planning. Processes of communication to express the needs of national constituencies are lacking. The list of weaknesses is a long one.

Scarcely a day goes by in Washington without the arrival of some delegation of urban representatives coming to tell the federal government how thwarted they are in trying to enlist the support of state legislatures in dealing with city problems. Variations among the 91,000 units of local government in the country compound the confusion. And the concept of national policy is blurred by all kinds of vague definitions.

## PUZZLE OF FEDERAL POWER

What do we mean by a federal program—is it the movement of funds "en bloc," or is it also attaching to a program guidelines for stimulating subunits in the culture? What is the nature of state responsibility, especially with reference to contemporary city growth? How can true representation be achieved in a context of population mobility? What can be done to rationalize tax structures in terms of emerging social realities? All these are questions that need answering before the federal system can respond effectively to the demands of late twentieth-century life in the United States.

It is a time when development appears more and more to be an exercise in equalization of opportunity and the delivery of services. A Mississippi child can expect to have $230 spent on his education this year while, for a child in New York's Westchester County, the outlay will be $1100. The new compensatory education programs of the federal government are only a beginning when it comes to re-dressing these inequalities and making up for more subtle depriva-tions in the distribution of competence and the quality of public and private leadership.

The hesitancy of national policy toward development reflects in part the newness of certain realizations of power on the part of the government. This year, for example, about $17 billion will be spent on research and development in the United States, two-thirds of the money coming from the federal government. It is easy to see that this investment carries with it the potentiality for significant control over the rapidity and nature of change in America. The nation has already learned how to speed up or slow down the economy by man-agement of the monetary system. The allocation of research money to stabilize or redirect social development represents yet another extension of governmental purpose over the national character and destiny.

It is currently a source of widespread uneasiness. Fear of being manipulated has arisen in many sectors of the national community. Universities are tense about the impact of so many categorical pro-grams on their institutional integrity. The public at large has shown a spirit of rebellion at the suggestion of controls over foreign travel. As yet, the federal system has no adequate mechanisms for responding to conflicts and resistances arising from its regulation of change. Here again, it is being challenged by new social realities.

It is an axiom of democratic theory that government's respon-sibility is to do for people what they cannot do for themselves. In this spirit, the federal government has become a chief agent in stimulat-ing action in its own substructures as well as in the informal sub-units of society by taking a large part in the channeling of resources. And here, again and again, it runs into conflicts with its clientele. Failures of consensus have dogged the poverty program from the be-ginning. They also hamper the development efforts of the Office of Education.

Some of these contests for control call for the development of new avenues of participation for the citizenry at large. Others might be solved by better coordination. The government investment—the stimulus to action—in education, for example, has been a series of separate efforts, some in lower and some in higher education. Communication between the two levels has been lacking, and the separation of elementary and secondary school people from those representing higher education has grown steadily more acute and problematical.

Such pressures and trouble spots are not, however, the whole story of the federal system in contemporary America. There are many promising new developments at all levels of its operation. Regional expressions of federal, state, and local planning and program execution proliferate on every side. Besides the Appalachian Regional Authority previously cited, there are the numerous regional medical programs; indeed, there has been no single new piece of legislation in recent years that has not paid deference to the idea of regionalism in the delivery of health services.

Regional emphases are no more prominent than federal efforts to revitalize state and local institutions. The Model Cities Act, the Public Works and Economic Development Act of 1965, to name a few at random, and the growing number of titles in federal legislation which aim to upgrade the strength and self-confidence of states and municipalities illustrate the trend. Almost all legislation on education includes provisions designed to help local people retrain themselves and improve their institutions for more vigorous participation in development programs.

Everywhere, there is evidence of a real rise in confidence in state-wide planning. Even in a relatively small state like West Virginia, the concept of the growth center has taken hold, and administrative and other resources are now being deployed in terms of sophisticated statewide strategies.

Also, there are new forms of cooperation between the governors of the states. The heightened interest of the governors in social and economic development is apparent; so is their increased willingness to take a stand on matters of human services. Lower officials of the state governments show a similar readiness to reach across state lines and collaborate with their counterparts elsewhere.

In the wake of these changes, the old boundaries between public and private are dissolving. The concept of the private college as opposed to the public institution is no longer useful, and the obsolescence of the distinction is noticeable in many other sectors of society as well. Some of the recent experiments in ghetto rehabilitation have brought together business, unofficial community groups, and old-line governmental institutions. Some of the most imaginative contributions to progress in vocational training are coming from business rather than from the traditional strongholds of education. Indeed, some students of American education argue that curriculum development at the elementary and secondary levels of schooling should be put out by contract to bidders, so that the competition of independent entrepreneurs could let in new ideas and free education from some of the rigidities now so characteristic of it.

These are only a few examples of how change within our federal system is as much a matter of innovation and bright hope as of strain, anachronism, and inadequacy. People have been worrying about the adaptability of the system since the days of the Founding Fathers, but no less distinguished a Federalist than James Madison himself expressed confidence in its continuing capacity to serve the nation. He said, "If the people should, in the future, become more partial to the federal than to other more local forms of government, the change can only result from such manifest and irresistible truth of a better administration as will overcome all their antecedent propensities. In that case, the people ought not to shirk their responsibilities; they should not be precluded from giving most of their confidence where they may discover it to be most deserved."

It is also useful to remember that unrest can be a sign of progress. In fact, protest and progress often go hand in hand. As Eric Hoffer, the longshoreman-essayist has observed, really desperate situations produce no uprisings. It is only when things are improving that people have the energy and optimism to be rebellious and demanding. "Discontent," says Hoffer, "is likely to be highest when misery is just bearable . . . when conditions have so improved that an ideal state seems almost within reach."

American federalism has withstood many pressures in its still short history. Caught now between the dynamisms of hope and indignation, it faces what may well be its most critical testing. What happens to the federal system of the United States, and how it weathers the storms of today and tomorrow may well decide whether the future is dominated by realized hope or by indignation turned to despair.

# CHAPTER TWELVE

# PROGRAM CONTROL AND LINKAGE: A SELECTED PANEL REACTS TO CHAPTERS TEN AND ELEVEN

A REACTION PANEL of three was asked to comment on the Ratchford and Miller chapters, with the authors replying to the comments. The panel members were Eber Eldridge, Extension Economist at Iowa State University; M. E. John, Head, Department of Agricultural Economics and Rural Sociology, The Pennsylvania State University; and Lee Taylor, Assistant Director of Research at the Agricultural Experiment Station, Cornell University. A transcript of the discussion follows.

DR. JOHN: Regardless of our concern for federalism there will be new national programs sponsored by our federal government. We have noticed that many times these programs are launched, whether through indirect methods, through our state government, or through direct approaches, before we have the essential trained personnel to adequately carry out these programs, and before we have had time to conduct the necessary research or even to assemble the research that we already have. I wonder if we might not launch these programs in a two-step manner. The first step would be after the enabling act is passed, with money appropriated to carry on a training program for at least the first year and to bring together the present research that has a significant bearing upon the program itself. Then maybe we ought to start out with a pilot program before we begin on a broader scale. A good illustration is the OEO program that caught many counties and many state workers off balance.

DR. MILLER: I mentioned in my paper that the whole question of manpower is a very serious one. There are times when I wonder even if Congress granted all requested funds for response to the urban questions of today, would we get very far, simply because of a lack of people. I am talking about manpower to do the job—to stay with the job. Read the *New York Times* and you will find that the average tenure of people in the urban programs runs only a few months. People may be around for part of the planning, but as likely as not they will not be around for the action. I am uneasy, also, about how legislation is enacted. The way mass media bring these problems to us seems to require public officials to have a slogan in front of them for new enactments. This contributes to the formation of consensus, to be sure. But legislation that starts as a slogan may imply more than it can deliver, and it may be executed without reference to needed manpower, community structures, and coordination of other investments that have already been made in the particular area. Most people agree that the downward and outward communication in the federal sector is much better than the arrangements that feed back experience and information on what the needs are and what the criteria should be in responding to them.

DR. TAYLOR: As a result of experiences I have had in the last two years, I am concerned about the social systems of research and development, about the environment in which we work. Recently I have had the experience of meeting with colleagues throughout Latin America to discuss the state of sociological research there. I am examining similar circumstances in this country. It is clear from these international and national experiences that we have not been imaginative, even in the land-grant university structures, in organizing for idea relevance in the social sciences in urbanized society, although these land-grant structures may have been imaginative for production agriculture.

Preceding chapters have discussed government and university systems. These systems are parts of one urbanized social organization as we see them. They are really not separate, but only elements of a total societal configuration. We are concerned in this framework with how we move dynamically forward in relating university and government social scientists—idea people—to the practical problems and intellectual challenges of society.

We cite two types of needed research supports for social science excellence, and invite a discussion of their viability. First, we need to develop mechanisms whereby the social science researchers, and sociologists in particular, can have extensive off-campus mobility to research site locations. By this we mean normative structures are needed to move social science researchers to on-location sites. Large libraries and extensive field experiment stations tend to be restrictive to one geographical area. Accordingly, imaginative normative structures need to be developed which allow social science researchers to move from the university, into the field, and back to the university again. In short, the action for social sciences can be any place in society, but is certainly not limited to the physical and geographical location of the university. The first need, then, is for the development of a normative mechanism for an off-campus mobility to on-location research sites.

A second need is for new kinds of laboratory or consortium structures which will specifically facilitate large and small numbers of leading social scientists and their research assistants to come together for short (multiweek) and longer (multiyear) periods of time to design and carry out research on specific problem subjects in multiple regions of a society or societies. The intent of this need area is to avoid bits-and-pieces research by enabling research scholars at their respective universities to assemble jointly for mounting major, and when appropriate large, society-wide research projects in such subject areas as poverty, urban riots, outdoor recreation, water resources, etc.

Can we discuss the relevance of these need areas and suggest ways whereby the combined support of government and universities might be brought to bear for the creation of imaginative and excellent social science research systems?

DR. RATCHFORD: I will comment, but you should know that I tend to be considered somewhat of a Turk by my colleagues and my answer will further prove it. I think the universities are more at fault than the federal establishment in this respect. We need to find some ways to act in concert as contrasted to each one operating independently and cutting each other's throats. I could give you many examples where the federal establishment gets caught in a scrap between two or more universities and says "to heck with all of them." I would have been most delighted to have either or both but wanted no part of the scrap. There is some experimentation going on in this respect. In the experiment stations and extension you originally had this concept, but they have become so deeply institutionalized that there is little flexibility. Let me be more specific about extension. We need some way that the universities can speak as a unit—an action unit not a lobbying unit—where they can pool resources and move resources back and forth between each other.

Now for the second part of the question. There is a steady flow of university faculty to Washington to serve as consultants and handle special assignments. I doubt if a national program has been developed in recent years that has not had a significant input of university resources. Many times this has been without the official sponsorship of the university. This problem must be handled internally by the universities. Parts of the federal establishment have taken recognition of the problem. Efforts are being made to pull into some central focus research and extension activities. There is a national council which is supposed to look at all the federal extension activities and make some recommendations for coordination. The same is happening in research. It is a matter of both the federal establishment and the universities getting themselves organized for continuing a dialogue on these problems.

DR. MILLER: Without trying to overlap Bryce Ratchford's comments,

I will attempt to draw four issues. They come from a discussion context—seminars that I have been engaged in for a few months with people who have great concern over the interplay of the university with society. I got interested in this because I found that few people had much awareness of the service of land-grant institutions to rural society.

The first issue is: "Should federal support flow largely without constraints, guidelines, and directions from the federal sector?" Should it be given to the local units, in this case the university, to somehow work out flexible systems with communities? Some people are worried that the universities will not be responsive and that without guidelines, you will simply have a vast waste of funds.

The second issue is: "Do you get the job done by a given segment of the university that is dedicated and prepared to do this particular work? Or do you call upon the university as a whole?" No one would deny that there would be an interplay if you took either one of these, but there is a difference of opinion about whether it is possible to build an agricultural college structure—experiment station, extension elements, and all—into the university to do the urban job as was done somewhat in rural society, or whether it is necessary to take the whole university along for that ride.

The third issue is: "Do you give federal support directly to the academic people or, in the urban situation, do you have to join academic institutions in a larger framework of public, political, and private elements of sponsorship?"

The fourth issue is: "How do you free and make flexible and dynamic the resources in the life of institutions?" We have not handled the concept of the institute in university life very well. The institute was a way to work around the rigidities of the departments, the schools, and colleges; but the institute turned out to be just as rigid and it became not unlike a department in the program of the parent institution. These are the four issues that have come out of these discussions on the interplay of higher education in modern society.

DR. ELDRIDGE: You mentioned the prevailing feelings on the third issue—granting money directly to universities, but was there a prevailing feeling on the other three issues?

DR. MILLER: There is a belief that funds should respond to the flexibility found in given settings, and which allow for inventive approaches. I think when the federal government comes up with so much money and puts a little bit here and a little bit there that it dissipates the effectiveness. We activate groups, and before long they run right into other groups that have been activated by other federal agencies, and how to gain consensus among them becomes an issue. Our discussions divide on whether a unit of the university has to have the main job of doing this. Also, they are divided on the value of a set of institutions similar to the land-grant type in dealing with the vastness of modern urban problems. They do agree that some dynamic new agreements within the life of the university have to be made so that talent can be used for certain periods of time, disbanded, and reassembled as needed.

DR. RATCHFORD: I can add one point from our own experience. I checked recently and found that we had 147 separate contracts with units of government in the state of Missouri. This included school systems, community action agencies, county government, and state government, which proves we are beginning to do what Paul Miller suggests. This has created a lot of red tape, but it has made the university more responsive and relevant to these governmental units which in turn have a greater interest in the university. After all they know they have some money invested in the university and are concerned about the outcome.

DR. MILLER: The proponents of the view that would support a comprehensive entity in which the universities are included argue that the university will do better on the problems of complex urban society if services are purchased from them. Some people say that we may have to create new structures that are somewhat like universities but which are centers of confidence that may even be in the business sector. The argument is that if the university can deliver in the urban setting, all right—if it cannot, then other groups should be contracted to do the job.

DR. TAYLOR: Are we still looking imaginatively at the university as an idea system of both students and faculty on this? In other words, is this an either-or situation? Are there not circumstances in which direct contracts to universities and agencies are desirable and other circumstances where money should be granted to the total university as an internal foundation? The internal foundation funds would be used with greater flexibility than other grant systems. They would be used to generate and support new kinds of ideas relevant to the challenges of urbanized society.

DR. RATCHFORD: Well, I suppose some combination may be the answer. The university needs some basic support to acquire basic competence to make good use of mission-type funds, so I do not think there is any particular conflict here.

I have a question about your beginning point of the universities serving as an "idea center." The question is specifically to what extent do they really serve in this role. A lot of ideas come out of a university; but how hard does the university work to make them into a coherent plan and then implement it? This relates to the point I was talking about—commitment. I can speak with feeling on this. I hear time and again that the only thing we are concerned about is publishing. Ideas do come out but I do not know whether we are really geared up and whether we do not actually stifle ideas by becoming so institutionalized.

DR. ELDRIDGE: If we assume the problem in focus is education for social and economic development, there appeared to be an underlying area of agreement in both the Miller and Ratchford chapters. Both agree that the university has not done the job. Furthermore, both seem to agree to the disturbing conclusion that the university might not direct itself to this type of education.

It is true that we have a complicated government structure—within and between levels of government as Paul Miller described. It is true as Bryce Ratchford wrote that we have an economic system where private decisions are made for economic gain without regard to social costs of society. It is true that we have an extension service whose primary claim to fame is teaching physical sciences to farmers for private individual gain.

It is also true that university administrators have been saying for over twenty years that the university must change its focus—yet, we agree that little has happened. How long will the public wait? How long can we afford to wait?

There appears to be a hint in both chapters that this educational job might be attempted outside the university. Dr. Ratchford said, "We can do it—assuming that we want to," this implying that universities might not, in fact, want to. He also said, "We have the brain power, the capability to set up a system" to do the job. He did not say this system would be within the university. Dr. Miller suggested that discussion has taken place within the federal government about the possibility of establishing "centers" for research and development outside the university.

My question is, Is it time to consider a new idea, an innovation, a social invention, to deal with this problem, just as the land-grant system was created to deal with a problem of the day?

DR. RATCHFORD: This is one of the basic problems of a university which arises from the way we operate with basically the faculty being "the university." It seems that we must move slowly, yet we move too slowly for the decision-makers, activists by nature, who are faced with pressing problems that will not wait five years to get solved. I think tremendous progress has been made in the last several years in moving the university in the direction we want to see it go. It has occurred largely, however, by buying. I mean by this that federal funds were made available for very restricted uses, but the faculty had to buy the restrictions to get the funds—and they did. It has been the buying rather than real desire that has propelled us into it. The only thing that bothers me is that we still may move so slowly, although I think there is some evidence of acceleration, that time will run out. I think we are accepted in rural areas as a developmental arm. You meet with a rural group and somewhere in the discussion somebody is going to say, "What does the university have on this? Let's talk to some university person. Let's talk to Joe Blow." Sure it is not universal but it is quite different in an urban setting. It is more likely to be: "For God's sake, don't go to the university."

DR. JOHN: Is not one of our problems due to having a conflict in interest and training between the research-oriented and action-oriented personnel? The research faculty are becoming better trained, more specialized. They want to get on with their work in their specialized fields. At the same time the university is being bombarded to deal with certain applied practical problems facing a rapidly changing society. These trends are going on at the same time. As a result, frequently the highly scientifically oriented are a little disturbed that they have to be involved in the more action-oriented programs. We have a tendency to develop specialization—action oriented versus research oriented. A division develops with the research-oriented person given higher status than the action-oriented.

DR. MILLER: There are many things we fail to understand about the urban setting. Who are the people who are doing the sort of a macro-sociology, if it may be called this, of what happened to the whole land-grant movement over the course of a century? What are the institutional instruments by which one effects linkage?

Three things loom as important. One is embodied in the notion of control. I mean control in the sense of planning, of getting some kind of comprehensive conception of how elements relate to each other and work together, some notion of where the manpower can be found. As I look back at the land-grant movement there was a great deal of control vested in the university. Plans were developed; plans were reconciled; decision-makers made choices about whether investments should go into soil research or into livestock research. But there was some form of plan and degree of social guidance.

The second consideration refers to the lack of "memory" in the society. The universities have, in their way, added to this; I believe they have done all they could. They were asked to stress the production of knowledge. But if you overdo the production of knowledge, then the question is: How do you get some kind of a conception from the whole of it? Conceptions of the whole at, say, the federal level in planning policies are very difficult to come by. Streams of highly specialized knowledge exist but there are few mechanisms or people who really put them together in formats for use by policy makers.

The third point is the concept of linkage. As I look at what universities are trying to do in the urban community today, they are really doing extensions of themselves in a sense. They are getting projects and groups of people that they feel comfortable with. That reminds me of when I went into the inner-city areas of Baltimore. I went into schools and I talked with health people. I started to see the lack of planning, the lack of linkage between university and community, and the lack of "memory" in the sense of being able to get at what had happened before and how this could be digested and codified and shared in a teaching sense with the larger community.

In our day, the university somehow does not bridge these communication gaps. Accordingly, these are the three concepts that I think we ought to look at in connection with applying the land-grant idea: the systems of planning and memory, making it possible to build upon what we learned yesterday and, finally, institutional linkages.

# CHAPTER THIRTEEN

# DOMESTIC DEVELOPMENT: BECOMING A POSTINDUSTRIAL SOCIETY

## E. WALTER COWARD, JR., GEORGE M. BEAL and RONALD C. POWERS

EACH BOOK needs an ending. Sometimes the ending is simply the last chapter. In the case of this book, we shall attempt to transform the last chapter into an ending through conscious planning. Our ending has two purposes. First, we seek to bring some parsimony to the wide-ranging discussions included in each of the sections of the book by commenting on the general themes that characterize these sec-

**E. WALTER COWARD, JR.** is Assistant Professor of Rural Sociology at The Pennsylvania State University. He holds the Ph.D. in sociology from Iowa State University. He has worked with programs of agricultural and rural development in Latin America and South and Southeast Asia. Publications related to development include: **Emerging Patterns of Commercial Farming in a Subsistence Economy** (Ames: Iowa State University, Rural Sociology Report 69, 1967), and **Planning Agricultural Development: The Matter of Priorities** (Journal of Developing Areas, October, 1971).

**GEORGE M. BEAL** is Professor and Chairman, Department of Sociology, Iowa State University. He holds the Ph.D. in sociology from Iowa State University. Publications related to the sociology of development in which he is one of the authors include: **India's Food Crisis and Steps to Meet It** (Ford Foundation, India, 1958); **Social Action and Interaction in Program Planning** (Ames: Iowa State University Press, 1966); **Extension Organization for Multicounty Development Areas** (Ames: Iowa State University, Rural Sociology Report 75, 1968); **Adoption of Agricultural Technology by the Indians of Guatemala** (Ames: Iowa State University, Rural Sociology Report 62, 1967).

**RONALD C. POWERS**—see page 184.

tions. Second, we want to comment on the ideas exposed in the chapters by the authors. In such commenting we intend to suggest additional concepts, frames of reference, and models that can be applied to the particular questions being considered. In seeking these two objectives our procedures will be to follow the topics as arranged in the major sections. This chapter will also deal with two additional topics: 1) the societal setting of domestic development and 2) the role of sociology in development.

## WHAT IS DEVELOPMENT?

In Section One the authors dealt with the problem of describing and defining development in sociological terms; identifying development relative to other phenomena, including other sociological phenomena. There are several general themes with which two or more of the authors have dealt in their chapters. These themes revolve around the questions: 1) How do sociologists define development, the goals of development, and the means for achieving such goals? 2) What is the sociological unit to which development applies? and 3) What procedures can be used to observe development?

### Attempts to Define Development

Each of the authors has attempted to define and elaborate the concept of development. Such an allocation of scholarly resources apparently is required in the absence of a widely accepted sociological conceptualization of development. In addition to general lack of agreement on a definition of development there is further ambiguity when concepts such as modernization and industrialization are used. (34, 38)

The definitions of development presented in this section appear to be somewhat more general or abstract than other definitions commonly used in the "development literature." One might hypothesize that the intended focus on domestic (U.S.) development in this book required the authors to conceptualize development in a manner that would include both the development within a technologically complex and structurally differentiated society as well as within societies with less complexity and differentiation.

In the development literature, definitions of development frequently reflect the particular conditions and situations faced by developing nations: political instability, low levels of technology, gemeinschaft social relations, the absence of a viable industrial sector or the predominance of traditional patterns of agricultural production. With these conditions in mind, development has often been defined in rather specific terms as the "process of transition from a social system displaying one form of economic organization to one displaying a different, presumably 'more advanced' economic organization." (22, p. 6)

Another prior approach to the discussion of development that is limited in its application to domestic development is the concept of modernization which rests on the assumption that development is a phenomenon that takes place in the *Tiers Monde*. The essence of modernization is that change is irreversibly in the direction of the structures of modernized societies. (11, p. 1; the First and Second Worlds of Horowitz, 21) Levy (26) sees modernization as the process of "invasion" or "subversion" of the structures of nonmodernized societies by the structure of modernized societies. Such definitions of modernization link development with a particular set of historical events (still occurring) involving diffusion from modernized to nonmodernized societies. It seems clear that conceptualization of development as a modernization process in the sense of Eisenstadt or Levy is not inclusive enough for a focus on domestic development in which the concern is with the nature and direction of further change within a modernized society.[1]

The authors in the first section of the book strive to conceptualize development in general terms that are applicable to the phenomena of development in both modern and nonmodern societies. Their definitions somewhat transcend reference to any particular social sector and deal with development as it applies to society.

For example, Geiger defines development as differentiation and balance in the society. Using a Parsonsian perspective, he speaks of the developed society as one which is maximally differentiated and maximally integrated. Maximizing these two dimensions requires the articulation of a magnitude and rate of interchange between the subsystems of society that prevent the occurrence of lags or gaps.

Havens begins with the basic premise of the existence of status-role differentiation in society. A major condition of this differentiation is that some status roles have authority associated with them, while others do not. Out of this situation emerges a variable level of conflict between those with and those without authority. This conflict is managed or regulated by patterns of social control. From these assumptions or perspectives Havens derives a view of societal development. The developed society has two major characteristics: 1) through instrumental, voluntary associations the members of society gain access to various positions of authority and/or have the

---

[1] There is a sense in which the modernization process does have implications for domestic development, although we believe that typical consideration of the modernization does not include this dimension. It is likely that in the long run the modernization of the developing nations will create an international environment with potential for affecting the course and form of further development within the United States.

ability to influence policy-making and decisions, and 2) conflict be-tween groups is low in intensity and its regulation is low in violence (this second condition follows Dahrendorf, 9).

Warner links his definition of the developed society with the concept of life chances. The developed society is one in which the members of the society are able to maximize goals that they value and minimize situations that they perceive to have negative value.

Eberts and Young approach the definition of development in a somewhat different manner, using the results of cluster analysis to suggest the dimensions of the concept. Obviously, this approach is not atheoretical since the selection of items to be considered in the cluster analysis is derived from conceptual considerations. Their analysis leads to the conclusions that from the sociological perspective the developed society is a structurally complex society.

A similar definition of development is used by Capener and Brown. They view development as structural change that makes a social system more effective in relating to its environment for the achievement of goals.

It is apparently difficult to conceptualize development without considering the causes, conditions, or processes that lead to develop-ment. Later we will comment on these factors. However, at this point the discussion will be limited to a review of the author's concep-tualization of development in the process sense.

We conclude that Havens views the development process as one in which voluntary associations which seek to attain instrumental goals are formed and are successful in attaining these goals. These goals, either by accident or design, are consistent with the broad goal of societal development. The factors related to the emergence of such associations will be part of the later discussion of the causes of devel-opment.

Warner conceptualizes seven components to be used in identify-ing development in process. Paraphrasing Warner, the development process refers to: 1) some amount of increase, 2) in the life chances, 3) of some people, 4) which is produced by some organization or set of organizations, 5) at some cost, 6) to some group of people, and 7) at the expense of some other alternatives.

## Man's Orientation to the Future

The authors have attempted to cast their definitions of develop-ment in general terms that will be applicable to a wide range of empirical development settings. A basic dimension underlying most definitions of development is that of a futuristic view; certain goals or consequences are valued, and social modifications are initiated to achieve these goals. This prospective dimension of development is related to basic notions that we have about man and his behavior. Of primary relevance to understanding development is the purposive, goal-oriented, future-oriented nature of man. The telic nature of man, coupled with his ability to communicate via abstractions, results in an ability to perceptually construct futures, a variety of alternative futures that may be. It is such perceptions of possible futures, widely held by the members of a social system or held by the key decision-makers of the system, that are at the core of development phenomena.

From this it is suggested that an important aspect of the sociology of development is what Bell has called "images of the future." (Cf. 27) These images will direct the actions that men now engage in. To extend Thomas, via Merton's self-fulfilling prophecy, it is not only true that the present is as men perceive it, but the future will, at least partly, become what men now perceive it to be. From the assumption of the purposefulness of man, Gabor's (16) statement seems acceptable: we cannot predict the future, *but we can invent it.*

Men invent the future in the sense that currently held images of the future provide a basis and purpose to present actions; these actions culminate in a future state of affairs more or less like the images originally held. In this framework, levels of development may be conceptualized, and perhaps empirically observed, as the extent to which the present state of affairs is congruent with previously stated goals. At any point in time, this level of development may be very high, but will not preclude future developmental impetus by the specification of new, as yet unattained goals.

This future orientation suggests the difference between change and development which is approximated in Etzioni's distinction between change and transformation. (12, pp. 120–22) Etzioni views change as a response to environmental forces while transformation implies anticipatory adjustments rather than reactionary adjustments. Transformation refers to the ability to adjust the system before there is the pressing need to make such adjustments. It refers to a "self-triggered" impetus for change rather than an "environmentally-triggered" impetus.

It is man's impetus to achieve stated goals, as yet unrealized, that is at the motivational core of development activities. Development, from a sociological point of view, may be seen as the identification of goals, the planning of strategies, and the modification of social structures so as to increase a social system's goal-attainment ability.

The difficulty of conceptually defining these goals, and of specifying empirical measures for many of these goals, is recognized as an important aspect of development. In fact, these problems may be a major deterrent to attaining development goals. For example, the hypothesis that intangible goals result in goal displacement and low goal attainment may have high relevance to the development process. (7,44)

## The Sociological Unit of Development

Most of the authors in this section are concerned with the phenomenon that they call *societal development*. Much as early sociologists focused on society as the unit of social change the authors, perhaps influenced by this earlier approach, suggest that society is the unit of developmental change. Societal change is the major, although not exclusive, unit of focus. Using what may be considered a more general level conceptual approach, Geiger, Warner, Eberts, and Young indicate that they view development as structural change in social systems generally. Warner's main focus is on agencies. Havens emphasizes formal voluntary associations. Eberts and Young analyze development using communities as the unit of analysis.

Perhaps the relevant point is that as sociologists the authors do not limit the role of sociology to a focus such as the sociology of economic development, or the sociology of political development. In the Parsonsian tradition they appear to assume that the economy and the policy can be subsumed as parts of the general social system and therefore are really "special" cases of the general phenomena of societal development. Warner writes that societal development is not a unitary variable; the concept designates a category of different types or kinds of development. These kinds of development might refer to economic development, political development, and other specific types.

Societal development implies a holistic approach to development. It can lead to a focus such as suggested by Geiger whereby societal development is defined in terms of balance among the parts— or the movement toward such balance. It may also lead to a focus on the potential consequences for individuals of a new social organization of a society, as compared to the opportunities of the current social organization. Examples of this focus are Warner's concern for a society that offers improved life chances and Havens's goal of a society in which the imposition of wills is managed.

Societal development as used in this section is not to be equated with *social development* as used in the ubiquitous phrase, social and economic development. Social development frequently is used to deal with development in the noneconomic, nonpolitical, or miscellaneous sectors of society. In this sense social development has sometimes referred to the development of social welfare services, public health services, religious services, or educational opportunities. The concept of societal development is intended to subsume these aspects of social development, as well as of economic and political development.

However, this general focus on societal development has disadvantages. One disadvantage is that relatively little attention is given to the multitude of other units that conceptually and empirically can be demonstrated as relevant to development. There are many territorially based units currently engaged in development activities, e.g., model city areas, counties, multicounty areas, growth center areas, states, and regions. The narrow range of sociological units for implementing development which are identified may be related to the tendency of some authors to disassociate the sociology of development from economic and political development. In the process little attention is given to the sociology of economic and political systems. Little is said about complex bureaucracies that reach from federal to local units with their many levels of status roles, authority, responsibility and decision loci, or other units in the political institution such as federal, state, and local governments, legislatures, political parties, judicial systems, and many types of newly created administrative units. In the economic sphere there are a myriad of social systems to be considered: corporations, cooperatives, marketing and distribution systems. Little emphasis is given to the sociological aspects of what is judged by some to be a crucial element of development, the educational system and its component subsystems.

The institutionalized patterns of religion, cultural arts, and recreation may have roles to play, depending on the specified goals of development. These too could be considered as units of development and each observed and perhaps planned from a sociological perspective.

In summary, focus on societal development is intended to deal with a set of questions that may not be apparent if some small social unit is the focus. It is also intended to deal with a set of questions that cannot be considered from the partial development perspective of economic development or political development, even less so from the specialized perspectives of the sociology of economic or political development. This larger, societal question is posed by Havens: "Toward what tangible goals should society be oriented that will allow the maximum contribution of all mankind to these goals?"

## The Cybernetic Social System

As just suggested, some of the authors in Section One proceed with the selection of society as the unit of development analysis. Even so, their discussions focus on the role of selected categories or systems of society in the development process: for example, Havens discusses voluntary organizations, Warner emphasizes governmental agencies, and the observation unit of Eberts and Young is the community.

We suggest that there are advantages to maintaining an abstract approach to the developmental unit of analysis, namely, considering the unit of analysis to be simply social systems. Such, of course, would not be unusual given the wide use of social system theory in contemporary sociology. Its application to the analysis of development has two particular advantages. First, it allows the researcher to maintain a more constant conceptual framework across the variety of social units that engage in development activities: small towns, metropolitan areas, multicounty groups, states, voluntary organizations, agencies, organizational sets, and other social groups. Second, the social system concept suggests exploring the applicability of general systems theory to the conceptualization of development.

A major notion of the general systems approach (or the cybernetic assumption) is the articulation of a system process whereby goals and outcomes are compared and, if found to be divergent, result in system alterations to reduce the divergence. There has been a recent sociological convergence of interest in cybernetic views of social behavior which emphasize the adjusting features of a social unit. Parsons in his recent discussion of social evolution has given some emphasis to cybernetic approaches. (36) Etzioni indicates that his theory of the active society rests in part on cybernetic assumptions. (12, ix)

We have suggested that, from the perspective of the individual, development arises because of the future-orientation that characterizes individuals. From a system point of view, development arises from the emergent property[2] of system *self-regulation*. Etzioni (12, p. 45) describes this system process as control: "The process of specifying preferred states of affairs and revising ongoing processes so as to move in the direction of these preferred states."

Conceptualizing development as a kind of planned change, or goal-oriented change links with these cybernetic ideas and further suggests that theories of social change with an emphasis on decision-making processes might be highly applicable to theories of development. Bell has recently mentioned a theory of change in which the process of decision-making is a prominent feature. (3, p. 41) He refers to the theory as a "cybernetic-decisional model of social change." As Bell describes the theory it is one that emphasizes "belief, values, images of the future, decision-making and individual as well as collective action, as these impinge on and alter social structures."

Some current trends suggest that the postindustrial society is moving in the direction of becoming an increasingly cybernetic system: one in which goals are specified, actions taken, and results monitored and used as the basis for future action. As Taviss (42, p. 521) indicates, a key feature of the postindustrial society is the "ethos of planning and the increased use of knowledge in policy-making." In addition to the use of knowledge to formulate policy, its use to improve feedback information relating means and ends is reflected in various techniques of scientific decision-making that are currently popular, an example being the PPBS approach. Such techniques can,

[2] Etzioni describes an emergent property as one added (or removed) by a transition from one level of analysis to another, e.g., from role analysis to system analysis. (12, p. 45)

of course, go awry such that the provision of feedback information becomes an end itself, or such that the indicators measured by the feedback information are substituted for original goals.

An example of the demand for planning is reflected in a recent *New York Times* editorial which called for the following government actions: "a national migration policy to direct the flow of people which now eddies haphazardly from rural backwater to city slum; a national land policy to plan the development of future suburbs and new towns; a national housing policy with much tougher controls on land speculators and featherbedding construction unions."[3]

## Factors Related to the Development Process

As some, however tentative, conceptualization of development has occurred, consideration of the sociological factors related to the process of development can proceed. To state the obvious, the explanatory factors that are initially considered will vary in relation to the concept of development stated. The verification of factors related to development is ultimately a problem of empirical observation. For such empirical observation to occur successfully two conditions need to be met: 1) one must have available an empirical measure of development, and 2) one must approach the analysis with an unusually sophisticated methodology. Each of these points is discussed below.

The chapters by Havens and Warner most explicitly deal with the theoretical statement of factors related to the development process. Both the chapter by Geiger and that by Eberts and Young are limited to a discussion of the components of development and not with the "related or correlated problems of causal factors in development."

Havens describes the following two necessary, but not sufficient, factors related to the development process: 1) communication and 2) relative deprivation. *Communication* is necessary for members of society to gain knowledge of new alternatives (both goals and means) to their situation. This new knowledge must lead to perceptions of *relative deprivation,* a feeling that present alternatives are inferior to newly learned alternatives, as a prelude to desire for change by individuals.

In addition to these two necessary factors, a set of sufficient conditions was identified by Havens which basically involves the emergence of instrumental voluntary organizations as mechanisms for implementing and achieving newly valued alternatives. Left conspicuously unspecified are the conditions under which communication and relative deprivation lead to the formation of voluntary associations.

This set of necessary and sufficient conditions is viewed by Havens as only one set of many that will lead to economic development. These

[3] Quoted in Taviss. (42)

conditions are unique as a set of factors leading to the view of societal development held by Havens.

For Warner the question is, How are life chances increased? Development is a product of social organization since it is through social organization that mutual enhancement of effort and a degree of protection from costs are provided for the individual. From a given level, life chances may be increased by alterations in social organization. Such alterations, in the form of new social organization, may derive from 1) consequences of technological change, 2) crises, 3) the entrepreneurship of individuals, 4) social movements, and 5) challenge groups. An important variable limiting the effect of alterations in the social structure on development is the process of institutionalization in which organizations increasingly give priority to system maintenance over original goals.

In addition to the social structural factors related to development, which Havens and Warner discuss, one also can consider the social psychological factors that are related. Hobbs in his discussion of social change refers to the behaviorist perspective of social change as illustrated in the work of Lerner and Martindale. The behaviorist view introduces into the discussion social psychological factors such as motivations and aspirations. It may also be noted that Geiger identifies one perspective of development as that which focuses on the individual and the relationship of personality features to societal development. Although the social psychological approach is not emphasized by the authors in Section One, there is considerable sociological interest in this approach as documented by Geiger.

*The Observation of Development.* As mentioned previously, the empirical observation of factors related to development requires an operational measure of the dependent variable, development.

The observation of development is, of course, highly dependent on the conceptualization of development from which one proceeds. Some conceptualizations may not provide an adequate basis for observation. It may generally be true that our concepts of development provide a better basis for the observation of a state of development, or some degree of development, but a somewhat inadequate basis for observing the development process.

We suggest that the observation of development will require an abstract conceptualization and empirical indicator(s) that deal with the following questions:

a. *What kind of change(s)?* Technology? Increased income per capita? Better social services? Increased number of voluntary associations? Value orientations? Beliefs and sentiments? Norms? Forms of social power?

b. *In what social units?* Individuals? Status Roles? Kinship groups?

    Communities? Societies? Units of governments? Firms? Market systems?

c. *Over what period of time?* Months? Years? Decades?

d. *Caused by what set of factors?* Natural disasters? Wars? Legislation? Adult education? Market forces? Socialization? Governmental planning?

    Such questions illustrate the circularity of the development process when considered in the long run. For example, is an increase in the number of voluntary organizations to be conceptualized as a kind of developmental change, or a cause of developmental change, or both?

    In Chapter 5 Eberts and Young describe their observation of developmental changes in New York State. Their research is premised on the answers that they provided to the questions just presented.

    In answer to the kind of change to be observed they have selected changes in the "objective or structural conditions and properties of social units." Their social units of analysis are communities in New York: cities, villages, and urbanized areas with over 2,500 population in 1950. In their diachronic analysis the researchers used a ten-year span (1950–1960) as the period of time in which to observe change. A review of the fifteen items used in their cluster analysis indicates that most of the structural changes they measured would be highly related to the articulation of market forces and governmental planning— as opposed to natural disasters or wars. Stated succinctly, Eberts and Young operationally define the development process as structural changes that occurred in communities over a ten-year period, largely in response to various mechanisms of nonascriptive and indirect allocation of social roles and activities, e.g., markets, bureaucracies, and publics. (Eisenstadt, 11, pp. 8–9)

    Whether one agrees with the particular answers implied in the Eberts and Young chapter, the point is that the researcher implicitly or explicitly provides answers to these questions as he proceeds with his research. If this is true, we suggest that a conscious effort to answer these questions is required for development research.

    The empirical identification of factors related to development is central to two requirements, the elaboration of theoretical notions of development and the creation of action strategies. As noted in both Sections One and Two, there is a "knowledge gap" particularly with reference to what some have called "models of changing"—an understanding of the dynamics of the development process and identification of points of leverage for the management of change. Now, to provide fill for this kind of knowledge gap will require research conceptualized and operationalized with the intention of answering more than: Is there a relationship?

    The construction of models of developing introduces the need to analyze the complex network of direct and indirect causal relationships among the parts and processes of a social system. This procedure involves the usual steps of research: the selection of theoretical frameworks, with specified concepts, the operationalization of concepts, the selection of research design, and the analysis of data. At a general level there are several requirements for the sociological analysis of development. Most of these are needed, and increasingly are used, procedures in other areas of sociological research.

## Models of Developing

Sociological models of development must deal with *multivariable* relationships. Two-variable associations are considered grossly inadequate except as a prelude to more complex interrelationships. At both the conceptual and empirical levels the approach must be in terms of multivariable complexity. One technique that may be suitable in meeting these criteria is path model analysis. Although path model analysis is generally thought of as a technique of data analysis, it can also be helpful in the more conceptual aspects of model building. With the path model approach in mind the theorist-researcher can conceptualize not only a set of variables that are believed to be related to development but also can conceptualize the interrelationships among these "independent" variables. A major advantage of this approach to multivariable analysis is that one can deal with both the direct and indirect effects of a given variable on the dependent variable being considered. From the strategy view, the specification of direct and indirect effects contributes to the assessment of the relative payoff likely if certain variables are manipulated as compared to others.

A second requirement is that models of development must deal with the *form* of relationships among the variables being considered. Frequently at the conceptual level the form of relationships is not explicitly stated, while at the empirical level data are analyzed using the assumptions of linear relationships. The assumption of linear relationships is not necessary at the conceptual level of model building and given the availability of various mathematical transformations is not necessary at the empirical level. The same comments are applicable to the assumptions of additivity.

A third requirement is that models of developing are longitudinal in nature and allow for development to act both as an "independent" and as a "dependent" variable. This idea is, of course, related to the modern systems conceptualization of a social system in that over time current activity, e.g., some development activity, affects the outcome of some future activity, e.g., some new level or rate of development activities.

Longitudinal studies would also be useful in testing the predictability of models. A model could be used, for example, to predict the pattern of changes in a small community as it becomes a "defense" town. Such predictions could then be compared with the actual changes observed in longitudinal analysis and discrepancies used as a basis for modifying the model.

In summary, models of the development process need to approximate the "structural models" suggested by Heise. (19, pp. 41–44) In a structural model the theorist attempts to specify relationships so as to predict the effect of change in one variable of the system on other variables in the system. As Heise notes, such a structural model requires both to specify the network of causal paths, direct and indirect, that exist between variables in the model, and to identify the parameters of these relationships.

Heise illustrates the above points: "Given a structural model, it is possible to calculate how a change in any one variable in the system will affect the values of other variables. Suppose, for example, it were possible to specify and measure the causal relations in Parsons's AGIL System. Then, given the model, it would be possible to say precisely what effects one-unit increase in integration would have on an organization's level of adaptation, goal attainment, and pattern maintenance."

The feasibility of such models in sociology is becoming increasingly attainable. Such models are a necessary requirement for the specification of models of developing. Such models will also lead to rejection of the suggested synonymity between talk and theory-building.

## SOCIOLOGICAL KNOWLEDGE AND DEVELOPMENT

It has been widely suggested that development is planned social change. In Section One, the major emphasis was on the *change* aspect of development: the types of social structural modifications associated with development. In Section Two, the emphasis shifts to the *planned* aspect of development. If development is planned social change then, *ipso facto*, the concept of planning is central to development. Planning is, of course, highly consistent with the view of development as attempts to invent the future. As Rothweel (39, p. ix) indicates, "Planning suggests a systematic attempt to shape the future."

Ozbekhan (35, pp. 214–19) conceptualizes planning as composed of three major components: "The 'normative plan,' which deals with the *oughts* and defines the goals on which all policy rests; the 'strategic plan,' which formulates what in the light of elected oughts, or chosen policies, we *can* actually do; and finally the 'operational plan,' which establishes how, when, and in what sequence of action we will implement the strategies that have been accepted as capable of satisfying the policies."

Ozbekhan recognizes that in most current planning processes the normative planning element is not usually included and emphasis is on strategic and operational planning. His observation is valid for our discussions in Section Two, which deal with the application of sociological propositions and models to strategic planning, i.e., what general procedures to follow to achieve selected goals.

It is this partial participation in the planning process, via the specification of strategies, that characterizes much current sociological involvement in development planning. Participation in normative planning, or what is frequently referred to as policy-making is minor. (39, p. ix) Since our current involvement is largely with strategies of development, we will first comment on that topic. Later, we will discuss participation in the policy-making process.

There is agreement that the conceptual models of social change available in sociology frequently have low utility for use in designing strategies of development. Largely this low utility derives from the purposes they fulfill as analytical tools of academicians. The essence of their limitation is captured in Powers's statement: "Sociology has an abundance of theories of change . . . but few theories of changing." Capener and Brown refer to the statement by Beers that sociology is more adequate for "observing and analyzing" than for "advising on action." No doubt the fact that much sociological research is postdictive rather than predictive is a factor that explains the low utility of current models.

There are at least two major dimensions on which theories of change and theories of changing may differ: the causal versus relational dimension and the explanatory (or statistically predictive) versus manipulatable dimension. There are few conceptual relationships that sociologists present as empirically supported causal relationship. While sociologists may think causally, at the empirical level relationships are typically analyzed in a correlational sense. If social science practitioners perform their tasks in the manner suggested by Capener and Brown, including the notion that strategy implementation may "constitute experimentation or proposition testing," one result could be the future availability of the needed causal models. The important point is that the models required for strategy-building are more possible as there is an increasing interplay between sociological theorists and practitioners.

Regarding the second dimension of difference, it may generally be true that models designed for explanation of change or development may include a different set of variables than models designed for strategy-building. The explanatory set is more inclusive than the strategy set, since the latter may preferably focus only on those variables which are potentially controllable by the strategy planner. In any case, the controllable variables are a subtest of the explanatory variables. Consequently, it is probable that further identification of controllable variables will contribute to explanatory models, although the opposite approach may not identify additional controllable variables.

In the absence of theories of changing, the application of theory to strategy-building will be more tedious and less suggestive than desired. The authors in this section presume, however, that even this application is required and useful.

### A Package of Models Is Required

The notion that any existing single sociological model is inadequate to the broad requirements of designing development strategy is found in several parts of this section. Capener and Brown indicate that components of a variety of sociological theories need to be utilized in designing the multidimensional strategies of development. Powers writes of the need for models that can be "conceptually coupled with each other" so as to deal with the complexity of the developmental context. Gross's proposition that segmented developmental plans are more successful than comprehensive plans may be a reflection of the inadequacy of theoretical models conceptually broad enough to support such plans.

How such a package of models is to be translated into a multidimensional strategy is a legitimate question. To call for applied social scientists who are eclectics is a possible solution; however, another "strategy" of strategy-building may be the use of planning teams (even within an individual perspective such as sociology).

### Strategies from Partial Information

The authors in Section Two (perhaps not unexpectedly) state two general ideas: 1) sociological theories can be applied to problems of strategy building, and 2) sociological theories, in their present form, are less than adequate for building action strategies. What are the alternatives given this set of conditions? Obviously, it may not be desirable to stop designing strategies until more adequate sociological theories are available. As mentioned previously, there is a real possibility that such improved theory will come about partially as a consequence of applying current theory to operationalizing strategy and planning feedback for theory verification. Another alternative suggested by Etzioni is learning "how to act under partial information."

(13, pp. 31–33) In Etzioni's view the development of social action strategies by sociologists even under conditions of partial information is preferable to the development of strategies by those without the sociologist's perspective.

## Values and the Planning Process

As Taviss (42, p. 534) observes, one important consequence of the planning ethos in the United States is that it emphasizes the importance of values and goals. Satisfactory planning requires a more rigorous statement of one's values and goals. Rothweel (39, p. ix) says, "The first stage at which the policy sciences can contribute to policy-making is one at which the process is especially vulnerable—the clarification of objectives." One element of goal clarification may be to determine if stated objectives can be operationalized to empirical phenomena. Planning attempts also clarify value inconsistencies and conflicts since one is often required to choose between two or more values.

There are two basic issues surrounding the process of policy-making and its intimate link with values and goals to which sociology is relevant. First is the basic question: What are values? From a social system point of view, values are sometimes viewed as shared definitions of the desirable and sometimes considered as the goals of particular power groups (s) in the system. Within our own society, at least, one can conceptualize values evolving from the interaction of power groups and the general public. The sociologist's contribution to conceptualizing values is highly relevant to the critical question: What values are to be the basis for policy-making? Involved is the basic elitist-populist dichotomy. In our complex, postindustrial society, what is the optimum mix of experts and the general public in the formation of policy? Can sociology suggest other alternatives to these participants? Assuming the desirability of having both kinds of participants: What can sociologists say about the design of structural mechanisms to facilitate this dual participation?

One alternative that has been suggested is "advocacy planning." (10, pp. 173–79) This is a planning approach designed to link the expert and various interest groups. It provides an expert to work with a particular interest group and organize its goals into a plan that will be able to compete with alternative plans, particularly those being submitted by public agencies. Advocacy planning is one structural technique for allowing multiple value systems to participate in rational planning decisions. The increased importance of public planning may require the design of additional mechanisms.

A second major issue is the identification of planning outcomes with the policy values that were to be satisfied. We refer to a feedback process by which the actual consequences of planning are compared with the intended consequences. When comparison indicates a discrepancy the causes of such will need to be considered. Sociology can contribute to this basic problem by providing a perspective on the wide range of social consequences that derive from any particular set of actions.[4] Sociology may also provide information as to why a particular strategy failed to achieve its intended objective.

In a way, what we are suggesting is an extension of the conceptualization of development that applies to the sociologist both as observer and as participant. As an observer of development, the sociologist needs to include observation of the processes by which a system selects goals; operationally, the policy-making procedure and the procedure by which the system evaluates goal attainment—the feedback process. As a participant in development the sociologist needs to consider his role in policy-making, as well as his strategist role.

Sociologists can contribute to an understanding of the relationship of values to individual behavior: information of utility to the discipline and to the selection of strategy. Sociologists can also contribute to the pool of values held by society: a policy-influencing role. Extending Ozbekhan's (35) observation that in our society "can" (e.g., go to the moon) frequently becomes "ought" (e.g., go to the moon), the demonstrated ability of social scientists to manage some social process may become translated into a value that such a process ought to be managed. The latter point illustrates the impact that knowledge can have on values.

Another impact that knowledge may have on values derives from the situation that individuals hold a series of values, some of which are assumed as causally related in a means-ends fashion; thus, we may value education because we believe it is related to higher income which we also value. If knowledge can demonstrate that one assumed causal relationship is not valid, i.e., suppose it was shown that education does not lead to higher income, then presumably we would cease to value education or provide a new justification for valuing it. Robin Williams (47, p. 30) suggests this point: "A society in which the store of knowledge concerning the consequences of action is large and is rapidly increasing is a society in which received norms and their 'justifying' values will be increasingly subjected to questioning and reformation."

As we become increasingly aware of the consequences of implementing certain values, as is required in effective planning, it may be desirable to pause and reconsider existing values.

---

[4] Moynihan's (32, p. 193) comment is relevant to this point: "The role of social science lies not in the formulation of social policy, but in the measurement of its results."

## Values in Conflict

Previously, we implied the possible conflicts arising from the statement of values by elitist groups versus the general public. That there may be conflict among various interest groups in the public is obvious. Here we would point out the equally important dilemma of conflict among the set of values commonly held by some planning unit. As long as they remain abstractions, values may retain a sense of congruity. However, when extended into action programs conflicts may appear. As an example, consider the conflict in values presented by the prospects of "corporation farming." On the one hand, corporation farming appeals to values such as efficiency and large-scale production while, on the other hand, opposing agrarian values, such as the importance of the family farm. The proposal for a negative income tax appeals to our value of efficiency but is incongruent with our value on achievement through hard work. Planning, as a process of rigorously selecting and stating values to be satisfied, will frequently produce such value conflicts.

Two important points about value conflicts are suggested in earlier chapters. Gross in his chapter suggests the proposition that "planned development is a form of social conflict." Our discussion suggests why this may frequently be the case. A second point emerges when Havens suggests that one goal of societal development is societal control, but not elimination, of conflict. For Havens, one important mechanism of control is the proliferation of voluntary organizations through which societal decision-making can be influenced. At this point, it is not clear how the plural interests of various voluntary organizations will be translated into policy that has broad acceptance. In a "less planned" situation it appears probable that the existence of interest groups can achieve a voice in decision-making, since decisions may be somewhat ad hoc and nonintegrated. However, in a situation of planning where actions are more clearly identified with underlying values and there is an effort to evaluate actions based on their presumed relevance to selected values, voluntary organizations may find it increasingly difficult to participate in decision-making. Given the increased planning ethos and its increasingly rigorous forms of decision-making (e.g., the PPBS approach[5]), we wonder if the proliferation of voluntary organizations in their present form will continue to be a key mechanism for private citizens to influence public decision-making. Taviss (42) has suggested that voluntary organizations may have to become increasingly centralized and undemocratic much as labor unions did, in order to act effectively. The formality of decision-making involved in planning processes may also require additional social arrangements to allow voluntary organizations to adequately

[5] "PPBS Comes to Washington," Held. (20, pp. 102–15)

link with planning units. This problem will be to arrive at the best means of coordinating the diverse preference patterns to arrive at compromise goals and means for reaching them satisfactory to the society as a whole.[6]

In dealing with this coordination problem it is important to recognize that the concept of optimizing behavior, while used extensively in economics, is a broad behavioral concept that has application in noneconomic settings. Although a social calculus applicable to these optimizing problems is not well refined as yet, the optimizing principle is generally applicable.[7]

While working on sociological inputs for the design of strategies to implement development activities we suggest that there is an additional need: the development of strategies for policy-making.

## PRESENT INSTITUTIONAL PATTERNS AND DEVELOPMENT

### Some Limits of Present Organizations

Each of the authors in Section Three points to needed adjustments in the particular social sector that he is describing: Miller speaks of adjustments needed to correct the insularity of government agencies; Ratchford delineates a number of required adjustments in university structure; Klemme talks of broadening the goals of the private sector to increase social responsibility. None of these implementors of development is currently organized to effectively plan and implement development. Goals and structure are intimately related, and each of the authors suggests that participation in development will require new forms of organization.

Miller has questioned the applicability of the federal system of government as an implementor of development. There is little question that government actions can initiate social change: consider the impact of the extension service on agriculture or the impact of highway location on community growth. The question is whether government can initiate actions to bring about changes designed to satisfy agreed upon values: Can it plan for development?

The planning orientation of development raises some important questions about the American political system. (Cf. Taviss, 42, p. 533) There are at least two basic issues that arise. First is the question of coordination: the "management muddle" to which Miller refers. Planning frequently requires some degree of coordination which is difficult to achieve in our system of federalism and separation of powers. The

---

[6] Roland Warren (45) presents a useful discussion of the problems of allocating resources among the many interest groups of a community.

[7] Some views of such a social calculus are presented by Coleman. (8)

second question deals with the ability of government to be anticipating as opposed to only reactionary in its activities. In Etzioni's (12) terms, can government be transformatory in nature, adjusting the system before there is the pressing need to make such adjustments? It may be somewhat easier for government to receive a public mandate to react to existing problems than to act in anticipation of future problems. This seems especially true with regard to the legal arm of government. Most new laws that are passed are in reaction to existing problems rather than as a deterrent to future problems (e.g., civil rights legislation). Support for government activities that are anticipatory in nature may be highly dependent on the widespread acceptance of the value of public planning.

The increasing overlap of the public and private sectors of the economy is characteristic of the domestic scene. One consequence of this boundary blurring is that the private sector of the economy increasingly incorporates goals that are not a part of the profit-maximization value. As Klemme indicates, the role of business in the post-industrial society centers on the notion of social responsibility.

Carl Kaysen (23, p. 218) illustrates what it may mean for a corporation to achieve goals of social responsibility: "Instead of the research and medical staff of a pharmaceutical house asking of a possible new drug only, can we sell it? Will it pass FDA standards? they might ask in addition, will it do something for medicine that existing drugs do not do? enough to be worth the effort of development and marketing?"

Klemme's comments and Kaysen's illustration point out that the private sector of the economy increasingly may be making allocative decisions based on criteria other than the traditional market. The important implication of this is the potential need for some non-market mechanism to regulate the allocation of a firm's resources. The general enlargement of business objectives toward social responsibility is an additional positive factor for the potential involvement of business as an implementor of development. A key question that remains is the coordination of these social responsibility objectives so that the allocation of resources by the business sector contributes to some planned objectives.

It is interesting to compare concepts set forth in Sections One and Two which stress the importance of structural change in development with the observations presented in Section Three by three representatives of significant social sectors. For example, Warner's discussion of development as an increase in life chances brought about by the action of new or reorganized institutional agencies and voluntary agencies is highly consistent with the concerns of Miller, Ratchford, and Klemme. The chapters in Section Three confirm Warner's perception of organizational constraints to development, e.g., their heritage of previous commitments or procedures.

## The Coordination Issue

Sections One and Three also overlap in their concern with problems of coordination. It is the nature of development, and the currently available strategies to achieve development, that decisions and actions are required by a variety of decision-making and implementing units that are mutually affecting, but are not always structurally integrated or systemically linked. Ratchford describes one of the development roles of the university as providing information to decision-making units that will improve the coordination between such units. Even within Gross's proposition that planning for a rather narrow range of activities is the preferred procedure, one frequently may still be confronted with numerous decision-making units.

We point out that this particular constraint was suggested in Warner's notion that development is at least partially dependent on the achievements possible as organizations act coordinately within organizational sets. Just as individuals can achieve mutual enhancement by participation in groups it is suggested that organizations achieve the mutual enhancement of its objectives by interacting with some other groups or organizations. Thus, the problem of coordination which is central to the process of planned development is readily transferable to the important conceptual problem of interorganizational analysis.

There is current with sociology the notion that key dimensions of social change include the processes of segmentation, differentiation, and integration. (Cf. Smelser, 41) Of these three processes it appears that the least attention has been given to the process of integration. We suggest that one important aspect of the sociology of development is the understanding of integration processes within and among highly differentiated social systems.

## DIMENSIONS OF THE DOMESTIC SCENE

We have previously mentioned the attempted uniqueness of this book's focus on domestic development. It may be significant to note that even though the attempt was to focus the content of this book on domestic development, much of the content is based upon and/or deals with the historical perspective of social change and development in the developing nations. The widespread terminology that divides nations into developing and developed has suggested to many that development is a process that is articulated, almost exclusively, in the developing nations. Typically, we have proceeded as though development referred to the process of becoming an industrial state but did not apply to any postindustrial modifications. One result has been little scholarly interest in analyzing the development process in the United States, even though a legion of public and private agencies were actively promoting development programs.

Moore (30) has indicated that we have missed a great deal by not observing development in our own industrial society and indicates the ubiquitous occurrence of planned development: "Change that is clearly related toward a goal and undertaken with an eye to reshaping the future along the lines of various private and public interests is a phenomenon of increasing importance and magnitude. This is conspicuously true of newly developing areas, but also true of central governments, other public bodies, and private associations in economically advanced countries."

Weidner (46) supports this view that our scholarly perspective of development has suffered from our limitation of research activities to the less-developed countries. In Weidner's view, development applies to the "most sophisticated, prosperous, and technologically advanced populations." (46, p. 241)

Thus we conclude that focus on domestic development is not faulty but mandatory. From a scholarly viewpoint, it is a needed complement to present theory-building and research activities based on the development phenomena in the developing nations.

As scholars turn their attention to domestic development there is a tendency to define domestic development problems and needs in terms of experience in the less-developed nations: a kind of reverse flow of knowledge from the developing to the developed nations. The applicability of this reverse transfer of knowledge is, of course, highly dependent on the similarity between the developing and developed nations on at least three bases: 1) the goals or objectives of the development programs, and 2) the social conditions from which development is to proceed, and 3) the social systems existent or potentially available to carry out development. The three are highly related since where the nation now stands will have obvious influence on where it intends to go and organizationally how it intends to get there. On these criteria there are both similarities and great differences between developing and developed nations.

One important difference is that the developing nations generally have an existing future model toward which they are oriented: typically some form, perhaps modified, of the industrial society of the West. This model of the future exists in the sense that there now are nations that possess major characteristics which these developing nations intend to have. As Bennis and Slater (4, p. 125) indicate: "One advantage of life in a so-called developing society, beset by poverty and disease, is the ability to 'see' the future, as expressed in the great industrialized states."

However, when we turn to the subject of domestic development the model of the future is considerably more abstract and largely requires projecting a state of affairs for which there is no existing empirical reference. In general, the development goals of the developing and developed nations are divergent since the former are largely pre-occupied with either achieving increased production of commodities or achieving a viable governmental organization. Many of the problems faced by the preindustrial nations are past problems of the post-industrial nations. For example, in the transition from a preindustrial society to an industrial one they frequently emphasize restructuring the social organization to create a variety of highly goal-oriented formal organizations, particularly the rise of the corporation in the economic sector. In the postindustrial society many of these problems have been resolved and a new set of problems has emerged. To illustrate, in contrast to the differentiation involved in the preindustrial transition, a key process in the postindustrial transition is the integration that Etzioni (12, p. 7) refers to as a "comprehensive overlayer of societal guidance."

### Views of U.S. Society

Conceptualizing and investigating the process of domestic development must begin with an understanding of the major characteristics of current American society and the implications that these have for the development process.

As Capener and Brown remind us, early development in America was generated by the force of rugged individualism. From this we have arrived at a situation in which government, particularly the federal government, is a dominant force affecting the direction and rate of developmental change. Nevertheless, some sociologists continue to emphasize the importance of proliferating voluntary organizations as a means of achieving developmental change. Such a strategy views the loci of impetus for development as the grass roots. However, there is much evidence that the current impetus for domestic development is not from the grass roots but from the top down, from various bureaucratic structures of government; e.g., consider the loci of impetus for Appalachian development, social security, medicare, welfare programs, and urban renewal.

Moynihan (32, ch. 2) argues this point in his thesis of the professionalization of reform. It is Moynihan's view that since the middle of this century efforts to change the American social system increasingly arise from the initiatives of professionals concerned with a problem rather than from those to whom the problem immediately applies.

A critical question to be answered, preparatory to dealing with domestic development is: What are the significant features of American society? What is the nature and balance of its institutional composition? What are its centers of decision-making? What are its mechanisms of social control? Is it an active society (Etzioni, 12); a temporary society (Bennis and Slater, 4); a postindustrial society (Bell, 2); a service economy (Fuchs, 15, pp. 7–17); a modest society (Boulding, 6, pp. 36–44); or a new industrial state (Galbraith, 17)? Or is it some combination of two or more of these "societies"?

Each of the authors referred to provides a distinctive view of some general feature of American society: among them are some common denominators that stand out sharply.

The term postindustrial (Bell, 2) is sometimes used to portray our current status and the near-at-hand future. Our society obviously is not postindustrial in the sense that we are no longer industrialized but rather in the sense that we have achieved high levels of industrialization in our production processes and consequently are able to allocate a relatively smaller portion of our resources to industrial production. Our society is postindustrial in the sense implied by Gross: with relatively high economic prosperity our goals become increasingly noneconomic, or at least shift from concern with economic growth to concern with economic distribution. This gets at the core of the problem: What are values and goals of the postindustrial society? We have spoken of development as inventing the future and we now ask, What is the future to which postindustrial society is directed?

*Social Purpose and the Industrial System.* As Galbraith (17) has painted the picture, the current American landscape is one in which an industrial system (composed of the 500–600 largest corporations) dominates to the extent that its goals, expansion of output and consumption, and technological advance are the dominant goals of society.[8] The extreme case of dominance by the industrial system is as Galbraith (17, p. 398) states: "Our wants will be managed in accordance with the needs of the industrial system; the policies of the state will be subject to similar influence; education will be adapted to industrial need; the disciplines required by the industrial system will be the conventional morality of the community."

For Galbraith the desirable future is a new industrial state in which postindustrial implies the end of dominance by the industrial system in defining social purposes. In Galbraith's view the industrial system and its goals will acquire proper perspective as society identifies goals other than "the production of goods and income by progressively more advanced technological methods." (17, p. 399)

*Postbureaucratic Organization.* Bennis and Slater (4) have provided a provocative view of the nature of future social organization. For them the key characteristic of social organization will be temporary systems. In contrast to present forms of bureaucracy with their pyramidal authority structure and their static arrangement of status roles,

[8] Fuchs (15) has indicated he considers Galbraith's thesis of large corporation dominance a myth.

Bennis and Slater envision organizations in which the status roles will be combined and recombined into work groups in response to tasks to be performed. As they describe: "Adaptive, problem-solving, temporary systems of diverse specialists, linked together by coordinating and task-evaluating executive specialists in an organic flux—this is the organization form that will gradually replace bureaucracy as we know it . . . 'adaptive structures.'"

Prototypes of this organization form are to be seen in the aerospace industry and in aerospace centers. Some have been so bold as to suggest that we need similarly structured centers for the achievement of societal development, e.g., centers for institutional innovation.

It is interesting to contemplate the relevance of adaptive structures to Warner's discussion of organizational constraints for the implementation of development. Would the temporary system form applied to governmental agencies assist them in becoming more adaptive and responsive to changing problems? Whatever the answer to these questions, domestic development needs to be discussed in the context of this emerging characteristic of social organization in American society.

*The Active Society.* For Etzioni (12) the major feature of the postmodern society will be its increasing potential to be "master of itself," particularly, to control its technological sector. The active society is one which is "responsive to its changing membership, one engaged in an intensive and perpetual self transformation" (12, p. viii), one characterized by societal self-control.

What is to be the mechanism of this societal self-control? In an analogy to the two revolutions in the realm of machines, the mechanization of work and the mechanization of control of the machines that work, Etzioni (12, p. 7) suggests two revolutions in the social realm: "The first societal revolution came with the development of the corporation, or modern organization in general, which provided the sociological machine, the more effective way of 'getting things done.' The second societal revolution involves the control by second-order organizations of first organizations which do the work—in other words, the introduction of a comprehensive overlayer of societal guidance."

The potential for societal control is closely related to the increased knowledge that society has about itself. The postmodern ability to create knowledge via instruments, such as the computer, and organizations specializing in producing and processing knowledge, provides society with an expanded knowledge base for planning changes and increased confidence for making such decisions.

Etzioni's view of American society is that it will increasingly approximate the cybernetic model. As such, there will be increased efforts to improve society's control of its future. One mechanism of societal control will be the creation of "second-order" organizations designed to be both responsive to society and controlling "first-order" organizations.

Such second-order organizations could take the form suggested by Bennis and Slater: temporary and adaptive. They could also partially resolve the problem depicted by Galbraith by bringing some social control to the first-order organizations that comprise the industrial system. Second-order organizations also relevant to our earlier discussions on the need for coordination, integration, and interorganizational relations.

Again, we suggest that discussions of domestic development, particularly discussions of social structural modifications needed to achieve development, should be pursued with conceptualizations such as Etzioni's in mind. Considering the discussions of Section Three we might ask: To what extent will government agencies perform as second-order organizations over other public and private groups? Under what circumstances should the university perform the role of second-order organization? What organizations should perform this role in the economic sector? Miller has commented on the need for some unit to provide control in the sense of planning, a control center that might function much as the land-grant university has done for agricultural research. Such questions may be at the core of understanding domestic development.

*The Postindustrial Society.* Bell (2) refers to the postindustrial society and identifies its most salient feature as knowledge. Knowledge which allows man to: "anticipate change, measure the course of its direction and impact, control it and even shape it for predetermined ends." (2, p. 55)

American society is for the first time a national society in which national decisions are made by government rather than in the marketplace. Concomitant with that shift is the nation's trend toward becoming a communal society in which many groups seek to establish their social rights. These features, combined with our increasing future orientation, result in a situation in which government planning becomes increasingly ubiquitous and necessary.

Planning is a dilemma since, while apparently necessary and desirable, it also clarifies the latent conflict between social choices and individual values. Even though the postindustrial society is characterized by knowledge, there is one critical item of knowledge that we do not now have: "We have no social calculus which gives us a true sense of the entire costs and benefits of our public initiatives." (2, p. 103)

The postindustrial society, then, is one in which planning will take on increased importance. Such planning will be directed toward the achievement of some values and not others with resultant conflict among various value advocates.

Our conceptualizations of domestic development will need to accommodate the features of the postindustrial society which Bell describes.

We have briefly commented on the features of the current American society identified by four prominent social scientists. Their views are significant because they have attempted to capture the major societal characteristics and have glimpsed the significant changes that lie ahead. We have suggested that an understanding of domestic development must proceed from an adequate understanding of where we now are, the best estimate of where current trends will lead us, and, even more intriguing, where we want to be in the future. There is an interesting dilemma in understanding the domestic context of development as against the context of development in the preindustrial nations. On the one hand, our ability to comprehend the nuances of culture should be greater in our own society than in some other society. On the other hand, the social scale and complexity of the domestic scene may override the advantages gained from the cultural familiarity. Experience with development processes in the developing nations may be a complement to one's understanding of domestic development but certainly will not be a sufficient basis for such understanding.

## THE SOCIOLOGIST'S ROLE IN DEVELOPMENTAL CHANGE

Thus far we have progressed through a series of discussions dealing with development goals and developmental processes as they apply to a broad range of societal activities. We have also discussed the difficult task of moving from theory to strategy: from our general explanations of human behavior to the specification of actions to be taken to achieve a specific purpose. And we have looked at a sample of current development roles and activities from three major institutions of society. We now turn to the question: What is the role and contribution of sociology to development? One provocative reply to this question has been provided by Earl Heady.[9] As most readers know, or may soon discover, Heady is an economist. Some sociologists have been critical of economics for dominating the field of development, and may resent the sociological role being defined by an economist. However, a careful reading of Heady's comments should lead to much less concern with boundary maintenance between the disciplines and an awesome recognition of the challenges, opportunities, and expectations facing sociologists. Ultimately, sociologists must define their

[9] Professor of Economics; Charles F. Curtiss Distinguished Professor in Agriculture; Executive Director, Center for Agricultural and Economic Development, Iowa State University.

own role but Heady's comments are one point of departure. He anticipates the following contributions from sociology:

This book opens and reemphasizes several new and alternative dimensions of development. These dimensions pose important questions: what development really is and whether it can be truly measured and expressed in the rather simple arithmetic of economists, which reflects one set of variables but leaves aside several other sets; what aggregative goals in development are or should be in terms of levels and rates, and in terms of components as reflected in institutions and social development—as compared to economic development in the usual sense; what social and political forces promote and initiate sustained development, or provide it only in special forms, particular directions and sporadic bursts in order that the interests of particular values, historic orientations, and social orders will be preserved or promoted; and how the mechanisms and social avenues for development can be created once its goals and nature can be more nearly characterized and defined in terms of an aggregation of elements represented by increments of G.N.P., social participation, group and national or society status, social systems, and other vectors of developmental space.

This broader concept of development, its expression or measurement through aggregation over both conventional economic quantities, and the numerous elements or sets of social phenomena, variables, systems or institutions, is extremely important and significant. At least to me one general thread of implication, one seeming to run through the book, is that economic development, in its usual and rather mechanical measurement and expression, is but one of the components of the process—but not necessarily the overriding one if development is to be continuous, pursued at optimum rates yet undetermined, and include the full set of elements which results in overall societal development, and the progress of societies and groups towards yet-to-be specified ends of welfare.

At its extreme in mechanical expression, economic development is measured in rates of growth and levels of gross national products, in productivities of aggregate resource categories, and other rather unhuman, nonpeople, and nonsocial indices; but some of the sociological variables presented seem to fall into the same category. As emphasized in this book, economic growth is not synonymous with social or society development. Neither is economic development a general concept containing a subconcept social development, the relation being more nearly the opposite. Social development perhaps is inseparably interlocked at "both ends" of economic development; first in providing the institutional, leadership, organizational, social, authoritative relationships, and other catalytic ingredients that lead to the spawning of economic development; and second, along with economic development, in serving as an inseparable component of total or society development, economic development *per se* being somewhat meaningless without or unless accompanied by the latter.

This book has dealt with development in its broadest and most complex social meaning. This does not mean economic development in the conventional sense is unimportant; it is a necessary ingredient of "total" development and certain facets of social development cannot occur without it. It needs to be pursued for this reason, as well as for the materialistic purposes of more food, more houses, and other consumer goods for individual utility. But in the longer stretch of time, economic and social development, including the institutions and relationships which are not either but promote both, are technical complements. Absence or slow rates of one restrain the other in progress towards society development—whether this be a discrete goal or a continuum only in the sense of direction. As mentioned above, I proclaim the importance of economic development in this overall attainment. Yet I think the "thread and emphasis" on the cultural, social, and institutional elements are important, both for better attaining desired rates and levels of economic growth and for defining the place of it in total social development as a more nearly ultimate end of societies. The acceptance and thrust of economic growth or development in terms of conventional measurements have become so great that it perhaps has come blindly to prevail as an end *per se,* with dominance over all other processes in which societies participate or wish to promote. And perhaps for this reason, we cannot even guarantee that economic growth held so highly as an end can ever have permanent attainment, as long as it is given such great dominance over other social processes or societal goals. High growth rates are quite frequently interrupted by revolutions, just as revolutions are initiated to attain growth. Yet neither will be permanently absent or present, unless other social development and goals also prevail.

These statements apply particularly and broadly to underdeveloped nations and societies, but their implications also are concrete and close to home. To illustrate, Bryce Ratchford (Chapter 10) spoke of the land-grant universities and their attainment in promoting national economic growth in the development of agriculture. He also posed the possibility that while society at large gained from this development, farmers did not necessarily do so. There is obvious empirical basis for this proposition. Of course agricultural policies have brought redress to some, but far from all, persons who otherwise bear the costs or burdens of this contribution to national development. Yet the somewhat blind and dominating embracing of economic growth as the ultimate of all social process or goals stands to warp the emphasis of our public institutions and university faculties, services, and departments. The agricultural college is an example. It has long been emphasized, especially through functions of the cooperative extension services, as the "peoples' college," designed to solve their problems. In some areas, it has served importantly in this. But its main thrust has been on the technical and economic growth aspects of development. At one stage of economic development (e.g., lower consumer incomes and consequent high demand elasticities as population and per capita income increased) this emphasis on technical and economic development alone was highly consistent with aggregate and net development. But it is no longer so, partly because gross economic development, as expressed through the conventional technological and economic parameters of greater labor productivity and capital-labor substitution, has progressed far enough that we are dropping below a critical threshold level in many rural communities.

The threshold level of central importance is population in farms and rural areas, but it is only one of a cluster of associated social variables. Nationally, and, as expressed in G.N.P. arithmetic measurements, economic growth progresses apace as yields go up, biological and mechanical inputs substitute for labor. Consumers gain vastly as the real price of food declines and resources are not only freed but are forced to migrate occupationally and geographically, so that further forward thrusts can occur in the output of goods and services in other sectors. Left alone without offsetting policies, the advanced farm innovators gain in profit. But the remainder of farmers realize an income decline because of the low price elasticity of demand, as they are forced to adopt the technology and output springs forward. Employment and value of product advances rapidly in the chemical, machinery, and other developing sectors which "fabricate" the modern physical inputs that characterize development in the sense of greater output and labor replacement in agriculture. But the generation of gains and losses again are simultaneous—gains to the stockholders, managers, and workers who are favored in the developmental processes as characterized in gross national product and the output of the chemical and machinery sectors, but losses to the workers replaced from agriculture. Or, in other mechanical measurements, capital assets mushroom in the suburbs of cities where new plants are located to process the modern inputs for agriculture while, as part of the chain, capital assets melt away in country towns as the rural labor force dwindles, sales of rural businesses decline accordingly, country stores are boarded up, and empty dwellings go through the dismal deterioration of broken windows, collapsed chimneys, crumbling foundations, and buckled roofs—capital gains in one sector and capital losses in another. A crucial extension of this linkage is in the replacement of southern farm workers who end up in large cities helping to raise the existing capital of the latter (although this is not alone the cause of the migration or the only group involved). But perhaps equally or even more important, at least for some age and economic groups, is the evaporation of institutions, relationships, and social mechanisms which provide the structure and services of a community.

All individuals and groups want economic growth—at least I have found no one who would go on record against it—but certainly not at the expense of all other facets of economic welfare, social development, and participation. Growth could be had, perhaps at the very fastest rate, through an effective dictatorial slave economy wherein investments were made in the health, food, housing, and education of people purely as intellectual and biological resources, apart from their own participation, individual roles, and welfare. No one wants this. Yet a few of the economic-growth devout handle the arithmetic of it as though it should have priority over all other facets of economic and social progress or processes and are willing to promote it without regard to solution of the broad social problems it creates. In that public institution claimed to be the public solver of peoples' problems, the agricultural experiment station, we now have calculations going forward to rank research and projects solely or mainly on their estimated contribution to growth—either as gross national product added or resources saved. These calculations are largely devoid of elements relating to people, social relationships, and institutions—or perhaps even relating much to the agricultural sector.

So it is true at both ends of the growth scale of highly underdeveloped and highly developed countries that economic growth does not stand alone as "God of all things." It is not synonymous with development in an overall and complete societal sense, to be promoted over all else regardless of its consequences and the distribution of gains and costs therefrom. We do not know what its rate should be for optimal social welfare and perhaps even our arithmetic to measure it is erroneous—in the sense that it adds only positive elements, excluding entirely those negative elements which relate to the incidence of sacrifices stemming from it and erosion it brings to social overhead capital, institutions, and systems of some sectors.

At the higher scale of economic development, it is obvious that economics alone has little prospect, or perhaps even any important tools, for solving the broad social problems which are created by further and rapid growth. It could, of course, do better if it withdrew a bit from growth orientation and devoted more resources to the economic problems created by further growth.[10] To be sure, growth is desired for its own sake, but not at the expense of other economic and social goals and processes. At the lower end of the scale, the underdeveloped countries, the case is not clear that the most important remaining task is to specify which economic variables should be manipulated and by how much. The model can be specified in highly mechanistic and sophisticated fashion. The variables so specified are known and their magnitudes are of great quantitative importance in attaining high rates and sustained levels of development. There is no mystery here, but as I have indicated elsewhere the question of "how to get the show on the road" more nearly is a mystery of how to identify and create the institutions, authoritative roles and relationships, cultural orientations, leadership, and public acceptance which in fact allow and activate the manipulations of economic variables and incentives so that the process is underway. It is clearly obvious that to initiate and sustain development, commodity prices must be favorably upward, technological inputs or resource prices favorably downward, capital supplies large enough to convert cultivators from subsistence to commercial standing (in order that they respond in the market), and firm or tenure structure of a form giving favorable cost-payoff relationship. These are not mysteries, but how to create the institutions, leadership and motivations which create them are.

I am not abandoning economics and economic growth or development. I am only emphasizing the obvious, as others in this book have, that some extent of economic growth goals *per se* and alone is of prime importance and can stand alone in promoting development and advances of social welfare. But beyond this extent, it has little power by itself and the task is more importantly that of broader social phenomena and science.

Economics has some advantage in the "exactness" of its models and arithmetic. Quantities are put together which are impressive, even though they leave aside some of the social and people elements of change. Other social sciences frequently, and perhaps typically, have the broader and more basic social problems formulated, but their variables are less exact and more difficult to manipulate in an aggregative policy sense. (It is harder to quantify a sociological variable such as development of an organization in a manner to impress authorities and "tell a story," although it has been developed and is important. To show increases in yields, labor productivity or farm sales is easier and more impressive, even where less urgent and important.) Whereas the calculus of economics is sometimes too mechanistic to come to grips with the real problem or crucial variables and phenomena, the models of other social sciences perhaps are not yet fully specified or sufficiently measured and quantified to solve, on a large scale, the more basic problems they identify. Obviously, we need some "crossing" of the powers and attributes of such disciplines as sociology and economics if

[10] Heady has commented elsewhere on "complete programs" and analyses necessary to be certain that the sum of gains and losses is positive: Earl O. Heady, *A Primer on Food, Agriculture and Public Policy.* New York: Random House, 1967. Pp. 86–104; and Earl O. Heady, *Problems and Policies of Agriculture in Developed Countries.* Oslo: Johnson and Nielson, 1967. Pp. 97–102.

we are fully to identify problems and specify models to solve the broader aspects of development. How should this be done? Should the sociologists identify the broader problem and assign economists the more mechanical tasks of calculation? Should interdisciplinary task forces be assigned to most major problems of the realm? Should the sociologist become less reluctant and take over more of the tools of economists, which also are increasingly those borrowed from or common to other fields?

Some of all would be useful. But the major task is to get more sociological resources devoted to the core problems of development. This need prevails at both ends of the scale; in countries such as the U.S. wherein economic development gives rise to complex "second run" problems—income burdens of people released from agriculture, decay of institutions in rural communities, and even an element of urban strife, and certainly in the less developed countries where the more mechanical variables of economics are more obvious but they cannot be fully or effectively activated until the necessary institutions, social interactions and relationships have been established.

Perhaps the greatest need is "not to let the momentum die" at this point. This book should be looked upon as the foundation, or perhaps only as the excavation for the foundation, of a structure to be erected in the future. Sociologists can and should obtain and focus appropriate efforts and resources on the field to make it tangible and operative. Economic development is a well-established subdiscipline of economics. But it is very recent, being established only in the postwar period as a result of some concentrated effort on its theories and world-wide attempts to attain it. Perhaps the sociology of development, as a subdiscipline, or the broad field of societal development, has the same opportunity in the next 20 years, since it is now increasingly recognized that the broader concept of augmented societies or societal development is a more ultimate and urgent goal than economic development, and that certain goals in economic development cannot even be attained without the broader environment and progress.

These chapters have emphasized that development has both positive and negative elements. Economics tends to measure only the gross positive ones. But one of the broader problems of development is the distribution of the gains and sacrifices it brings. Even without the negative elements or sacrifices, the existence of numerous sociological variables—such as institutions and participation—requires that some model should be developed which incorporates an overall aggregate goal or measure. Such a measure is an objective function in which the various sociological and economic variables would be given relevant weights, both positive and negative. Then an optimal path in development might be better prescribed, with each of the sociological variables augmented just by the right amount. This type of model, I believe, is needed in sociological analyses of development for the future. Progress is, will, and should be made in quantification of sociological variables in a predictive sense. However, it seems to me that sociologists also should be developing normative-type models of the type suggested. Then, given the overall directive of optimizing development in all its important sociological facets (activities) as well as its fewer economic variables, sociologists could prescribe an optimal path. I believe this possibility is real, and it is another reason I would like to see the momentum go ahead from here. Now, perhaps there is need among sociologists, or by sociologists and economists together, to hold some specialized workshops on developing such models.

In this same vein, I believe sociologists can conceivably develop policy models. Under these, and following quantification of more of the sociological variables, public authorities and communities might specify goals in terms of attainment of various levels and mixes of sociologic (and economic) target variables. The sociologists might then specify which instrumental variables should be manipulated, and by how much, to attain these combination goals. This possibility also is real as quantification goes further, and is another reason for intensive workshops.

This book has covered a tremendous range, as should be the case in an "initial relating" of the general concepts, actual measurement, and quantification of variables, operations at the level of regional, community and institutional development and the engagement and organization of our universities and other intellectual resources to help in the task. But each of these general areas represents a broad coverage. It is likely that intensive workshops should be held in most of them, with some interaction among sociologists, economists and political scientists as the broader theories and framework of societal development (the broader social framework of development) is interrelated with and superimposed on economic development. The goal would be to interchange and integrate concepts and tools, but also to provide identification of the sociological variables, processes, and institutions necessary to get the desired kinds and amounts of economic development.

These papers have dealt mainly with development in the U.S. and North America, although some facets of problems in less developed countries have been mentioned. Even this is a broad area, needing to be broken down into analyses of less extensive regions or economies. Special attention now needs to be given separately to sociological developmental aspects, variables and processes of developing rural regions and communities, declining rural communities and urban centers, and developing regions of economies such as the U.S. But equally, there needs to be further concentration on these topics and variables for less developed countries. Each provides subject matter for a useful workshop.

There is much ground yet to be plowed. The important thing is that any momentum should not be lost. Sociologists have in their hands the opportunity to step up this momentum, with great gain to society in progress on all fronts of societal development.

One major thesis in discussing the participation of sociologists in developmental change is that role is not simply to identify sociocultural barriers to economic development but to pursue the broader question of developing a framework of societal development, of which economic development may be one important part. In this view the sociology of development is not merely a variant of economic sociology that deals with developing social action strategies to achieve economic goals—the sociology of development is concerned with the process of identifying noneconomic societal goals and the relationship of economic goals to these. Since development deals with planned activities aimed at specified objectives, another important dimension of the sociology of development is assessment of the societal impact of a given activity. Did it accomplish what was intended? Did it have consequences, desirable or undesirable, other than those intended?

The participation of sociologists in development could have important implications for the discipline by accentuating trends that are already underway: for example, increased interest in applied sociology, increased interest in policy research and model building, and increased interest in macrosociology. Increased interest in the application of sociology to the public problems and decision-making is evident among both sociologists and public decision-makers. (Cf. Lazarsfeld et al., 24) Sociological participation in designing development strategies could affect that trend. The noneconomic social sciences are increasingly being received as, at least, potential policy sciences (Lerner and Lasswell, 25) and involvement in development would lead sociology to becoming a policy-oriented science. (Weidner, 46, p. 235) There is current interest in macrosociology (cf. Etzioni, 13) and such focus will be necessary if we are to accomplish objectives such as an "aggregate goal for development that has sociological dimensions" (see Heady's previous comments).

To illustrate the different posture that may be required of sociology as it participates in development we will compare the posture of rural sociological research regarding the adoption of technology (adoption-diffusion research) with a development posture. First, adoption-diffusion research has not been concerned with the value of new technology to the agricultural sector. Such value questions would be a part of sociological involvement in development policy. Second, adoption-diffusion research has given little attention to the overall impact and consequences of new technology on the agricultural sector. In development research such impact would be assessed and related to previously defined goals. And third, adoption-diffusion researchers have done little strategy translating since they frequently worked closely with a unit specifically designed to make such application (the Cooperative Extension Service). In much development work such translating units will not exist so that development will require increased strategy involvement by sociologists.

## Some General Questions

Development is inventing the future. It derives from the goal-oriented characteristic of man and the organizations that he creates and the ability that he has to abstractly consider a state of events that are not existent in this time and/or place. From this perspective several general questions arise for the sociology of development.

1) What can sociology contribute to the pool of images of the future held by society? What sociological variables could be a part of images of the future? What societal goals are desirable from the sociological perspective?

2) What can sociology contribute to the prediction of futures under different assumptions regarding inputs, organizational structures, and strategies for change?

3) What can sociology contribute to the effective and efficient achievement of future states of the system as envisioned in current images of the future? What social systems provide the greatest potential for reaching desired futures? What sociological strategies can be applied for the achievement of development goals?

4) What can sociology contribute to the articulation of feedback processes to monitor the impact of planned development? What sociological frameworks can be utilized to measure the "total" consequences of a development activity?

There are two basic ways in which sociology can contribute to the pool of images of the future: 1) by observing and projecting current social trends and detailing their likely impacts on future states of the system, and 2) by constructing alternative models of the future based on two sets of constraints—the current state of the system and the currently held values.

Observing and projecting social trends link directly with the contemporary interest in social indicators. (Bauer, 1; Gross, 18; U.S. Dept. HEW, 43) Projecting trends obviously is highly dependent on accurately assessing the current state of the society with regard to these trends. The attempt to operationalize social indicators reflects the inadequacy of the present informational system to provide the needed statistical series. Biderman (5) vividly illustrates this inadequacy by showing that of the 81 domestic goals delineated by the President's Commission on Goals (37) there are 48 that can be monitored with existing statistical series—and many of these to a relatively limited extent.

A major preliminary, and continuing, problem with the collection of these social indicators is delineating the critical dimensions of society to be measured. As Biderman (5, p. 71) has asked, "How can one assess the adequacy of our measure of state (of the nation) when we do not have prior knowledge to guide us in determining what should be measured?" In the same volume with Biderman's question, Gross (18) presents his framework of one such ideal system of social statistics. Gross outlines seven major structural elements around which social data should be collected, ranging from the number and characteristics of people to the nature of internal relations.

Social scientists are at work on the problem of creating a system of social indicators. Their success is a prerequisite to our effectively projecting images of the future based on current conditions. Social indicators are also relevant to the feedback process. The availability of social indicators will be an important feedback to society and its decision-makers and can provide the basis for intrusions designed to alter trends indicated by the social indicators. Bauer (1, p. 35) has commented on this aspect: "It should be remembered that if a phenomenon is measured, and the measure is available, the phenomenon is more likely to be taken into consideration in the formation of policy."

This dual utility of social indicators for the observation of trends and as a basis for the initiation of action to manage such observed trends is conceptualized by Moore and Sheldon (31, p. 144) as *monitoring* social change:[11] "Monitoring social change we mean in the full, ambiguous sense of the term. We are concerned with 'tuning in' with recording and verifying the messages we may get or produce relating to structural alterations. But we are also concerned with the use of such information for entry into the system, to alter the magnitudes, speed or even direction of change in terms of explicit, normative criteria."

Sociologists can also contribute to society's images of the future by constructing alternative models of the future. While such alternative models are not necessarily utopias, their construction is related to questions raised by Moore (29) in his discussion of "The Utility of Utopias." The construction of preferable futures intrudes on a boundary problem which sociology has confronted on other occasions. Can a value-free social science say anything about goals? (Moore, 29, p. 771) Moore contends that there are certain panhuman goals or values—for example, health is preferred to sickness, longevity to early death, material well-being to poverty, low levels of conflict to high—and that these can serve as a base for the construction of alternative future conditions. One might also consider constructing alternative futures on the basis of values not presently widely held by the members of society. In such a situation, it becomes mandatory for the sociologist to explicitly state the values on which his alternatives are based.

All of these questions and proposed assignments for the sociology of development suggest a general area of sociological activity that is relatively dormant (or perhaps not yet conceived)—the exploration and prediction of alternative outcomes under changing social parameters. Several of the authors in this book have suggested such a role: Miller suggests, in addition to the study of existing systems, delineating desired states and suggesting future systems to achieve these ends; Ratchford calls for procedures to analyze the probable consequences of new technology before it is introduced.

That such "research" will require different analytical techniques than those now used for testing relational hypotheses is obvious. In some cases, new techniques may need to be created. In other cases, techniques not now widely used may become increasingly important. One example of the latter is the technique of computer simulation.

---

[11] For their more recent discussion see Sheldon and Moore. (40)

The increased availability of Heise's "structural models," and the increased demand for sociologists to conduct projective research could give prominence to this research technique.

## Some Specific Tasks

Heady suggests a major problem is "to get more sociological resources devoted to the core problems of development." Most sociologists are teachers and/or researchers. Increasingly there are sociologists who perform practitioner roles. It is from one or more of these status roles, perhaps modified, that sociologists will attempt to meet society's demand "not only for greater understanding of, but for relevant assistance in, the resolution of overburdening societal problems." (Capener and Brown, ch. 7) Typically, "understanding of" is the function of research activities, "resolution of" can be seen as the function of the practitioner, and the teaching role somewhat overlaps both.

*Research on Development.* Thomas Ford (14) has expressed a number of pertinent ideas regarding types of developmental research. In his view, there are three types: 1) basic policy research, 2) strategic research, and 3) tactical research.

Policy research inquires into the assumptions behind and potential consequences of values and goals embedded in policy decisions. The assessment of consequences includes considering outcomes in relation to stated objectives as well as the relationship of outcomes to other values and goals in society.

Strategy research proceeds within a framework of policy and the policy objectives are taken as given. Strategy research deals with the question of alternative general strategies to achieve policy goals. Examples of strategy research include feasibility studies, general background research, and some evaluation research. Tactical research assumes previous decisions on both policy and strategy—and asks the question of *how* to implement a given strategy.

The relative allocation of sociological resources to these three types of development research is problematic with regard to optimizing the role of sociologists in development. Tactical research may be appealing because tactical questions appear susceptible to our research methods. But as Ford (14, p. 13) notes, the long-run payoff of tactical research may be negligible if strategies and policies are weak or untested.

Sociologists' preferences among the types of development research, of course, may be constrained by factors unrelated to their assessment of priorities. Problems of funding and time pressures, important in conducting tactical research, may be even more important constraints on policy and strategy research. (14, p. 9)

*Practitioners of Development.* We have already noted the increased interest in applied sociology. In the case of development, with our relatively unsophisticated, and certainly untested, sociological propositions regarding development, there is special potential for practitioners to contribute to the model-building process. Miller and Reissman (28, p. 277) have commented on this general contribution of applied sociology: "We believe there is a great need for professionals to be trained more inductively in the field and for theory to be built upon this type of clinical experience."

There is need for the profession of sociology to admit the role of practitioner with full rights and privileges; practitioners who are competent. In Zetterberg's (48, p. 18) terms: "Competent in translating scientific theory into practice. The defining characteristic of a scientifically competent practitioner is not his contribution to scientific knowledge and methodology, but his use of scientific knowledge in solving problems repeatedly encountered in his occupation."

Part of the admission process will involve rewarding these translating skills as well as the more scientific contributions. John[12] has commented on the current strains in sociology which are in part caused by the increased research specialization within sociology and the concurrent increase in demands on the university to deal with social problems. Balanced participation by sociology in the development field will require solutions to such strains.

The role of social critic is a fourth role that has been suggested.[13] The intimacy of sociologists with their own and their colleagues' work may compel them to be rather humble about their possible contributions to understanding development. Nevertheless, as Haller points out, sociologists do "have a way of looking at the world which is not the common property of everybody," but which would make a useful contribution to society's knowledge. The role of the social critic is performed by 1) applying our best sociological thinking to interpret what's going on around us and 2) communicating these interpretations to others, e.g., general publics,[14] interest groups, policy makers, and administrators.

## Inventing the Future of Development Sociology

There is within sociology increased concern with the development field and increased acceptance of the orientations that sociology will need to adopt in order to participate in development: two such orientations are the policy orientation and the applied orientation.

---

[12] See his comments in the Discussion section at the end of Chapter 12.
[13] Archibald Haller, Department of Rural Sociology, University of Wisconsin, made this suggestion.
[14] One systematic and available procedure for pursuing this role is the periodical, *The Public Interest.*

It is very likely that the domestic environment will continue to provide stimulants for the rise of development sociology. The other important determinant must, of course, come from within sociology, in particular from those sociologists who choose to participate in development sociology. We believe one important social mechanism to aid development sociologists will be future conferences and seminars focusing on development topics specialized and general, such as methodology, policy research, or aggregate indicators of societal development.

While such special topics would be useful approaches for future deliberation we also suggest that there is need for future conferences, seminars, and writing in which a broader view of development is pursued. The first direction in which to expand is suggested by one of Gross's propositions (see Chapter 6) and discussed in Haller's summary comments. Gross suggested, "Domestic growth and foreign expansion are mutually supporting." We may or may not agree that societal development, as well as economic development, is dependent on some form of foreign expansion. Nevertheless, we are likely to accept Haller's suggestion that we need to consider the reciprocal influences between our domestic development activities and our foreign policy or international activities. Future explorations need to consider domestic development in this macro-setting.

A second obvious direction for expansion is to involve other social science disciplines in working conferences and seminars designed to achieve objectives of mutual interest. Such meetings could deal with specific topics, e.g., national migration policy, but would provide a mechanism for multidisciplinary discussions.

Although attempted focus throughout this book has been largely on the sociological view, we have seen this as a short-run rather than long-run strategy. There will continue to be a need for both types of discussions: the within-sociology discussions of development and the across-social-sciences discussions of development.

In Chapter 7, Capener and Brown refer to Myrdal's (33, p. 235) comments regarding the requirements for understanding development. We conclude with Myrdal's comments: "A worth-while theory of development and underdevelopment, if it can ever be formulated, would have to be based on ideas distilled from the broadest empirical knowledge of social change in all its manifold aspects, acquired under the greatest freedom from tradition-bound predilections."

## REFERENCES

1. Bauer, Raymond A., ed. *Social Indicators*. Cambridge, Mass.: The M.I.T. Press, 1966.
2. Bell, Daniel. "Notes on the Post-Industrial Society (1)." *The Public Interest* 6:24–35; 7:102–18, 1967.

3. Bell, Wendell. "Teachers, Students, and Ideas, a Personal Account." *American Behavioral Scientist* 12 (1968): 41–52.
4. Bennis, Warren G., and Slater, Philip E. *The Temporary Society.* New York: Harper and Row, 1968.
5. Biderman, Albert D. "Social Indicators and Goals." In *Social Indicators,* edited by Raymond A. Bauer. Cambridge, Mass.: The M.I.T. Press, 1966.
6. Boulding, Kenneth E. "Is Scarcity Dead?" *The Public Interest* 5 (1966): 36–44.
7. Brooks, Ralph M.; Coward, E. Walter, Jr.; and Beal, George M. "Some Effects of Intangible Goals on Extension's Resource Development Programs." Paper presented at Rural Sociological Society Meetings, 1969, at San Francisco.
8. Coleman, James. "The Possibility of a Social Welfare Function." *American Economic Review* 61 (1966): 1105–22.
9. Dahrendorf, Ralf. *Class and Class Conflict in Industrial Society.* Stanford, Calif.: Stanford University Press, 1959.
10. Davidoff, Paul. "Normative Planning." In *Planning for Diversity and Choice,* edited by Stanford Anderson. Cambridge, Mass.: The M.I.T. Press, 1968.
11. Eisenstadt, S. N. *Modernization, Protest and Change.* Englewood Cliffs, N.J.: Prentice-Hall, 1966.
12. Etzioni, Amitai. *The Active Society.* New York: The Free Press, 1968.
13. ———. "Social Analysis and Social Action." *American Behavioral Scientist* 12 (1968): 31–33.
14. Ford, Thomas. *Social Research and Developmental Change: The Critical Gap.* Mimeographed. Lexington: Department of Sociology, University of Kentucky. n.d.
15. Fuchs, Victor. "The First Service Economy." *The Public Interest* 2 (1966): 7–17.
16. Gabor, Dennis. *Inventing the Future.* New York: Alfred A. Knopf, 1964.
17. Galbraith, John K. *The New Industrial State.* Boston: Houghton Mifflin Company, 1967.
18. Gross, Bertram M. *The State of the Nation.* New York: Tavistock Publications, 1966.
19. Heise, David R. "Problems in Path Analysis and Causal Inference." In *Sociological Methodology,* edited by Edgar F. Borgotta. San Francisco: Jossey-Bass, 1969.
20. Held, Virginia. "PPBS Comes to Washington." *The Public Interest* 4 (1966): 102–15.
21. Horowitz, Irving L. *Three Worlds of Development: The Theory and Practice of Interactional Stratification.* New York: Oxford University Press, 1966.
22. Hoselitz, Bert. *Sociological Aspects of Economic Growth.* Glencoe, Ill.: The Free Press, 1960.
23. Kaysen, Carl. "The Business Corporation as a Creator of Values." In *Human Values and Economic Policy,* edited by Sidney Hook. New York: New York University Press, 1967.
24. Lazarsfeld, Paul F.; Sewall, William H.; and Wilensky, Harold L., eds. *The Uses of Sociology.* New York: Basic Books, 1967.
25. Lerner, Daniel, and Lasswell, Harold D., eds. *The Policy Sciences: Recent Developments in Scope and Method.* Stanford, Calif.: Stanford University Press, 1951.
26. Levy, Marion J. *Modernization and the Structure of Societies.* Vols. I and II. Princeton, N.J.: Princeton University Press, 1966.

27. Mau, James A. *Social Change and Images of the Future.* New York: Pitman Publishing Corporation, 1969.
28. Miller, S. M., and Riessman, Frank. *Social Class and Social Policy.* New York: Basic Books, 1968.
29. Moore, Wilbert E. "The Utility of Utopias." *The American Sociological Review* 31 (1966): 765–72.
30. ———. "Developmental Change in Urban Industrial Societies." In *Perspectives in Developmental Change,* edited by Art Gallaher. Lexington: University of Kentucky Press, 1968.
31. ———, and Sheldon, Eleanor. "Monitoring Social Change: A Conceptual and Programmatic Statement." In *Proceedings of the Social Statistics Section.* American Statistical Association, 1965.
32. Moynihan, Daniel P. *Maximum Feasible Misunderstanding.* New York: The Free Press, 1969.
33. Myrdal, Gunnar. *Value in Social Theory.* New York: Harper, 1958.
34. Nettl, J. P., and Robertson, Roland. "Industrialization, Development and Modernization." *British Journal of Sociology* 17 (1966): 274–91.
35. Ozbekhan, Hasan. "The Triumph of Technology: 'Can' Implies 'Ought'." In *Planning for Diversity and Choice,* edited by Stanford Anderson. Cambridge, Mass.: The M.I.T. Press, 1968.
36. Parsons, Talcott. *Societies: Evolutionary and Comparative Perspectives.* Englewood Cliffs, N.J.: Prentice-Hall, 1967.
37. President's Commission on Goals. *Goals for Americans.* Englewood Cliffs, N.J.: Prentice-Hall, 1960.
38. Riggs, Fred M. *Administration in Developing Countries: The Theory of Prismatic Society.* Boston: Houghton Mifflin, 1964.
39. Rothweel, Charles E. "Forward." In *The Policy Sciences: Recent Developments in Scope and Method,* edited by Daniel Lerner and Harold D. Lasswell. Stanford, Calif.: Stanford University Press, 1951.
40. Sheldon, Eleanor B., and Moore, Wilbert E., eds. *Indicators of Social Change: Concepts and Measurements.* New York: Russell Sage Foundation, 1968.
41. Smelser, Neil J. *The Sociology of Economic Life.* Englewood Cliffs, N.J.: Prentice-Hall, 1963.
42. Taviss, Irene. "The Technological Society: Some Challenges for Social Science." *Social Research* 35 (1968): 521–39.
43. United States Department of Health, Education and Welfare. *Toward a Social Report.* Washington, D.C.: U.S. Government Printing Office, 1969.
44. Warner, W. Keith, and Havens, A. Eugene. "Goal Displacement and the Intangibility of Organizational Goals." *Administrative Science Quarterly* 12 (1968): 539–55.
45. Warren, Roland L. "The Interorganizational Field as a Focus of Investigation." *Administrative Science Quarterly* 12 (1967): 396–419.
46. Weidner, Edward. "Developmental Change and the Social Sciences: Conclusion." In *Perspectives in Developmental Change,* edited by Art Gallaher. Lexington: University of Kentucky Press, 1968.
47. Williams, Robin. "Individual and Group Values." In *Social Goals and Indicators for American Society.* (Annals of the American Academy of Political and Social Sciences Vol. 371), edited by Bertram M. Gross. May, 1967.
48. Zetterberg, Hans L. *Social Theory and Social Practice.* New York: Bedminister Press, 1962.

# INDEX